THE GAMES MUST GO ON

AVERY BRUNDAGE AND THE OLYMPIC MOVEMENT

Avery Brundage reading his "games-must-go-on" speech at Munich in 1972.

THE GAMES MUST GO ON

AVERY BRUNDAGE AND THE OLYMPIC MOVEMENT

ALLEN GUTTMANN

COLUMBIA UNIVERSITY PRESS
NEW YORK   1984

Unless otherwise noted, the photographs in this book are from
Avery Brundage Collection (University of Illinois Archives).

Library of Congress Cataloging in Publication Data

Guttmann, Allen.
  The games must go on.

  Includes bibliographical references and index.
  1. Brundage, Avery.   2. International Olympic
Committee—Presidents—Biography.   I. Title.
GV721.2.B78G87   1983   796.4'8'0924   [B]   83–5360
ISBN 0–231–05444–0

Columbia University Press
New York   Guildford, Surrey

To Rudolf and Klara Bargen

CONTENTS

Illustrations appear as a group after page 144

PREFACE

Munich, September 6, 1972. Standing before the mourning thousands gathered together in the Olympic Stadium and before the countless millions watching on television, Avery Brundage, president of the International Olympic Committee, announced to the world, "The games must go on." The murder of eleven Israeli athletes by a band of Palestinian terrorists must not be allowed to break off the celebration of the XX Olympiad. Although Brundage had been a public figure for decades, this was the most visible, and probably also the most controversial, of his public moments. It was natural then to ask, in approval or in indignation, who this man Brundage was.

He was usually seen by those Americans who were aware of him at all as a crusty octogenarian bureaucrat given to sour statements about amateurism and its corruption. A spoilsport. An anachronism. He felt more at home in Europe than in America and the ordinary European sports fan was more likely than the American spectator to have some notion of what Brundage had accomplished as a member, vice president, and—from 1952 to 1972—president of the International Olympic Committee. Hadn't he advocated that the Soviet Union be brought into the Olympics? Hadn't he forced the temporary unity of the teams from divided Germany? Hadn't he tried vainly to keep South Africa and Rhodesia within the Olympic movement? Hadn't he become a kind of ceremonial figure, always there to open and close the games, at Helsinki and Melbourne, at Rome and Tokyo, at Mexico City and Munich, not to mention all those other occasions when he stood, an aged man in fur cap and frosty spectacles, opening and closing the winter games?

By 1972, thousands of photographs and millions of words had made Avery Brundage internationally famous. Speeches, articles, and interviews had spread his views of amateur athletics far and wide. His opinions were headline news: BRUNDAGE SAYS GAMES ARE ENDANGERED! But who was he? How did he come to be the world's most important sports administrator? Why did he seem invariably to believe that the games *had* to go on—despite Adolf Hitler's rise to power and his position as host to the 1936 games in Berlin, despite Japan's invasion of China and Germany's of Poland, despite the Soviet Union's crushing of the Hungarian Revolution, despite the political divisions that split China, Korea, and Germany into mutually hostile political fragments, despite racism in South Africa and nationalism in Indonesia and civil unrest in Mexico, despite Palestinian terror committed within the Olympic Village itself?

Brundage's speeches are an obvious source of insight into his beliefs. Opening the 62nd Session of the International Olympic Committee in Tokyo on October 6, 1964, he repeated statements which had already become familiar themes in his addresses and interviews: "The Olympic Movement is a 20th Century religion, a religion with universal appeal which incorporates all the basic values of other religions, a modern, exciting, virile, dynamic religion." It is a religion of which Pierre de Coubertin, the French "renovator" of the Olympics, was the prophet, for Coubertin's idealism had "kindled a torch that will enlighten the world."[1] If Coubertin was the revered prophet, then Brundage himself must rank, at the very least, as a high priest at the altar of Olympism. His speeches, articles, and interviews demonstrate that his convictions were indeed religious in that they represented his deepest and most fundamental values, but the innumerable, repetitious published statements fail to tell us how it happened that Brundage arrived at his convictions, convictions obviously shared by millions of others who have grown misty-eyed at the lighting of the Olympic flame, whose hearts have beat faster with the hoisting of the victor's national flag. In order to understand that moment in Munich when the games *had* to go on, it is necessary to study both the public career and the private person. It is necessary to describe the athlete, the businessman, the art collector, the bureaucrat, and to speculate as well about the Brundage that Brundage rarely spoke of. The game is worth the candle. To understand Brundage is to gain insight not only into the history of the modern Olympics but also into the "religion of Olympism" which made the games possible. To understand Brundage is to realize why the Olympic Games may well go on long after the "religion of Olympism" has become a mockery.

ACKNOWLEDGMENTS

For no other scholarly project have I required and received as much help as for this one. The cooperation of the President, the Director, and many of the members of the International Olympic Committee was indispensable. For their letters and interviews, and for their permission to consult archival material, quote from letters, and reprint photographs, I am grateful to Juan Antonio Samaranch, Monique Berlioux, Sir Adetokunbo Ademola, Sir Reginald Alexander, Syed Wajid Ali, Royotara Azuma, Comte Jean de Beaumont, Lance Cross, Arpad Csanadi, Willi Daume, Gustaf Dyrssen, Bo Ekelund, Gunnar Ericsson, the Marquess of Exeter, Raymond Gafner, Herman van Karnebeek, Kiba M'Baye, Manfred von Mautner Markhof, Lord Arthur Porritt, J. W. Rangell, Douglas F. Roby, Alexandro Sipercu, Jan Staubo, Giorgio di Stefani, Vladimir Stoytchev, and Prince Tsuneyoshi Takeda. For similar assistance I wish to thank Yvon d'Argencé, Maynard Brichford, Dennis Brutus, Liselott Diem, K. S. Duncan, Leonore Edstrøm, David D. Henry, J. B. Holt, Anselmo Lopez, Ulrich Müller, C. Robert Paul, Jr., Dagmar Püschel, Kenneth L. Roper, Frederick J. Ruegsegger, Ilse-Marie Sabath, Gudmund Schack, Walther Tröger, and Wilhelmina Kirby Waller. I am also indebted, for many kinds of help, to Wolfgang Decker, Henning Eichberg, Robert M. Goodhue, Ommo Grupe, Chadwick and Betty Hansen, Hugh Hawkins, Sunichi Hirai, Manfred Lämmer, Hans and Ulrike Lenk, John Loy, Günther Lüschen, Gordon N. Ray, Steven A. Riess, George Stade, Egon Steinkamp, James and Carline Stottlar, Melinda Takeuchi, and John William Ward. I have also been aided by the American Council of Learned Societies, the American Philosophical Society, the British Olympic Association, the Bundesinstitut für Sportwissenschaft, the Chicago Historical Society, the Comité Olímpico Español, the Deutsche Forschungsgemeinschaft, the International Amateur Athletic Federation, the Nationales Olympisches Komitee für Deutschland, the U.S. Olympic Committee, and the University of Illinois Alumni Office. I am especially thankful to the University of Illinois Archives, which made available to me the Avery Brundage Collection, to Amherst College and the John Simon Guggenheim Foundation, which made possible an entire year of travel and research, and to my wife, Doris Bargen, who often interrupted her own scholarly work to help me with mine.

THE GAMES MUST GO ON
AVERY BRUNDAGE AND THE OLYMPIC MOVEMENT

CHAPTER I

EARLY YEARS OF A SELF-MADE MAN

No matter how carefully we assemble the facts, autobiography involves us, inevitably, in myth. In our anecdotes as well as in our multivolume memoirs, we create the selves we then present, more or less sincerely, to the world. In the myth that Brundage created about Brundage, there is no genesis. As he told it in interviews and in an unfinished autobiographical manuscript, the story begins *in medias res*. Rather like the youthful Benjamin Franklin, whom every American remembers as an unknown runaway walking into Philadelphia and munching the rolls purchased with his last penny, Avery Brundage first appears in mythic time as an eighteen-year-old freshman arriving at the University of Illinois in Champaign-Urbana. He appears on campus, pursues a rigorous course of studies in civil engineering, demonstrates his athletic skill in several sports, and goes on after graduation to the 1912 Olympic Games and then to a highly remunerative career in the construction industry. But where did the eighteen-year-old freshman come from? Benjamin Franklin tells us in his *Autobiography* about his childhood in Boston, but Brundage was invariably reticent about his origins. He did disclose to interviewers and to editors some information about his family and his childhood and his life before his arrival at the university, but he said remarkably little and this reluctance to discuss his origins was intentional. "I have never paid much attention to the genealogy of the Brundage family."[1]

He was, like Franklin, the "epitome of the self-made man."[2] He might well have quoted the famous words from the first paragraph of Franklin's *Autobiography*: "From the poverty and obscurity in which I was born and in which I passed my earliest years, I have raised myself to a state of affluence and some degree of celebrity in the world." Brundage, the self-made man, was proud of his ascent from humble origins and annoyed by the frequent mistaken references to inherited wealth and aristocratic ease. When Arnold Lunn, a sportsman who should have known better, referred in *Ski Survey* to Brundage as "the son of a wealthy father," Brundage seems to have let the error go without comment,[3] but a German magazine's criticism of his "life of ease" brought a tart letter to I.O.C. Chancellor Otto Mayer, "you may inform them that every penny that I have ever had has been earned through my own efforts."[4]

Brundage's origins were humble enough. He was born in Detroit on September 28, 1887. His father, Charles, was a stonecutter from Campbelltown, New York; his mother, Minnie Lloyd Brundage, was from Buffalo. He was named for a friend of his father, about whom Avery remarked, "I never met the man." An older brother died in infancy. A younger brother, Chester, was born November 7, 1891. When Avery was five, the family moved to Chicago and split apart. Since Brundage ordered that his mother's diary be burned after his own death, we shall probably never know the details of his father's departure, but the mere fact that Brundage wanted the diary destroyed is psychologically important. Unquestionably, the desertion was a traumatic event for a five-year-old boy.[5]

Avery and Chester were reared mostly by their aunts and uncles, one of whom became a prominent figure in Illinois politics. Edward Jackson Brundage left school at fourteen and later worked his way through the Chicago College of Law, graduating in 1893, at the age of twenty-four.[6] His political career began with election to the state legislature as a Republican, in 1898, and culminated with his successful campaign to become Attorney General of Illinois in 1916. Late in his life, Avery told a friend that he had been the pet of the family,[7] but, apart from a letter of recommendation written in 1917, there is little evidence that Uncle Edward took any special interest in his nephew. Avery bequeathed to the University of Illinois an album with 311 photographs of Uncle Edward's family. Although Chester appears twice, there is apparently no snapshot of Avery. Did he remove them? Was he never photographed with his Uncle Edward, his Aunt Germaine, and his four cousins? One can only speculate.

When he was twelve, Avery became a newsboy, like the lucky, plucky heroes of Horatio Alger. He rose before dawn and trudged the streets of Carl Sandburg's "Stormy, husky, brawling/City of the Big Shoulders." Unlike Alger's streetboys, Avery was able to stay in school. He attended Sherwood Public School and then R. T. Crane Manual Training School (the school subsequently made a second contribution to the history of sports—George Halas of the Chicago Bears). To attend this intensive vocational school, with classes that went daily from eight to five, Avery had to travel seven miles by cable car (after having finished with his paper route). He was a good student. At thirteen, he won an essay competition sponsored by William Randolph Hearst's newspaper chain and was rewarded by a trip to Washington to attend William McKinley's second inauguration as President of the United States. Avery voyaged into the imagined world of the stamp collector as well, but he could scarcely have thought then that he would one day stand in post offices in Buenos Aires and in Warsaw, mailing home his letters and postcards, "Correo Aereo," "Poczka Polska."[8]

He was forced to begin wearing spectacles by the age of ten— an event traumatic enough for him to single it out for inclusion in a brief list of the most important events of his life; he overcame this visual handicap with typical determination. Like another myopic boy, Theodore Roosevelt, he became an athlete. (Did Avery know of Roosevelt's boxing and big-game hunting when he attended McKinley's inauguration and watched the spectacled New Yorker take the vice-presidential oath?) In a magazine article written for *The American Boy* in 1919, Avery described his enthusiasm for sports and revealed what that enthusiasm meant psychologically:

I liked to play football, baseball, basketball and all of the other games as well, but track and field events appealed to me particularly because they are a demonstration of individual skill and supremacy. The track athlete stands or falls on his own merits.[9]

And what else is a self-made man if not one who stands or falls on his own merits? One need not be a believer in Freudian psychoanalysis to suspect that Brundage recognized in childhood that sports, especially individual sports like track and field, are a paradigm of objective achievement. Their ideal, if not their practice, is that of equal opportunity to demonstrate an achievement about which there can be no difference of opinion. Upon the cinder track, the ascriptive characteristics of birth and background are formally irrelevant and a badly disadvantaged young man can outperform his social superiors.

Crane School, located in what had been a factory, had no gymnasium, swimming pool, or athletic grounds. Looking back, Brundage was especially proud of his ability to have improvised what today's athletes take for granted:

I found that I could practice many of the different events in the back yard or on a vacant lot, whenever I had a few spare moments, suiting my own convenience, without waiting to gather a team together. It was easy to dig a sand pit to jump into and to make a pair of jumping standards; a heavy stone served for a shot, a large iron washer for a discus, and a ball of lead and a piece of wire for a hammer. . . . Afterward, in manual training school, I cast a regular shot and a hammer.[10]

Determination was rewarded. During his senior year he was mentioned in the sports pages of the Chicago papers as "the find of the season."[11] His picture began to appear, in track-and-field togs, with spectacles.

At Crane School, Brundage studied English and German, history and "political economy," mathematics and natural science. Enrolling in the university in the fall of 1905, Brundage majored in civil engineering and had a heavy academic load, including courses in mechanics, hydraulics, bridge design, and electrical engineering. Although he received a few grades in the "C" range (railroad structures, masonry construction, tunneling), his record was an excellent one that earned him membership in the honor societies of Tau Beta Pi (1908) and Sigma Chi (1909). His senior project was a study of the specifications for bridges.[12] Although his training in applied science occasionally revealed itself, especially in the 1930s, in an enthusiasm for technological advance in sports—starting blocks for the sprints, electrical timing devices—he was always humanistically rather than scientifically inclined.[13] He found time for a number of courses in the humanities: logic, rhetoric and advanced composition, German, psychology. In his junior year he wrote an article for the engineers' journal, *The Technograph*, "Is There Something Wrong with Current Engineering Education?" He warned against narrowly technical training; the engineer who cares only for his calculations "loses all connection with anything but this little circle in which he moves, and the great outside world means as little to him as Hyperion, the seventh satellite of Saturn, does to any ordinary citizen."[14] With Franklinian energy, Brundage practiced what he preached. In his sophomore year he campaigned to become editor of the yearbook, *The Illio*. He was, however, then pledged to Sigma Alpha Epsilon social fraternity, which jeopardized his chances. "Like most of the college elections in those days," he later recalled, "there was a definite division between the fraternity members and the so-called 'barbarians,' of which there were several times as many."[15] When the editor of the *Daily Illini* offered to keep secret the fact that Brundage was pledged to the fraternity, Brundage replied characteristically, "If they do not want to vote for me, as I am, I do not want their votes."[16] Despite his experience editing the high school paper *Science and Craft*, despite his "up-to-date campaign methods," which included printed cards listing his qualifications and a huge sign suspended at the main campus corner of Wright and Green, he was defeated by H. M. Railsback, 302 to 125. Undaunted by the rebuff, Brundage later worked for *The Illio* board and became a member of the campus literary society, *The Scribbler's Club*. Among the other youthful scribblers was Carl Van Doren, who went on to become a distinguished man of letters (and a biographer of Benjamin Franklin). When the Scribbler's Club sponsored a magazine in Brundage's senior year, he became its editor in chief.[17]

In the midst of these activities, sports were not forgotten. A classmate recalled a typical scene:

I remember . . . math class and how you would return to your seat after completing a problem at the blackboard, reach for your Chicago Tribune from a back pocket, tilt your chair against the wall, and then read the Sports pages for 15 minutes while the rest of us were still laboring to finish our assignments.[18]

Appropriately enough, it was as an athlete that Brundage made his first appearance in the *Daily Illini* on October 15, 1905, when he placed third in the intramural broad-jump competition. (He did better a year later, winning with a leap of 19′4″.) He went on to play intramural lacrosse and football, varsity basketball, and, of course, to become a star in the track-and-field events that were his specialty. In his junior year he defeated fellow engineering student R. W. Reische and became student manager of the track team and a member of the Athletic Association. He joined other student managers in an attempt to protect the integrity of athletic achievement: "Resolved, that it is the sentiment of this Board that the wearing of [school] colors by students not members of varsity teams should be discountenanced as prejudicial to the best athletic interests of the university."[19] School colors worn by those who hadn't earned the right to wear them may seem a minor matter today, when teenagers who never heard of Cambridge or New Haven wear sweatshirts emblazoned with HARVARD (in blue) or YALE (in crimson), but to Brundage the unearned colors represented a forged identity or inauthenticity that he loathed. The orange-and-blue controversy foreshadowed the strife over Olympic symbolism that would obsess him fifty years later.

By his senior year, Brundage was a track star about whom the *Daily Illini* raved, after his performance in a dual meet against Purdue (May 8, 1909),

Avery Brundage, long a star performer for Illinois, inaugurated his last collegiate track season with a versatile bundle of performances. He appeared in an altogether new light, athletically speaking, when he tied for first with [James K.] Richie and [Ludlow J.] Washburn, also of Illinois, in the high jump. He scored first in the discus, first in the shot put, and made third in the hammer throw. [Of] the total score of eighty points he garnered fourteen for the Varsity.[20]

When Coach Harry Gill's team won the Intercollegiate Conference title on June 5, Brundage clearly delighted in the opportunity to write about the success to which he had contributed; in *The Illio* he told how the team thwarted the University of Chicago, then coached by the already redoubtable Amos Alonzo Stagg, on Chicago's own field:

One of the most satisfying events to the Orange and Blue partisans was the relay race. The wily Stagg had anticipated that this would be the deciding event of the meet . . . and had reserved all his quarter-milers, not running a man in the 440, to cinch the event. The Illinois team, with only one fresh man [J. Verne] Richards, who ran a wonderful race—[James Q.] Pettigrew, [James T.] Hanley, and [Carl J.] Rohrer had all participated in grueling contests—assumed the lead on the first lap, and were never headed, completely outclassing the fresh Maroon racers and thoroughly discomfiting the astute Alonzo.[21]

Brundage briefly mentioned his own victory in the discus with a throw of 127'.[22]

Since Brundage finished the year as chairman of the university's paramount social event, the Senior Stag, one might conclude that the athlete-editor-writer-organizer was an extroverted and socially successful young man. Perhaps he was. There are apparently no letters and no diaries or memoirs to reveal an adolescent crisis of the kind that Erik Erikson anatomized in *Young Man Luther*. There is, however, one bit of evidence that strongly suggests a young man Brundage other than the one who stares intently at us from the yearbook photographs of the track team and the Scribbler's Club and *The Illio* board and the Phoenix Honorary Society. In addition to the public face, rather stern even then, there is the private self revealed in a short story which Brundage published in *The Scribbler* for April 1909, just before his graduation. It is the only piece of fiction that he ever published. It can be read as the fictionalized dramatization of the youthful author's secret self.

When *The Scribbler* was founded, it was announced as "partly of a humorous nature,"[23] but the title of Brundage's story is "The Retribution." In it, one hears a somewhat ominous note. Retribution for what? Against whom? The protagonist is a man in his late twenties, a certain Allan Nordaunt, whose name suggests a combination of "dauntless" and "mordant." Conjectures about fictional names are always a little uncertain, but the characterizations of the story are not conjectural at all. Nordaunt is poised, calm, sophisticated, commanding, and mysterious. Alice Stuphen, the lovely girl whom Nordaunt once courted in vain, is overwhelmed when her spurned suitor returns after years abroad. "She still thrilled with the fascination of his presence, the presence that had so enthralled her years ago. Nordaunt certainly had a winning way with most women when he chose to exercise it, which was seldom." Belatedly, Alice realizes, "His virile personality was positively captivating and grew upon one with time." The situation is as naïvely imagined as the characters. Nordaunt has returned to America after what the author refers to (with a Biblical allusion?) as "his seven years' sojourn on the other side of the world." He had left America when fickle Alice broke off their engagement in order foolishly to accept the insincere attentions of a banker's son. Shortly after Nordaunt's heartbroken departure, the wealthy rival jilted Alice in order to marry a girl from New York. It was necessary for Nordaunt to overcome his grief, which he did, manfully: "The grim lines about his mouth and the firm set to his jaw testified to his success in the battle, and the business he managed benefitted by the new strength of will engendered in the conflict."[27] Now, at a dinner party given in his honor, the young man radiates sophistication, charm, and self-confidence and attracts the admiration of everyone present. The details of the scene are hackneyed and sophomoric. As the salad dishes are carried away, Nordaunt muses beneath the candalabrum and decides against sherry. "Notwithstanding his life among the quasi-Latin peoples of the south countries he had not developed a taste for smooth wines—he preferred champagnes and other charged liquors." Thanks to his strength of will and force of character, he is able to win Alice's breathless love and to bring her to the point where she indirectly but unmistakably proposes marriage. After she sighs to him, "I never realized what your friendship meant until I lost it,"[24] he takes her in his arms, kisses her, and, the very next day, departs for Buenos Aires. Alone. It is her turn to suffer from unrequited love. It is just the kind of bitter retribution that many an adolescent, caught in the stormy weather of romantic love, has dreamed of. In the wish-fulfillment fantasy one can see with almost painful clarity the shy and sensitive Avery Brundage known only to his closest friends.

It may be that Brundage actually was disappointed by a young woman who preferred some banker's untrustworthy son, but it seems more likely that the fantasy was more general in nature. It was young Brundage's way of demonstrating his determination to succeed, to overcome his shyness and the handicaps of poverty, to become the envied center of attention, to conquer the world by the force of his will. What is most intriguing about the story is the conclusion. Nordaunt chooses revenge rather than a more conventional boy-gets-girl happy ending. There are those who have wondered if Brundage's idealism verged upon the punitive when those whom he loved—the amateur athletes of the world—failed to live up to his high expectations. Paavo Nurmi, Eleanor Holm Jarrett, Karl Schranz—they all felt his retribution.

Whether or not there really was a young woman in Champaign or Urbana or Chicago to be an Alice Stuphen to Brundage's Allan Nordaunt, the engineer-author did not marry until 1927, eighteen years after his graduation from the university. For the first twelve of those years, until 1921, he lived with his mother at 110 South Dearborn Street in Chicago. He quickly earned enough to support the both of them in reasonable comfort.[25]

While still a student, in the summers of 1906 and 1907, Brundage worked as a surveyor's instrumentman for a railroad construction firm and then as an assistant superintendent for a building contractor. Upon graduation from the university, in 1909, he became a superintendent for the famous Chicago architectural firm of Holabird & Roche. After Chicago's master builder, Daniel H. Burnham, William Holabird and Martin Roche were the most successful architects in the Windy City, known today for their designs of the City Hall and County Courthouse, the Wrigley Building, the Rand-McNally Building, the Palmolive Building, the Daily News Building, the Board of Trade, and a number of hotels, including one that was later to be owned by Avery Brundage (the LaSalle Hotel, built in 1908–1909). Brundage worked on none of these projects but listed other large commissions for whose construction he had some responsibility—The Republic Building, the A. M. Rothschild Store, the Hotel Sherman.[26]

In these years, and later, when he was an independent builder, he was upset by the thefts and bribery which seem to have been common in Chicago's construction industry. His first job required him to superintend and inspect the building of a skyscraper "ornamented with beautiful Indiana limestone trim." When he tried to reject a shipment of limestone that was not up to specifications, he was offered some words of wisdom by the general contractor: "Better think about that young fellow. . . . the stone mason is the nephew of the architect." When he was on his own as a constructor, he secured a $500,000 certified check in order to bid on a public-works job and was told that his politically naïve effort was a waste of time. A friend of his was asked, "Who is this Brundage fellow who has never been in to see the boss?" "After that," wrote Brundage, "I gave up any ideas I might have had of landing public works contracts."[27] His integrity was all the more admirable when one remembers that his Uncle Edward, leader of the "North Side" faction of Chicago's Republican Party and Attorney General of Illinois from 1916 to 1924, was in a position to help an ambitious relative.

Curiously, Uncle Edward was also in a position to tell young Avery something about unfairness in the milieu of professional sports. When tickets for the 1908 World Series between the Chicago Cubs and the Detroit Tigers were to go on sale at Spalding's Sporting Goods Store, scalpers managed to corner the market so quickly that Mayor Frederick Busse was unable to buy a ticket. He was about to close the ballpark—in the middle of Edward Brundage's district—for alleged violations of the building code when Uncle Edward interceded and, presumably, arranged for the Mayor's needs to be met.[28] Avery Brundage's lifelong aversion to commercialized sports may have had its origins in dinnertable anecdotes about the unsavory ties between professional baseball and organized crime, ties which later involved the Chicago White Sox in the worst scandal ever to besmirch American sports.

From uneasy involvement in "the gross social and economic injustices in the imperfect world in which we live."[29] Brundage found refuge in *amateur* athletics. He became a member of the Chicago Athletic Association's famous "Cherry Circle" team. (Uniforms bore a cherry-colored "C" in a circle of the same color.) Since he was not truly talented in any single discipline, he doggedly went out for all of them at once and became, like his former track coach at Illinois, Harry Gill, a specialist in the "all-round" competitions which were then the American version of the decathlon. The events, contested on a single day, were the 100-yard dash, the high jump and the broad jump, the hammer-throw, the pole-vault, the 120-yard high hurdles, the mile run, the 880-yard walk, and the 56-pound-weight throw. Brundage later described the walk as "the closest a man can come to experiencing the pangs of childbirth."[30] Commenting on the weight-throw, Brundage noted that "sometimes the weight would throw you farther than you could throw it."[31] He entered the 1910 All-round Championship, held at Marshall Field in Chicago on August 13, 1910, on the spur of the moment. Never having pole-vaulted, he quickly practiced and cleared 8' before the day of the meet. In the contest itself, he made 10' on his third and last try, "landing on my head and nearly breaking my neck."[32] F. C. Thompson of Los Angeles won with 7,009 points, but Brundage was a very respectable third with 6,038.5.[33] Encouraged by success, he ignored the advice of Cherry Circle coach Martin Delaney and overtrained for the 1911 championship. "I soon had visions of a new world record." He went stale ten days before the meet and came in fourth, "and thus early in life I came to appreciate the Delphic precepts *meden agon* or 'nothing too much' and *gnothi sottan* or 'know thyself.'"[34] Undeterred by disappointment, he began to think ahead to the most important athletic event of his life, the Olympic Games of 1912.

CHAPTER II

COUBERTIN AND THE OLYMPIC IDEAL

Although the flames of the altar of Zeus at Olympia were extinguished by Christian ardor at the end of the fourth or the beginning of the fifth century (historians are unsure whether Theodosius I or II finally ended the pagan celebrations), the memory of the games lingered on throughout the Middle Ages and the Renaissance. There were even attempts to revive the ancient athletic competitions. Robert Dover of Shropshire, for instance, inaugurated annual "Olympick Games" in the Coteswolds in the seventeenth century. (They were more Olympic in the eyes of the poets describing them than in the choice of events, which were English folk games.[1]) On several occasions in the nineteenth century, the Greeks themselves—fired by nationalism after their successful struggle for independence from the Turks—staged "Olympic" contests, but the games failed to win the world's notice. From 1852, however, when the German scholar Ernst Curtius called for a revival of the games, interest increased until Pierre de Coubertin was able, in 1894, to establish the International Olympic Committee which, in turn, made possible the inauguration of the modern cycle at Athens in 1896.[2]

Coubertin's original motives were a mixture of nationalism and internationalism. Born in Paris at 20, rue Odinot, on January 1, 1863, the French nobleman was essentially an educator—or at least a propagandist of education. Upset and humiliated by the French defeat in 1871 at the hands of the more disciplined and better equipped Prussians, Coubertin assumed that the Prussian dedication to physical education had been a crucial factor in his own nation's military defeat. One counter to the Germanic system of gymnastic exercises was the English tradition of schoolboy sports. Coubertin visited England in 1883 and concluded that the playing fields of Eton might decide the *next* battle even if they hadn't really influenced the outcome at Waterloo. He wrote *L'Éducation en Angleterre* (1887) and launched a whole series of organizations devoted to physical education and sports. "Rebronzer la France!" became the motto for the generation which had seen French hegemony disappear in the face of Prussian military might.

Coubertin the revanchiste did not, however, remain unmoved by the international ideals of modern sports. In the course of time, he became less and less chauvinistic and more dedicated to the concept of international good will and cooperation. When Pascal Grousset founded the nationalistic Ligue Nationale de l'Éducation Physique (1888), Coubertin responded by launching the Union des Sociétés Françaises de Sports Athlétiques (1889). In his mind, the Olympic Games gradually came to be an instrument of ecumenicism—so much so that he moved his residence and the office of the International Olympic Committee to Lausanne, Switzerland, in 1915 in order to demonstrate Olympism's neutrality during the World War.[3]

How much of Coubertin's internationalism was evident in the 1890s is uncertain, but he did announce at the fifth anniversary celebration of the Union des Sociétés Françaises de Sports Athlétiques, "It is necessary to internationalize sports; it is necessary to revive the Olympic Games."[4] With the "renovation" of the games very much on his mind, he invited foreign as well as French scholars and educators (but not athletes) to the Sorbonne for an international conference on the principles of amateurism. Seventy-eight delegates attended, from nine countries.[5] (The French themselves, comments one of the Baron's biographers, showed "absolute indifference.")[6] The conference opened on June 16, 1894, and covered a number of topics before Coubertin skillfully guided attention to the realization of his dream. Always mindful of symbolism and ceremony, he arranged for the conference to hear a performance of the ancient "Hymn to Apollo," discovered the previous year at Delphi, transcribed by the classicist Théodore Reinach, set to music by Gabriel Fauré, and exquisitely sung by Jeanne Remacle of the Opéra Français. "If the Olympic Games have been reborn, it was perhaps during those instants when every heart beat as one."[7] Coubertin suggested reviving the games and the delegates, on June 23, responded unanimously to his appeal. They accepted Père Henri-Martin Didon's suggestion for a motto: "Citius, Altius, Fortius" ("faster, higher, stronger"), words engraved on the entrance to Père Didon's lycée, Albert le Grand. Coubertin was authorized to establish an International Olympic Committee (I.O.C.) and to work with it for the revival of the games at Athens in 1896. For his colleagues, he chose Generals Viktor Balck of Sweden and Alexander Butowsky of Russia, Demetrius Bikelas of Greece, Chancellor Jiri Guth-Jarkovsky of Bohemia, Ferenc Kemeny of Hungary, William Milligan Sloane of the United States, and eight others, none of whom seems to have shown up in Athens for the second session of the I.O.C. In his *Mémoires Olympiques*, Coubertin described the I.O.C. as a nucleus of active members, a wider group of men of "bonne volonté," and a "façade" of more or less useful men who gave the committee the benefit of their prestige.[8] The committee's first president was a diplomatic choice, Demetrius Bikelas of Greece, whose chief function was to stir his countrymen's enthusiasm for the new venture while Coubertin worked feverishly to find rules and regulations acceptable to athletes from a dozen different countries.[9]

Preparations for the games were beset with difficulties and the Baron had to rush off to Athens in November of 1894 to try to solve some of them. Since the Greek government under Prime Minister Charilaos Tricoupis was hostile to the notion of hosting the games, it was fortunate that Tricoupis was forced from office in January 1895 and replaced by Theodoros Deligiannes. Enthusiastic support from Crown Prince Constantine and his brother George was an invaluable asset to Coubertin, and it was another stroke of luck that the wealthy Alexandrine businessman, George Averoff, was moved to demonstrate his Hellenism with the gift of a refurbished Olympic stadium in Athens. The ancient stadium of Herodes Atticus was reconstructed and readied for the modern athletes.

Difficulties of another sort were caused by the Germans, whose most important athletic organization, Die Deutsche Turnerschaft, was committed to the national tradition of gymnastics (*Turnen*) and quite hostile to modern sports, which the Deutsche Turnerschaft saw as liberal, internationalist, and English in their inspiration. Fortunately for Coubertin, an influential professor of chemistry, Willibald Gebhardt, founder of the Deutscher Bund für Spiel und Sport (1895), got wind of the projected games and offered his support. In 1896 he became the fifteenth member of the I.O.C. In him, Coubertin had an immensely helpful colleague.

In all, twelve nations responded to the I.O.C.'s invitation. The thirteen-member American team was made up principally of four students from Princeton, where I.O.C. member William Milligan Sloane taught French history, and of five members of the Boston Athletic Association. Despite a scattering of articles in American magazines, there was little interest in the games. Perhaps the excitement of the presidential campaign pitting William Jennings Bryan against William McKinley preoccupied the American public. The level of academic support outside of Professor Sloane's Princeton office is indicated by the experience of James B. Connolly, a Harvard undergraduate:

When his dean advised him not to risk the trip, since he might not be readmitted, Connolly replied, "I am not resigning and I am not making application to reenter, But I *am* going to the Olympic Games, so I am through with Harvard right now. Good day, sir."[10]

The American group was nonetheless the largest except for the Greek team. The British numbered only six, including Edwin Flack, a well-known distance runner from Australia, and J. P. Boland, an English tourist who decided on the spur of the moment to enter the tennis competition in singles and in doubles (he won both, the second with a German partner, a bit of internationalism no longer allowed). The greatest disappointment for Coubertin was the French team, which "consisted of two cyclists, some fencers, a runner, and a couple of French tourists . . . who happened to be in Athens in the spring of 1896."[11] It was "a motley handful."[12] Thanks to Gebhardt's heroic exertions, the Germans sent three track-and-field athletes and ten brave gymnasts who defied the Deutsche Turnerschaft's boycott and suffered suspension as their punishment.

As the opening day approached, Coubertin was lyrically ecstatic. In a letter dated March 26, he wrote:

The Athenian spring is double this year. It warms not only the clear atmosphere but the soul of the populace. It pushes up sweet-smelling flowers between the stones of the Parthenon. . . . The sun shines, and the Olympic games are here. The fears and ironies of the year just past have disappeared. The skeptics have been eliminated; the Olympic games have not a single enemy.[13]

On the opening day, also the anniversary of Greek independence, nearly half of the entire city of Athens crowded into the stadium or gathered on the hills surrounding it, but the games themselves threatened to become a major disappointment for the Greeks as the Americans swept the track-and-field events. Thomas Burke of the Boston Athletic Association won the 100-meter and the 400-meter races while his fellow Bostonians, Thomas Curtis, Ellery Clark, William Hoyt, and James Connolly won the hurdles, the jumps, and the pole vault. Even the discus prize eluded the Greek athletes as Robert Garrett, a junior from Princeton who had never even seen a discus until a few weeks before the games, outthrew Panagiotis Paraskevopoulos with a toss of 29.15 meters. (Garrett also bested his Greek rival, Miltiades Gouskos, in the shot put.) The German gymnasts and the French cyclists triumphed as had been expected, but Greek athletes had their moments of success in fencing and shooting, and Nike, goddess of victory, saved the day for the happy hosts. The marathon, invented for the 1896 games in commemoration of the legendary courier's run of 490 B.C., was won by a Greek peasant, Spiridon Loues, whose entry into the stadium brought the young princes down from the stands and on to the track, where they accompanied their triumphant countryman to the finish. The games ended in a series of banquets and speeches. Reports published in various European and American journals were laudatory. Although Coubertin was treatedly badly by the Greeks, who behaved as if the revival of the games had been entirely *their* idea, his dream had been realized.

At least in part. Coubertin took satisfaction in the fact that athletes of many different countries had participated in the contests, but he must have been somewhat disappointed that the French had not turned out in greater numbers and that they had not been more impressively represented among the victors. Runner Albin Lermusieux attracted less attention for his athletic prowess than for his hurriedly drawing on a pair of white gloves just before the 100-meter race; he explained to the astonished Thomas Curtis, "Ah-ha! Zat is because I run for ze king!"[14] Coubertin's countrymen continued to disappoint him; they "took to Olympics very slowly."[15] It was perhaps significant that Coubertin's account, "The Olympic Games of 1896," was published not in France but rather in an American journal, *Century*, for November 1896. Even the official journal of the Union des Sociétés Françaises de Sports Athlétiques sneered at its founder's efforts: "At this moment, the Olympic Games have gathered a rather second-rate group of athletes in Athens. . . . This fact is enough for us to give the games the small place they deserve in the resurrection of the ancient Olympic Games."[16]

Even greater were the setbacks of 1900, when the games were celebrated in Paris. It was the year of an *exposition universelle* and Coubertin reluctantly agreed to allow the athletic competitions to be held in conjunction with the exposition, which ran from April 15 to October 15. Since the French bureaucracy was far more concerned for the commercial aspects of the fair, the athletic events were, in effect, lost in the shuffle. Indeed, Commissioner Alfred Picart disliked sports. Facilities were wretched; the competitions stretched out over a period of four months; they were badly publicized; they attracted little attention; they were marred by disputes.

Perhaps Coubertin took comfort in the fact that the games were held at all.

Once again, the Americans dominated the track-and-field events. Alvin Kraenzlein was especially impressive, winning the 110-meter hurdles and the 200-meter dash as well as the long jump and the 60-meter dash. Another American, Ray Ewry, won three gold medals in events that now strike us, for no good reason, as quaint: the standing high, long, and triple jumps. French athletic honor was saved by fifteen medals in fencing, twelve in shooting, and at least another twelve in archery (records are incomplete). In the absence of the German gymnasts, the French won medals there too.

Unfortunately for international good will, a number of American athletes from Princeton, Yale, and other universities refused to compete on July 15 because it was the Sabbath; the French thought little of their suggestions that events be contested on July 14 instead (Bastille Day). The marathon also caused resentments. Originally planned as a run from Versailles to Paris, the route was changed at the last minute to one that twisted and wound through Paris. The race was won by Michel Theato, a Frenchman, but the victor appeared remarkably unspotted by the puddle-strewn course. Walter Tewksbury, the American who won gold medals in the 200 meters and in the 400-meter hurdles, commented, "There wasn't a drop of mud on the three Frenchmen. Everyone else in the race was drenched with the stuff."[17] Arthur Newton of the New York Athletic Club, who came in fifth, claimed to have passed the Frenchmen early in the race, only to find them there ahead of him at the finish. Explanations for these mysteries come quickly to mind.

It may have been owing to such episodes as these that the I.O.C. held its fourth session in Paris in May of 1901 and took up the question of the standardization of rules and regulations. Should the I.O.C. attempt to take charge of this formidable task (as Coubertin had done in 1896)? Gebhardt urged that this be done, but Coubertin successfully argued that the matter be left to the national sports federations, which might then be encouraged to form international organizations (like the Fédération Internationale de Gymnastique, which had been founded in 1881). The relationships among the I.O.C., the national federations, and the international ones were to occupy Coubertin and his successors, including Avery Brundage, for many years to come.

The less than overwhelming success of the Parisian games made 1904 seem a crucial year. The I.O.C. accepted Chicago's offer to host the games. St. Louis, however, was planning its famous fair ("Meet me in St. Louis, Louis, meet me at the fair!") and threatening to stage rival games. When Henry Gurrer, president of the organizing committee, wrote on November 26, 1902, that Chicago was ready to surrender the honor to St. Louis, the I.O.C. decided that the games were fated to be held on the banks of the Mississippi rather than on the shores of Lake Michigan (where the seventeen-year-old Brundage might have been among the spectators). Despite its dread of a second Olympiad lost in the hustle and bustle of a world's fair, the I.O.C. authorized the change.

It was a bad mistake. For one thing, the middle West—Chicago or St. Louis—was simply too far for most Europeans. Their devotion to Olympism, or their pecuniary resources, were insufficient to bring them across the Atlantic and then an additional 1,000 miles into the interior of the continent. In fact, Coubertin himself remained in France and the I.O.C. held its official session in London rather than in St. Louis. The majority of the athletes were from the United States and Americans monopolized the track-and-field events, winning 64 of the 69 medals. Americans harvested *all* of the medals in archery, boxing, cycling, and free-style wrestling, and picked up another 29 in rowing.

The games had their highpoints, of course. Ray Ewry, for instance, astonished the spectators with a duplication of his victories in the three standing jumps. World records were set in the 200-meter, 400-meter, 800-meter, and 1500-meter races. There were also the usual disputes. Fred Lorz was wildly cheered as the winner of the marathon until it became known that he had traveled much of the distance in a truck. The lowpoint of the entire summer was surely the "Anthropological Days" in August, when a group of not very carefully chosen "aborigines" from the side shows of the fair competed among themselves in track-and-field events and then in their native sports. The achievements were generally unimpressive, and the impression given was one that certainly supported the popular white-supremacist beliefs of the day. Watching pygmies engaged in a mud-fight, American, British, French, and German spectators might well have felt that their nations were morally right to bring modern sports (as well as the rest of civilization) to the Philippines, to East Africa, to Indo-China, and to the islands of the Pacific. Coubertin's comment had overtones of resignation:

In no place but America would one have dared place such events on a program—but to Americans everything is permissible, their youthful exuberance calling certainly for the indulgence of the ancient Greek ancestors, if, by chance, they found themselves at that time among the amused spectators.[18]

At the sixth session of the I.O.C., held in London in June of 1904, the main item of business to be settled was the site of the 1908 games. Although Gebhardt hoped to bring them to Berlin, Coubertin preferred a more classical spot. "I desired Rome," he later commented, "only because I wanted Olympism, after its return from the excursion to utilitarian America, to don once again the sumptuous toga, woven of art and philosophy, in which I had always wanted to clothe her."[19] As it turned out, the Italians found the task of organization beyond them. Fortunately, the British Olympic Association, founded in London in 1905, stepped in and offered to act as hosts. "To the British must go all the credit for first placing the organization of the games upon a firm and businesslike basis."[20] The organizing committee defined the term amateur to its satisfaction and let the national federations decide whether or not their athletes lived up to the rules; they established official entry dates and the right of the organizing committee to refuse entry; they placed limits on the number of entries from any one country. In short, the British found temporary answers to problems that still bedevil the I.O.C.

There was, nonetheless, a series of petty disputes.[21] Tensions between Ireland and England, which led to ill will between the hosts and the numerous Irish-Americans representing the United

States, were responsible for many difficulties. The American (and the Swedish) flags were, initially, not displayed in the stadium. During the opening ceremony, the American flag was not dipped for the English monarch (and hasn't been dipped since). The officials, all of whom were supplied by the hosts, were accused of rank partiality, especially where American athletes were involved. Wyndham Halswelle of Great Britain won the 400 meters in a "walkover" because the other finalists, both Americans, wished to protest the judges' disqualification of their countryman, J. C. Carpenter. The marathon was a memorable fiasco. The Italian contestant Dorando Pietri was the first to enter the stadium at Wimbledon, but he was too exhausted to last the final few yards. As he staggered toward the finish and then fell to the ground, he was lifted bodily by the officials and dragged across the goal. (A photograph of the exhausted runner and the helpful officials is one of the most famous in Olympic history.) American protests, scorned at first as signs of poor sportsmanship, eventually prevailed, but the British managed to steal the limelight from the American winner, John Hayes; a special trophy was presented to Pietri by Queen Alexandra. As late as 1972, British authors still refused to credit Hayes with his hard-earned victory.[22]

In the years between 1908 and 1912, the I.O.C. grappled with the problems of amateurism. Since professional fencers had competed in 1896 and 1900, and the victorious American cyclists of 1904 were also paid performers, the problem seemed acute. At an Olympic Congress organized in Brussels in 1905 by the newly elected Belgian member, Henri Comte de Baillet-Latour, everyone seemed to agree that it was indeed hard to agree on a definition of amateurism. Albert Comte de Bertier de Sauvigny of France reported on amateurism at the tenth session of the I.O.C. (Berlin, 1909), and the matter was referred to a committee consisting of Thomas A. Cook of Great Britain, Jules de Muzza of Hungary, and William Milligan Sloane of the United States. (When the committee reported back a year later in Luxembourg, a new committee was named to study the matter further.) It was undoubtedly a relief to turn to the more determinable question of the site for 1912.

Stockholm was chosen even though boxing was illegal in Sweden and had to be omitted from the program. Although women had competed in tennis in 1900 and in 1908 and in archery and yachting in 1908, Coubertin protested a move to increase their presence in 1912. He found their participation "impractical, uninteresting, unaesthetic, and incorrect."[23] Nonetheless, the I.O.C. decided at Luxembourg to admit women to the games as swimmers and as tennis players.

One result of the disputes in London was that the I.O.C. wisely decided to carry its internationalism one step further and to insist that the officials for 1912 be provided not by the host nation alone but by all the nations represented in the relevant international federations. The careful planning of logistics which had made the 1908 Olympics a more or less smoothly run affair continued in 1912. The facilities were excellent; the Swedes built a grand new stadium of brick and undressed granite, in the form of a "U," with seating capacity of 27,000. Led by the engineer Sigfrid Edstrøm, the Swedes were ready to mount the most successful of prewar games. When King Gustav V welcomed the youth of the world on the fifth of May, the stage was set for Jim Thorpe—and Avery Brundage.

CHAPTER III

STOCKHOLM
AND AFTER

Before the celebration of the 1908 Olympics in London, Brundage had not been particularly interested in the games, but one of his friends, Wilbur G. Burroughs, won a place on the team that went to England, wrote about his experiences in the *Daily Illini* ("Every Judge was an Englishman"), and undoubtedly talked at length to the other members of the Illinois track-and-field squad.[1] Having "specialized" in the all-round competitions in 1910 and 1911, Brundage now entered the tryouts for the pentathlon and the decathlon, events which appeared on the Olympic program for the first time in 1908. On May 16, 1912, he won the Western tryouts for the pentathlon. He outdid his only rival in the long jump (21'4.5") and the javelin throw (137'6") and he performed well in the 200-meter dash and the discus throw, but his time over 1500 meters was a slow 5:46.8. A week later, he competed against four others in the tryouts for the decathlon, which consisted of races over 100, 400, and 1500 meters, the 110-meter hurdles, the long and high jumps, the pole vault, the shot put, and the discus and javelin throws. Although he won none of the ten events, he finished an overall second to Eugene Shobinger and qualified for the team.[2]

His excitement was evident even sixty years later when he began chapter 1 of his unfinished manuscript autobiography by describing his "unbounded elation" upon receiving a telegram from James E.

Sullivan, secretary of the American Olympic Committee. In Brundage's memory, the text read: "You have been chosen a member of the U.S. team for the games of the Vth Olympiad in Stockholm."[3] Actually, the telegram read: "You have been selected a member of the American Team[.] [R]eport at Hotel Hermitage Newyork not later than Wednesday morning June 12th to compete in Olympic Fund benefit games to be held on that day. Bring club or college flag for decoration of boat."[4] Brundage's memory culled away the prosaic details and rewrote the telegram in romantic form.

In order to take advantage of the marvelous opportunity, Brundage was forced to resign his position with Holabird & Roche, a sacrifice which certainly reinforced his conviction that amateur sports demand a moral as well as a physical commitment. The sacrifice was one which he, ever afterward, expected others to make.

He packed his bags and departed for New York and Stockholm. The team, 164 strong (including officials), sailed on the *Finland*, embarking on June 14. The passenger list includes not only "Avery Brundage" but also "Mrs. Brundage," which has led at least one scholar to assume that Minnie Lloyd Brundage accompanied her twenty-four-year-old son to Sweden.[5] It is far more likely that Brundage brought along a female companion about whom nothing more is known or that the passenger list was simply in error. It is a minor mystery which Brundage did not resolve in the manuscript autobiography.

During the ten-day voyage across the Atlantic, the team trained on a special 100-yard cork track and in a canvas swimming pool, in the middle of which swimmers were suspended from the waist by a rope. Distance runners trotted around and around the deck while tennis players practiced on "an imaginary tennis court."[6] James E. Sullivan's official account of the voyage emphasizes dedication and youthful high spirits, but Brundage noted the presence of large appetites too: "Exposure to the unlimited menus on shipboard was fatal to some and several hopes of Olympic victory foundered at the bounteous dinner table."[7] Perhaps Brundage, who never weighed much more than 190, underestimated the caloric needs of the weight men, whom he jocularly referred to as the "Irish Whales."[8]

The boat docked in Antwerp and the athletes were generously welcomed by Belgian sportsmen, who offered them the use of the facilities at the Beershot Athletic Club. The Americans took them up on this despite the heavy rain. Two days later, on June 26, they sailed for Stockholm. Passage through the "alluring archipelago" was pleasant, but there was no Olympic Village in Stockholm and the team was "cooped up" on shipboard.[9] The cabins were small and hot, and "members of the team, after their events were finished, disturbed the others by their boisterous return late in the evening."[10] Long summer days made the nights seem especially short.

Nonetheless, when King Gustav V opened the games on July 6, there was "an electric excitement in the air."[11] The spectators joined the athletes in singing "A Mighty Fortress Is Our God." The weather was glorious and Secretary Sullivan was moved very nearly to poetry: "a bright warm sun shone on the arena, making the flags of all nations ruffling in the breeze resemble an enormous multicolored bow."[12] Brundage was apparently more struck by the display of organizational mastery: "I was a young engineer just from the university. The efficiency and almost mathematical precision with which the events were handled and the formal correctness of the arrangements made a great impression on me."[13] Looking backward, Brundage noted, "Four of the men who were to lead and guide the Olympic Movement for the next sixty years were there in Stockholm," but he was but one of 2,541 competitors and had no opportunity then to meet Coubertin or his successors, the Belgian count, Henri de Baillet-Latour, and the Swedish engineer, Sigfrid Edstrøm.[14] Among the throng were also Carl Diem and Karl Ritter von Halt, German athletes and sports administrators who were eventually to be numbered among Brundage's closest friends. By strange coincidence, the Finnish team included a gymnast, Karl Gustav Wahamaki, whose daughter was destined to give birth, forty years later, to Avery Brundage's only children.

Although the Swedish team was the most successful when all the events are taken into account, the Americans once again dominated the track and field, sweeping all three places in the 110-meter hurdles, in the 100-meter and 800-meter races, in the pole vault and the shot put. Contrary to earlier predictions, James Meredith, a student at Mercersburg Academy, beat out his favored countrymen, Melvin Sheppard and Ira Davenport, and won the 800-meter race in world-record time (1:51.9). Brundage was thrilled by Meredith's will power and remarked years later that the memory of the race was more vivid for him than the works of Michelangelo or Rembrandt.[15] Brundage was also excited by the great Finnish runner, Hannes Kolehmainen, who won easily in the 10,000 meters and in the cross-country contests but who barely vanquished France's Jean Bouin in the 5,000 meters. Indeed, Kolehmainen's margin was only .10 second.

Among Brundage's rivals in the pentathlon was Jim Thorpe, whose performance in the Eastern Try-Outs in New York had been scarcely if at all better than Brundage's back in Chicago. Now, Brundage improved his efforts, but the Indian athlete seemed inspired by the Olympics. It was all Brundage could do to come in sixth in the pentathlon. It was by no means a shameful outcome, but the decathlon proved to be a catastrophe which bothered Brundage for the rest of his life. Realizing that he was far behind in points, Brundage dropped out rather than run the 1500-meter race, which he hated. "This failure to finish the competition was unforgiveable."[16] It was an uncharacteristic lack of will. It was ever afterwards an occasion for self-reproach. Thirty-five years later, Brundage praised Philip Noel-Baker because the Englishman had run the 1500 meters in Stockholm despite a painful injury. Noel-Baker had "stayed the race" as Brundage had not.[17]

Although Brundage worried about his own moral lapse, others have remembered Thorpe's achievement and have written elo-

Table 1. Pentathlon Results, 1912

	Broad Jump	Javelin	200 Meters	Discus	1500 Meters
Brundage	21'7.05"	140'7.00"	24.4 sec.	113'10.9"	5 min. 12.9 sec.
Thorpe	23'2.70"	153'2.95"	22.9 sec.	116'8.4"	4 min. 44.8 sec.

quently of his introduction to the admiring Swedish monarch ("Sir, you are the greatest athlete in the world!") and indignantly of the sorry aftermath of the Olympics, when it was disclosed that Thorpe had played semiprofessional summer baseball while at the Carlisle Indian School. (Far more serious violations at the school itself have since been discovered; while allegedly a student, Thorpe had been paid to play football.[18]) Since he had violated the amateur code as it was then construed, he was stripped of his medals. An abject appeal, written for him by his famous mentor, G. S. ("Pop") Warner, was in vain, and it was not until 1982 that the I.O.C., under pressure from the United States Olympic Committee, finally reversed its original verdict. Those who feel that Thorpe had been treated unjustly have hinted that Brundage's adament opposition to the Indian athlete's reinstatement had been motivated by resentment that Thorpe had beaten him in 1912.[19] It was Brundage's misfortune not only to have competed against a legend but also to believe that the fateful punishment meted out to the hero was fully justified by the hero's moral inadequacy.

My account of Brundage's participation in the 1912 games has been chronological. His own was not. The unpublished autobiography tentatively entitled "The Olympic Story" begins with the arrival of Sullivan's telegram and then moves backward in time to describe Brundage's enthusiasm for sports while still a high–school and a college student. After a description of the team and of the voyage to Stockholm comes a burst of praise for the Olympic ideal:

What social, racial, religious or political prejudices of any kind might have existed, were soon forgotten and sportsmen from all over the world, with different ideas, assorted viewpoints, and various manners of living, mingled on the field and off with the utmost friendliness, transported by an overflowing Olympic spirit.

An account of the competition follows, interrupted by memories of his experience as a construction supervisor and as a young businessman. The contrast is stark. Whether Brundage consciously intended the dramatic structure or not, there is a thematic opposition in the chapter between business and sports. Immediately after describing the corruption and dishonesty of the construction industry, he attempts to sum up the meaning of the Olympic movement. Against the dark background of "the gross social and economic injustices of the imperfect world in which we live," he projects the shining image of ideal Olympism:

All were judged and judged solely on their merit, regardless of social position, wealth, family connections, race, religion, color or political affiliation. Here was no commercial connivery nor political chicanery. The rules were the same for everyone, respected by all, and enforced impartially.

The chapter concludes with a declaration of faith: "My conversion, along with many others, to Coubertin's religion, the Olympic Movement, was complete." The key terms are all there in the prose. On the one hand, the ascriptive characteristics of birth; on the other hand, the achievements of individual merit. Against the sordid backdrop of connivery, chicanery, dishonesty, corruption, unfairness, and injustice, the bright clarity of fair play and impartial rules. It was the birth of a dream.

The participants, wrote Brundage, left Stockholm "with wider horizons,"[20] and he was in search of still wider ones. He applied in Stockholm for a passport and set out with Lewis R. Anderson, J. Duncan, and J. R. Case, all track-and-field men, for Finland (then ruled by the Russians).[21] The American athletes were shown about by A. R. Taipaly.[22] In either Stockholm or Helsinki, Brundage met Lauri Pihkala, soon to become famous for his contributions to the study and the administration of sports,[23] later one of Brundage's most faithful and philosophic correspondents. The Americans competed in Helsinki on July 20–22, 1912, and then journeyed on to St. Petersburg, where the Russians' hospitality was exuberant. Vodka was served just before the track meet and "one of our wild Irish discus throwers nearly decapitated a Grand Duke who was too close to the scene of [the] action."[24] Brundage was in no great danger of decapitation, but the facilities in St. Petersburg were primitive and he broke his wrist "in a jumping pit which was not a pit at all but a pile of shavings."[25] He continued on with the others to Moscow, Kiev, and Odessa, but he was unable to compete. He paid a brief visit to Izmir (then known as Smyrna) on the west coast of Turkey, but his exact itinerary is uncertain.[26] Notes which he drew up on "Travel to 1932" describe a trajectory from Antwerp to Stockholm to Helsinki, but the line ends with a tantalizing "Viborg, Etc."[27] He probably stopped in Istanbul en route from Odessa to Izmir. From the Turkish port the likeliest route was by ship to Athens, Brindisi, or Venice, and then by train to Paris. A chronology drawn up in 1971 by Karl Adolf Scherer and amended in 1972 by Brundage refers to a "Reise ins zaristische Rußland" ("journey to Czarist Russia"), to which Brundage added in ink, "and all Europe."[28]

Upon returning to the United States, Brundage had to find work, which he did, apparently without great difficulty. He became a superintendent for the construction firm of John Griffiths and Son. Living frugally with his mother, he repaid the loans that had made his trip abroad possible. He then saved $2,000 and borrowed additional money in order to launch his own construction firm in 1915.

In an article published in the *Big Ten Weekly*, he asked rhetorically, "Why Die When You Graduate?" He chided college players who dropped completely out of sports after graduation and urged them to join private athletic clubs where they might continue to compete well into middle age.[29] Despite the demands of his growing business, he remained highly active in competitive sports. Of his training schedule, it was reported, "From May until October he puts in two hours every night exercising under the moon and stars. In winter the same two hours are spent in a gymnasium where he varies his routine by playing a great deal of handball."[30]

His finest athletic achievements came after the disappointments in Stockholm. In 1914 he represented the Chicago Athletic Association in the "all-round" competition held that year in Birmingham, Alabama. In the ten events he scored 6,999 points while his closest rival, the local favorite, Gilbert Ritchie, managed only 6,743. The Birmingham *News* marveled at Brundage's prowess:

With an air of confidence, Brundage stepped upon the field accompanied by his manager at 1:30 o'clock. His lithe form and sinewy limbs bespoke of fitness. His carriage cried out confidence. His poise displayed courage and ability. From the opening event to the 100-yard dash, the spectators realized that Brundage was a winner and almost in a class by himself.[31]

It was a triumph that Brundage was able to repeat in 1916 and 1918 with a total of 6,468.75 points (at Newark, New Jersey) and 6,708.5 points (at Chicago's Great Lakes Naval Training Station). Still smarting from the self-inflicted wounds of Stockholm, he felt somewhat redeemed by these three victories. Patrick McDonald, the shot-put winner at Stockholm and, at 6'5" and 280 pounds, one of the."Irish whales," congratulated Brundage with a mighty slap on the back and heavy-handed wit, "Avery, me boy, had you only a few drops of Irish blood, you might well be a pretty good athlete."[32] McDonald's kidding amused Brundage, but a newspaper comment must have hurt him; reporting on Brundage's 1916 victory over Alma Richards, who had won a gold medal at Stockholm in the high jump, the Cairo (Illinois) *Herald* remarked, "The Chicagoan is not a Jim Thorpe . . . by any means but at the same time he gave a good performance."[33] Thorpe's shadow was to haunt Brundage for the rest of his life. Still, headlines in the Chicago papers undoubtedly helped the Avery Brundage Company as well as the Avery Brundage psyche.

In retrospect, the psyche is more interesting, if harder to be certain about, than the performances in the ten events of the "all-round." Brundage's coach at the Chicago Athletic Association, Martin Delaney, felt that Brundage trained too strenuously, tried too hard, wanted victory so much that psychological strain often hindered him. Ironically, the win in 1914 was Brundage's athletic zenith, because a foot injury incurred that summer forced him to rest for a couple of weeks, long enough for him to achieve his maximum on the day of the meet.[34] When Brundage later warned young athletes, with an analogy drawn from the physics of metals, not to strain themselves beyond the "elastic limit," he spoke from experience.[35]

Delaney also noted another important characteristic. Brundage was extremely upset when his opponents cheated. Although Delaney didn't speculate on this, it is clear that cheaters jeopardize precisely that ideal world of fair play and justice that Brundage sought in sports. The cheater was the moral equivalent of the dishonest businessman and the politician on the take. Jumping the gun was like slipping the superintendent a bribe. Brundage eventually learned to control his highly emotional reactions to the walker who ran or the runner who used his elbows against a rival, but he always detested cheaters as apostates from the religion of sports.

Track-and-field championships are for young men. At thirty-one, Brundage had shown remarkable durability, but it was time to switch the focus of his active (if not his passive) involvement in sports. He had played handball for years (the American version, not the European team sport); now he concentrated on it and represented the Chicago Athletic Association in local and national tournaments. He was the hometown champion and the president of Chicago's Handball League. It was a game at which he excelled— as an individual. He was ranked among the nation's ten best players and took one of two games against Angelo Trulio, 1932's national champion, by a score of 21–19 (after a loss of 21–16). Since Brundage was then forty-six years old, the New York *Times* seems to have overdone its understatement: "Brundage Shows Skill as Handball Player."[36] Until age and injury slowed him, in his sixties, he continued to be an avid, if not a fanatic, player.

As he was an active athlete and a respected businessman, it was no surprise when Brundage began to play an increasingly important role in sports administration. He became a member of the board of directors of the Chicago Athletic Association, which enabled him to become active in the Central Amateur Athletic Association and then in the national organization of which the Central Association was a part, the Amateur Athletic Union (A.A.U.). By the time of his election as president of the A.A.U., in 1928, he had become disaffected from the Chicago club. The reasons were characteristic. In 1928 the club dropped track and field from its schedule of competition. In 1931, the Board of Directors considered abandoning ice hockey and swimming as well. Brundage felt strongly that the club had been neglecting its younger members and had been becoming primarily a social rather than an athletic institution. The name "Chicago Athletic Association" summoned up images of obese bankers, cigar smoke, and whisky on the rocks rather than the picture of lean young men in Cherry Circle track suits. When Brundage failed to persuade other members of the Board to return to earlier policies, he resigned.[37] An athletic association whose members cared more for jiggers than for dashes was no better than a fraud.

When Brundage began in 1919 to assume administrative responsibilities within the Amateur Athletic Union, the A.A.U. was roughly as old as he was. Dissension within the National Association of Amateur Athletes of America (N.A.A.A.A.), which had been founded by a group of New York athletic clubs in 1879, led to the formation of the A.A.U. on January 21, 1888. The new organization quickly adopted restrictive rules which made it impossible for members to participate in meets it did not sponsor. By the end of 1889, the organization had grown to over 10,000 members and was able to absorb the membership of the faltering N.A.A.A.A. The A.A.U. had, in effect, "gained control of amateur athletics" in the United States.[38] Specifically, the group claimed jurisdiction over twenty-three different sports, including track and field.

Affiliation with the A.A.U. was attained through club membership, but clubs like the famed New York Athletic Club, founded in 1868, began to play a less dominant role in sports as colleges and universities, and even high schools, became increasingly involved in athletics. Unlike the Germans and French, whose amateur sports are organized through private clubs and sports federations, Americans chose to institutionalize sports within the educational system, with fateful consequences. The colleges and universities, not clubs like the Chicago Athletic Association, were destined to control amateur athletics in the United States. This meant that active participation tended to end abruptly with graduation from high school or college. A further development was that the professionalization of American coaches, employed by schools and colleges, put the student-athlete under the control of an older man whose occupational concerns were not always congruent with those of his young charges.

As early as 1875, thirteen years before the founding of the A.A.U., the most prestigious eastern colleges formed the Intercollegiate Association of Amateur Athletes of America (I.C.A.A.A.A.). When the brutality and dishonesty of intercollegiate football brought about the crisis of 1905, at which time many universities abolished the game and others asked how it might be brought under control, Chancellor H. M. McCracken of New York University invited delegates from twenty institutions to a conference which, in turn, led to a larger conference and the formation in 1906 of the Intercollegiate Athletic Association of the United States. Renamed the National Collegiate Athletic Association in 1910, this organization has slowly come to dominate amateur sports in the United States. In order to do this, the N.C.A.A. has had to supplant the A.A.U. in many of the sports which the older organization once governed. As one scholar has noted, "although it was not evident in 1906, the relations between these two sports bodies were to have a great deal to do with the shaping of amateur athletics in the United States."[39] Comparing A.A.U. officers with those of the N.C.A.A., one of the former remarked proudly that sports were an *avocation* for the A.A.U. and a *vocation* for the rival group.[40] Realizing that officials who volunteered their services on behalf of athletic clubs were no match for salaried professional coaches backed by the financial resources of the nation's universities (and aided in their recruitment by the adoption of a physical-education requirement), James E. Sullivan of the A.A.U. suggested an alliance in 1906, but the college-based organization rejected the offer. Controversies developed in which each group used the weapon which came most quickly to hand—the disbarment of its members from competitions sponsored by the other. The conflict, troublesome at first, became dormant during World War I, then flared up more intensely than ever in the 1920s, when the strife centered on control of the American Olympic Committee.

This committee, which came to life every four years in order to arrange for American participation in the Olympic Games, had originally been the creature of the A.A.U. (The committee which selected Avery Brundage and sent him to Stockholm had been picked by James E. Sullivan of the A.A.U.) As the N.C.A.A. began to overshadow the A.A.U. nationally, the latter organization was able to rely upon support from the *international* sports organizations for whom the American type of school-based sports seemed an aberration rather than an inevitability. The N.C.A.A. sought to limit if not to end the A.A.U.'s control of the American Olympic Committee. The opportunity came when mismanagement of the team sent to the Olympic Games at Antwerp in 1920 caused a public scandal. Scores of athletes returned from the Belgian city on a commercial ocean liner rather than on the troopship chartered by the Olympic committee. The N.C.A.A. decided the time was ripe for a call to reform. At its annual convention, December 29, 1920, the group resolved that the American Olympic Committee (A.O.C.) be restructured. Gustavus Town Kirby of the A.A.U. also suggested a reorganization scheme, which the A.O.C. accepted on February 5, 1921; but the Reorganization Committee, which met on May 4, voted to *reduce* the N.C.A.A.'s share of delegates at the proposed convention from 16 to 3 (the A.A.U. was to have 33 delegates), which, of course, infuriated the collegiate group led by Palmer Pierce of West Point. It is quite possible that the A.A.U. hoped by this insult to provoke the N.C.A.A. into a boycott. If this was the strategy, it worked—at least in the short run. The A.A.U. went ahead and formed the American Olympic Association on November 25, 1921, without participation by the N.C.A.A. The A.O.A. then chose Robert M. Thompson of the A.A.U. as its president and elected a nine-member Executive Committee that included seven of its own members—and Palmer Pierce of the N.C.A.A. The leaders of the collegiate group quite naturally resisted this kind of co-option, but they did attend the A.O.A. meeting of November 22, 1922, at which time the constitution was amended to increase the number of N.C.A.A. representatives and those of the newly formed National Amateur Athletic Federation. The result was "the most representative body in the history of . . .

Olympic participation."[41] Avery Brundage, one of the original members of the A.O.A., was then active in both the A.A.U. and the N.C.A.A. Although his deepest loyalty was with the former organization, he devoutly wished for an end to the squabbles which were victimizing the amateur athlete and weakening the Olympic movement.

The bright hopes of 1922 lasted until 1923. When the fighting resumed, it was, as usual, the athletes who became the casualties. University of Southern California track star Charles Paddock was invited to a Y.M.C.A.-sponsored meet in Paris, and Palmer Pierce of the N.C.A.A. announced that the runner had "a perfect right to start," but the A.A.U. ruled that *no* American athletes were to compete in Europe that summer. Paddock went to Paris despite the ban, tied the world's record for 150 meters, and told newsmen, "The A.A.U. hasn't any authority over members of the National Collegiate Association and can't dictate to them."[42] He was suspended by the A.A.U. The controversy raged on into 1924, when Paddock was reinstated.

The year 1925 was the lull before the storm. At the A.O.A. convention on November 17, 1926, the A.A.U. faction managed to change the rules so that a simple majority rather than a two-thirds vote was adequate to replace officers and committee members in case of death, disability, or resignation. This apparently trivial bureaucratic issue triggered enough resentment at the N.C.A.A.'s 21st annual convention for the group to withdraw its representatives from the A.O.A. (December 30, 1926). In August of the following year, the death of William C. Prout of the A.A.U. left the A.O.A. presidency vacant. General Douglas MacArthur was chosen to replace him. Under MacArthur's vigorous leadership, the A.O.A. established the quadrennial American Olympic Committee which then selected the team for the IX Olympiad and sent it to Amsterdam. MacArthur's comments on his administrative problems (which were soon to become Avery Brundage's), were stoic: "To abstain from the conflicting interest of various sports bodies and yet to demand of all support for the Olympic movement has been a problem which at times appeared insurmountable."[43] He laid down his burdens as president of the A.O.A. and Brundage assumed them.

The prestigious New York Athletic Club had been the principal force behind the foundation of the A.A.U. and easterners continued to dominate the organization. Brundage was the first president from the "West" (from the banks of the Charles, the Hudson, or the Schuylkill, Chicago represented the West), and he was proud that *he* was the one to have made the A.A.U. a truly national organization.[44] National it had to be if it were not to be overwhelmed by the N.C.A.A.

Brundage had been chairman of the A.A.U.'s handball committee (1925–1927) and had been elected second vice president in 1925 (under A.A.U. President Murray Hulbert and Vice President W. F. Humphrey). In 1926 and 1927, Brundage rose to be Hulbert's first vice president. His own presidency began in 1928 and lasted, except for the year 1933, to 1935. He saw the creation of bureaucratic harmony as one of his main tasks. Delegates from both the A.A.U. and the N.C.A.A. met at New York's Hotel Astor on April 15, 1929, at which time the A.A.U. surrendered to its rival the right to certify college students (provided they did not compete against athletes suspended by the A.A.U.). In a speech given at the Hotel Sherman in the fall of 1929, Brundage tactfully concluded his hymn to amateurism with a quotation from Charles Kennedy, the Princeton professor who was then president of the N.C.A.A.[45] Gustavus Town Kirby, the venerable sports administrator who had been vice president of the committee that sent Brundage to Stockholm, passed on to Brundage peace feelers from Kennedy: "Kennedy feels that if you and he and I could sit down once in a while around a conference table we could settle all difficulties between A.A.U. and collegiate interests."[46] Brundage decided to strike while the iron was hot and thus to forge unity within the American Olympic Association, of which he had become president in 1928. Decades later, Brundage recalled the sequence of events which led to the reconciliation:

I was first elected President of the National AAU in 1928, after [the Games of the IX Olympiad in Amsterdam], succeeding Judge Murray Hulbert of New York City, and at the next meeting of the American Olympic

Association I was elected President, and Chairman of the American Olympic Committee, as they were called at that time. One of my first objectives in this office was to adjust the differences between the AAU and the NCAA. I arranged a meeting between them at Gus. Kirby's home in Westchester County. We stayed there three or four days and rewrote the constitution of the Olympic Committee to give the NCAA more representation. As a result there was peace between the two organizations for twenty-five years.[47]

Actually, the five-man committee on which Brundage served, along with Kennedy, Kirby, A. C. Gilbert and G. Randolph Manning, seems to have met frequently in 1930 before it was able to come to an agreement. In any event, the constitution worked out by the five men was unanimously adopted by the American Olympic Association. "The war between the N.C.A.A. and the A.A.U. that had raged for a decade over registration of athletes and America's Olympic participation had come to an end."[48] The unanimous vote was on November 19, 1930. A little more than a month later, on December 31, Brundage made a conciliatory address to the 25th-anniversary celebration of the N.C.A.A. His enthusiastic remarks on the creation of "a race of athletes imbued with the virile philosophy of sport" were not likely to offend anyone in the collegiate group.[49] In his report to the A.A.U., November 16, 1931, he boasted that "our Union has never been in better shape physically, mentally, and morally than it is today."[50] Hostilities had diminished to the point where people differed mostly over how much credit was due President Brundage and how much President Kennedy. The controversy over jurisdiction and governance and control of the Olympic Committee erupted with renewed virulence in the 1960s, but it was no longer Brundage's responsibility to find a settlement.

Preparations for the Olympic Games of 1932, which took place in Los Angeles, were carried out in what Kennedy referred to as "spirit of harmony and cooperation."[51] Preparations for the *next* Olympics, scheduled for Berlin in 1936, were to be accompanied by a controversy so stormy that the troubles of the 1920s seemed, in comparison, a tempest in a teapot, but no one, in the good mood of the moment, was able to see that far over the peaceful horizon.

CHAPTER IV

MONEY AND LOVE

The Avery Brundage Company was begun in 1915. Economically considered, it was a good time and a good place. The twenties were, after the short postwar depression, boom times, especially on the shores of Lake Michigan. Although Chicago grew somewhat less frantically than Miami Beach, its growth was nonetheless spectacular. From 1918 to 1926, the population of Chicago increased 35 percent. The land values increased by over 150 percent, the value of new buildings by 1000 percent, and the number of lots subdivided in the entire metropolitan region increased 3000 percent.[1]

Unlike Miami Beach, the Windy City had the advantage of at least a modicum of planning. Thanks to the vision of Daniel Burnham and his associates, Chicago had an overall design for urban life as well as the energy and creativity which had already made the city foremost in the world architecturally. Built along the shore of Lake Michigan, the city had immense natural resources which Burnham's plan used well. Most American cities turned their shorelines over to private investors who exploited the land as they saw fit, but Chicago's lakefront was reserved for parks—for the Art Institute, the Field Museum of Natural History, the Shedd Aquarium, the Adler Planetarium, and Soldiers Field Stadium. The city's most concentrated business section lay within the world-famous "Loop" made by the downtown convergence of the elevated tracks of the urban transport system. The city's residential areas, ranging from fashionable Oak Park and Evanston to the "inerradicable cancer"[2] of the South Side's black ghetto, fanned out from the Loop and a vast ring of parklands surrounded the entire complex. Burnham's dream was of a unified city which provided for relaxation and cultural development as well as economic exploitation. Although no great architect arrived on the scene in Brundage's day, as Louis Sullivan and Frank Lloyd Wright had a generation earlier, there were firms like Holabird & Roche and architects like Bertram Goodhue who contributed aesthetically to Chicago's skyline.

Burnham's Chicago was also, in the 1920s, Al Capone's Chicago. Although organized crime in Chicago was centered in the bootlegger-and-speakeasy subculture created by Prohibition, there was— as we have seen—dishonesty and corruption enough in the construction industry for Brundage to limit his activity to the private sector. He built factories, hotels, and apartment buildings. Although his firm constructed the Walker Hotel, which had been designed by Daniel Burnham, Brundage's role was utilitarian rather than aesthetic. While others designed, he built. He was not all that selective about his commissions (except that he did not bid on municipal projects) and he left specialization to more established firms. He was soon known as a man who took any job and who performed that job efficiently and honestly. Efficiency was demonstrated when he carried out Albert Kahn's plans for the Ford Motor Company's assembly plant at 126th Street and Torrence Avenue. Work was begun in January of 1923, in the dead of a Middle Western winter, and by April the framework was complete. The entire plant was ready for full operation in October, without cost overruns.[3] Honesty was dramatically demonstrated when Brundage put up a building for the University of Chicago and returned money which was left over when the costs were lower than the bid had been.[4] Another kind of honesty was displayed when a corrupt superintendent asked for a bribe of $100,000, which he offered to split with Brundage. Pretending to agree, Brundage informed the superintendent's boss, paid in marked banknotes, and—we can be certain—took personal satisfaction when the bribe-taker was arrested.[5] Here was one occasion where the belief in "fair play" made a difference in the world of business. With an oblique reference to a fellow Illinoisan, Brundage was known to his associates as "Honest Ave."

Brundage had begun his own firm at a time when American neutrality was threatened by the war in Europe that had broken out in 1914. When the United States, no longer "too proud to fight," entered the war in 1917, Chester Brundage, who had followed his older brother through the University of Illinois, enlisted in the army and served in France as a captain in the 108th Engineers.[6] Avery also attempted to volunteer but was turned down because of his poor eyesight.[7] There was correspondence concerning a post in Washington with Bernard Baruch's War Industries Board, but nothing seems to have come of this.[8] The end of the war in November 1918 probably forestalled the move to Washington.

On Brundage's application for a commission in the U.S. Army Ordnance Officers' Reserve Corps, dated December 28, 1917, he listed his income as "between $10,000 and $20,000" a year.[9] It was "no handicap," he commented later, "to be all-round champion of America, which gave one an entree almost everywhere,"[10] a curious admission on the part of one who never tired of maintaining that athletes should never use their sports for material advantage of any sort whatsoever. That he was also a 32nd-degree Mason probably helped as well.[11] When he turned the Avery Brundage Company into a corporation in April of 1926, the company was capitalized at $250,000 and Brundage was also director of the South Chicago Coal and Dock Company, capitalized at $750,000.[12] To the readers of the Chicago Athletic Association's journal, *The Cherry Cirle*, Brundage announced proudly, "There is all the room in the world for advancement in this business."[13] At this time his company was at work on eight new buildings in downtown Chicago, half of all the city's major construction projects at that time.[14] A year later, on June 30, 1927, *Hill's Reports* listed Brundage's net worth as in excess of $1,000,000.[15] The self-made man had come a long way.

Brundage was especially proud of the apartment houses he built. The brochure he published as part of his firm's publicity featured pictures of a whole series of them: 3800 Sheridan Road ("A striking apartment building in a conspicuous location"), the Shoreland

Hotel ("One of the largest and finest residential hotels in Chicago"), 5000 East End Avenue ("The tallest apartment building in Chicago"), the Sheridan-Brompton Apartments ("One of the largest apartment buildings in Chicago"), etc. The Sheridan-Brompton project was one where the Brundage Company's swiftness was appreciated. Interest on stocks and bonds cost the owners of the site $500 a day; they anticipated a rental income of $40,000 a month once the apartments were ready for occupancy. Brundage finished the job in four months.[16]

When the Great Crash of 1929 signaled the end of the protracted boom of the 1920s, Brundage managed to persevere. Although he was at one point financially ruined, he refused to take advantage of the bankruptcy laws. "I was going around with my chest out and not a nickel in my pocket, but no one knew that except my accountant and my secretary."[17] Typically, Brundage attributed his courage to his athletic background:

A banker sportsman friend and I (we were both broke at the time), counted 39 men we knew who, overcome by the disaster that had left them penniless, had shot and killed themselves or jumped out of skyscraper windows, one of them owing me a couple of hundred thousand dollars. Not one of them, we noted, had had the character building discipline of competitive sport.[18]

Whatever the source of his determination, he paid his debts and scraped money together to acquire the assets of liquidated firms. He laid the basis for a second fortune to replace the one lost in what Edmund Wilson called "the American Earthquake."

He was in a good position to buy up the assets of bankrupt firms because he was made chairman of a committee which watched over liquidations and reorganizations. It was a sign of trust that his business associates chose him for this position and it was a point of honor with him that he refused to purchase properties whose liquidation his committee had supervised. Indicted for alleged corruption, Brundage emerged from the trial as a paragon of civic virtue:

It was as chairman of the H. O. Stone Bondholder's Protective Committee that Avery Brundage's name became slightly tainted. The committee was in the process of reorganizing distressed corporations when Brundage and

Colonel Horatio B. Hackett, a member of the committee, were accused of having divided between them an appraisal fee of $23,104.87. Archie H. Cohen, referee in bankruptcy, made the recommendation that Brundage and Hackett, along with four other members of the committee, be removed ". . . because they have shown themselves unworthy of their trust." This recommendation was filed in the United States District Court in Chicago. The case went to court and the attorneys for the bondholder's committee explained that the fee received by Hackett and Brundage, instead of being divided between them, had been paid out to various unemployed men who were given the appraisal jobs by the committee. The judge then threw the case out of court.[19]

What is certain is that Chicago's business community subsequently expressed gratitude for Brundage's having made the financial disaster of the Depression somewhat less devastating than it might have been. If Brundage thought back on his sophomoric short story, "The Retribution," he must have smiled to think how many banker's sons were ready to pay tribute to a nobody become somebody.

Brundage's most important property was acquired after the Depression. In 1940, Chicago's LaSalle Hotel was taken over by the Roanoke Real Estate Company, which Brundage had established to replace his construction firm.[20] The hotel eventually became famous in the specialized world of international sports administration because Brundage's office was there; Olympic matters were discussed in letters flown back and forth between the LaSalle Hotel and Lausanne's Chateau de Vidy (in those old-fashioned times letters took three days instead of two weeks). Brundage invested heavily in the modernization of the hotel and became emotionally involved with the place. The employees seem to have been genuinely fond of him, to have recognized that the hotel meant more than income to its owner, perhaps because it symbolized Brundage's ability to act as host where once he was too lowly to have been a guest. When the building was swept by fire on June 5, 1946, fifty-six persons were killed and Brundage was deeply distressed. His many letters describing the tragedy were almost formulaic, as if he wanted to exorcise his sense of guilt:

How such a thing could happen in a fireproof building, I do not know. It is incredible. When I look at it, I still cannot believe it. Of course, ninety percent of the loss of life was caused by panic and hysteria; the fire was out in less than half an hour and over a thousand guests, including a blind girl and her dog, were evacuated safely down the fire escapes.[21]

It is impossible to know how personally responsible Brundage felt, but the fire was certainly not an event that he easily recovered from. And it was, unfortunately, not the last time that destructive flames were to sweep through his home.

The LaSalle Hotel, which was restored after the fire, was not the only investment. Brundage bought the 1,000-bed Cosmopolitan Hotel in Denver and owned stocks and bonds in various companies. His choices were not always happy ones:

He bought a small oil company which had shown promise, but when the well caught fire and burned he became a retired oil man. Likewise, he bought a silver mine in the most remote corner of Nevada, but when the production costs turned out to be greater than the profits, and when bandits continually raided his mine, he abandoned that, too.[22]

In 1953 he acquired shares in Chicago's Susquehanna Corporation and he eventually served as the chairman of its board of directors, but he left the organization when speculators began to take it over.[23]

By this time, Brundage had acquired an assistant who was of inestimable value to him both in his economic affairs and in his Olympic administration. In 1950 he met Frederick J. ("Fritz") Ruegsegger, a twenty-nine-year-old Swiss who had worked in France and Spain before coming to the United States in 1948 and taking various business positions. The two men met in California while Ruegsegger was working for an investment firm. While he was in the process of giving Brundage advice on some investments in California and Nevada, Brundage surprised him by asking suddenly if the Swiss would work for him. Ruegsegger asked Brundage about his background and remarked that he didn't know if Brundage was qualified to become his employer. Needless to say, Brundage was startled, but Ruegsegger was persuaded and the relationship lasted until Brundage's death.[24]

In some ways, Ruegsegger seems to have become the younger brother that Brundage had lacked. Chester Brundage, clearly ov-

ershadowed by his dynamic and successful older brother, had failed
in the enterprises that Avery had set up for him and was finally
taken into the construction company and then into the Roanoke
Real Estate Company. Chester never married. He seems to have
been in every respect a colorless personality. His death on March
28, 1954, went almost unnoticed. Ruegsegger was a true cosmopolitan—sophisticated, well informed, able to speak several lan-
guages, at ease with titled Europeans and moneyed Americans. In
later years he was said to resemble Henry Kissinger, an apt comparison for one who served as Avery Brundage's "Secretary of
State." Although Ruegsegger puckishly referred to his boss as "Mr.
B.," the relationship was a warm and affectionate one. Like the
prototypical Swiss banker, Ruegsegger avoided publicity, but he
gradually assumed responsibility for Brundage's financial affairs.
Ruegsegger commented on him, somewhat obliquely, in recalling
a comic episode:

One evening over dinner Brundage asked me why I'd never asked for a
raise, what with inflation and everything. "I don't have to because I raise
myself." Brundage was taken aback and slightly stunned. He stammered,
"But how can you do this?" I answered "Easy, when you are gone, I run
everything. I have the executive power to make all decisions." Brundage
thought for a moment, then leaned over his soup, cupping his mouth,
"May I inquire how much you make?"

Brundage was presumably content with the answer, and with Ruegsegger's management of his financial affairs. In his last will and
testament, no beneficiary was more generously rewarded than
Ruegsegger.[25]

Chicago remained the center of Brundage's business life, but he
began, in 1941, to invest in California. He had visited the state in
1915, when the A.A.U. held its national track-and-field championships in San Francisco and when the city put on the Pan-Pacific
Exposition. In 1941, as fears of a Japanese invasion sent property
values tumbling, Brundage decided to take advantage of others'
timidity. He purchased a home in Santa Barbara at 715 Ashley
Road. Nine years later he bought the nearby Montecito Country
Club. In 1949 he acquired the "Restaurante del Paseo" and adjacent

properties, including the historic de la Guerra mansion and several dozen shops and offices. The Santa Barbara *News-Press* reported a sale price of around $450,000. In 1956, Brundage bought the Montecito Hotel.[26]

Brundage's home, "La Piñeta," was actually a palatial mansion, a work of art which housed a large portion of his Asian art collection. La Piñeta was obviously a source of great pride. Built in a more or less Hispanic style then common in Southern California, it had ample room for Brundage not only to display his Japanese and Chinese jades and bronzes but also to entertain such members of the I.O.C. who might venture to Santa Barbara. In his notebooks, Brundage wrote, *"OLD CHINESE SAYINGS.* If you want to be happy for one day, get drunk, for one week, get yourself a concubine, forever, make yourself a garden."[27] The gardens which surrounded La Piñeta were spectacular, with hedges, walkways, pools, a fountain, sculptures. There were also signs that Brundage was no Chinese sage. In the spring of 1953, after the I.O.C. session at Mexico City, he invited the whole committee to Santa Barbara. As they arrived at La Piñeta, they were struck by the large Olympic flag displayed over the entrance to the mansion.

By the time Brundage bought La Piñeta, he had found someone to act as its gracious hostess. From the time of his graduation from the university in 1909 to her death in 1921, Brundage had lived with his mother. In the years of his economic rise, he was romantically involved with several women but not inclined to marry. On a one-page typed document, "TRAVEL TO 1932," Brundage added a note in long-hand, "Margaret 9/18/17."[28] Margaret may have been a *femme fatale* important enough to be entered along with his pre-1932 athletic tours and a Caribbean cruise, but Avery was not the *poète maudit* destined to immortalize her. The Avery–Margaret story must be left to our imagination.

By 1927 Brundage was a millionaire, ready to act upon Jane Austen's sage maxim: "It is a truth universally acknowledged that a single man in possession of a good fortune, must be in want of a wife." Indeed, the wife he found seems almost to have stepped out of *Pride and Prejudice* or *Sense and Sensibility*. Elizabeth Dunlap

was the musically talented daughter of Charles C. Dunlap, a Chicago banker. Three years younger than her husband, she was slim,
brownhaired, a graduate of the University of Chicago. Trained as
a soprano, she was fond of Schubert's *Lieder* and passionate about
Bach. She often performed for La Piñeta's visitors. (This interest
in music may not have been a major source of her charm, for him;
he once remarked of a performance of Wagner's *Die Walküre*, it
"started at 7 o'clock, at 10:00 P.M. I looked at my watch and it
registered exactly 8 o'clock."[29]) If the forty-year-old Brundage was
overcome by passion, it was a stroke of good luck that his bride
was quite acceptable socially.[30]

He had more than enough time to weigh the pros and cons of
matrimony versus a bachelor's life when he and four other wealthy
sportsmen chartered a boat for a wilderness adventure. Accompanied by Percy H. Batten, Arthur B. Modine, George W. Smith,
and R. W. Tansill, he set off for Alaska on the *Ethel*, Captain Carl
Isakson in charge. The group hoped to bring back ten kodiak bears
for Chicago's Field Museum of Natural History. In order to avoid
the late-summer fogs of the Pacific Northwest, they sailed from
Seattle on May 2nd, stopped at Victoria, British Columbia, and
took the "inside passage" to Juneau, "tying up nights in order not
to miss any of the superb scenery." The scenery was spectacular,
"an everchanging panorama of delightful vistas" with mountain for-
ests, waterfalls, glaciers. From Juneau they sailed by the St. Elias
range, "unsurpassed for scenic grandeur." When they reached King
Cove and Cold Bay, they left the boat and spent two strenuous
weeks inland, hunting the kodiak bears. At this time, Brundage's
mood changed drastically: there was "a perpetual tumult of wind,
rain, sleet, fog, hail, and mist that makes up what is about as un-
pleasant a climate as you could find anywhere." He concluded,
"This part of Alaska is fit only for bears." On the way back, the
Ethel sailed to Seward and then the party took the train five hundred
miles north to Fairbanks, where they boarded a river steamer and
went westward down the Tenana River to the Yukon River. From
there, the adventurers went eastward up the Yukon for a thousand
miles to the Arctic Circle and then "up" to Dawson (upstream but

actually in a southeasterly direction) in Canada's Yukon Territory. From Dawson the men made their way by river boat and train back down to the coast. At Skagway, a little north of Juneau, they had their rendezvous with Captain Isakson and the *Ethel*. By this time, they had had enough of wilderness and Theodore Roosevelt's "strenuous life." They boarded not the *Ethel* but "the largest and best steamer on the run and engaged the most palatial suite of state-rooms to be had for our return journey." Nature, however, was not quite done with them. Their ship nearly capsized in a hurricane that caught them in Chugach Gulf between Afognak Island and the Kenai Peninsula. By the time the trip was over, on August 7, they had had "enough of sailing the ocean in a small boat to last the members . . . for the rest of their natural lives." They had also come to appreciate the courage of Arctic explorers. *The Homecomer*, the trade journal of the construction industry, had teased Brundage about the voyage: "Avery Brundage . . . is such a born eskimo that he cannot get his fill of winter in Cook County and must needs trek off to Alaska to find a climate snappy enough to suit his taste,"[31] but Brundage was, in writing up the account for the Chicago Athletic Association's *Cherry Circle*, as romantic as he ever allowed himself to be on non-Olympic themes: "we came to know, as a passenger on a larger boat rarely [does], a little of the spell of the sea which enthralls the heart of a sailor and drags him back to his calling no matter how far from it he drifts."[32]

Once back in Chicago, Brundage began seriously to court Elizabeth Dunlap and the two were engaged on December 6 and married on December 22, 1927. After a month-long honeymoon in Bermuda, they moved into a ten-room apartment on the top floor of 229 Lake Shore Drive. He said of her, generously, that she was the person responsible for the beautiful and the pleasant in life, but there is no way to know from his matter-of-fact letters what sort of relationship the two of them had. She appears in his Olympic correspondence as hostess, sender of greetings, receiver of mementos, and, occasionally, as a dedicated shopper. Writing to Daniel J. Ferris, secretary-treasurer of the A.A.U., Brundage requested reimbursement for some European expenses and added jestingly,

"Worst of all, I exposed Mrs. Brundage to the shopping temptations of Paris for ten days."[33] When Joseph Raycroft sent Brundage a photograph of an ancient Greek statue that he thought might represent "the Goddess of Sports," Raycroft added that Brundage could probably hang the photograph in his study without making Elizabeth jealous.[34] Avery and Elizabeth probably exchanged letters, especially in the months of separation between their meeting and their marriage, but the letters seem no longer to exist. Friends have described Elizabeth Brundage as a good woman, deeply devoted to her husband. They have also commented that she was not particularly attractive and that she was sometimes tipsy from a drink too many. In a material sense, Brundage certainly cared for his wife, but she had to settle for his less than complete devotion. It hurt her deeply when she discovered, after seventeen years of marriage, that he had been unfaithful.

She learned of the affair when Herb Caen, a columnist for the San Francisco *Examiner*, referred to a nationally known sports figure, married, who was involved with a "beautiful blonde . . . import from a Scandinavian country." When the article appeared on November 1, 1954, Brundage had known Lilian Linnea Dresden for six years. Daughter of Karl Gustav Wahamaki, an Olympic gymnast from the 1912 games in Stockholm, she was born April 21, 1919, in Helsinki. She had lived in Shanghai with her parents and her younger brother Leo while her father served as Finnish consul.[35] Lilian had become Mrs. Dresden when she married Elliott Dresden in Fort Worth, Texas, on September 7, 1948, at which time she already had a son, Karl Paulin, apparently from an earlier marriage. The relationship with Elliott Dresden lasted only for ten days and the marriage was subsequently annulled on September 14, 1952,[36] but Lilian kept her husband's name.

Although Brundage was rumored to have had numerous affairs with women in several different countries, the relationship with Lilian Dresden was different. On August 27, 1951, she entered Mills Memorial Hospital in San Mateo, California, and gave birth to a boy, Avery Gregory Dresden. On August 19, 1952, a second son was born, Gary Toro Dresden.[37] On the birth certificate, the father's name is withheld. Brundage was extremely anxious to keep the births secret, in order, he alleged, to protect his marriage.[38] Acknowledging his paternity and setting up a trust fund to provide for the boys (and to prevent Lilian's deportation as an alien without means of support), he stipulated that Lilian and the boys keep his secret and that they renounce all further claims to his estate.[39] That Brundage was not childless remained a closely kept secret until after his death (at which time the sons contested the will and received an additional out-of-court settlement).[40] At the time when the San Francisco newspaper printed its "humorous" reference to her as a "blonde keptive," Lilian and her sons were living in a house in Redwood City. (The house was in the name of Brundage's secretary, Frances Blakely, who—according to Ruegsegger citing Elizabeth Brundage—had once hoped to marry Avery herself.[41])

What is most significant about the entire episode is not that Avery Brundage, like many another famous man, had committed adultery. It is rather that he refused to acknowledge his sons publicly and kept their existence hidden from many of his closest friends, one of whom "fell off his chair" when a lawyer introduced himself as attorney for Avery Brundage's sons.[42] Although Brundage indicated that he wanted to protect his marriage, he had other motives as well. In 1951 and 1952 he was in line for election to the office of I.O.C. president and he feared that adverse publicity might ruin his chances. One can judge such fears harshly, as William Oscar Johnson does in "Avery Brundage: The Man Behind the Mask," the *Sports Illustrated* article that publicized Brundage's private life,[43] but one must constantly bear in mind that Brundage's commitment to the religion of Olympism was truly fanatic. He assumed that exposure as an adulterer would have damaged the Olympic movement as well as the president of the I.O.C.[44] Inevitably, idealism and selfishness are tangled together here, but it is important not to underestimate Brundage's devotion to the ideal.

Reciprocally, the existence of Lilian Dresden's boys may well have intensified Brundage's paternalism as well as causing him guilt for doing to *his* boys what his own father had done to Chester and to him. Lacking legitimate children and unready to acknowledge

the sons he did have, Brundage must have been all the more ready
to see the amateur athletes of the world as his spiritual sons and
daughters. The love that he was psychologically unable to offer
Avery Gregory and Gary Toro was bestowed upon all the other
young men and women whom he felt to be somehow *his*, his to be
proud of, his to scold, his to honor when they fulfilled his dreams,
his to cast off in anger when they betrayed his ideals. What bio-
logical children could possibly have competed with "the youth of
the world" summoned quadrennially to gather together under the
Olympic rings?

CHAPTER V

THE OLYMPIC MOVEMENT FROM ANTWERP TO LOS ANGELES

The "guns of August" finally fell silent on November 11, 1918, but the hostilities continued as the victors wrangled at Versailles, divided the spoils, and created a League of Nations which can be seen as a brave hope or as the cynical crust tossed to a world hungering for peace. The war had interrupted the modern Olympic sequence (as wars had not in ancient times). The games of 1916, planned for Berlin, were never held. Olympic idealism was a casualty in another sense as well. When the I.O.C. convened in Lausanne in 1919 and decided to hold the games the following year, at Antwerp, the leaders of the Olympic movement concluded that wartime feelings had been too embittered to allow the defeated nations to compete against the victors—if any nation can be said to have been victorious in a conflict that devastated the continent and left millions dead. Abandoning his belief in the universality of the Olympic movement, Coubertin allayed his conscience with the legal fiction that the Belgians, not the I.O.C., had made the decision to exclude the Germans and the Austrians:

The problem of German participation was discussed. Solemnly to proclaim any kind of ostracism in the wake of a conflict which had just drenched Europe in blood would have been a violation of the Olympic constitution as it then was. The solution was quite simple. There was, for each Olympiad, an Organizing Committee which, according to the formula employed since 1896, sent out the invitations. Antwerp was thus the master of the situation without any direct violation of the fundamental principle of universality.[1]

Four years later, at its 21st Session (Rome, 1923), the I.O.C. was confronted with the question again, and again chose to evade it. The decision was left to the French hosts of the 1924 games. Paris spurned Berlin. In fact, the I.O.C. decided in Rome to postpone until 1924 the election of new members from Germany to replace those who had died or resigned from the committee. The Germans resumed their soccer rivalry with the neutral Swiss in 1920 and played their former enemies, the Italians, in 1923, but they had to wait until 1928 before they once again took their place in the Olympic parade.[2] When the problem recurred after World War II, Sigfrid Edström and Avery Brundage would find themselves almost as helpless as Coubertin had been.

Despite the brevity of the "lead time" and the shortages caused by the war, Antwerp's games are generally considered to have been a success. Charles Paddock ("the world's fastest human") won the 100 meters as expected and ran the first lap for the successful 400-meter relay team, but the days of American track-and-field domination were apparently over. The British won five gold medals in these events to the Americans' nine and the Finns, who were the sensation of the games, won eight. Hannes Kolehmainen, who had returned from Stockholm with three gold medals, set an Olympic record in the marathon, but the games were most memorable for the appearance of Paavo Nurmi. The "flying Finn" was victorious over 10,000 meters in both the flat and the cross-country races (and he earned a third gold medal in the cross-country relay). It was Nurmi's manner as much as anything else which impressed the spectators—he said little, he trained with a stopwatch in his hand, he became a symbol of mechanical (some said joyless) perfection.

At the 19th Session of the I.O.C., held concurrently with the

Olympic Congress in Lausanne in 1921, Coubertin announced his intention to retire as president of the committee and asked, as "une faveur exceptionelle," that the 1924 games be celebrated in Paris, his "ville natale."[3] The majority thought this appropriate, but the enraged Italian delegates, who had favored Rome, stormed out of the congress. At this session, the committee decided to begin publication of the *Bulletin du C.I.O.* and to establish a Executive Commission, the first members of which were Baron Godefroy de Blonay (Switzerland), Jiri Guth-Jarkovsky (Bohemia), Comte Henri de Baillet-Latour (Belgium), Sigfrid Edstrøm (Sweden), and Comte Melchior de Polignac (France).

Sharp disagreements divided the committee when it turned to the question of winter sports. Ice skating had been included in the 1908 games and ice hockey in those of 1920. Should there be special winter games apart from the summer festival? The Scandinavian countries and the British were in favor of the innovation. They had invented these sports (as *sports* rather than as utilitarian or noncompetitive recreational activities) and they saw no reason why an antiquarian homage to the Greeks should prevent full recognition of skiing and skating. The opposition, which included Coubertin and was later to include Brundage, argued that winter sports were restricted by the facts of geography to a small group of nations. Winter sports could never be said to gather together "the youth of the world" as running, jumping, throwing, lifting, wrestling, and swimming did. The argument was resolved in favor of the winter games and the first of the series was celebrated at Chamonix from January 24 to February 4, 1924. It established the tradition that the winter games precede the summer contests, which were to remain the climax of each Olympiad.

The first winter games were successful but fairly uneventful. To no one's great surprise, the Norwegians won eleven of the medals for skiing (with Finland's Tapano Niku taking the bronze for the 18-kilometer race) and the Finns were first in four of the five speed-skating contests (with Charles Jewtraw of the United States first over 500 meters).

The summer games of 1924, held in Paris, were an even greater triumph for Paavo Nurmi than those of 1920 had been. He set an Olympic record for 5,000 meters (14'31.2"), won the 10,000-meter cross-country race, and was part of Finland's winning teams in the 3,000-meter relay and the 10,000-meter cross-country relay. The only athlete to rival Nurmi was Johnny Weissmüller, who swam 100 meters in Olympic-record and 400 meters in world-record times.

At the Olympic Congress in Lausanne in 1921, the I.O.C. had reaffirmed its stand against the publication of point tables, which they rightly saw as an invitation to chauvinism, but it was impossible to ignore the outbreaks of nationalism at the games. When the American rugby team unexpectedly defeated the French in a roughly played game, the losing players congratulated the victors, but fights broke out among the angry spectators.[4] When France's Lucien Gaudin claimed a touch against the Italian fencer Bino Bini, the latter denied the claim; when the jury awarded the match to Gaudin, the entire Italian team marched out singing the Fascist anthem. The Italian fencers won the team title in sabers, but Oreste Puliti was disqualified for life when the team was accused of collusion in individual matches and Puliti challenged one of the accusers to a duel in earnest.[5]

Brundage had been too involved in his construction company to have gone to Antwerp in 1920 for the games of the VII Olympiad, but he was on hand—as a spectator—in 1924. By this time he was a member of the American Olympic Association, but he seems not to have had the chance in Paris to become personally acquainted with Coubertin. He did take the opportunity to travel again in Europe after twelve active years in the United States. He went from Paris to Vienna, where he spent the Fourth of July, returned to Paris by train and then flew to London. It was the first of his countless flights. In all, the trip lasted five weeks, from June 13 to July 21.

Between the games in Paris and those in Amsterdam four years later, the bureaucratic tendency to regularize and standardize accelerated. The Executive Board began holding meetings with representatives of the national Olympic committees and the international sports federations. The I.O.C. organized an important Olympic Congress which took place in Prague, May 26–28, 1925.[6] The amateur rule, which had always been (and still is) an insoluble problem (because misconceived as a question of money rather than as a question of time), received a new formation: "An amateur is one who devotes himself to sport for sport's sake without deriving from it, directly or indirectly, the means of existence. A professional is one who derives the means of existence entirely or partly from sport."[7]

One of the most important events of the Congress was the election of Coubertin's successor. In the first round, which included 13 absentee ballots, Belgium's Comte Henri de Baillet-Latour received 17 votes of a possible 40; in the second round, he received 19 out of a total of 27 votes and was thus elected to an eight-year term.[8] Born on March 1, 1876, the Count was thirteen years younger than the Baron he succeeded. Elected to the I.O.C. in 1903, he organized the Belgian Olympic Committee a year later and, in 1905, acted as host for the Olympic Congress held in Brussels. His conception of the Olympic movement differed scarcely from that of Coubertin.

While the I.O.C. evolved in a familiar pattern, organizational challenges sprang up around it. Unhappy with the world of "bourgeois sports," the working class had, even in the nineteenth century, founded its own class-conscious sports organizations, the most important of which was Germany's Arbeiter-Turnerbund, long associated with the Social Democratic Party. Although the Arbeiter-Turnerbund had been founded in 1893, it originally resisted the impulse to competition and initially opposed the Olympic Games. It was reluctant to sponsor local, regional, and national contests, but the fascination of modern sports was too much for the ideology of cooperation. In 1920, an organization akin to the I.O.C. was formed, the Luzerner Sport-Internationale (LSI). In 1925, the first *Arbeiterolympiade* was celebrated at Frankfurt (July 24–28, 1925).[9] The pomp and ceremony were, in form if not in content, reminiscent of Olympic ritual.[10] Despite the exclusion of the Communists, who founded their own Rote Sport-Internationale (RSI) in 1922, the event was a success and plans were made for subsequent celebrations.

A second and even more important challenge came from another more or less excluded group. The prejudice against female athletes had long roots, reaching back at least to the early nineteenth century.[11] When Phokian Clias published the first book devoted to women's sports and exercises, *Kalisthenie* (1829), his emphasis was on graceful movement rather than on strenuous competition. The criteria for women's physical education long remained hygienic and aesthetic rather than athletic. In *Die Weibliche Turnkunst* (1855), Moritz Kloß warned that excessive exercise might endanger a girl's health: "The aesthetic element ought to dominate these exercises, for girls generally have a tendency to graceful, ornamental presentation."[12] And Germany at this time was more advanced and progressive than the United States. Hysterical fear of "masculine" development was a bugaboo which haunted the nineteenth and early twentieth centuries. Indeed, the irrational dread of "Amazon" muscularity can be traced from the beginnings of modern sports to the most recent Olympics.

Coubertin shared fully the prejudices of his age on this matter and opposed the participation of female athletes in the Olympic Games. He "had not planned for the admission of women, did not want women to be admitted, and fought against their admission for more than thirty years."[13] This call to the "youth of the world" was meant for male ears alone. Coubertin reluctantly acceded to the inclusion of female swimmers in 1912, but track and field remained a masculine preserve. The I.O.C. resolved in 1924, upon a motion from France's Comte Justinien de Clary, that "as far as the participation of women in the Olympic Games is concerned, the status quo ought to be maintained. . . . In no case will the committee accept . . . women's competitions in fencing."[14]

In response to such obdurateness, an equally obdurate Frenchwoman, Alice Milliat, decided that women should take matters into their own hands. On October 31, 1921, she founded the Fédération Sportive Féminine Internationale (F.S.F.I.) and promptly began a

series of international championships for women.[15] The first
F.S.F.I.-sponsored track-and-field championship took place at the
Stade Pershing in Paris on August 20, 1922. It consisted of eleven
events, including a 1,000-meter race. Twenty thousand spectators
watched the contests.

Sigfrid Edstrøm, founder and president of the International Amateur Athletic Federation as well as member of the I.O.C.'s Executive Commission, was unhappy about the "Premiers Jeux Olympiques Féminins du Monde" and wished that the F.S.F.I. would
simply vanish,[16] but Mme. Milliat was resolute and Edstrøm concluded that cooperation was the better part of valor. Negotiating
for both the I.A.A.F. and the I.O.C., he reached an agreement
with Milliat in 1926 under which the F.S.F.I. was to control wom-
en's sports but under the rules and regulations of the I.A.A.F.
(revised if necessary to conform to women's needs). Milliat also
agreed not to use the word "Olympic" in reference to events sponsored by the F.S.F.I.[17] On April 5, 1926, the I.O.C. voted at its
Lisbon session to "permit the admission of women to a restricted
number of athletic events at the Games."[18] Gymnastics as well as
track and field were to be allowed on an experimental basis, but
the former was limited to team competitions and the latter to five
events (as opposed to the eleven contested by the F.S.F.I. in Paris
in 1922).

The experiment was only a partial success. The 800-meter race
was said to have been a disaster because several of the women collapsed during or immediately after the race. Many men, forgetting
the agonized contortions of male runners or assuming that athletic
agony ought to be limited by gender, concluded that women's track
and field was a mistake. The 800-meter race was removed from the
Olympic program, not to reappear until 1960. The long, still-un-
finished dispute over women's sports was one in which Brundage
was to take an active and frequently misunderstood part.

In the men's events of 1928, Paavo Nurmi triumphed again over
10,000 meters but came in second to his countrymen Ville Ritola
in the 5,000 meters and Toivo Loukola in the 3,000-meter steeple-
chase. Weissmüller lowered his own Olympic record in the 100-

meter swim to 58.6 seconds and won again in the 200-meter relay. Believing as he did in the universality of Olympism, Brundage was especially pleased when the triple-jumper Mikio Oda became the first Japanese athlete to return from the games with a gold medal.[19]

The winter games at St. Moritz were largely an exhibition of Scandinavian skills. The most memorable performer was Sonja Henie, who swirled and glided her way to the first of her three gold medals for figure skating. While she eventually dazzled millions as an ice-show performer and then as a film star, her professionalism made her one of Brundage's perennial symbols for the materialistic betrayal of Olympic values.

At the I.O.C.'s 21st session, in Rome in 1923, William May Garland of Los Angeles, elected the previous year as a member from the United States, presented so effective a case for his home town as host for 1932 that the members rose in a body to accept the bid by acclamation and "M. Garland remercie avec émotion ses colleagues."[20] The enthusiasm in Rome was not shared by the Easterners who dominated the American Olympic Association. "They had considerable doubt," recalled Brundage, "that these inexperienced provincials (anyplace west of the Alleghenies was still considered Indian country) were competent to handle a sport event of this magnitude."[21] The Easterners plotted to take over the organizing committee in Los Angeles and "the explosion on the shores of the Pacific at this announcement was loud and noisy."[22] Brundage, who had found a way to end the feud between the A.A.U. and the N.C.A.A., was made president of the American Olympic Association and of the U.S. Olympic Committee, the first "Westerner" to hold that office. "One of my first actions was a trip to Los Angeles to try to make peace."[23] Peace was made.

With the organizing committee in Los Angeles preparing the facilities, the I.O.C. returned to the question of female participation. President Baillet-Latour argued in the Executive Commission for limiting them to gymnastics, swimming, tennis, and figure skating, but the decision was postponed until after the important Olympic Congress scheduled for Berlin in 1930.[24] The victory of the "feminists" at the 29th Session in Barcelona, in 1931, was prepared for by the impressive demonstrations of the women athletes who performed for the delegates in Berlin. A vivid account of these performances was written by Brundage's friend Gustavus Town Kirby:

I personally saw groups of young girls in the scantiest kind of clothing, trotting around the fields or running tracks, engaging in 100 metre runs, taking part in the broad jump, and hopping about in all kinds of athletic and gymnastic movements; and to my direct statement as to whether or not such character of exercise was not bad for them, the answer invariably was that on the contrary, it was good for them.[25]

Kirby, whose involvement in the Olympic movement dated back to the 1890s, looked upon nude swimming and sunbathing with an open-mindedness surprising even to himself:

To my inquiry as to whether or not this intermingling of the sexes in a nude condition did not make for immorality, the answer was a positive "No.". . . Irrespective of the moral question, there is no gainsaying the fact that the boys and girls and youth of Germany are today to a large extent well developed and bronzed.[26]

Brundage, who was present as a delegate from the A.A.U. and the I.A.A.F. (as well as the Fédération Internationale de Handball), was similarly impressed. Later that summer, when football coach Knute Rockne of Notre Dame ridiculed Kirby and referred to the 800-meter race at Amsterdam in 1928 as "a pitiful spectacle and a reproach to anyone who had anything to do with putting on a race of this kind,"[27] Brundage joined the fray on Kirby's side:

Anyone who observed the exhibitions put on by girl athletes in connection with the Olympic Congress in Berlin would be a strong advocate for sports of all kinds for girls under proper supervision. They are really doing some wonderful things in the athletic line in Germany today. We could well take a few pointers for them.[28]

Since the program of the Congress included a dance, "Lauf der Frauen und Männer," performed in Berlin's magnificent Opernhaus by physical-education students leaping and twisting to music by Johann Sebastian Bach, the delegates might well have been overwhelmed by evidence of female physicality.[29]

Just how impressed the I.O.C. was became clear when the votes were cast. When the I.A.A.F. met to consider track-and-field participation, Baillet-Latour proposed that women be eliminated from the Los Angeles games and Kirby promptly moved that, in the event Baillet-Latour's proposal was adopted, a special congress be called to consider the elimination of *men's* events as well.[30] The I.A.A.F., with Brundage sitting on the Committee on Women's Sports, voted to continue the women's program in 1932.[31] When the Olympic Congress finally voted, the delegates endorsed participation in gymnastics, swimming, tennis, and skating (all by a vote of 26–1), fencing (19–8), and track and field (17–1 with 1 abstention).[32] Although one of the American delegates, Ernest Lee Jahncke, was unhappy about this outcome, Brundage shared Kirby's pleasure. Mme. Milliat had reason to be both pleased and apprehensive. Edström, officially recognizing F.S.F.I. records on behalf of the I.A.A.F., eventually managed to coopt Milliat's organization. He thanked her for her work and promised to urge the I.O.C. to enlarge its program of women's sports, but it would be decades before female participation approached equality.[33]

The second summer games held in the United States were a vast improvement over the near-fiasco of St. Louis in 1904. For the first time, the organizing committee established an Olympic Village, which encouraged the athletes of the entire world to mix and mingle, but the sunny prospects were clouded over by a crisis within the I.A.A.F. Immediately before the games, the I.A.A.F. disqualified Paavo Nurmi for allegedly having accepted monetary compensation. The Executive Committee was made up of Edström, Bo Ekelund (Sweden), Brundage's close friend Karl Ritter von Halt (Germany), and Brundage himself.[34] The Finnish reaction to the disqualification was chauvinistic and there were threats of immediate withdrawal from the games and Edström's power company, Asea Electric, was boycotted in Finland,[35] but the I.A.A.F. was firm in its decision and the I.O.C. honored the firmness even though Nurmi was probably the most famous athlete in the world.

President Herbert Hoover—another self-made man and an engineer—was one of Brundage's political heroes, but Hoover was no sportsman and had no enthusiasm for the Olympics. He sent Vice President Charles Curtis to Los Angeles to welcome the assembled athletes. Athletically, the 1932 games were remarkable for Mildred ("Babe") Didrikson's stellar performances in track and field, where she won the 80-meter hurdles and the javelin (both new world records) and came in second in the high jump (after a disqualified jump in which her feet were said to have been in the wrong position). Almost as remarkable were the achievements of the Afro-American runners and the Japanese swimmers. Eddie Tolan set one world record and two Olympic records in the 100 meters and the 200 meters while his teammate Ralph Metcalfe came in second and third. As for the Japanese:

The Japanese men suddenly emerged as the best swimmers in the world. Four different Japanese won individual events, and three of them broke Olympic records; their 800-meter relay quartet cracked the Olympic mark by an amazing thirty-eight seconds. Even more amazing was the youthfulness of the flying fish from Japan: Kusuo Kitamura, who won the strenuous 1,500-meter free style, was only fourteen; Masaji Kiyokawa, the 100-meter backstroke champion, was sixteen; and Yasuji Miyazaki, the 100-meter free style champion, was seventeen.[36]

Since the Indian field-hockey team trounced the Americans by a score of 24–1 and carried off a gold medal while the Argentines Juan Zabala and Santiago Lovell were the winners in the marathon and in heavyweight boxing, it was clear that the Olympics were no longer limited to the Americans and Europeans who had invented them. Little by little, the ideal of cosmopolitan inclusiveness (on *Western* terms) was approached.

There was, after Los Angeles, a mood of justified satisfaction in Olympic circles. The mood was not to last. Events in Europe precipitated the most serious crisis the Olympic movement had yet encountered. That the movement survived was in large part due to Avery Brundage.

CHAPTER VI

"THE NAZI OLYMPICS"

At its 29th Session in Barcelona (April 1931) the I.O.C. had been unable to select the venue for the 1936 games, but a subsequent mail ballot showed 43 votes for Berlin and only 16 for Barcelona (and 8 abstentions).[1] Like the treaties of Locarno and Rappallo, which formalized the acceptance of the Weimar Republic within European political culture, the choice ratified the reintegration of Germany within international sports. When the I.O.C.'s decision was announced, on May 13, 1931, Heinrich Brüning was Chancellor of Germany and a centrist coalition ruled; when the games were actually held, the National Socialists were in power and Adolf Hitler was Chancellor. It was not what the I.O.C. had expected.

The Nazis themselves were, despite frequent statements to the contrary by subsequent commentators, not enthusiastic about sports. Ideologically, they were far closer to the indigenous German tradition of *Turnen*—i.e., to the gymnastics movement inspired by the early-nineteenth-century prophet of nationalism Friedrich Ludwig Jahn. Although Jahn himself had liberal as well as conservative tendencies, the more liberal of his followers went into exile after the failure of the Revolution of 1848. (Many of the *Turner* emigrated to Chicago, where they created a flourishing gymnastics movement by the time of Brundage's childhood arrival there.) The *Turner* who remained in Germany became increasingly conservative, nationalistic, and romantic. They were loyal to Kaiser Wilhelm, to German *Kultur*, which they wished to spread both within Europe and overseas, and to an intuitive, irrationalist *Weltanschauung*. It was, therefore, inevitable that Die Deutsche Turnerschaft was hostile to the development of modern sports with their internationalism, their quantification, their obsession with records. Since the Olympic Games were from the very start internationalist, since the motto "altius, citius, fortius" embodied the progressive and competitive aspects of modern sports that Die Deutsche Turnerschaft had resisted, it was no wonder that the organization was, as we have seen, initially hostile to the games and never more than half-heartedly committed to them.[2]

The Nazis adhered to a *Weltanschauung* even more romantic than that of rival nationalist movements and were at first contemptuously dismissive of modern sports ("What Jews praise is poison for us"[3]). Hitler made an exception for boxing, which he saw as a display of physical courage and as a metaphor for the *Existenzkampf*, but his relationship to other sports was minimal. As one historian remarked, "Sports were quite alien to Hitler's inner self."[4] Consequently, informed observers had every reason to wonder about the new regime and its attitude vis-à-vis the Olympic Games planned for Berlin.

Among the most worried were, quite naturally, the president and the secretary of the organizing committee, Theodor Lewald and Carl Diem. Lewald, son of a Berlin lawyer and civil servant, had been a member of the I.O.C. since 1924 and served also as president of the national Olympic committee (and as chairman of the Deutscher Reichsausschuß für Leibesübungen, the closest German equivalent to the A.A.U.). Although Lewald typified the best in the austere Prussian tradition of public service, he had reason to be anxious about his personal safety as well as about the future of the Olympic movement; his father had converted from Judaism to Christianity and the Nazi journal *Völkischer Beobachter* had begun to cry out for his dismissal.[5] The secretary of the organizing committee, Carl Diem, was a self-made man whose father, like Avery Brundage's, had deserted the family. Young Diem had made his own way, initially as a sports journalist. He discovered that he had organizational as well as reportorial talent and, by the age of thirty, he was captain of the German team which competed at the Stockholm Olympics in 1912. Despite his lack of formal education, he eventually developed into a remarkable scholar, still known for his comprehensive world history of sports (published in 1960) and for a large number of monographs on sport history. In 1920, with support from Lewald and the Deutscher Reichsausschuß für Leibesübungen, he founded the Deutsche Hochschule für Leibesübungen, a university dedicated to the scientific study of sports. Although Diem was enough the child of his times to have been an ardent nationalist in the 1920s, he was definitely a proponent of modern sports rather than of *Turnen* and he was not bigoted about the achievements of other nations. He was an admirer of American sports, which he felt to be better organized than German sports. In 1930 he published *Sport in Amerika*, a glowing account of the playgrounds, athletic clubs, Y.M.C.A.'s, and—especially—collegiate gymnasia, field houses, tracks, and pools which he and Lewald visited during a five–week tour of the United States in 1929.[6]

Since Diem became an intimate friend of Avery Brundage and a key figure in the stormy controversy over American participation in the 1936 Olympics, it is necessary to say a word more about the American tour of 1929. Diem and Lewald arrived in Chicago by train on May 19 and were met at the station by Brundage, who invited them to tea with various notables from Chicago's large German-American community. Brundage and Diem had a further chance to become acquainted the next day at a dinner at the Hotel Atlantic. They got on extremely well and Diem was subsequently touched that Brundage gladly traveled the 900 miles to New York in order to preside at the farewell banquet held on June 9 at the posh Astor Hotel.[7]

The Nazi seizure of power jeopardized Diem's position within German sports. Since the faculty of the Deutsche Hochschule für Leibesübungen included several Jews, and Diem's wife Liselott was of partially Jewish ancestry, Diem was denounced by the Nazis as a "weißer Jude ("white Jew").[8] Given the endangered position of both the president and the secretary of the organizing committee and the shrill hostility of the Nazis to sports in general and the

Olympics in particular, no one was very optimistic about the 1936 games. On March 16, 1933, one day after the New York *Times* began to question the appropriateness of Berlin as the Olympic site, Lewald was received by Hitler at the Reichskanzlei. To Lewald's astonishment and relief, Hitler did not order an immediate end to the preparations. This was not because he had suddenly changed his mind about modern sports and Olympic ideals but because propaganda minister Josef Goebbels, who was at the audience in the Reichskanzlei, had realized that the games were a splendid opportunity to demonstrate German organizational talent and physical prowess. Lewald was forced to resign from his post with the Deutscher Reichsausschuß für Leibesübungen, but Baillet-Latour personally intervened with Hitler in order to stipulate that Lewald continue to serve as president of the organizing committee. Diem lost his post at the Deutsche Hochschule für Leibesübungen but was allowed to continue as secretary of the organizing group. In April, Lewald was optimistic (or dishonest) enough to write to Brundage that "there will not be the slightest discrimination made in the Berlin Games because of religion or race and furthermore . . . every participant has the fullest assurance of a kind, hearty, and courteous reception."[9] On October 5, Hitler toured the site of the games, inspected the progress in construction, and became positively lyrical about the prospects. He promised the startled committee the full financial support of his regime, a sum later set at 20,000,000 Reichsmarks. "Lewald and Diem were unable to believe their ears."[10]

Hitler's willingness to act as host allayed one set of anxieties and aroused another. The I.O.C. was not at all certain that the Nazis were ready to abandon their Fascist principles in order to stage the games by Olympic rules, which clearly forbid racial or religious discrimination. General Charles Sherrill, one of the three American members of the I.O.C., wrote to the American Jewish Congress and reassured them, "Rest assured that I will stoutly maintain the American principle that all citizens are equal under all laws."[11] As Sherrill and twenty-eight other members of the I.O.C. assembled in Vienna on June 7, 1933, the discrepancy between Nazi doctrine and Olympic rulebook was a central issue. Baillet-Latour, reelected president at this session by a nearly unanimous vote, joined Sherrill and William May Garland as the two Americans questioned Lewald and Karl Ritter von Halt about Jewish participation. The crux of the matter was not the acceptance of Jewish athletes on foreign teams but rather the right of *German* Jews to try out for their national team. Lewald and von Halt were able to secure a written guarantee from the Reichsinnenministerium that German Jews did indeed have this right: "All the laws regulating the Olympic Games shall be observed. As a principle German Jews shall not be excluded from German Teams at the Games of the XIth Olympiad."[12] Sherrill was surprised at his own unexpected success. He told A.A.U. official Frederick W. Rubien all about it on June 11. It had been the hardest fight he had ever been through. The Germans had yielded slowly and initially offered merely to publish the Olympic rules, but Sherrill had pushed them until they telephoned Berlin and came through with a formal written statement of acceptance for Jewish athletes within the German team. He informed Rubien that he had had to persuade his British colleague on the Executive Board, Lord Aberdare, that the I.O.C. was indeed within its rights to demand that the makeup of the German team conform to rule. The victory, thought Sherrill, was complete.[13]

It was not. The reliability of Nazi guarantees, written or oral, was called into question by the discrimination against Jewish athletes, who were allowed to use public sports facilities but who were expelled from the private sports clubs which were the center of German athletics. Since Brundage had followed Douglas MacArthur as president of the American Olympic Association, Bernard S. Deutsch of the American Jewish Congress addressed an open letter to him to alert him to this violation of the spirit if not the letter of the guarantees offered by the Reichsministerium.[14] Brundage had already written Kirby on May 31, 1933, that the "very foundation of the modern Olympic revival will be undermined if individual countries are allowed to restrict participation by reason of class, creed or race,"[15] but he seems not to have answered Deutsch's letter because it was his principle to reply to all private communications but not to public statements. It was Kirby who pressed the issue. In his forty years as an advocate of amateur sports, he was an unusually eloquent defender of the principle of equality. To a fellow member of the American Olympic Committee, he wrote, "I am and have been always very serious in my conclusion that sport is the only true democracy. . . ." It doesn't matter "whether you are rich as Croesus or as poor as Job's turkey."[16] To Kirby, religious discrimination was even worse than economic disadvantage. For the convention of the American Olympic Committee on November 22, he prepared a resolution which threatened a boycott unless German Jews were allowed in fact as well as theory to "train, prepare for and participate in the Olympic Games of 1936."[17] Brundage expressed reservations about the forthright tone of the resolution and Kirby defended his stand with characteristic vigor: "Undoubtedly it is generally wiser to 'let sleeping dogs lie,' but unfortunately these dogs are not sleeping, they are growling and snarling and snipping and all but biting." Kirby admired and had affection for Lewald and Diem, but "the democracy of sport . . . is bigger than Lewald or Diem or Brundage or Rubien—and certainly than Kirby."[18] The A.O.A. passed a somewhat milder version of Kirby's resolution.

Even as the A.O.A. deliberated, Reichssportführer Hans von Tschammer und Osten issued a statement that Jews were not barred from sports clubs by any official *governmental* decree,[19] but Brundage was not reassured by the sophistical distinction. He wrote to Baillet-Latour, "The German authorities have displayed a singular lack of astuteness in all of their publicity. On this subject, every news dispatch that has come from Germany seems to indicate that the Hitlerites do not intend to live up to the pledges given to the I.O.C. at Vienna."[20] Brundage kept his worries private because he did not want to cause unnecessary difficulties for his friends Lewald and Diem and von Halt. Kirby, however, refused to ignore the frequent newspaper reports of discrimination against Jewish athletes. He was among the Madison Square Garden speakers at an anti-Nazi rally held by the American Jewish Committee on March 6, 1934.

When the I.O.C. convened in Athens on May 15, 1934, Britain's Lord Aberdare, who had earlier been ready to accept German assurances, now expressed concern about reports from Germany and asked his German colleagues "if the pledge given in Vienna last year had been given practical application and if it really was possible for Jews to go into training with the object of participating in the Olympic Games."[21] Garland asked the same question and Lewald and von Halt declared officially:

It goes without saying that the Pledges given by Germany in Vienna in 1933 to admit to the German Olympic team German Sportsmen of Non-Aryan origin, provided they have the necessary capability, will be strictly observed and facilities for preparation will be given to all sportsmen.[22]

For that purpose, the Deutscher Leichtathletik-Verband ("German Track and Field Association") had invited Jewish sports organizations to submit the names of potential Olympic team members.

The I.O.C. was satisfied. The American Olympic Association was not. When it met on June 14, it postponed acceptance of the official German invitation to the games until after an on-the-spot investigation by President Brundage. His American colleagues may have expected a dispassionate appraisal of the situation, but the German consulate in Chicago reported on September 3 to its embassy in Washington that Brundage's mission was to "find in Germany . . . what he lacked in America."[23] The consulate assumed that Brundage's mind was already made up—in Germany's favor.

Brundage wrote Diem that he and Elizabeth meant to sail on the S. S. New York of the Hamburg-American Line on July 25 and indicated his desire to talk with Sportführer von Tschammer und Osten as well as with leaders of Jewish sports organizations.[24] The primary purpose of the trip to Europe, however, was not the investigation of Nazi discrimination but attendance at the I.A.A.F. congress in Stockholm in late August. The Brundages arrived at the German port of Cuxhaven on August 3 and went on to Scandinavia, where they spent most of the month. They traveled as far north as Norway's North Cape, where Elizabeth was so seriously ill that Avery "for a time . . . despaired of her life."[25] She recovered somewhat while they were in Stockholm for the conference, but she may not have accompanied her husband on his first trip to the Soviet Union, where he was impressed by the effort to modernize physical education as well as factory production.

When the I.A.A.F. meetings began with festivities at Edstrøm's villa, Vestoräas, about sixty miles from Stockholm, Brundage and Diem began to discuss the German problem. During lunch at Stockholm's Grand Hotel, Brundage met with Diem, von Halt, Lewald, and Justus W. Meyerhof, a Jewish member of the Berliner Sport-Club. Diem made notes on the discussion:

We showed Brundage documents indicating that the Jews are able to participate freely in sports and to train for the Olympic team. Meyerhof told us that he had offered to resign from the Berliner Sport-Club but that the resignation had not been accepted. I was seldom as proud of my club as at that moment. Brundage was visibly impressed. He plans to speak with leaders of Jewish sports when he visits Berlin.[26]

That evening, August 29, the Brundages dined with Diem, von Halt, and Sigfrid and Ruth Edstrøm at the elegant Gyldenen Freden. Over coffee and cognac, after the ladies had retired, Edstrøm and Brundage offered Diem *Bruderschaft*, which moved Diem immensely.[27]

Before seeing Diem again in Berlin, the Brundages went south. Postcards from "A" and "E" to Elizabeth's niece, Jean Harper, tell of perfect September weather in Venice.[28] While touring Italy and Yugoslavia, Brundage had ample time to ponder Edstrøm's thoughts on the Jewish problem, i.e., that

As regards the persecution of the Jews in Germany I am not at all in favor of said action, but I fully understand that an alteration had to take place. As it was in Germany, a great part of the German nation was led by the Jews and not by the Germans themselves. Even in the U.S.A. the day may come when you will have to stop the activities of the Jews. They are intelligent and unscrupulous. Many of my friends are Jews so you must not think that I am against them, but they must be kept within certain limits.[29]

The on-the-spot investigation of German conditions did not begin until September 13, the day after the Brundages' arrival in

Koenigsberg in East Prussia. Since Brundage did not speak German well, he was forced to rely on interpreters. It was an additional drawback that he was never allowed to talk alone with representatives of the Jewish sports clubs. He met Reichssportführer von Tschammer und Osten and "liked him very much" and listened carefully when he was told that there was no discrimination and that Jewish athletes were quite likely to make the team.[30] This was also the message communicated by Brundage's oldest German friend, Karl Ritter von Halt. Brundage's report to the American Olympic Association was strongly in favor of accepting the invitation. To the press he announced, "I was given positive assurance in writing by Tschammer [und] Osten, Germany's official Olympic representative [an error], that there will be no discrimination against Jews. You can't ask more than that and I think the guarantee will be fulfilled."[31] Brundage's doubts about the Reichssportführer's sincerity were stifled by the intensity of his faith in the importance of the games. Further assurances came in the form of a letter sent by Rudolf Hess to Baillet-Latour, in which Hess informed the I.O.C. president that the law of August 16, 1934, which forbade all contact between Nazis and Jews, did not apply to sports.[32]

The eighteen-member American Olympic Committee met in New York on September 26, one day after Brundage's return from Europe, and resolved unanimously (even the skeptical Kirby was now convinced) that "in the light of the report of President Brundage and the attitude and assurances of the German Olympic Committee and the representatives of the German Government . . . , we accept the invitation of the German Olympic Committee."[33] Any hopes that this decision might terminate the controversy quickly evaporated. The New York *Times* for September 27 was full of bad news (from Brundage's perspective): Samuel Untermyer of the Anti-Defamation League, listing instances of Nazi persecution of Jewish athletes, called for a boycott of the games; Representative Emanuel Celler of New York charged that Brundage had "prejudged the situation before he sailed from America. The Reich Sports Commissars have snared and deluded him."[34] The A.A.U. held its annual convention December 7–9 and voted to postpone acceptance of the German invitation—a clear sign that Untermyer and Celler were not the only holdouts. For Brundage, who was accustomed to a more subservient A.A.U., the vote was tantamount to a declaration of no confidence. Passions flamed; the lines hardened.

By mid-1935 an intensive boycott campaign was in full swing. Brundage's position had always been that sports and politics should be strictly separate: "The A.O.C. must not be involved in political, racial, religious or sociological controversies."[35] (By "sociological," of course, he meant "social.") All that could be asked of the Nazi regime, from his perspective, was that it accept Olympic rules and allow German Jews to try out for the German team, and the highest German officials had promised that this would indeed be the case. What was good enough for him was also good enough for Pierre de Coubertin, whom the German organizing committee assiduously courted. Although the founder was scrupulous about not attending either the sessions of the I.O.C. or the games themselves, he did agree, after a visit to Lausanne by Diem and Lewald, to record a radio message that the organizers were able to use, on August 4, 1935, as the first of a broadcast series publicizing the Berlin games.[36]

Brundage explained his view of the matter in a sixteen-page pamphlet, "Fair Play for American Athletes," published by the A.O.C. He asked if the American athlete was to be made "a martyr to a cause not his own" and he repeated his arguments about the separation of sports from politics and religion. American athletes should not become needlessly involved in "the present Jew-Nazi altercation." The entire problem, in his eyes, was that opponents of the Nazi regime were not satisfied with Olympic rules; they really wanted a boycott to undermine Nazism; they meant to use the games as a political weapon.

Brundage was not wholly inaccurate. It was inevitable that the boycott movement attracted anti-Nazis of all sorts, including those totally uninterested in sports. The Communist Party was active in all anti-Nazi campaigns (until the Molotov–von Ribbentrop Pact of 1939) and American Jews were naturally eager to express their opposition to Hitler by whatever means were available. But, in

Brundage's mind, *all* of the pro-boycott camp had enlisted for political reasons and "all of the real sport leaders in the United States are unanimously in favor of participation in the Olympic Games which are above all considerations of politics, race, color or creed."[37] Criticism of his position he casually dismissed as "obviously written by a Jew or someone who has succumbed to the Jewish propaganda."[38] Writing to I.O.C. president Baillet-Latour, he referred to the "Jewish proposal to boycott the Games,"[39] as if only Jews had reason to oppose Nazism.

Brundage's relations with Charles Ornstein, a Jewish member of the A.O.C., deteriorated into petty hostility and his friendship with Judge Jeremiah T. Mahoney, Brundage's successor as A.A.U. president, turned into enmity. Guido von Mengden, press secretary for the Reichsbund für Leibesübungen, denounced Mahoney as a "powerful Jewish financier." Brundage, somewhat better informed about ethnicity in America,[40] characterized the Roman Catholic judge's opposition to the games as politically motivated. Mahoney had mayoral ambitions in New York and New York was notoriously "overpopulated" with Jewish voters. Therefore, Mahoney must have been insincere. Brundage refused to acknowledge that Roman Catholics had excellent reasons to fear Hitler, who had made no secret of his neopaganism or of his hatred for the church he had been born into. The Catholic journal *Commonweal* was for a boycott (as was the Protestant publication *Christian Century*); in July of 1935 the Catholic War Veterans appealed to the A.O.C. to nullify its agreement with the Germans.[41] The boycott movement included a number of politically prominent Catholics such as James Curley and David I. Walsh of Massachusetts and Fiorello LaGuardia and Al Smith of New York; and a Gallup Poll taken in March of 1935 showed 43 percent of the entire population in favor of a boycott, but Brundage continued obstinately to see a conspiracy of Jews and Communists. This was not the *result* of anti-Semitism, which seems not have been a part of Brundage's makeup prior to the fight over the boycott, but rather the *cause* of it.[42] On this question, Kirby wrote Brundage one of the harshest letters Brundage ever received: "I take it that the fundamental difference between you and me is that you are a Jew hater and Jew baiter and I am neither."[43] It was the battle over the acceptance or rejection of the invitation to Berlin that turned Brundage—for a period of several years—into an anti-Semite. Having been assured by men he knew and trusted that the German government accepted the Olympic rules, believing as he did that the games were the most important international institution of the century, a force for peace and reconciliation among peoples, he simply failed to understand that there were men of good will who did not agree with him. He was unable to imagine motives that were other than biased by ethnic identity or political radicalism. Once he had made up his own mind, he attributed to opponents the most despicable of motives and an almost satanic insincerity.

As a result, his statements became nearly hysterical. Writing as president of the A.O.C. and addressing the "sport-loving public of the United States," he announced that "there will be teams representing the United States in the 1936 Games" and he lashed out at the opposition:

The bitter feelings engendered, the attempted coercion and intimidation by fair means or foul, the vicious and insidious propaganda which are being used in this campaign largely by individuals who have never learned the lessons of amateur sport and thus do not hesitate to use methods contrary to all codes of sportsmanship, are an indication of what may be expected if religious, racial, class or political issues are allowed to intrude in the council halls of sport where they have no place. . . . Many of the individuals and organizations active in the present campaign to boycott the Olympics have Communistic antecedents. Radicals and Communists must keep their hands off American sport.[44]

Mahoney's chief contribution to the "vicious and insidious propaganda" was a pamphlet entitled "Germany Has Violated the Olympic Code" (1935). Writing in the form of an open letter to Lewald, Mahoney cited specific cases—the expulsion of Jews from sports clubs and from public facilities, the ban on competition between Jews and other Germans, the exclusion of world-class highjumper Gretel Bergmann from the Olympic team. Every allegation has been verified by subsequent scholarship.

Mahoney had the facts, Brundage had the votes. Mahoney and Ornstein offered a boycott motion at the annual meetings of the Metropolitan Association of the A.A.U., October 8, 1935, and the motion was tabled, 77–32.[45] On December 6, the national organization met, also in New York, which Brundage thought disadvantageous for his side of the quarrel. He had earlier written to Garland, "You can't imagine what the situation is in New York City, where because of the fact that 30% or 40% of the population is Jewish, the newspapers are half given up to the German situation."[46] In London, Carl Diem wrote anxiously in his diary, "Today, the American Olympic Committee is meeting in New York to decide the question of its participation in the Olympic Games."[47]

Diem and Brundage had reason to worry, for the vote was close, but the motion to investigate further failed by 58¼ to 55¾ and the A.A.U. formally accepted the invitation to participate in the winter games at Garmisch-Partenkirchen and the summer games in Berlin. It was one of the bitterest struggles of Brundage's career and one which he never forgot. Decades later, he still referred to "the viciousness of the contest to prevent a United States team from participating" and to the "great victory for Olympic principles."[48] And, decades later, he was still referred to as "an avowed admirer of Hitler."[49]

While Brundage was winning his victory in the United States, his opponents had carried the battle elsewhere. The third American member of the I.O.C. (in addition to Sherrill and Garland) was Ernest Lee Jahncke. Former Assistant Secretary of the Navy under President Herbert Hoover, Jahncke was clearly not a man tarred by Brundage's somewhat wild brush. No more than Jeremiah Mahoney was he a Jew or a Communist. On November 27, the New York *Times* printed his appeal to Baillet-Latour: the

plain and undeniable fact is that the Nazis have consistently and persistently violated their pledges. Of this they have been convicted out of their own mouths and by the testimony of impartial and experienced American and English newspaper correspondents. . . . It is plainly your duty to hold the Nazi sports authorities accountable for the violation of their pledges. . . . I do not doubt that you have received all sorts of assurances from the Nazi sports authorities. Ever since they gave us their pledges in June, 1933, they have been lavish with their promises. The difficulty is that they have been stingy with their performance of them.

However much you would like us to believe that the Germans have kept their pledges, the fact is that the Nazi sports authorities have dissolved Catholic sports clubs and have denied Germany's Jewish athletes adequate opportunity to condition themselves for competition in the Olympic elimination contests and this, of course, is equivalent to excluding them as a group from the German team. . . .

Does it surprise you that under these conditions few non-Aryan athletes have been able to attain Olympic form? Or that under these conditions the Reichssportführer is willing to assure you that such athletes who hold "sufficient records" will be admitted to the elimination contests?

No one pretends that the Games should be taken away from Germany merely because Jews are not admitted to Nazi sport clubs. The point, my dear Count, is that by excluding them from those clubs the Nazis have . . . excluded them from the use of training facilities and opportunities for competition. . . .

Let me urge upon you that you place your great talents and influence in the service of the spirit of fair play and chivalry instead of the service of brutality, force and power. Let me beseech you to seize your opportunity to take your rightful place in the history of the Olympics alongside of de Coubertin instead of Hitler.[50]

Baillet-Latour, who had previously informed Brundage that he was ready to come to the United States in order to combat personally the Jewish campaign to prevent American participation in the games, found Jahncke's letter discourteous and answered him in anger. Baillet-Latour informed Jahncke that the president's duty was to execute the decisions of the committee.[51] The Count saw Jahncke as a traitor who was for inexplicably spiteful reasons unable to accept the personal assurances of honorable men like Diem, Lewald, von Halt, Brundage, and, of course, Baillet-Latour himself. He asked Jahncke to resign from the I.O.C. and, when Jahncke refused, arranged for him to be expelled.

Meanwhile, all was not well in the United States either, despite the favorable vote of the A.A.U. It was not easy to raise money for any purpose in a depression. The bitterness of the fight over participation had soured many potential contributors, especially among the normally philanthropic Jewish population. Three months before the team was supposed to depart, Kirby, Treasurer of the A.O.A., wrote dolefully, "We are in a hell of a hole financially."[52] Until the last minute, it was uncertain whether or not the entire team would be able to make the journey to Berlin. It was a sign of the times, and of the mood, that the official report of the A.O.C. listed contributions as small as ten cents.

Protest took other forms than the withholding of customary contributions. Mahoney, Ornstein, and others who favored a boycott staged alternative games, the rather pretentiously named "World Labour Athletic Carnival," August 15–16, 1936, at Randall's Island, New York.[53] Although Dietrich Wortmann of the A.A.U.'s Foreign Relations Committee complained about the use of the A.A.U.'s name in connection with this meet, A.A.U. secretary Daniel J. Ferris defended the right of the opposition to go ahead with official sanction.[54] That Wortmann stooped to such petty harassment indicates the intensity of passions aroused by the boycott fight. Ferris wrote Brundage on the matter but seems not to have received a reply. Radical groups, meanwhile, planned a much more elaborate workers' "Olimpiada" in Barcelona, but the outbreak of the Spanish Civil War in July of 1936 interrupted the event just as the athletes had begun to arrive.[55] And the drama in Berlin was so spectacular that its rivals have been almost completely forgotten.

Difficulties dogged Brundage's heels even on shipboard, but they were of a nonpolitical nature. Eleanor Holm Jarrett was a veteran swimmer who had already competed in two Olympics. As a fifteen-year-old she had tied for 5th place in the 100-meter backstroke at Amsterdam and she had won the event with a world record at Los Angeles in 1932. Now a married woman of twenty-two, she asked for and was denied permission to join the passengers in first-class accommodations (at her own expense). She showed no inclination to abide by the strict rules governing behavior while aboard the S.S. Manhattan. According to her roommate, she went to a party and returned to their cabin at 6:00 A.M., intoxicated. Although placed on probation, Jarrett was allegedly found drunk by the chaperone of the women's team. That Jarrett smoked, gambled, and missed meals added to the officials' horror.[56] The A.O.C. decided to withdraw her from competition and Brundage refused to alter the decision even after he was handed a petition signed by 220 coaches and athletes. Since Eleanor Holm Jarrett was a very beautiful woman as well as a great athlete, the press reacted gleefully ("Eleanor Bares Olympic Story") and newspapers published cheesecake photographs of the "water nymph."[57] Brundage has appeared, ever since, in the guise of a killjoy.[58]

Brundage had other, more important worries. Counting on the repeated guarantees of his German friends and carried along by his own belief in Olympism, he had risked his moral authority on behalf of the games. If the Nazis failed to keep their promises, what then? In countless letters and speeches, he later claimed that the Nazis *did* keep their word, that they followed the Olympic rules, that German Jews who qualified athletically for the competitions were indeed allowed to compete. It is certainly true that the Nazis invited two "half-Jews" (i.e., athletes of mixed religious background) to participate. Helene Mayer, who had won a gold medal in fencing in 1928, was brought back to Germany from Los Angeles, where she had lived for a number of years (she had won three national championships in the United States). Rudi Ball was invited to play on the ice hockey team. Since Nazi law did not yet define *Mischlinge* as Jews, Mayer and Ball were, technically, *not* examples of good faith. More important, Jewish athletes of Olympic calibre *were* barred from the games. Gretel Bergmann had highjumped 1.60 meters that summer, four centimeters better than her "Aryan" rival, Elfriede Kaun, but Bergmann was kept from the Olympic team on the pretext that she was not a member of an officially recognized sports club. This was an anticipation of "catch-22" because her club, Stuttgarter Schild, was barred from membership in the official Fachamt für Leichtathletik ("Special Office for Track and Field") presided over by none other than Brundage's close friend, I.O.C. member Karl Ritter von Halt. Other Jews who might have won places on the team were intimidated or lacked facilities to train and failed to achieve their potential. Even before the games began,

Lewald confessed to an American consul, George Messersmith, that he had lied to the American Olympic Committee.[59]

One must give Baillet-Latour some credit for doing his best to hold the Nazis to their word. Although he had written Brundage that he was not personally fond of Jews,[60] he did attempt to force the Nazis to admit qualified Jews to the team and he, on at least two occasions, forced a change in Hitler's policies. When Baillet-Latour heard, shortly before the beginning of the winter games, that the streets and roads of Garmisch-Partenkirchen were placarded with anti-Semitic signs, he demanded that the placards be removed—and they were.[61] At the summer games, Baillet-Latour intervened dramatically in a frequently misreported and misunderstood incident.

In legend, the incident concerned Jessie Owens. It is alleged that Hitler refused to offer Owens his hand after the first of his four track-and-field victories. In actuality, Hitler never had a chance to refuse to congratulate Owens. As Karl Ritter von Halt related the episode in 1955, Hans von Tschammer und Osten brought the first victors, who happened to be Germans and Finns, to Hitler's box, where the Führer congratulated them. Baillet-Latour was furious at this form of favoritism and complained the next day to von Halt and was accompanied by him to call upon Hitler, whom the Belgian then scolded for this infraction of Olympic protocol. Hitler excused himself and subsequently greeted German victors in private.[62] In Brundage's trenchant sports imagery, "Hitler backed water fast."[63]

Were the games a propaganda triumph for the Nazis? The question is not easily answered. Predictably, Brundage was sure that they were not: "It is true that the Hitler regime made every effort to use for its own purposes this great festival of the youth of the world, but it was arranged and controlled entirely and exclusively by non-Nazis for the benefit of non-Nazis."[64] In his official report to the A.O.C., Brundage asserted that the games had been a contribution to "international peace and harmony."[65] A great deal more needs to be said. Hitler had told Diem and Lewald that he wanted to impress the world with the magnificence of the games, and the world was impressed. The facilities, especially the Olympic stadium itself, were monumental and the pageantry, which can still be vicariously experienced in Leni Riefenstahl's documentary *Olympia*, was truly extraordinary. Among Diem's inspired innovations was an enormous iron bell upon which was inscribed, *Ich rufe die Jugend der Welt* (I call the youth of the world). It was also Diem's inspiration that a torch be lit by the rays of the sun at the altar of Zeus in Olympia and carried by a relay of thousands of runners to the stadium in Berlin, where it was used to ignite the Olympic flame. (The idea came from a passage in Plutarch's *Life of Numa Pompilius*, where the flame is ignited at the altar of Athena, not Zeus.[66])

The enthusiasm of the mostly German crowd was enormous as it greeted the world's athletes. The 383 members of the American team, the men in white trousers and blue coats, the women in white skirts and blue jackets, were led into the stadium by A.O.C. President Brundage. They were welcomed by the crowd, as were the other foreign teams. The various athletic events were contested with a minimum of controversy and the athletic achievements were stellar. The organizing committee arranged a splendid series of social, cultural, and artistic events for the public and, with the help of the German government, entertained the I.O.C. royally. There was, for instance, a huge dinner party for 2,000 at the famed Pfaueninsel ("Peacock Island") and a reception at the opening of a new museum containing the spectacularly beautiful Hellenistic altar from the Temple of Zeus at Pergamon.[67] The most impressive of Diem's many artistic contributions was *Olympische Jugend*, a Festspiel with dances choreographed by Mary Wigman to music composed by Carl Orff and Werner Egk; the performers included a chorus of a thousand, sixty male dancers, and eighty female dancers. Small wonder that thousands of ordinary tourists left with a sense of aesthetic fulfillment, a conviction of German efficiency, and a vague impression that National Socialism was not the horror that they had imagined it to be on the basis of newspaper or newsreel reports. The swastika was very much in evidence, but Hitler's role had been minimized. Baillet-Latour told Hitler bluntly that the host was limited to a single sentence which Baillet-Latour had typed up for him to speak. Intentionally or not, Hitler's response was comic: "Count, I'll take the trouble to learn it by heart."[68]

The strongest evidence for Brundage's assertion that the games were not a propaganda triumph is the fact that Jesse Owens was unquestionably the star of the games. Setting a world record of 10.3 seconds for 100 meters and an Olympic record of 20.7 seconds for 200 meters, he went on to jump an astonishing 8.06 meters and to help set still another world record in the 400-meter relay. One of the most respected of British journals noted that "The German spectators, like all others, have fallen completely under the spell of the American Negro Jesse Owens, who is . . . the hero of these games."[69] When the Nazi periodical *Der Angriff* sneered at the Negro athletes as America's *schwarze Hilfstruppe* (black auxiliaries), the editors were immediately rebuked by the propaganda ministry, which had specifically ordered that the black athletes not be insulted.[70] In 1937, the press was directed to portray Owens favorably. The popular picture-and-text series sponsored by the German cigarette firm Reemtsma featured no fewer than seven glossy paste-in photographs of Owens, including one of him lying on the grass chatting shoulder-to-shoulder with the German jumper Luz Long, whose generous advice helped Owens to his world-record long-jump.[71] Owens was described in the text as the *Wunderathlet* of the games and the most popular of all the track-and-field athletes.[72] He also appears in Leni Riefenstahl's film as if he were a real Olympian, a divinity, the god of sports. Gerard de Houville's review of the film was aptly entitled "Les Dieux du stade"; Owens, he wrote, was "beau comme une statue de bronze animée."[73] In the film the camera focuses on Owens as it focused on no other athlete, not even Glenn Morris, the American winner of the decathlon. Propaganda minister Goebbels, whose office secretly financed the film, demanded that Riefenstahl cut the footage devoted to Owens, but she bravely refused, relying on Hitler's favor to protect her from Goebbels' ire.[74] Ironically, neither Owens nor any other black champion was pictured in the Atlanta *Constitution*, the most liberal of Southern newspapers.

It was also ironical that the American coaches Lawson Robertson and Dean Cromwell violated "customary standards of sportsmanship . . . and the feelings of individuals" by cutting Marty Glickman and Sam Stoller, the only Jews on the American track team, from the 400-meter relay, which consisted of Owens, Ralph Metcalf, Frank Wykoff, and Foy Draper. The reason for the coaches' substitution was probably the tendency to favor athletes from one's own university rather than anti-Semitism. Draper was a student and Cromwell his coach at the University of Southern California.[75]

To the degree that Owens made a mockery of the Nazi myth of "Nordic" superiority, the games were not a propaganda coup, but the overall impression of the games must have added to Hitler's prestige. Pierre de Coubertin himself, in an interview published by the Parisian paper *Le Journal*, remarked that the games had been organized with "Hitlerian strength and discipline."[76]

Propaganda coup or not, the games were unquestionably an important step on Avery Brundage's path to Olympic leadership. On the first day of the 35th Session, July 30, the wrath of the I.O.C. against dissenter Jahncke was expressed in its vote to expel him: 49–0. Garland abstained, but he expressed his disapproval of his American colleague. (Charles Sherrill, the third American member, had died suddenly on June 25.) Jahncke was gone and the I.O.C. now consisted of like-minded men in agreement with one another, at least in regard to the correctness of their decision to keep the games in Garmisch-Partenkirchen and Berlin. Who had a better right to represent the I.O.C. in the United States than the man who had fought like a lion to frustrate the boycott and bring the American team to Berlin? Brundage was elected unanimously and the official notes specifically record that his election was "en remplacement de M. Lee Jahncke."[77]

CHAPTER VII

PRESERVING THE IDEAL, 1936–1948

Brundage's election to the I.O.C. was doubtless a moment of sweet satisfaction, but it caused him a certain amount of pain as well. For years, Gustavus Kirby had had one overriding ambition—to become a member of the I.O.C. The election of the younger man, whom Kirby looked upon rather as a protégé, represented another in a long string of disappointments. Edstrøm thought Kirby had been passed by because of a quarrel with Coubertin in Lausanne in 1921.[1] In a confidential letter, William May Garland noted that the outspoken Kirby had clashed with Baillet-Latour as well.[2] Even before Brundage's election, which was a foregone conclusion by the summer of 1936, Kirby wrote to him, "Speaking quite candidly, I should like to become a member of the I.O.C., and I honestly feel that I deserve . . . such appointment."[3] After Brundage's election, Kirby apparently sent him an embittered letter which seems not to have been preserved but which A. C. Gilbert referred to in an effort to soothe the older man.[4] At the Berlin session, Baillet-Latour quite naturally turned to Garland and Brundage for advice on replacing the suddenly deceased Charles Sherrill. Kirby was upset at the thought that Brundage might have recommended someone else, which would have been "another great disappointment, to be borne without quitting or grousing,"[5] but Brundage reassured him that he had advanced no other name.[6] Kirby appealed for support again, early in 1937, but Frederic R. Coudert, a wealthy lawyer, became the third American member (after Garland managed to forgive him for his political support of Franklin Roosevelt in the recent national election).[7]

Brundage's star was in the ascendancy internationally, but there was a brief period in 1937 when his authority at home was shaky. At the A.A.U.'s annual convention in December of 1935, Brundage had run for and was once again elected president of the organization, but a year later the tables were turned, and Mahoney defeated the candidate of Brundage's faction, Major Patrick J. Walsh, by a vote of 199 3/7 to 127 4/7.[8] Brundage attributed defeat not to second thoughts about the correctness of American participation in Berlin but rather to the fact that he and his supporters had been in Germany at the games while "Jews, politicians, promoters, and radicals" were hard at work conspiring against him.[9] He felt that the A.A.U. was in danger unless the forces of evil were curbed. Kirby was so involved emotionally that he ostentatiously refused to sit at the same table with Mahoney and it was all that Brundage and Gilbert could do to save their friend from expulsion at the hands of the Mahoney faction from Kirby's office as treasurer of the A.O.A.[10] Brundage's backers regained the majority at the 1937 A.A.U. convention and he was able to inform Edstrøm on December 6 that Judge William Hoyt had replaced "the Mahoney gang,"[11] but it was years before the wounds of the boycott fight healed.

There was less friction among the Olympians. Coudert was formally taken into the select group at the 36th Session (Warsaw, June 7–11, 1937). At this time, Edstrøm became vice president, following the late Baron Godefroy de Blonay of Switzerland, and—despite his lack of seniority—Brundage stepped into Blonay's place on the Executive Board.[12] There were changes of a different sort at the next session, which took place in Egypt in March of 1938. Brundage's trusted friend Lewald was forced by his own government to resign from the I.O.C. and was replaced by the Nazis with General Walter von Reichenau. The committee clung to the hypocritical notion that *it* and not the Nazis had made the decision.

On his way to Egypt for the session, Brundage attended the

I.A.A.F. meetings in Paris (February 28 and March 1). It was an opportunity for good talks among close friends. He and Elizabeth stayed at the Hotel Bristol, 112 Faubourg St. Honoré, as did Karl Ritter von Halt, Bo Ekelund, Sigfrid Edstrøm, and their wives.[13]

The "Cairo" session was not held only in Cairo but also in various other locations. The committee visited the pyramids on March 11 and then departed by train for Upper Egypt. They spent an entire week, March 12 to 19, returning by boat down the Nile from Aswan. It was a chance to see both the tomb of Tutankhamen and the marvelous murals of Beni-Hassan, which provide the most detailed of all glimpses into the athletic life of ancient Egypt. From Cairo, which they reached on the 19th, the members hurried off to Alexandria and its spectacular Greco-Roman museum. On the 22nd, the group went on to Athens and then to Olympia, where they solemnly buried the heart of Coubertin (who had died peacefully on September 2, 1937, on a park bench in Lausanne). Brundage was deeply stirred by the visit to Olympia: "we wandered through the ruins of the old structures which housed the athletes and officials, now overgrown with trees, shrubs and wild flowers." He admired the statue of Hermes by Praxiteles, which stands in the little museum in Olympia, and called it "perhaps the most beautiful male figure known." He was captivated by the olive groves, the profusion of blossoming fruit trees, the snow-clad mountains, and the sea sparkling under the Mediterranean sun.[14] On the 26th, he departed on the steamer *Grimani*, bound for Italy. Since he cordially thanked his Italian colleague, Alberto Bonacossa, for the use of an automobile while in Rome, he must have stopped in the Eternal City either on the way to Cairo or on the return trip from Athens.[15]

If there was a metaphorical cloud in the dazzlingly blue African sky beneath which the business of the session took place, it was the possibility that the games of the XII Olympiad might have to be relocated. The participation of the Japanese team in Los Angeles and Berlin (where the male swimmers continued to excel and Naota Tajima won the triple jump and Kitei Son the marathon) was rightly seen as a symbol of Olympic internationalism. The next step in the I.O.C.'s missionary program was to award the 1940 games to an Asian host, and Japan was the obvious choice as the only Asian nation with the economic resources and the administrative skills necessary for the task. The decision, in which the newly elected Brundage had participated, was made at the Berlin session in 1936. Japan's government, however, had fallen into the hands of the military and the military was obsessed by geopolitical anxieties. Believing that territorial expansion was the prerequisite for economic survival, the Japanese had seized Manchuria in 1931 (*before* the I.O.C. decision to award the games) and invaded China in 1937. The pretext was the defense of Japanese rights allegedly violated by the Chinese (who were actually bogged down in a Nationalist-Communist civil war). The result was a war for empire that ended only when the Emperor, stunned and grieved by the nuclear obliteration of Hiroshima and Nagasaki, forced the still reluctant military to lay down their arms.

A. C. Gilbert—an Olympian from the 1908 games, a member of the A.O.A., a toy manufacturer famous for Erector Sets—was among those who felt that imperialist Japan had forfeited the right to hold the games. He wrote to Brundage in February of 1938 and expressed the hope that the I.O.C. would postpone the games because of Japan's war in China, but Brundage, the most strongly pro-Japanese member of the I.O.C., disagreed, acknowledging, however, that "it is difficult indeed to keep the public clear on the point that politics have no part in the Olympic movement."[16] When the I.O.C. met in March, China's C. T. Wang, who did not attend the meetings in Egypt, cabled a request that the games be held elsewhere and the British Amateur Athletic Association voted for a boycott in the event that the war continued into 1940,[17] but the I.O.C. did not see the Japanese invasion as a relevant issue. "Then as now, the I.O.C. considered war and peace pragmatically, as an organizational question."[18]

Three months later, after his return from the Mediterranean, Brundage suggested to Kirby that Chinese athletes be given safe-conduct passes in order to compete with the others in Japan.[19] Only three days after this bizarrely idealistic letter to Kirby, the Chicago

papers carried the news that another prominent athletic administrator, William J. Bingham of Harvard, had resigned from the
A.O.A. to protest the plans to go ahead despite the war. Reporters
asked Brundage to comment and they probably wrote the answer
down in advance: "The work of the committee will go on just the
same."[20] Within a month, however, it was evident that the Olympiad was not going to be celebrated in Tokyo and Sapporo after
all. It was not that the I.O.C. had qualms or that there was a boycott
movement comparable to that of 1934–36. The Japanese themselves
decided that the games were a costly distraction. *The Japan Advertiser*
(Tokyo) revealed on July 15, 1938, that the government had already
decided to renounce the games. The paper quoted Count Michimasa Soyeshima of the organizing committee: "There is nothing to
do but to say we can't help it." The Count then resigned from the
I.O.C. Edstrøm, who was visiting Chicago at the time, asked Brundage to cable for a confirmation of the newspaper story. On the
16th, Dr. M. Nagai told Brundage the bad news: the organizers
were asking the I.O.C. to release them from their commitment.[21]

The I.O.C. was not caught wholly unprepared. Contingency
plans had already been made to transfer the games to Helsinki.
I.O.C. member Ernst Krogius had promised Helsinki as a substitute site for the summer games and responded quickly to Baillet-
Latour's official request that Finland host the games.[22] By mid-
August the Finns had a committee headed by J. R. Rangell, director
of the Finnish Bank, vice president of the national Olympic committee, and (since the Cairo Session) member of the I.O.C.[23] When
the I.O.C. met in London the following June, the winter games
were awarded to Garmisch-Partenkirchen; since the vote was unanimous, there was proof positive that there were no second thoughts
about the "Nazi Olympics" of 1936.

Then came September 1, 1939. For Brundage, the outbreak of
World War II was "the suicide of a culture."[24] To Kirby he la-
mented, "Like you, with so many dear friends on both sides, this
wholly unnecessary war makes me feel very sad," but he went on
characteristically, "We must redouble our efforts and not relax."[25]
Initially, his sympathies lay with the Axis powers. He felt that the

Roosevelt administration had been too committed "to the British and French Empires" and that the film industry and the press had preached "a hatred of Germany." Brundage thought that the United States had attempted to antagonize Japan, "a country which, in my opinion, honestly wants to be friendly. Germany has been insulted on every possible occasion by our public officials."[26]

Brundage persisted in the illusion that the games might yet be saved. He was certainly not alone. Edstrøm wrote to him that Lord Aberdare of Great Britain and the Marquis Melchior de Polignac of France wanted to cancel the games but the Finns wished to go ahead if the United States agreed to send a team. Edstrøm reported that he, Karl Ritter von Halt, and Italy's Count Alberto Bonacossa were all "keen on having the Games."[27] They were not to be. The Germans withdrew their invitation for the winter games in November 1939 and the last, illusory hopes for the summer games were blasted into oblivion by the Soviet Union's "criminal invasion of Finland"[28] on November 30. The Finnish organizing committee renounced the games officially on April 23, 1940, but even Brundage realized the renunciation was only a formality.[29]

Brundage's instinctive reaction to the threat to the games was to seek alternatives. As early as 1937 he had discussed with various A.A.U. officials the possibility of Pan-American Games, similar to the Olympic Games but restricted to the nations of the western hemisphere. "When it became apparent that the Games of the XII Olympiad scheduled for Tokyo in 1940 could not be held, the latent interest in the Pan-American Games which had existed in many countries was brought to life."[30] Brundage, writing in 1964, named Argentina's Rudolfo G. Valenzuela, Chief Justice of the Argentine Supreme Court, as the leader of the movement to inaugurate the games,[31] but Brundage was certainly the most active of the North Americans. In August of 1940, he flew to Buenos Aires for a conference attended by representatives of sixteen Latin American nations.

It was an ambitious journey which began with a flight (on Pan American Airways) from Chicago on August 14. He was in Port au Prince, Haiti, on the 15th, in Rio de Janeiro on the 20th, in São

Paulo on the 23rd. He spent the end of the month in Buenos Aires. "Although I was the only one there who was not Latin American," recalled Brundage, "I had the honor of being elected president."[32] Juan Carlos Palacios of Argentina was named head of the organizing committee for the first games, planned for Buenos Aires in 1942. Brundage returned by way of Santiago (Chile), Lima (Peru), and Quito (Ecuador). He seems also to have stopped in Bolivia and Colombia. He was utterly exhausted when he arrived home, and fifteen pounds below his normal weight, but he was pleased to have been able to meet with innumerable Latin American sportsmen, with many of whom he would later work not only on the Pan-American Games Commission but also within the I.O.C. Indeed, the arduous journey established him as the middle man between Lausanne and all of Latin America.

One of the first things that Brundage arranged for upon his return to Chicago was a change in names. The American Olympic Association became the United States of America Sports Federation and the U.S.A.S.F. letterhead announced that this organization was also the organizer of both the United States Olympic Committee (formed quadrennially to take an American team to the Olympics) and the United States Pan-American Games Committee. On December 3, 1941, Brundage announced in an NBC radio broadcast. "The Olympic flame is temporarily extinguished and the world looks to the western hemisphere to keep alive the fine traditions of amateur sport."[33] Four days later, of course, the United States was at war.

Secretary of State Cordell Hull had originally been supportive of the Pan-American Games (with the laissez-faire proviso that they be left strictly to private and not governmental initiative),[34] but the Japanese attack on Pearl Harbor radically altered circumstances. Asa S. Bushnell, who directed the "Sports Section" within Nelson Rockefeller's Office of Inter-American Affairs, now questioned the appropriateness of the Pan-American Games, but Brundage refused to abandon hope: "I cannot understand the reason for the action referred to in your letter of February 24th. I should think the recommendation would be for participation."[35] Bushnell explained his stand in some detail, patiently, as if to a child: the danger with American participation in the Pan-American Games was that it might seem frivolous in light of the nation's involvement in World War II.[36] By this time, the decision had been made—by the U.S. government. Assistant Secretary of State Sumner Welles wrote to James F. Simms of the United States of America Sport Federation to inform him that "all-out war effort" forbade diversion of transportation for the long voyage to Buenos Aires.[37] Simms replied that the U.S.A.S.F. was both surprised and grieved.[38] Protests to Welles and to Roosevelt were useless. Brundage took this newest disappointment hard and worried about adverse reactions in Latin America: "The proud, suspicious and nationalistic Argentineans will take it as a deliberate slight.[39]

The Pan-American Games *were* celebrated in Buenos Aires and Brundage was there—in 1951. If the "proud, suspicious and nationalistic" Latin Americans were insulted by the North Americans' wartime priorities, they kept it to themselves. Brundage remained president of the Games Commission until the second quadrennial games were celebrated in Mexico City in 1955. The events continued for the rest of Brundage's life to concern him. He was proud of his role as founder, but the Pan-American Games never rivaled the Olympic Games in his heart of hearts. They lacked both universality and a tradition linking them with classical antiquity. They were bound to seem, to some degree, imitative.

Brundage had done his best to preserve the Olympics from the ravages of war, but he was a citizen as well as a sports administrator and he was active in that role as well. Fearful that the United States might be dragged into European conflict by the Roosevelt administration, Brundage had become an ardently outspoken isolationist in the years between Hitler's invasion of Poland and Japan's attack on Pearl Harbor.

The Middle West was the heartland of isolationism, not because it was geographically isolated from foreign affairs or because it was culturally provincial but because the Middle West was the home of millions of Irish-Americans who had no desire to fight for what they saw as British interests and of millions of German-Americans for whom World War I had been a traumatic conflict of loyalties. The latter group was especially important. The "Germans" who farmed in Minnesota or brewed in Milwaukee or baked in Chicago had been proud of their ethnic identity and had maintained a good deal of their original culture. Initially sympathetic to the German cause in 1914, they were forced to choose in 1917 between their *Vaterland* and their new home. They chose America and they fought loyally in the American Expeditionary Force, but the psychological dilemma was severe and they were not eager to suffer it again. The political results are still referred to as "isolationism," but they might better be described as the consequence of divided nationalism.

Brundage's ancestry was not German, but he had been drawn toward German culture while still a student at the University of Illinois. His friendships with Diem, von Halt, and Lewald made him increasingly pro-German. Having become emotionally as well as administratively committed to the 1936 games, having suffered personal abuse and the loss of friendship because of his stance, having gone to Berlin to witness the spectacle and having experienced there his induction into the I.O.C., he was an active partisan of German culture. In the heat of the battle over the boycott, he seemed to many to have gone beyond the honorable defense of German culture and to have become a shameless apologist for the Nazis. In a much-publicized speech in Madison Square Garden on October 4, 1936, he praised the National Socialists for their opposition to Communism. Addressing the German-American Bund, he spoke intemperately and unwisely: "We can learn much from Germany. We, too, if we wish to preserve our institutions, must stamp out communism. We, too, must take steps to arrest the decline of patriotism." Headlines screamed in Chicago: BE LIKE NAZIS, BRUNDAGE PLEA and AMERICA MUST FOLLOW NAZI EXAMPLE—BRUNDAGE.[40] Small wonder that he was denounced as pro-Nazi.

His sense of injustice grew more intense when Leni Riefenstahl's documentary film, *Olympia*, was not publicly screened in the United States. It was, he wrote Garland, an "outrage."[41] Simms thought that the film had no commercial possibilities because it was too long, had too many shots of Hitler and other Nazi leaders, and included moments of nudity in the rhapsodic introductory scenes; but Brundage replied that the "objectionable features . . . have been eliminated from the American edition," by which he seems to have referred to deletions of propaganda footage and cuts made in the introduction, which originally included a hauntingly beautiful dance by a group of naked girls.[42] Brundage and Kirby were both sure whom to blame for the rejection of the film by the cinema industry. To a German correspondent who had raved about *Olympia*, Brundage replied that the film couldn't be shown commercially because "unfortunately the theaters and moving picture companies are almost all owned by Jews."[43] Kirby, who referred to Riefenstahl as "your beautiful affinity," thought that Jews were simply too influential in the United States for the A.O.A. to risk alienating them by sponsoring the film, but Brundage went ahead with private showings.[44] When Riefenstahl visited Chicago in December of 1938, he introduced her and her art to a group of forty or fifty persons at the Chicago Engineers Club.[45] Garland arranged for a similar screening in Los Angeles and wrote Brundage that he thought the film appeared to have more American than German propaganda.[46] Brundage's determination to see that justice was done led him successfully to propose in 1939 that his "beautiful affinity" receive an Olympic diploma from the I.O.C. in recognition of her contribution to "les idéals olympiques."[47]

There was some truth in Brundage's allegation that the motion-picture industry was controlled by American Jews (they were very prominent among producers, directors, and actors), just as there had been some truth in his charges that American Jews were in the forefront of the boycott campaign of 1934–36, but he became completely unbalanced on the topic of Jewish influence. He began collecting anti-Semitic literature. Pamphlets like Robert Edmondson's "The Proof of a Jewish Conspiracy To Communize America and Rule the World" (1935), magazines like *The American Gentile*, and copies of Hitler's speeches were filed away (along with a number of Jewish publications).[48] His letters contained frequent references to the materialism of Jews and to their inability to understand fair play and good sportsmanship. After a trip to Cuba he wrote himself a memorandum and noted, "Jews drive out gentiles and Spanish in Cuba. Cuban wouldn't sell his house—they created a club next door and made it so noisy and such a nuisance he has to get out. Police stop racket, but in ten days at it again."[49]

Mildly anti-Semitic comments by Baillet-Latour and Edström have already been cited apropos of the attempt to force Nazi authorities to open the German Olympic team to Jewish athletes. In comparison to their remarks, those of Count Clarence von Rosen— I.O.C. member from Sweden—were extreme. He wrote Brundage in 1947, after the murder of six million Jews had become common knowledge, that Jews are responsible for all the world's trouble, that the Talmud binds them to a campaign against Christianity, and that Communism is but the political form of Judaism.[50] Corresponding with Rosen and dining with him in Chicago and in Djursholm did Brundage no good.

Consonant with this tendency to anti-Semitism, Brundage blamed the Jews for allegedly driving the United States into involvement in World War II. Once again, one must admit in all fairness that Brundage was not wholly wrong. Many American Jews were in fact advocates of intervention. Many had called for an end to the American embargo against the Spanish republic when that republic was attacked by native and foreign Fascists. As Hitler's reign of terror was extended geographically to include most of the European continent, American Jews were unquestionably more eager than their fellow citizens for American involvement in the war. That they were influential enough to have *caused* American involvement is quite another proposition.

In May of 1937, Brundage came upon an article in *The American Mercury* which gave more or less coherent focus to his blurred thoughts on foreign affairs. "The Red Road to War," written by Harold Lord Varney, was a fairly astute analysis of Stalin's foreign policy in the Popular Front period (which Varney referred to by its other common name, the United Front). Fearful of Hitler, Stalin did indeed, from 1935 to 1939, attempt to make common cause with the western democracies and American Communists like Earl Browder did indeed go about the country explaining that "Communism is twentieth-century Americanism." Varney, however, went on inaccurately to assert that Jews were a central factor in Stalin's foreign policy:

Already, a powerful racial group, controlling enormous publicity resources, was building up a new demonism around Hitler. To impartial minds, such a reaction on the part of world Jewry was quite understandable. It was obvious to the Moscow master-minds that it would merely be necessary to hitch Communism onto the bandwagon of mounting anti-Hitlerism to give Stalinism a halo instead of a stigma.[51]

In Varney's view, it was "in Russia's military rebirth that Europe finds its most appalling challenge."[52] Liberals who thought Hitler and Mussolini posed the greater threat had simply been taken in by Stalin's cynical propaganda. "The Russian bear, now caparisoned in his crimson Marxian raiment, is advancing upon historic Europe with all the resistless momentum of a glacial slide."[53] Brundage may or may not have smiled at the image of a red-caped, ursine avalanche, but he surely took pleasure in a comment toward the end of the article:

Mr. Avery Brundage, endeavoring as president of the American Olympic Committtee to maintain the tradition of American sportsmanship by supporting the Olympic Games when they were held in a Fascist nation, drew down upon himself the most venomous campaign of abuse ever experienced by an American sportsman.[54]

After such welcome words, Brundage wrote to Varney, "This is the most accurate analysis of international politics and their repercussions in the United States that I have yet seen."[55] He wrote the editor of *The American Mercury* and ordered 1,000 copies of the article, which he began to mail to his many correspondents.[56] When Varney came to the United States, Brundage invited him to dine at the New York Athletic Club and introduced him to Major John L. Griffith, president of the N.C.A.A.[57] When war came to Europe, Brundage thought that Hitler was only partly to blame. For a fervent anti-Communist he made the oddly Marxist observation, "The real difficulty is that France and England see their commercial supremacy challenged once more by the Germans."[58]

It was, therefore, a combination of anti-Communist, philo-Germanic, and anti-Semitic motives, added to the traumatic fear that a prolonged war might destroy forever the Olympic movement, which impelled Brundage to an increasingly active political role. He spoke out publicly at a rally at Chicago's Soldiers Field on August 4, 1940. He introduced the principal speaker, Charles Lindbergh, who was not only the prototypical German-American isolationist but also a symbol of the kind of individual achievement that Brundage most admired. Brundage condemned the "stupid, dishonest and criminal politics" of those who risked war. Predictably, he turned to the world of amateur sports as the shining contrast to the sordid worlds of politics and business:

What we need more than anything else in the United States today is a citizenship motivated by the same spirit that actuates an amateur sportsman. A body of "amateur" citizens who really love their country, who contribute to it and are not always taking from it. . . . The time is too short to give all of these principles in detail today, but adoption of this virile, dynamic . . . philosophy of amateur sport and of its code of fair play and good sportsmanship will prevent us from becoming a soft, aimless, lazy aggregation of dollar chasing . . . pleasure seekers.[59]

The rally was sponsored by the "Citizens Keep America Out of War Committee" rather than the more famous "America First" movement, but the cast of speakers was the same. (In addition to Lindbergh, Senators Bennett Champ Clark and Patrick McCarran spoke.) There was considerable isolationist sentiment in Chicago, home of hundreds of thousands of Irish- and German-Americans, but there were also many Poles, Czechs, and others who felt that the United States ought to be at England's side in the fight against Hitler. Some charged that Brundage and Lindbergh posed as isolationists but were actually pro-Nazi, a tactic which roused Brundage's indignation. "One of the cleverest tricks of the Communists and Jews in 1939," he wrote in one of his miscellaneous folders of notes, "was the smearing of 'America First' as pro-Nazi."[60] Brundage lacked the philosophical detachment to see that the reckless label he objected to was the counterpart of the reckless labels he had pinned on others. His readiness almost automatically to castigate the opposition as "Communists and Jews" was one that he only gradually and never fully overcame.

The election of 1940 seemed crucial for economic as well as foreign-policy issues, and Brundage became more politically involved than ever. To Garland he wrote, "Four more years of the present regime and there will be little left to save."[61] Long convinced that the Roosevelt administration was made up of "radical demagogues and crackpot brain trusters,"[62] he backed Wendell Willkie for the presidency and maintained that his domestic platform was just what the country needed:

Next November it will be decided whether we shall continue to follow the philosophy of our self-reliant forefathers which brought us liberty and more freedom than any other people ever enjoyed, and the highest standard of living ever known, or whether we shall pursue the policies which during the last eight years have destroyed the initiative of our people and broken the morale of an entire generation, have wasted billions of dollars and doubled the national debt, have kept ten to fifteen million unfortunate men out of work, have ploughed under crops and killed little pigs and have destroyed or sought to destroy cherished American institutions.[63]

In brief, returning the Republicans to office meant returning America to the nineteenth-century liberal-democratic values embodied in men like Henry Ford and Herbert Hoover and Avery Brundage. Two years after Willkie's defeat, which did not, after all, destroy America, Brundage described himself as "an old-fashioned rock-ribbed conservative Republican."[64] Brundage meant, of course, that he remained faithful to nineteenth-century liberalism with its central doctrine of individualism unhindered and unhelped by state intervention. The citizen should be like the athlete, free to win or lose on his own. He had little or no sense of the institutional structures which made individualism (and modern sports) possible.

The year 1944 brought another disappointment. Preferring Senator Robert Taft of Ohio to Governor Thomas E. Dewey of New York, Brundage was annoyed when the Republicans nominated the latter to run against Roosevelt in the last of Roosevelt's four campaigns. It seemed another case of Tweedledee and Tweedledum. He wrote the election off as "a farce. The people were sold down the river again. What is needed badly is sound and conservative leadership."[65] Although he had for decades used politics as the dark background against which to project the bright world of amateur sports or as the savage monster always looking for a chance to ravage the Olympic movement, Brundage was tempted in both 1942 and 1944 to run for political office. The Republicans sought him out as a candidate for Mayor of Chicago and then for Governor of Illinois, but he concluded, wisely, that he was not meant for electoral politics.[66] Although he had had a long career of voluntary civil service, and by no means just in the world of sports, he was not the sort to flatter an audience or to disguise his real opinions in smokescreens of gibberish.

In the early 1950s, he began to gather materials published by the Radical Right. It is impossible to know how much of what he read he actually believed. Did he think Dwight David Eisenhower was a "New Deal Stooge" or that "Zionists" were behind Alger Hiss and against Senator Joseph McCarthy?[67] He wrote himself a note that "holding back General MacArthur in the Korean War was a tremendous loss of face for the white race in all of Asia,"[68] but he must have realized that Harry Truman was not really under the voodoo spell of Communist advisors and had not "created a personal war in Korea on the sole advice of [Dean] Acheson."[69] Brundage feared the Communist Party of the United States and exaggerated its influence, but he was not gullible enough to tremble at "Red and Pink janissaries" in the White House.[70] Brundage was, however, convinced by much of the nonsense emanating from the Radical Right. In a speech which he gave on many occasions, he asked:

Why did we turn over to others all the fruits of the war . . . at Yalta and at Potsdam? How did Communists, or their friends, get into every department of our government during the war? . . . Who ordered the destruction, sale or abandonment of our war material, amounting it is estimated to $5 billion, following D-Day? Why was China betrayed? Why was MacArthur held back in Korea?[71]

The rhetorical questions were part of a litany sung by many in the 1950s, most notably, of course, by Senator Joseph McCarthy of Wisconsin.

The temporary nature of Brundage's radicalism needs to be emphasized. He ceased to collect right-wing documents and hate literature, and his speeches showed fewer and fewer traces of their influence. He never warmed to the appeals of Marxism, but he became, especially after his election to the presidency of the I.O.C., a better informed and a somewhat more sophisticated observer of the political scene. As president of an international organization, he was forced—like Roosevelt in World War II, like Truman during the Korean War—to compromise and to accept less than perfect solutions. By the late 1950s, fanatics began to target *him* for denunciation as a Communist dupe and stooge. To have become the victim of hysteria may have enabled him to sympathize a bit with the plight of others at whom the witch-hunters pointed their accusatory fingers. It may also be that Ruegsegger's influence brought Brundage to a more reasonable anti-Communism than that of *The American Gentile.*

Politics were always a secondary concern. In the early 1940s, Brundage's central purpose was to keep alive the Olympic flame. Throughout the terrible war that he had hoped to avoid or ignore, Brundage maintained the lines of communication holding together the I.O.C. and the less firmly established Pan-American Games Commission. Mails were slow and uncertain, but they allowed contacts that were vitally important to him. He and Edstrøm perceived themselves as keepers of the sacred flame, guardians of an ideal in whose name they were ready once again to act as soon as the madness ended. Since Belgium was occupied by the Germans, Baillet-Latour was less free than Brundage and Edstrøm to correspond with I.O.C. members outside the orbit of Axis power. Diem, von Halt, and von Tschammer und Osten visited the I.O.C. president in the winter of 1940–41, partly to comfort him, partly to explain to him Hitler's plans for the usurpation of power in the *Neue Ordnung* in postwar international sports.[72] When the Belgian died of a stroke on January 6, 1942, approximately a year after his son's death in an American plane crash, Edstrøm took over in his position as vice president. (He did not, however, assume the title of president.) He was able by virtue of Sweden's neutrality to play the role of

Olympic trustee more energetically than had been possible for Baillet-Latour. He was also, by temperament, an activist, and a better writer than Brundage, whose letters tended to be brief and hortatory rather than detailed, descriptive, or anecdotal.

The end of the fighting did not mean an end to the suffering. Europe was devastated and even Sweden had been reduced to austerity by disruptions in normal trade. Once it was possible to communicate again with the former enemy, Brundage widened his correspondent's role. When Greta von Halt reported that Karl had been killed in a P.O.W. camp, Brundage grieved, and then rejoiced when he learned that the rumor was false.[73] When Liselott Diem wrote of cold and hunger in Russian-occupied Berlin, he did what he could to help her, Carl, and their children.[74] She later remarked, quite simply, that he had fed her whole family.[75] He transformed himself into a one-man C.A.R.E. program and rushed packages off to England, Germany, Finland, and Sweden. He kept secretaries busy in Chicago's department stores searching out necessities like soap and needles and occasional luxuries like silk stockings and chocolate.

Even before the European phase of the war was over, Brundage began to resume personal contact with his colleagues. In November of 1944, Edstrøm managed to cross the Atlantic to New York, where Brundage met him. Since Edstrøm was then 74 years old (he had been born on November 21, 1870), he was worried about continuity within the I.O.C. if anything should happen to him during the "terrible guerre mondiale" and he suggested in a circular letter that Brundage become the second vice president.[76] The election took place by a mail ballot and Brundage officially assumed the office at the first postwar Executive Board meeting in London (August 21–24, 1945). Brundage, Edstrøm, and Britain's Lord Aberdare were the only members present, and Brundage felt himself lucky to have received special permission from the U.S. government to travel on the *Queen Elizabeth*, then a military transport.

England had suffered from the war and the hard times were by no means over. Although Brundage certainly sympathized with the English and had done more than most citizens to alleviate their want, he later amused A.A.U. delegates with a Mark Twain-like anecdote:

Among the items still on the menu was turkey. I had visions of a good old fashioned turkey dinner with all the trimmings. A waiter pushed alongside my table one of those great big covered silver services four feet across. A chef appeared and sharpened his knife. Two captains came over to watch. . . . The chef turned back the silver cover to display a turkey not quite the size of a large chicken. He sliced off two or three pieces about the size of the end of my thumb and that was the turkey dinner. They then pushed over another big silver service containing ten silver vegetable pots. I counted them. In the first were large potatoes, in the second medium sized potatoes, in the third small potatoes, and in the fourth mashed potatoes; eight of the ten pots held potatoes and the remaining two contained spinach.[77]

Not all the English were as resolute as the undaunted chef. In regards to a far more serious matter, Lord Aberdare had grown pessimistic. He wrote Brundage to ask if they really wanted to resume the games after the war, if the ideals of friendly rivalry and international brotherhood had not been degraded by the Nazi propaganda of 1936.[78] Despite his doubts, Aberdare let himself be persuaded by Brundage and Edstrøm and plans were made for the resumption of the interrupted sequence. Since Baltimore, Los Angeles, Minneapolis, Philadelphia, Lausanne, and London and all indicated a desire to host the 1948 games, the question was put to a mail ballot. On September 1, Edstrøm could report that London was the choice of the majority. The Executive Board had already decided, in the event that London was chosen, to award the winter games to St. Moritz in Switzerland.

After the Executive Board was done with its business, Brundage accompanied Edstrøm back to Stockholm for a meeting of the I.A.A.F. Then, in "order to show the Finns that they had some friends left in the world despite their undeserved misfortunes, I took the time to pay a visit to Helsinki."[79] Since he had long admired the Finns for their athleticism and was soon to fall in love with a young woman from Helsinki, the visit made sense. Afterwards, he returned to the United States by air. It was the first of countless transatlantic flights. The plane stopped for dinner in Iceland and for breakfast in Goose Bay, Labrador. "I am still a little bewildered after my overnight flight from Stockholm," he wrote to Bo Ekelund, "It is difficult to comprehend how one can be in Stockholm one day and in New York City the next."[80] Now that he was an I.O.C. vice president as well as a member of the Executive Board, such trips were destined to become routine. Eventually, as I.O.C. president, he was to make as many as thirteen transatlantic flights in a single year.[81] To an interviewer he remarked whimsically, "I vote in Chicago and own a beautiful house in Montecito. But I live in an airplane."[82]

At the first postwar I.O.C. session, held in Lausanne on September 4–6, 1946, Edström was elected president by acclamation, and Brundage became the first vice president, apparently without opposition. Since exactly half of the 26 members present were new to the committee (they had been proposed by the Executive Board), the I.O.C. was truly a different body from the one that had met in Cairo and made a pilgrimage to Olympia.

Perhaps it is more accurate to say that it was a different body collectively, but it contained many of the old members, and some of them now became the focus of dissension within the committee. Although the members liked to think of themselves as delegates *from* the I.O.C. *to* their respective homelands, that is, as men above and beyond the limitations of nationalism, it was extremely hard to forget that the member across the table had, only a few months earlier, worn the uniform of an enemy power. When that uniform represented an ideology as hideous as Fascism, passions were stirred. Karl Ritter von Halt, for instance, had administered track-and-field sports under the leadership of Reichssportführer von Tschammer und Osten and had also been head of the Deutsche Bank. Under pressure, he had joined the Nazi Party. Greta von Halt explained to Brundage that Karl had always rejected Hitler's policies and the war that evolved from them,[83] and Brundage loyally defended von Halt when he came under suspicion from the Allied High Commission for Germany. Brundage wrote to High Commissioner John J. McCloy that "Dr. von Halt is not a politician and was never a Nazi."[84] (In this same letter, he also defended Diem, whose collected speeches and essays, published in 1942 as *Die Olympische Flamme*, contained not only evidences of youthful chauvinism but also considerable obligatory praise for Hitler, which Diem later regretted.) Brundage was ready to begin again as if Hitler and Mussolini had never existed, but other members of the committee had different perceptions. P. W. Scharroo of Holland and Albert Mayer of Switzerland were among those who noted that von Halt had been an S.-A.-Gruppenführer in the war; Brundage dismissed such accusations as politically biased,[85] but the problem was not to be shrugged away.

The other German member to survive the war, Adolf Friedrich zu Mecklenburg, a member of the I.O.C. since 1926 and a brother-in-law of Queen Wilhelmina of Holland, had not been as closely tied to the Nazi regime as von Halt had been, but Scharroo objected strongly to inviting him to the 39th Session in Lausanne because Mecklenburg had been in constant communication with Josef Goebbels while serving as president of the Auslands-Presse-Klub (Foreign Press Club).[86] Edstrøm polled the Executive Board on this. Aberdare and Brundage did not vote, but Counts Bonacossa of Italy and Polignac of France both wanted Mecklenburg and he was invited to Lausanne.[87] Unfortunately, Bonacossa and Polignac were themselves rather under a cloud. The first had been a member of Mussolini's Fascisti, as had both his Italian colleagues, Count Paolo Thaon di Revel and General Giorgio Vaccaro.[88] The second had been imprisoned for six months by the French authorities in Occupied Germany.[89] The Marquess of Exeter (formerly Lord Burghley) had expressed considerable resentment about Polignac's continued prominence long before Scharroo made an issue of Nazi or Fascist ties.[90] Edstrøm, however, grew exasperated: "All I ask for is justice!"[91] Unlike jesting Pilate, Edstrøm did not go so far as to ask in this instance, "What is justice?"

The controversy smoldered on until the Vienna Session of May 3–5, 1951, when Scharroo and his Belgian colleague R. W. Seeldrayers demanded a vote on whether or not Mecklenburg and von Halt, who had both been members from the prewar Reich, had the right to represent the newly established Federal Republic of Germany. Had their mandate not expired with the government they had represented? Scharroo and Seeldrayers argued for new men with new views to represent the new political entity. Brundage, however, stood up for von Halt as "un parfait gentleman" and Edstrøm stubbornly refused to put the matter to a vote despite the protests from a number of members, including Prince Axel of Denmark, General Pahud de Mortanges of Holland, Baron de Trannoy of Belgium, Olaf Ditlev-Simonsen of Norway, Jerzy Loth of Poland, and Brooks Parker of the United States. As emotions intensified, Edstrøm played his trump card—he informed the committee that Mecklenburg and von Halt were actually present in Vienna and wanted to join them. Seeldrayers continued to protest, then Edstrøm stopped the debate with the announcement, "These are old friends whom we receive today" ("Ce sont de vieux amis que nous recevons aujourd'hui").[92] Not even a motion from the Italian Olympic Committee moved the I.O.C. to expel General Vaccaro, whose commitment to Fascism was an embarrassment to the members of the postwar Comite Olimpico Nazionale d'Italia (C.O.N.I.). With Vaccaro in mind, the Italians proposed that "national Olympic committees have the right to require the I.O.C. to substitute members who, in their opinion, are unable to fulfill a useful function in regard to the athletic organizations of their country."[93] The proposal was voted down. Fortunately, Vaccaro seems either to have lost interest in Olympic affairs or to have understood that he was persona non grata with his colleagues. He ceased to attend meetings and it was decided at the 44th Session in Copenhagen (1950) that he had resigned.[94]

There was some resentment against Japan as well as against the Fascist powers. When Brundage backed the membership of Royotaro Azuma at the 1950 session, Exeter opposed the move as premature and pointed out that Japan already had two members. Sir Harold Luxton of Australia commented with understatement that Japanese participation in the Olympics would be unpopular down under. Once again, Edstrøm was among those who argued for the inclusion of members representing the defeated powers and for speedy return to Olympic participation. He had asked Azuma to come to Copenhagen. He had obtained a recommendation from none other than General Douglas MacArthur, commander of the U.S. Army of Occupation. The controversy was resolved when the ailing Dr. M. Nagai resigned and Azuma was named not as a third but merely as a second member from Japan.[95]

All in all, however, the I.O.C. devoted comparatively little time to the question of wartime affiliations. It devoted a great deal of time to the jurisdictional dispute that one might term "The Great Ice Hockey Controversy." This controversy, in which Brundage played a central role, had its origins in 1930, when the A.A.U. became a member of the international federation governing amateur ice hockey, the Ligue Internationale de Hockey sur Glace (L.I.H.G.), which had been formed in 1908. Since the dispute was typical of the wrangles which plagued the I.O.C. and drove Brundage to the point of despair, a detailed account is called for.

Friction developed between the A.A.U. and commercial rink owners. As Brundage explained,

In its endeavors to maintain amateur standards, the A.A.U. . . . expelled the rink teams, which had become little more than farm teams for the professional league, and this led to the formation of the outlaw leagues, which have the effrontery to call themselves amateurs although they admittedly pay their players.[96]

The expelled groups formed the American Hockey Association in 1939 and applied to the L.I.H.G. for recognition as the national ice hockey federation for the United States. The A.H.A. was turned down at that time, but Canada and Great Britain joined the organization in forming what was dubbed the International Ice Hockey Association (1940). The L.I.H.G. ordered this rival organization to dissolve and the British affiliate dutifully dropped out but continued nonetheless to support the A.H.A. The Canadians and the Americans, led by Walter Brown, a Boston entrepreneur, continued to press for A.H.A. recognition by the L.I.H.G. even though their organization allowed amateurs to play against professionals, which violated A.A.U., L.I.H.G., and Olympic rules. Although Brundage appealed to British ice hockey officials to "see the light and withdraw from this unholy alliance,"[97] they continued to back the A.H.A. in the mid-1940s, as did the Canadians, the Swedes, and the Swiss.

At an L.I.H.G. congress in Prague in 1946, President Fritz Kraatz of Switzerland moved that national ice hockey federations be allowed to govern ice hockey alone and no other sport. The motion passed and the A.A.U., which governed a number of sports, lost its L.I.H.G. recognition.[98] John Hutchinson, the American representative in Prague, admitted that he found it hard to present the A.A.U.'s case because the discussion was in French.

The A.A.U., however, continued to have the support of the United States of America Sports Federation (the renamed A.O.A.) and of the I.O.C. In ex-President Brundage, the A.A.U. had a staunch backer. At the 40th I.O.C. Session in Stockholm (June 16–22, 1947), the Executive Board met with the international federations and tried to resolve the differences between the L.I.H.G. and the U.S. Olympic Committee, which was then preparing to send a team to the winter Olympics in St. Moritz. Edstrøm, Brundage, Kraatz, Exeter, Sidney Dawes of Canada, and Anton Johanson of Sweden met to avert the fiasco of two teams both claiming to represent the United States. In Brundage's version of the episode, L.I.H.G. President Kraatz had to leave early but promised to accept whatever agreement the others worked out. Kraatz denied that he had promised any such thing.[99] An impasse developed. As Edstrøm commented, the U.S. Olympic Committee was in a position to refuse its certification to the A.H.A.'s teams, but Kraatz was in a position, as president of the L.I.H.G., to cancel the entire ice hockey tournament at St. Moritz: "If there is no Ice Hockey," wrote Edstrøm to Brundage, "there can be no Winter Games."[100] Edstrøm felt that the Swiss had invested too much in the games for the I.O.C. to stop them.[101] He sought a compromise, but Brundage was adamant: "This is a battle in which the future of sport and the Olympic Games are at stake."[102] Kraatz, who is said to have remarked that he didn't care whether ice hockey appeared on the Olympic program or not because there was more profit in a world championship anyway, told Hutchinson that the L.I.H.G. had determined at its Zurich conference in September of 1947 that its teams would play only against the A.H.A. team in St. Moritz.[103] It was *his* final word. Brundage, fully involved in his crusade against play-for-pay hockey, was no more inclined to back down than Kraatz was: "We are sending our teams to Switzerland with the idea that the Olympic rules will be enforced and the outlaw ice hockey team will not be permitted to compete. If the outlaw ice hockey team is permitted to compete, our teams are to be withdrawn from the Games."[104]

January 30, 1948, approached and both hockey teams, that chosen by the A.H.A. and that selected by the U.S.O.C. through the A.A.U., arrived in St. Moritz. Brundage's three-page "MEMORANDUM: THE ICE HOCKEY CONTROVERSY AT ST. MORITZ" reveals his frustration and anger at what he saw as the appearance of professionalism within the sacred precincts of Olympism:

When I reached Switzerland I found that I was practically public enemy No. 1—there was little or no understanding of the point of view of the U.S.O.C. Most of the Press and Radio was bitterly against us, particularly the popular newspapers. . . . The matter was first presented to the I.O.C. executive committee, which was finally convinced after a long argument that neither . . . team was properly entered. The first disposition was to accept the A.H.A. team and to censure the U.S.O.C. for not forwarding their entries unsigned. Finally, after I showed them the copies of the correspondence indicating that we had sent on the A.H.A. entries unsigned on the same day that we had received them . . . , they agreed to withdraw both teams. Aberdare was our chief opponent in this discussion, relying on obscure technicalities and ignoring the broad issue that commercial organizations should not be allowed in the Games. . . .

The executive committee decided . . . that neither of the two teams from the United States [was] eligible for competition. The Swiss Organizing Committee and the L.I.H.G. both denounced this decision and defied it. The next day, in the first of the Games, the A.H.A. team was allowed to compete.

Brundage then described the I.O.C. session at which the Swiss organizing committee challenged the Executive Board's right to have made the decision excluding both teams.

Again I was actively opposed by Burghley [the Marquess of Exeter] and Seeldrayers. After hours of pettifogging on minor technicalities, ignoring all the broad questions at issue, the I.O.C. finally decided to take the matter into its own hands, disregarding the action of its executive committee.

Hours were spent in a full detailed presentation of the case from the point of view of the Swiss Organizing Committee, the L.I.H.G., and the U.S.O.C. The battle that I had to fight in the executive committee now had to be repeated with several clever opponents, Burghley and Seeldrayers the most vociferous. Every minor technicality that could be raised against us was invoked. While many were sympathetic to our point of view, we had no active support. Seeldrayers did everything possible to twist the argument against us. Instead of a meeting of sportsmen it became a battle of wits. The atmosphere was entirely different from any previous I.O.C. meetings that I ever attended. All my arguments for the purity of the Games were ignored or ridiculed as not being included in the rules. The position of a large number of the members veered from one side to the other . . . and I must say that until the ballots were counted, 16 to 10, I was never sure of victory. . . .

After the vote was taken the I.O.C. decided to send an unofficial committee, Burghley, Ekelund and Dawes, to meet with the Organizing Committee and the L.I.H.G., to endeavor to devise a satisfactory solution. Ice Hockey was thrown off the program, the L.I.H.G. was refused recognition by the I.O.C. and the Swiss Organizing Committee was censured for allowing the A.H.A. team to play. . . .

Brundage then lists those who voted against the U.S.O.C. and notes that Seeldrayers ostentatiously entertained Kraatz at dinner in the public dining room. The Swiss press and radio attacked the I.O.C. and Brundage feared that his colleagues might be weak enough to give way under pressure. The organizing committee returned to the I.O.C. and argued once more that ice hockey, the most popular and lucrative (in terms of spectators and admission tickets) of the winter sports, simply *had* to be reinstated. The I.O.C. gave way and the hockey tournament was allowed to remain on the program provided the A.H.A. games were disallowed. And then, a new betrayal:

After agreeing to this and thanking us, public announcement was made both by the Swiss Organizing Committee and the L.I.H.G. that if the

A.H.A. team won it would be recognized. How can one deal with this kind of people?

The impression became quite general after a while that the seat of the trouble was gate receipts, but whether the general public ever understood the controversy or not I am doubtful.[105]

Whether or not one agrees with Brundage on the principles involved—and he may well have been right to want to bar the A.H.A. as a commercial organization—one sees in his prose the same inability to imagine sincere opposition that distorted his view of the 1934–36 boycott controversy. While he fought for purity, his opponents on the I.O.C. hid behind pettifogging technicalities. Never a strong supporter of the winter games, he felt more deeply than ever that they were hopelessly infected by the viruses of commercialism and nationalism. The mood of the games was, in the view of I.O.C. Chancellor Otto Mayer, "empoisonnée."[106]

The ice hockey dispute dragged on for some years. Walter Brown's position, as head of the A.H.A. and owner of the Boston Celtics, was vividly expressed in a letter to A.A.U. Secretary Daniel J. Ferris when Brown characterized the A.A.U.'s hockey committee as a bunch of collegiate dilettantes.[107] At the I.O.C.'s Copenhagen Session in 1950, a committee was named to seek a resolution of the quarrel (Albert Mayer of Switzerland, Olaf Ditlev-Simonsen, Sidney Dawes, J. C. Patteson of Canada). The outcome was an agreement by which the selection of the 1952 team was to be made by a committee of four from the A.H.A., four from the U.S.O.C., and two professionals from the National Hockey League. Edström and Brundage accepted this, perhaps from weariness, but there remained considerable bitterness within the A.A.U. Rufus Trimble, chairman of the A.A.U.'s Ice Hockey Committee, accused Brundage and Edström of cooperating with professionals to destroy amateur ice hockey in the United States.[108] For Brundage to appear as the betrayer of amateurism was a curious reversal of roles.

As Brundage ruefully commented, the public neither knew nor cared about the principles for which he had fought in St. Moritz. What mattered for them was that the Canadians won the gold medal in ice hockey, that the Scandinavians triumphed once more in speed skating and men's skiing, that Dick Button's figures were judged the best, that Gretchen Fraser of the United States won the first gold medal ever awarded for women's slalom.

On July 17, 1948, Brundage sailed on the *America* for the summer games in London. Since European sports still suffered from the effects of the war—athletes killed in action, facilities reduced to rubble, food in short supply—it was inevitable that the United States would dominate many of the events. Since the I.O.C. once again, as in 1920 and 1924, barred the athletes from the defeated nations, American domination was all the easier. In men's track and field, the Americans ran off with ten gold medals (four more than the Swedes). In men's swimming and diving, they garnered all eight gold medals. The games were also remarkable for Emil Zatopek's first Olympic victory over 10,000 meters, but the most memorable performance of all was probably that of the Dutch athlete Francina Blankers-Koen.

As an eighteen-year-old, she had participated in Berlin in 1936 and tied for sixth in the high jump. Now, twelve years, one husband, and two children later, she earned gold medals in the 100-meter and 200-meter dashes, the 80-meter hurdles, and the 400-meter relay. She was unable to enter the long jump or the high jump, in both of which she held the world's record, because Olympic rules limited the number of events in which an individual could compete. Brundage had been active in the I.A.A.F.'s push to add the 200-meter race, the long jump, and (with qualms) the shot put to the women's events for 1948. He continued to grouse about unfeminine female shot-putters, but he was lyrical—at least in retrospect—about Fanny Blankers-Koen: "A new type of woman is appearing—lithe, supple, physically disciplined, strong, slender and efficient, like the Goddesses of ancient Greece. It is the day of the bikini and the mini skirt."[109] The extent of his opposition to women's athletics has been exaggerated.

During the games, the Brundages stayed at the Dorchester Hotel in Park Lane, their favorite London residence. Thanks to Douglas Roby of the U.S. Olympic Association, they had the use of a car loaned by the Ford Motor Company of Great Britain. At the official reception at Buckingham Palace, King George VI expressed admiration for Gustavus Kirby's team tie and down-to-earth Kirby offered it to him on the spot. The affable monarch suggested Kirby mail it to him later, which Kirby did.[110] Appearing at this and other festive occasions, watching the athletic contests, chatting with fellow members of the I.O.C., Brundage seemed to bask in a shared sense of reunion and renewal after the nightmare of World War II, but his genial greetings and official smiles disguised a troubled soul. He sought out his old friend Diem to reveal the anguish he normally masked. Diem, whom Edstrøm had personally invited to London as a guest of the I.O.C., wrote to his wife Liselott about a visit from their friend Brundage at the Cumberland Hotel on July 31: "Brundage visited me yesterday, in a depressed mood. He was a part of the Lindbergh party, which is taken to be Fascist. Hence, he has many enemies and these miserable creatures are at work everywhere. There is still a hate campaign against Germany against which no one takes energetic action."[111] Since there *were* men who never forgave Brundage for his opposition to the boycott campaign of 1934–36, and for his isolationism in 1939–40, one cannot dismiss Brundage's emotions as paranoid, but he was certainly naïve to have expected his opponents to forgive and forget. He had characterized them as "Communists and Jews" whose motives were alien to the world of fair play and good sportsmanship; it was inevitable that some were human-all-too-human enough to repay him in kind.

The pain that Brundage revealed to Diem was kept hidden from his colleagues in the I.O.C. At the 42nd Session, held during the summer games, there was little business aside from a long discussion about a proposed age-limit for members. The motion to force retirement at 70, made by New Zealand's Arthur Porritt, received 27 votes out of 42 and thus failed to achieve the requisite two-thirds majority. There was apparently very little acrimony and the committee adjourned with a good deal of satisfaction. The games had survived the war. The Brundages returned on the *Washington*, on August 20.

CHAPTER VIII

PRESIDENT AND APOSTLE OF AMATEURISM

As an adolescent fashioning his own track-and-field equipment in the high school machine shop, as a student working his way through the University of Illinois, as a civil engineer borrowing money to begin his own construction firm, Brundage was a self-made man in the Franklinian tradition. There came a time, however, when he became the beneficiary of what sociologists refer to as sponsored mobility. His sponsor was Sigfrid Edstrøm, the Swedish engineer, industrialist, amateur athlete (100 meters in 11 seconds), and sports administrator, president of the I.A.A.F. and member of the I.O.C. Executive Board since its creation in 1921. Married to an American, Edstrøm came often to the United States. In September of 1929, he visited Chicago, where his wife Ruth had once taught school, and discussed Olympic problems with Brundage.[1] The men got on so well that they later joined with Karl Ritter von Halt in a "beer society" that convened whenever the three veterans of the 1912 Olympics gathered on I.A.A.F. or I.O.C. business. In 1934 Edstrøm asked Brundage if he might suggest him as a member of the I.O.C.[2] Brundage, already on the Executive Committee of the I.A.A.F., was amenable. Eight years after Brundage's election to the I.O.C., Edstrøm nominated him as second vice president.[3] By this time, Brundage had also acted as vice president for a number of I.A.A.F. congresses.[4] At the first postwar meeting of the I.O.C., in Lausanne in 1946, Brundage became first vice president under President Edstrøm.[5] A pattern had been established.

Brundage was not the only person Edstrøm forwarded in office. He wrote to Brundage in 1945 that he and his Swedish I.A.A.F. colleague Bo Ekelund had offered the presidency of that international federation to Lord Burghley, later the Marquess of Exeter, who did indeed become Edstrøm's successor.[6] Edstrøm also sponsored Douglas Roby of Chicago and Detroit, who had first come to the Swede's attention in 1939 when Roby chaired Detroit's committee to bid for the 1944 games. After the war, Edstrøm visited Detroit and chanced to see a picture of Roby's grammarschool class in Chicago. Tears came to Edstrøm's eyes as he recognized the teachers; his American wife, Ruth Randall, had taught in Roby's school.[7] As president of the A.A.U., Roby was clearly well qualified for membership in the I.O.C., but he was, at the time of his election in 1952, definitely Edstrøm's choice and not Brundage's. The two Americans were destined for more than one confrontation.

Early in 1949, John Jewett Garland hastily scribbled Brundage a note about a conversation he had just had with Edstrøm in New York's Ritz-Carlton Hotel. The message was probably no surprise to Brundage. Edstrøm wanted him as his successor as I.O.C. president but expected opposition from some of the European members.[8] There was resistance within the committee to the notion of an American at the head of a committee which included enough of the titled European nobility to make up the equivalent of the House of Lords. There was also a feeling that Brundage was perhaps *too* ambitious. His courting of aristocracy was sometimes embarrassingly obvious. Once, for instance, while at lunch with Roby and Kenneth ("Tug") Wilson of the N.C.A.A., Brundage noticed Exeter entering the room with Prince Axel of Denmark; Brundage rose and, with scarcely a word of apology, abandoned his American colleagues in order to join the influential Europeans.[9] Perhaps it was simple tactlessness rather than ruthless ambition. Lord Porritt, Brundage's senior on the I.O.C. by two years, commented on the

American's aura of impersonality: "I knew him *very* well, but I never got close to him. I liked him and I trusted him, but I could never call him a friend." Brundage simply "couldn't mix." In Porritt's vivid metaphor, "He lived in a little castle of his own and you had to get the portcullis [up] before you could get in."[10] While Edström moved from table to table, chatting and joking with his colleagues, Brundage often sat alone with Ruegsegger. He had no small talk.[11]

Herman A. van Karnebeek, the Dutch member who also served on the Executive Board, tells a revealing story. Since Brundage seldom dined with his colleagues and was "never a man to sit at the bar, never," van Karnebeek once sent word to Brundage in his hotel room that he wished Brundage's company to help celebrate his birthday. Brundage came down and the birthday was celebrated, but the American later discovered that the Dutchman hadn't been born on that day. Amused rather than annoyed, Brundage presented van Karnebeek with a silver tray: "To the Jonkheer Herman A. van Karnebeek who invented a birthday in order that we might enjoy a pleasant celebration at Lausanne in March 1971. Avery Brundage."[12] It was typical of Brundage to have sent a memento rather than to have spoken his appreciation. Except with a narrow circle of friends—von Halt, Diem, Edström, Ruegsegger—he found it difficult to express more personal emotions. When his Italian colleague, Giorgio de Stefani, wrote to him of the tragic loss of his first child, there was apparently no written reply from Brundage nor does de Stefani recall a spoken response.[13] Despite his energetic involvement in Olympic and in countless other committees, Brundage was a loner. He "never visited anybody, never went to anybody's house."[14] If his colleagues in the I.O.C. were to be persuaded to accept him as Edström's successor, it was for his organizational ability, his energy, and his devotion to Olympism, not for his gregarious charm, his modesty, or his tactfulness.

John Jewett Garland, whose unanimous election to the I.O.C. as his father's replacement (in 1948) owed much to Brundage's patronage, became a kind of unofficial campaign manager for his benefactor. He wrote to Jean Ketseas, a Greek member, urging Brun-

APOSTLE OF AMATEURISM   II3

dage's election when Edstrøm retired.[15] Ketseas, in turn, reported
back to Garland that he had discussed the candidacy with Albert
Mayer of Switzerland, de Stefani of Italy, and Baron Pedro Ibarra
Mac-Mahon de Guell of Spain.[16] They apparently agreed that
Brundage was the best choice. In fact, Mayer wrote to Brundage
to assure him of his support.[17] Between Garland's note from the
Ritz-Carlton and Brundage's election at Helsinki in 1952, we can
be certain that Brundage and Edstrøm discussed prospects and stra-
tegies. They were surely encouraged when Brundage was reelected
vice president by acclamation in 1950 at the Copenhagen session.[18]

Meanwhile, shortly before the Helsinki vote, Mohammed Taher
Pacha of Egypt sent Brundage a letter from Geneva to inform him
that he had talked up Brundage's candidacy with Albert Mayer and
with Prince Franz-Josef of Lichtenstein; Taher Pasha was also in
correspondence with Manfred Mautner Ritter von Markhof of Austria and Karl Ritter von Halt, about whose ardent support there
could scarcely have been any doubt.[19] Immediately before the vote
to determine the new leader, Prince Axel of Denmark drew Brundage aside and explained to him for twenty minutes that "no American should be President of the IOC."[20] There were certainly others
who felt as Prince Axel did. When Brundage's name was put forward as the official candidate of the Executive Board, which then
consisted of Edstrøm and Brundage, ex officio, Scharroo of Holland, Armand Massard of France, Alberto Bonacossa of Italy, and
the Marquess of Exeter, Prince Axel rose to nominate Exeter (then
still known as Lord Burghley). Exeter, who had won a gold medal
in the 400-meter hurdles in Amsterdam in 1928 and was now president of the I.A.A.F., was a very strong and able candidate. Konstantin Andrianov of the Soviet Union seconded Exeter's nomi-
nation, after which he and Axel made speeches which Garland
thought to have had a major impact on the committee.[21] Axel
avoided comments on Brundage's personality and argued that the
I.O.C. was, after all, a *European* association within which the
United States was a latecomer.[22] (From Prince Axel's royal perch,
1896 must have been rather late in the game.) Andrianov was certainly suspicious of Brundage's outspoken anti-Communism and

may have been worried about Brundage's devotion to pure amateurism. Seeldrayers, one of the few Jews ever to be elected to the I.O.C, may have been bothered by Brundage's anti-Semitism and his eagerness to welcome back members whom Seeldrayers accused of collaboration with Hitler and Mussolini. Seeldrayers had also quarreled with Brundage during the "Great Ice Hockey Controversy" of 1947–1948. Sidney Dawes of Canada, Lord Porritt of New Zealand, and Lord Aberdare of Great Britain all spoke for Exeter who was, as Brundage noted, the "British Empire's" candidate.[23] Garland, who sent Brundage a lengthy analysis of the election, felt that the strongest factors in Brundage's favor were Albert Mayer's endorsement, the backing of the Executive Committee, Brundage's personal popularity, and the realization that he had for years labored in the vineyard of Olympism. Garland thought that the opposition's speeches actually helped Brundage through a boomerang effect.[24] Brundage's years of involvement with Latin American athletic festivals like the Central American Games, his leadership in the Pan-American Games Commission, and his proposal sponsorship of many of the South and Central American members earned him support among the Hispanic delegates from the western hemisphere.

The election was very close. Although the balloting was secret, Garland kept tabs on it and concluded that Brundage and Exeter were tied after 16 rounds, that Brundage was ahead by one vote after 21 rounds. The final tally was 30–17, with two blank ballots, on the 25th round. Among Brundage's papers is an annotated list of the membership as of 1952. Against the names of the delegates from the British Commonwealth and the Communist countries he wrote "BE" or "Iron." He concluded that the opposition had consisted of Lords Aberdare and Luke (Great Britain), Exeter himself, Lewis Luxton (Australia), Sidney Dawes (Canada), Lord Porritt (New Zealand), Konstantin Andrianov and Aleksei Romanov (U.S.S.R.), G. A. Gruss (Czechoslovakia), Jerzy Loth (Poland), Ferenc Mező (Hungary), Vladimir Stoytchev (Bulgaria), R. W. Seeldrayers (Belgium), Olaf Ditlev-Simonsen (Norway), and Bo Ekelund (Sweden).[25] The position taken by Ekelund, a protégé of

Edstrøm and a friend of Brundage, is hard to explain (if Brundage's surmise about his vote was correct). Perhaps Ekelund simply felt that Exeter would have been a better president.

After the balloting for president was concluded, Armand Massard of France defeated Exeter for vice president by a vote of 25–23; it was an attempt to preserve the balance between the French-speaking and the English-speaking members rather than a lack of confidence in Exeter.[26]

That Brundage had made the notation necessary to calculate who had been for him and who against can be seen as petty or even vindictive (one thinks back to the adolescent short-story, "The Retribution"), but Brundage's subsequent comportment as president suggests rather than he was determined to show even the skeptics that he was able to behave fairly or—as he would have phrased it—to demonstrate his belief in fair play and good sportsmanship. The difference between his relatively dispassionate acceptance of opposition in this case and his violent emotionalism during and after the boycott controversy of 1934–36 can be explained by the fact that he did not conceive of a vote for Exeter as an attack on the religion of Olympism. He was able to forgive skepticism about Avery Brundage more quickly than disbelief in the Olympic Games.

Now that he was actually Coubertin's successor, he intended to use his office as Theodore Roosevelt had used his—as "a bully pulpit." His inaugural address, delivered at a grand dinner given by the city of Lausanne on August 14, 1952, preached the sermon he had preached for thirty years and was to repeat for another twenty—amateurism.

In all of his many administrative roles as president of the A.A.U. and of the A.O.A., as member of the Executive Council of the I.A.A.F., and now, as president of the I.O.C., Brundage was unmistakably an idealist. His favorite quotation, used to sum up countless speeches, was from John Galsworthy:

Sport, which still keeps the flag of idealism flying, is perhaps the most saving grace in the world at the moment, with its spirit of rules kept, and regard for the adversary, whether the fight is going for or against. When, if ever, the spirit of sport, which is the spirit of fair play, reigns over international affairs, the cat force, which rules there now, will slink away, and human life emerge for the first time from the jungle.[27]

Paradoxically, sports represented an ideal form of conduct because sports were, for Brundage, a world apart: "Sport is recreation, it is a pastime or a diversion, it is play, it is action for amusement, it is free, spontaneous and joyous—it is the opposite of work."[28] If Brundage saw himself as a man with a mission, it was surely as the prophet of Coubertin's religion of Olympism, "a religion with universal appeal which incorporates all the basic values of other religions,"[29] a religion whose ethical component Brundage summed up in a single word: amateurism.

The amateur code, coming to us from antiquity, contributed to and strengthened by the noblest aspirations of great men of each generation, embraces the highest moral laws. No philosophy, no religion, preaches loftier sentiments.[30]

Despite the reference to the "amateur code" and the endless attempts to reduce this code to the I.O.C.'s eligibility rule, Brundage viewed the distinction between amateur and professional as "a thing of the spirit."[31] It "exists in the heart and not in the rule book."[32] The amateur plays for the sake of play, for the love of it, as the etymology of "amateur" implies, while professionals have some other motive, usually materialistic. There are those who compete "for the love of the game itself without thought of reward or payment of any kind," and they are free men; the others are "employees" and "entertainers . . . and there is no place for them in the Olympic Games."[33] Professional sports are "a branch of the entertainment business."[34] Although he sometimes attempted to be tactful and acknowledged the legitimacy of professional sports, the politeness went against the grain. Even as he insisted that he had no quarrel with honest professionals who didn't pretend to be amateurs, he called them "a troop of trained seals."[35]

An anecdote which Brundage used repeatedly to illustrate the difference that motives make told of an American tourist in an "underdeveloped" country who purchased an onyx carving as a souvenir. The price was low, a mere three dollars, and the tourist asked about the purchase of a large number of carvings for resale on the American market. How much would they cost if he ordered a thousand of them? The onyx-carver thought for a moment and then answered, "Five dollars each." To make one carving was an act of artistic expression, play; to make a thousand was work.[36] At moments, Brundage was ready to admit that a man like Babe Ruth was truly an amateur in spirit because the Babe seemed obviously in love with the game of baseball, eager to play on and on whether the Yankees paid him or not. Brundage was ready to count even Thomas Edison and Henry Ford among the amateurs in spirit because their vocations and avocations were one and the same.[37]

Latitudinarian in theory, Brundage tended to be the opposite in practice. In his fanatic desire to achieve absolute purity within the sacred realm of amateur sports, he insisted that a professional in *any* sport lost his amateur status in *all* sports. Brundage's friend Exeter asked if this definition of amateurism really made sense in the real world: "Why should a groom for a race horse not compete as an amateur swimmer? Why should a man who repairs racing bicycles not be eligible to compete as an amateur runner?"[38] Brundage wavered and then responded with a counterquestion: what about professional basketball and football players who want to compete in track and field?[39] Although Brundage did not name him, he might have asked about his nemesis: What about Jim Thorpe? The principle must not be compromised.

Behind the principle lay an implicit set of assumptions. For Brundage, amateurism was the expression of the concept of the Renaissance man who was expert in many activities but an expert, that is, a specialist, in none of them. In his critique of engineering education he had warned against narrowly technical training and he certainly drove himself to excel in fields as different as track-and-field sports, the construction industry, and the study of Asian art. Amateurism in this sense can be traced back to the Renaissance, to the world of Baldissare Castiglione's *Il Cortegiano*, to the courtier who danced, wrote sonnets, played the lute, and commanded armies on the field of battle, who was, however, neither a dancer nor a poet nor a musician nor a soldier. Behind this Renaissance concept of the talented amateur lay diffuse assumptions about society and social class, about the superiority of the aristocrat whose graceful ability was somehow innate and about the inferiority of all the others who painstakingly *acquired* skills. These assumptions about class and sports crystalized in Victorian England when the aristocracy and the upper middle class cooperated to formulate the amateur rule and to segregate *their* sports from the recreations of the hoi polloi.

Since the true spirit of amateurism was allegedly confined to those at the upper levels of society, the amateur rule was originally based upon the class divisions characteristic of Victorian society. The regulations of the Henley Regatta of 1879, for instance, read, "No person shall be considered an amateur oarsman or sculler . . . Who is or has been by trade or employment for wages, a mechanic, artisan, or laborer."[40] It was precisely this rule which enabled the organizers to exclude a certain John Kelley, whose daughter Grace became the Princess of Monaco and, incidently, the daughter-in-law of a member of the I.O.C. It was certainly not *this* definition of amateurism which attracted Brundage, who was of course ineligible for competition under Henley Regatta Rules, but the abandonment of definition by class membership led Brundage and others into the doomed quest for an adequate alternative.

The philosphical problem, which Brundage never fully understood, was that his ends and means were unrelated. It was quite impossible in the 1920s to believe that the *spirit* of amateurism—love of sports for their own sake—was confined to a distinct social class. Avery Brundage, the son of a stone mason, was as able to understand and be moved by the spirit of amateurism as was his friend and fellow Olympian the Marquess of Exeter. But how was one to discriminate in practice between those who did and those who did not participate with the spirit of amateurism? The attempted solution, of course, was to continue to rely upon sociological distinctions but to draw the line differently. *All* occupational categories, manual or not, became acceptable—except for one. The amateur athlete is the man or woman whose occupation lies some-where—anywhere—outside of sports. If one's income is not de-rived from sports, then one is, presumably, an amateur in spirit.

There is an attractive simplicity about this interpretation of the relationship between spirit and social category, but it runs counter to some of the most powerful tendencies of modern sports—the desire for victory and the mania for records. The more intensely athletes seek to win and the more obsessively they strive for records, the more they are driven to specialize in sports to the exclusion of other activities. Olympic champions seldom have time for the prac-tice of medicine or the demands of political office. In other words, top-level athletes are forced to professionalize in the sense that sports become not the avocation but the vocation, not the diversion of a summer afternoon but the preoccupation of the entire year. When players become specialists in their play, when they *train*, distinctions dissolve and categories are confounded. When the im-pulse to win, which is by definition an aspect of sports, and to set records, which is the most remarkable characteristic of modern sports, are intensified by nationalism, which has most emphatically been the case within the Olympic movement, then the commitment to athletic achievement can become almost suicidal. Where then is the amateur?

Brundage was keenly aware of the dangers of nationalism. When he and I.O.C. Chancellor Otto Mayer questioned the amateur sta-tus of the Italian cyclist Ercole Baldini, the Comite Olimpico Na-zionale d'Italia rushed to the defense of the accused, who continued to ride for Italy.[41] When Brundage sent the U.S. Olympic Com-mittee an article (from the A.A.U.'s own magazine!) in which it was reported that the U.S. Army allowed its Olympic candidates to train full time, Donald Hull answered on behalf of the U.S.O.C. that the athletes continued to fulfill their military duties, and there the matter ended.[42] When Brundage persuaded the I.O.C. to dis-qualify the famed Austrian skier Karl Schranz for his appearances in advertisements for ski manufacturers, the enraged Austrian re-sponse was directed against Brundage.

The American embassy in Vienna received bomb threats and dozens of protests. A fire was started at the door of one of the leading members of the Austrian Skiing Association because it was felt that he had not sufficiently protected Austria's interests. A well-known Austrian industrialist was singled out for vitriolic attacks because he had cabled a supportive message to Brundage. . . . His grandchildren were badly beaten at school, and his products were boycotted. Schranz was given the Order of Merit for Sports by the Austrian Council of Ministers, the first to be awarded.[43]

The head of the Austrian Olympic Committee, Heinz Pruckner, was forced to resign simply because he had allowed the Austrian team to continue after Schranz's disqualification.[44] The Austrian press was quick to publish photographs of advertisements featuring French and Swiss skiers and to accuse Brundage of partiality.[45]

It was painfully obvious to Brundage that national Olympic committees are not and never will be zealous in the enforcement of rules which encourage the spirit of amateurism but hamper the nation's athletes in their quest for medals.[46] In 1967, the Turkish Olympic Committee courageously decided not to field a soccer team in Mexico City the following year because they suspected many of the players of professionalism.[47] An admirable example, but few national committees have shown the same strictness. Bitterly aware of this, Brundage repeatedly remarked that "at least three persons have lied" if an ineligible athlete is certified.[48] It was an illogical assertion (because members of the national sports federation and the national Olympic committee might sincerely believe lies told by a dishonest athlete), but no historian of the modern Olympics can doubt that many national committees have certified athletes whom they knew to be paid professionals.

Brundage and his fellow believers in amateurism attempted repeatedly to preserve Olympism by diminishing nationalism within amateur sports. Specifically, there was a constant struggle over national flags and anthems, especially during the victory ceremony. In the first year of his presidency, Brundage told the representatives of the national Olympic committees that he thought it necessary to "replace the National Hymns by an Olympic Hymn, or sounding the trumpets during the Ceremony of presenting the medals," but the delegates voted "unanimously in favor of maintaining the status quo."[49] Albert Mayer offered Brundage some support,[50] but he too was forced by pressure from the national committees to withdraw his proposal to substitute a fanfare of trumpets for the national anthems.[51] Brundage led another serious reform effort in the 1960s. At the 56th Session of the I.O.C. at San Francisco, he suggested,

It might be better to use a fanfare of trumpets instead of national hymns in the victory ceremonies. When the Olympic flag is raised at the opening of the Games, perhaps all national flags should be lowered. Contestants in the Olympic Games should come . . . as sportsmen and not as representatives of a country.[52]

After years of discussion, the proposal to replace anthems with trumpet fanfare came to a vote at the 60th Session in Baden-Baden (1963). The proposal needed a rule-amending majority of two-thirds and was therefore defeated by a vote of 26–26. It was, ironically, the vociferous critics of "bourgeois nationalism" who resisted the reform. As Brundage's friend Willi Daume, a member from West Germany, commented, such resistance seemed inappropriate to men who proudly avow their freedom from nationalism by singing the "Internationale."[53]

There was also the quixotic attempt to pretend that nations did not contend for overall "victory" in the games. The I.O.C. refused to establish an official system of points by which to determine which nation "won." At the Helsinki session that elected him to the presidency, Brundage requested and received a resolution against point tables:

The I.O.C. deplores the practice in the newspapers of the world, of attributing and publishing tables of points showing national placings in the Olympic Games. This is entirely contrary to the rules and spirit of the Olympic Games, which are contests between individuals with no points scored.[54]

Despite this stand, the I.O.C. refused to encourage the formation of international teams (like the British-German combination which won the gold medal for tennis doubles in 1896) and the I.O.C. continued to organize the games through the national Olympic committees rather than through regional units (which might have had the additional advantage of roughly equal populations). When athletes in exile from Poland and other countries of the Warsaw Pact begged to be allowed to compete as an Olympic team under the five-ringed Olympic flag, the I.O.C. refused the request.[55] When the exiles pressed Brundage on this matter, he offered solace—"The I.O.C. looks with sympathy on the case"—but he returned to the familiar argument against this venture into internationalism: "the whole conception of the Olympic Games is based on National teams organized by National Olympic Committees."[56] It was not even possible temporarily to house athletes by sports rather than by nations and thus to internationalize the Olympic Village. Gaston Mullegg, the Swiss president of the Fédération Internationale d'Aviron suggested this and was quickly rebuffed by the I.O.C. The vote against his proposal was unanimous.[57] Ironically, it was because of politics that national teams finally did march behind the Olympic flag in 1980—in order to protest the Soviet Union's invasion of Afghanistan.

That nationalism imperils the spirit of amateurism was and is obvious. That the mania for records can do the same is less clear because this mania is not incompatible with participation in sports for the sake of sports. In other words, a definition which holds that sports are a category of play, i.e., that they are ends in themselves and not means to some other end (like earning a living), does *not* rule out total and even maniacal commitment to record-breaking. It is only when one adds, as Brundage did, that the autotelic activity must be an avocation apart from one's "normal" vocation that the quest for records begins to interfere with the pursuit of ordinary occupations. Brundage did of course demand that amateur sports be an avocation "purely incidental to the main business of life,"[58] and he was more or less consciously aware that there was a potential conflict between this criterion and the quest for records. His response was consistent. He valued amateurism higher than he did the setting of records and he blamed the press and the public for a misplaced emphasis.[59] Records are "the certain death of the amateur" because they are possible only on the basis of specialization.[60]

When critics attacked the choice of Mexico City as the site of the 1968 games and argued that the high altitude and rarefied atmosphere made it unlikely that distance runners would be able to set new records, Brundage answered that the Olympics are an athletic festival and that it is not necessary that records be broken.[61] The games had a mission which was more important than the quantified results of the contests. "The Olympic Games belong to all the world, not the part of it at sea level."[62]

In connection with these games, a member of the Belgian Olympic Committee pointed out that illegal drugs used at such altitudes were even more dangerous than under ordinary conditions.[63] Although the I.O.C. took the problem of drugs seriously and began to take measures against anabolic steroids and other agents (the first drug tests took place in Mexico City), Brundage was never as concerned about doping as he was about professionalization. Of course he condemned the athlete who popped pills in order to gain a competitive edge over a more sportsmanlike opponent, but drugs never seemed quite the image of evil that Mammon did.[64]

Since Brundage was unable to extirpate the deeper roots of professionalization, he had no alternative but to hack away at the branches. For fifty years he attacked the ramifications of wickedness in the form of sub-rosa cash payments, valuable gifts, income derived indirectly from athletic fame (e.g., money received for endorsements of products or from ghostwritten books), the establishment of special training camps, the combination of vocation and avocation in the role of coach-athlete, athletic scholarships, and payments for "broken time" (i.e., time lost from one's normal job).

Everyone involved in the administration of amateur sports agreed, at least publicly, that sub-rosa cash payments are a violation of the rules. Enforcement of the rule was another matter. Brundage quickly became notorious for his uncanny ability to detect violations. Newspaper reports incited him to letters of inquiry, to investigations, to expostulations, and—occasionally—to suspensions. Fame was no protection. The American runner Wes Santee was suspended by the A.A.U. and, after he had lost a court fight against the organization, he admitted that he had indeed received more than $10,000 in expense money, a practice he defended as common among world-class runners.[65] An even more famous runner, Finland's Paavo Nurmi, was accused of the same practice and was barred from the 1932 games in Los Angeles (Brundage seems in this instance to have felt that the penalty was excessive.)[66]

Since Brundage read numerous newspapers on a daily basis and received clipped newspaper and magazine articles from the *Times* of London, *La Prensa* (Buenos Aires), *L'Equipe* (Paris), *The Mainichi Times* (Tokyo), and countless other journals, he was able to fire off accusatory letters whenever a campaign was announced to give a house to the mother of a Brazilian triple-jumper, whenever an Argentinian soccer player or a Canadian figure skater was about to be presented with an automobile.[67] Even in social situations, where small talk was the lingua franca, Brundage was likely to raise the question of amateurism and payments in cash or kind. To Arpad Csanadi of Hungary, an authority on soccer, Brundage complained that the game was hopelessly commercialized. Csanadi parried with the comment that soccer was one of the world's most popular sports; of the millions who played, perhaps one or two percent were professionals. "But, Dr. Csanadi," retorted Brundage, "why do you bring only this two percent to the Olympic Games?"[68]

The campaign against commercialization was carried to the point where an undergraduate student of journalism was denied the right to publish an article on his experiences in sport.[69] England's sprinter Dorothy Hyman was forced to wait until retirement from sports before she published her memoirs and the American decathlon champion Bob Mathias was told not to wear an Olympic jersey when he appeared in an instructional film.[70] Denmark's Paul Elvstrøm sailed into metaphorically troubled waters when he, four times a victor in Olympic yacht races, failed to dissociate himself from publicity for the ship-building firm that he owned and that was his only means of livelihood.[71] Brundage's objection to horses named after commercial products brought forth a commentary from Prince Philip of England, who noted that it was difficult to clear equestrianism of this problem because manufacturers often named their products after the horses.[72]

The problem of endorsements became especially acute among world-class skiers as their sport became increasingly popular and ski manufacturers fought for a share in the lucrative market. Photographs of advertisements piled up on Brundage's desk. Letters went out. "Our office . . . is flooded with letters and telephone calls asking us whether or not the skiers whose names and pictures are . . . used as endorsements by manufacturers of skis and ski equipment . . . will be permitted to participate in the Olympic Winter Games at Sapporo in 1972."[73] The Fédération Internationale de Ski seemed totally disinclined to punish the violators of the amateur rule. There were showdowns at Grenoble in 1968 and at Sapporo in 1972, donnybrooks which became major episodes in Olympic history.

The establishment of training camps was another headache. The I.O.C. accepted them in principle and sought vainly to limit their scope. Prior to the 1964 winter games, Brundage wrote to J. Lyman Bingham to ask him if there was any truth in the rumor that the American speed skaters planned to train for a month in the United States and then again at Innsbruck; the answer was that *none* of the winter teams complied with the rules.[74] When the 1968 games were awarded to Mexico City, everyone familiar with the simple facts of geography and physiology knew that the elevation of this site placed insurmountable obstacles before cyclists, distance runners, and swimmers who had neither grown up at such a height nor had had the chance to acclimate themselves. The I.O.C. extended the limits on training camps to six weeks, but the Americans and doubtless many others simply violated the rules while Brundage, despite his bursts of rage, was helpless to prevent them.[75] Except in the rarest of cases, the I.O.C. felt compelled to accept the word of the national Olympic committees that there was no evidence of an infraction of the rules. In this specific instance, Brundage protested to Douglas Roby of the U.S. Olympic Committee that the Americans had broken the rules and Roby accused Brundage of enmity toward the United States and favortism in regards to Russian teams which trained twelve months a year.[76]

In principle, at least, it was possible to say whether a team trained together for six weeks or for a year, but the problem of the teacher-athlete was conceptually more difficult. The skier who was richly paid to "teach" a few hours a month, mostly by his or her brilliant example on the slopes, was unquestionably a paid professional, but what about the highschool biologist who was also responsible for a class of beginners? Brundage informed the Board of Governors of the A.A.U. that "ANYONE WHO TEACHES, TRAINS OR COACHES IN ANY SPORT FOR MONEY OR OTHER PECUNIARY CONSIDERATIONS RE-CEIVED EITHER DIRECTLY OR INDIRECTLY IS A PROFESSIONAL."[77] When the Fédération Internationale de Ski requested a modification of the rules in 1935, the I.O.C. refused to change its position and the F.I.S. went ahead on its own. At its 15th International Congress in February 1938, the F.I.S. declared that coaches and instructors remained amateurs. The gauntlet (or the ski glove) was thrown down and Brundage was furious against Arnold Lunn and N. R. Ostgaard, officials of the F.I.S., who had "poisoned the minds of a large section of the ski world."[78] The I.O.C. stood its ground in 1938 and the conflict brewed until the first postwar games approached. Alerted to the possibility that the F.I.S. might try to enter instructors as amateurs, Brundage responded fiercely:

An amateur is an amateur, and no pronouncement, sanction, decree or fiat of any organization, national or international, can alter that situation. Because the FIS allows paid teachers to participate in its events, does not make them amateurs.[79]

Given this austere view of the matter ("An amateur is an amateur"), Brundage felt that allowing the instructors to compete at St. Moritz would be "a world-wide scandal."[80] Eventually, the conflict was resolved. Marc Hodler of the F.I.S. suggested that part-time instructors of elementary skiing be deemed amateurs while others be regarded as paid professionals; Brundage accepted the compromise, which included the proviso that even part-time instructors not teach during the ninety days prior to the winter games, but he complained subsequently that the F.I.S. failed to live up to the terms of the agreement.[81] In his heart of hearts, he continued to believe that the teachers of a sport are professionals who have forfeited their right to appear as amateurs.

Although athletic scholarships are ipso facto rewards for athletic ability, hypocritical conventions enable universities to maintain that all the recipients are actually bona fide students (as, in fact, many of them are). Except for some not particularly welcome help from the Communist nations, Brundage was isolated in his fulminations against athletic scholarships. Having long felt that "the commercialization of College Football in our Universities is one of the worst of all evils because it exists, of all places, in educational institutions,"[82] Brundage decided in 1952 to make a full-scale assault upon the monster. His article, "The Fumbled Ball," went far beyond the assertion that many student-athletes were actually paid performers who rarely saw the inside of a classroom:

College football, originally a game incorporating the finest characteristics of the American way of life, has become a national scandal that smells to high heaven. . . . Educated people in Europe, in Latin America, and in the Orient, simply cannot understand why our institutions of higher learning should be football factories and farms for professional football leagues.[83]

On the narrow issue of athletic scholarships, Brundage seemed to be in a strong position because Rule 26 of the Olympic Charter did unmistakably prohibit them: "Individuals subsidized by governments, educational institutions, or business concerns because of their athletic ability are not amateurs."[84] Speaking to the I.O.C. at its 60th Session in 1963, Brundage was crystal clear:

Young men who because of their athletic ability are given scholarships and other benefits and advantages by educational institutions [are ineligible and] the argument that these young men might never get a college education is a non sequitur, and the fact that they keep up with their college work is not significant either. The gift of a scholarship worth several thousands of dollars is no different than a gift of several thousands of dollars in cash, and the truth is they are paid to participate.[85]

Brundage asked the universities to adhere to the rules and he called the attention of the A.A.U. to what he thought was the worst violation of all:

Many organizations and individuals in other countries have been annoyed by the proselyting which has brought foreign athletes to many of our colleges. Certainly *all* of these scholarships were mainly because of athletic ability, and *all* of these athletes are ineligible.[86]

The response of the universities was predictable. James Counsilman, famed swimming coach for Indiana University, reported that all Big 10 scholarships are given primarily for academic achievement and only secondarily for athletic ability.[87] Perhaps it is just as well that Brundage did not live to see the day when the University of Texas at El Paso fielded a championship cross-country team recruited entirely from Africa.[88] One suspects that the Africans were not sought out chiefly for their scholastic potential.

The most intractable of problems was that of "broken-time" payments. By the 1920s, everyone agreed that amateur athletes ought to be reimbursed for expenses incurred by travel to meets and matches, but the Fédération Internationale de Football Association (F.I.F.A.), which governs soccer, was not satisfied. Although the Olympic Congress held in Prague in 1925 opposed payments for broken time by a vote of 63–12, pressure from F.I.F.A., led by Louis Rimet of France, caused the I.O.C. Executive Board to waver from its course in 1927. Against the protests of Edström and General R. J. Kentish of Great Britain, F.I.F.A. was granted its request for broken-time compensation for the 1928 Olympics at Amsterdam.[89] (The British were so upset by F.I.F.A.'s demands that the Football Association withdrew from the international body until after World War II.) At the Olympic Congress held in Berlin in 1930, which Brundage attended as president of the A.A.U. and as a delegate from the I.A.A.F. and the Féderation Internationale de Handball, the delegates voted against broken-time payments by a resounding 90–20.[90] As a result, there were no soccer contests at the 1932 games in Los Angeles.

When the issue flared up again in the 1940s, Brundage continued to oppose the payments and regretted that the I.O.C. had weakly decided in 1938 to allow a special "indemnity" to the wife, mother, or father whose only means of support came from an athletic husband or son who lost time from work because of participation in sports.[91] (No provision was made for athletic wives or daughters who supported needy relatives.) In an article which appeared in the A.A.U. journal, *Amateur Athlete*, Brundage wrote, "Everyone knows that reimbursement for lost wages . . . is not compatible with amateurism."[92] But "everyone" did not know this, and the sports administrators of the Scandinavian countries were, in Brundage's eyes, "the ring leaders in the battle to legitimize payment for broken time."[93] Pressure mounted for such payments, but Brundage continued to repeat that amateurism is "an inflexible, an absolute and universal thing. It is rigid and unvarying and cannot be changed for any organization."[94] It is clear from Brundage's language ("absolute and universal") that the religion of Olympism, like Christianity, incorporates a good deal of Platonism.

Gaston Meyer, editor of the prestigious French sports daily *L'Equipe*, disagreed with Brundage and expressed what he ironically called *idées revolutionnaires*; Meyer maintained that it was foolish to forbid what was impossible to prevent.[95] This was a pragmatism for which Brundage had no patience.

One reason for Brundage's stubborn stand on the broken-time issue, and on all the other threats to the purity of the amateur ideal, was his obdurate conviction that 95 percent of all Olympic medals are won by "poor boys" (like Avery Brundage).[96] He asserted on more than one occasion that no rich boy had ever been an Olympic champion (which assertion must have astonished the Marquess of Exeter). Sports sociologists have shown repeatedly that, on the contrary, poor boys ("those of low socioeconomic status" is their preferred locution) are very much underrepresented at the Olympic Games, but Brundage simply ridiculed empirical studies of sports and blamed sociologists like Gregory Stone and Guenther Lueschen for not doing their scholarly work properly and for contaminating youth "by their laxity in enforcing regulations."[97] In a circular letter "On the Olympic Games and Payment for Broken Time," Brundage made his point *ad absurdum* and informed his colleagues that he had "never known nor even heard of one single athlete who was too poor to participate in the Olympic Games."[98] Perhaps one should not take him too literally; what he wanted to say was that *he* had sacrificed for the principles of amateurism and it had done him good.

Although Brundage warned that payments for broken time meant "the end of the Olympic Movement as it now exists,"[99] the majority either disagreed or wished radically to alter the movement. The dam was finally breached in June of 1962. At the 59th Session of the I.O.C., in Moscow, Rule 26 was revised:

The International Olympic Committee in principle is opposed to payments for broken time which it considers an infraction of olympic amateurism.

However, when a competitor can prove that his dependents are suffering hardship because of his (or her) loss of salary or wages while attending the Olympic Games, his national olympic committee may make a contribution to these dependents, but under no circumstances may it exceed the sum which he (or she) would have earned during his (or her) actual period of absence, which in turn must not exceed 30 days.[100]

Brundage took the defeat badly and condemned the action as "a deviation from pure amateurism." He asked the A.A.U. to renounce the benefits offered by the new rule:

If the Amateur Athletic Union of the United States would adopt a resolution to the effect that in a prosperous country like the United States of America there is so much pride when an athlete becomes a member of an Olympic team that dependents are always cared for privately and that there is, therefore, no need of invoking a rule of this kind, the effect would be most salutary.[101]

The A.A.U. did not agree.

By the time Brundage was to hand on to Lord Killanin the torch which had been passed to him by Coubertin, Baillet-Latour, and Edstrøm, the effort to achieve the spirit of amateurism through controls over the sources of income had clearly failed. In 1969, an I.O.C. commission headed by Rumania's Alexandru Siperco acknowledged that "olympic level performances cannot be anymore realized by practising sport as a game, or only for relaxation."[102] Non-Communist observers began increasingly to feel that the amateur rules served mainly as a handicap favoring the full-time athletes of the Communist countries who won easy victories over the more honest of their "capitalist" opponents. When the French journal *Le Miroir des Sports* accused the I.O.C. in general and Brundage in particular of hypocrisy and mendacity, Brundage sued in the French courts and won an award of one centime.[103] He framed the check, but there was no way to prevent an objective observer from coming to a somewhat less recklessly expressed conclusion that a chasm had opened between Olympic idealism and athletic practice. The Olympic oath threatened to become the very opposite of what Brundage hoped for. Deluded he may have been, but at least he had enough of a sense of humor to be ironic about his own stubborn idealism. In an interview with a Stockholm newspaper, he responded impishly to a question about his favorite literary hero: "I do not read many novels but Don Quijote is probably the closest to my ideal."[104] A steel statue of Cervantes' tilter at windmills stood in Brundage's house in Santa Barbara.[105]

CHAPTER IX

THE OLYMPIC GAMES AND THE COLD WAR

The Olympic movement had survived World War II, but the sense of satisfaction which had prevailed in London in 1948 was short-lived. It was soon apparent that Franklin Roosevelt's idealistic vision of a world peace secured by the United Nations was no more realizable than Woodrow Wilson's hopes for a League of Nations presiding over a world made safe for democracy. Russian soldiers stood guard in Berlin and Vienna and the Kremlin controlled all of eastern Europe. Russian tanks rolled into Prague to establish the Communist Party's rule and Russian tanks blocked Allied access to Berlin in an attempt to force the Americans, the British, and the French to abandon the isolated city. There was no peace in Europe, and Europe was not the only arena of combat. On the opposite side of the globe, the superpowers fought by proxy. Nationalists led by Chiang Kai-shek and Communists led by Mao Tse-tung were involved in a bloody struggle for political control of China's hundreds of millions of people. Wars were soon to begin in Korea and in Vietnam.

While political leaders began to adjust to the new balance of power by means of the North Atlantic Treaty Organization and the Warsaw Pact and, in the days of John Foster Dulles, with a whole alphabet soup of regional alliances, the members of the I.O.C. found themselves confronted with the same set of problems

on a smaller and less deadly scale. To what degree were they—
princes, counts, and barons, generals and wealthy businessmen—
ready to welcome Communist functionaries into the Olympic family? The I.O.C.'s own rules prohibit any kind of political discrimination, but rule books are not invariably an accurate guide to behavior. In the case of the smaller members of the Communist bloc—
Bulgaria, Czechoslovakia, Hungary, Poland, Rumania, Yugoslavia—there was apparently no difficulty. These nations had had
recognized national Olympic committees before the war and they
had participated in earlier Olympics. In some cases, there was personal continuity in that men who had worked in the national committees before the war were still active after 1945. (There were also
several I.O.C. members from eastern Europe who survived the
conflict, but none was an important figure in Olympic affairs.) In
short, the I.O.C. was not disposed to violate its own rules and
block participation by the smaller Slavic nations.

The Soviet Union was another matter. "The great problem" commented Edstrøm apropos of the first postwar session of the I.O.C.,
"will be the question of *Russia.*"[1] Although Czarist Russia had participated in the Olympic Games, the USSR had withdrawn from
"bourgeois" sports and had sponsored a rival to the Olympics in
the form of the Rote Sport-Internationale (R.S.I.). As early as 1923,
the I.O.C. had officially expressed its hope that Russian youth
would be able to join in future games.[2] Now, in the mid-1940s,
the Russians began to signal that they wished to return to the various international sports federations and to enter the Olympics.
Brundage was not the only I.O.C. member who felt an internal
psychological conflict between the universality proclaimed in
Olympic rhetoric and an intense dislike of the ideology institutionalized in the Soviet Union. He was ambivalent about the notion
of the hammer and sickle next to the Olympic rings.

Brundage had visited the Soviet Union in 1934. He was struck
then by the athletic progress made since his visit to Czarist Russia
immediately after the 1912 games in Stockholm. Popular enthusiasm for sports was evident and the efforts of the government to
provide facilities and organizational support compared well with

those of the West. Brundage's political convictions, however, remained untouched. He was a Middle Western adherent of the Republican Party, a believer in laissez-faire capitalism and in liberal
(not social) democracy. Communism was anathema to him in 1934
and he became—as we have seen—almost obsessively anti-Communist in the late 1930s. It is, however, a serious mistake to conclude, as a recent scholar has on the basis of a meticulous but narrow
study of the boycott controversy of 1934–36, that "Avery Brundage's Olympic movement was eternally mobilized against Communism. . . . His allegiance was not truly to the law [i.e., the
Olympic rules], as he imagined, but to any declared enemy of Communism."[3] When Brundage had to choose between his hostility to
Communism and his commitment to the ideal of Olympic universality, he chose the latter. He wanted the Russians in the Olympic
movement, Communists or not.

During the war he wrote to Britain's Lord Aberdare, "I agree
with you that the I.O.C. should be represented in Russia which
should also be a member of the International Sport Federations."[4]
(The peculiar wording results from the stubborn notion that I.O.C.
members were not representatives of their nations but rather represented Olympism to their fellow countrymen.) To Frederick W.
Rubien of the U.S.A.S.F. he explained, "If the Russians would
agree to live up to the rules and regulations of the Federations and
the International Olympic Committee there is no reason why they
should not be members."[5] A few months later he expressed the
same sentiments to Edström.[6]

In order for a nation to participate in the Olympic Games, it
must have a national Olympic committee recognized by the I.O.C.
That recognition depends, among other things, on the political independence of the national body from its own national government.
This rule, based on nineteenth-century liberal conceptions of the
supreme importance of private as opposed to governmental institutions, was easy to enforce in an era when governments were in-
different to the Olympic movement. In the postwar period, however, many governments realized the political implications of sports
and began to assert direct governmental control over their national

Olympic committees, often in the form of a ministry of sports. Brundage fretted about this nascent tendency as early as 1943: "Mixtures of politics and sports in various Latin American countries will probably lead to considerable trouble when Pan-American sport develops."[7] Brazil, for instance, established a National Council of Sports in 1941 and placed the council directly under the Minister of Education and Public Health.[8] Brundage found himself engaged in an apparently endless dispute with Latin American governments who routinely allowed the ministers of education or of sports to name the president of the national Olympic committee or even to occupy the post themselves.[9] At an Executive Board meeting in Lausanne, a worried Brundage told his colleagues about the instrusions of the military and of governments in South and Central America.[10]

The Soviet Union was undeniably among those governments which exercised close control over its national Olympic committee. Edstrøm was initially reluctant to accept the Communist model of Politburo control.[11] Brundage shared his suspicions and, in 1950, commented on this problem in a letter to Arnold Lunn, the British inventor of the ski slalom (and a rather fierce anti-Communist): "How there can possibly be a Russian Olympic Committee that is autonomous I do not understand."[12] Nonetheless, he and Edstrøm finally decided to ignore the obvious infraction of the rule by the Communists even as they struggled to enforce the rule in Latin America and in Europe (where governments began to take over their national Olympic committees in the 1950s and 1960s). The political autonomy of the Russian Olympic Committee became one of the polite fictions rampant in international affairs.

Recognition of a national committee by the I.O.C. was also dependent upon the presence within the former of representatives of national sports federations affiliated with the international federations recognized by the I.O.C. For example, most if not all national committees include representatives from the national soccer organization recognized by the Fédération Internationale de Football Association which the I.O.C. officially recognizes. The crux of the "Great Ice Hockey Controversy" of 1946–48 was that the U.S.

Olympic Committee recognized one hockey association while the L.I.H.G. recognized another. Since the USSR had national organizations for most of the Olympic sports, the first step on the road to Olympus was for these organizations to become affiliated with their respective international federations, which they began to do, but not always in the most routine or expected ways.

In September and November of 1945, Edstrøm wrote Aleksei Romanov and invited the Russians to join the I.A.A.F. There was no answer.[13] Then, immediately before the start of the European track-and-field championships in Oslo in August 1946, the Russians appeared—uninvited. Theoretical problems suddenly became practical ones. Arriving in Oslo, Brundage was grabbed by the Norwegian chairman of the organizing committee, who conveyed the "startling greeting. 'The Russians are here. What shall we do?' "[14] Brundage spoke at the airport with the Russian officials, who assured him that the athletes were all bona fide amateurs. The I.A.A.F., which of course sponsored the meet, generously allowed the thirty-five Russians to compete although the USSR was not at that time a member of the I.A.A.F. Had Brundage wished to be legalistic in order to be anti-Communist, he would have had no trouble at all, but he chose rather to bend the rules so that the Russians could slip through the barrier. Reporting on the incident to the I.O.C., he passed on his impression that the Russians seemed sincere in their desire to enter the Olympic movement.[15] The first step was for them belatedly to join the I.A.A.F. Unannounced appearances must not be allowed to become the order of the day. Edstrøm thought it proper that the I.A.A.F. should extend a friendly hand, but it was finally up to the Russians to seek official affiliation.[16]

The Russians complied, but they made their entry conditional upon I.A.A.F. acceptance of three demands: that Russian be made an official I.A.A.F. language, that a Russian be elected to the I.A.A.F. Executive Committee, and that Spain (then ruled by a Fascist government) be expelled from the organization. The I.A.A.F. rejected the three demands, which Brundage referred to as "impudent" and "arrogant,"[17] whereupon the Russians meekly dropped them. Their national track-and-field federation was promptly recognized.

By the end of 1947, the Russians were also members of the international federations for basketball, soccer, weight lifting, and wrestling. Technically, their national Olympic committee had fulfilled the prerequisites for I.O.C. recognition. For the I.O.C., the question now became one of amateurism, an ideal which Edstrøm felt was "not at all understood" in the USSR.[18] Since Russian champions were supported by the state and received large cash prizes for victories in international competition or for setting world records, Edstrøm's remark was an understatement. "We must be very careful," Brundage warned, "or the whole structure of amateur sport and the Olympic Games which we have labored so many years to create will be wrecked and ruined."[19]

Before the Russians had been let into the I.A.A.F., Exeter had gone to Moscow and discussed the prickly issue of "state amateurs" with Aleksei Romanov (soon to become an I.O.C. member for Russia). Exeter reported sanguinely that the Russians accepted the I.A.A.F. rules on amateurism.[20] The only difficulty was that the Russians insisted on amnesty for athletes who had received cash payments prior to July 1, 1947. Brundage opposed the amnesty but found himself a minority within the I.A.A.F.[21] One reason for the group's flexibility about novel interpretations of the amateur rule was given by Edstrøm: "Our young athletes all over Europe are crazy to have the Russian athletes participate."[22]

The Russians had not entered the federation soon enough for them to compete in the 1948 Olympics in London. When one of Brundage's correspondents expressed regret at their absence, Brundage had some temporary second thoughts on the matter: "I seriously doubt that it is possible to have friendly sport contacts with any country that adheres to the Communist system."[23] The problem was that the Communists always brought politics into sports.

The accusation deserves comment. In one sense, it was a naïve remark because all institutions have political implications. Values, even implicit ones, represent human choices and not the facts of nature. The I.O.C., for instance, asserted proudly on every possible occasion that the Olympic Games were a social movement which brought men and women together in friendly competition and which promoted the ideal of international peace. To ring the stadium with a hundred flags and to bring together the athletes of a hundred different nations was ipso facto an implicit political statement which Brundage's speeches made totally explicit. In crass terms, the I.O.C. continually made a political choice in which peaceful rather than martial competition was affirmed. In another sense, however, Brundage's accusation was justified. The Communists had somewhat different ideas about what particular political purposes the movement ought implicitly and explicitly to serve. By their lights, international good will was all very well, but it was also important to demonstrate the superiority of the Communist system. In other words, they disturbed what had been—except for the deviation of 1936—more or less a liberal consensus and they made men conscious of what had simply been taken for granted. By openly disagreeing about politics, they made it difficult to pretend that the I.O.C. had no politics. Brundage, however, managed to maintain the pretense. He continued to repeat to the day of his death the contradictory propositions that the Olympic movement was the most important social force of the twentieth century and that it was without political implications.

When the Russians finally did apply to the I.O.C. for recognition of their national Olympic committee, they issued their familiar triad of demands: acceptance of Russian as an official language, a seat on the Executive Board, and the expulsion of Spain from the Olympic Games. The Executive Board's response was that not even Spanish had been accepted as an official language although it was spoken through most of Latin America, that seats on the Executive Board were not awarded politically, and that the Russians were free to move Spain's ouster once they were members of the organization. The Russians dropped their demands and Brundage seemed rather surprised that the I.O.C. had so quickly tamed the fearsome bear: "For the first time the Russians made no demands nor were there any reservations in the application. They simply stated that they had examined our rules and regulations and accepted them."[24]

Although Brundage remained skeptical about the Russians' sincerity, he voted for their acceptance at the Vienna session of the I.O.C. in May 1951. There were three abstentions, but none of the members voted nay.[25] Neither in Brundage's "Olympic Story" nor in Otto Mayer's *À Travers les anneaux olympiques* is there any indication who the three abstainers were. The minutes of the session and the correspondence of the members keep the secret.

Whoever the abstainers were, Brundage was not among them. Indeed, he was at this time so eager for the Soviet Union's smooth entry into the Olympic movement that he was enraged at Douglas Roby, the newest American I.O.C. member, for some anti-Russian jibes published under Roby's name on the occasion of an A.A.U.-sponsored Russian–American track meet at Philadelphia's Franklin Field. (The remarks were actually not by Roby but by A.A.U. Secretary Daniel J. Ferris.) Irate Brundage shouted at Roby, "You ought to have known better than that!" In Roby's vivid metaphor, "Brundage got a hold of me and tore me all to pieces." Kirby, Mahoney, and Ornstein—all men familiar with Brundage's verbal assaults—interceded to make peace between the two Olympians.[26]

The first Russian members were definitely not chosen by the I.O.C. as *its* delegates to the Soviet Union. When the Russians announced that *they* intended to name their own I.O.C. members, Edstrøm huffed and puffed and banged his cane upon the table and lectured the Russians on the I.O.C. rules and ordered them out of the room. In privacy, the members laughed at the startled Russians, who were obviously not used to such treatment, but who were the new members to be if not the men chosen by the Kremlin? Whom did they know there? Brundage was among the few who had visited the Soviet Union, and his visit was nearly twenty years earlier. The rule was bent.[27] Konstantin Andrianov and Aleksei Romanov, elected in Vienna and at the next session in Oslo, were Soviet bureaucrats completely loyal to the Communist Party, which is not to say that they were not also believers in sports. They were the unofficial leaders of the other representatives from Eastern Europe and the I.O.C. was now politicized in the sense that there were now open disagreements along recognizably political lines. It was obvious that individual members had ceased simply to represent their own consciences. Armand Massard of France noted sarcastically that whenever the Russian members made a proposal they were backed by the other Communists, who rose, one after the other, to announce their assent.[28] Daniel J. Ferris told Brundage about an egregious instance of servility at an I.A.A.F. congress in Belgrade; the leader of the Russian delegation left his alphabetically assigned seat at the rear of the hall and sat in the front row where he was visible to the delegates from the satellite countries, and he looked about during the votes to make sure that all hands were dutifully raised.[29] Brundage complained about this subservience, but he accepted it as the price paid for the universalism of the Olympic movement.

It was hard for him, and it was even harder for him to blink the plain fact that the Soviet Union and its allies never intended to comply with the amateur rule as he construed it. The Soviet Union's top athletes were supported by the state and continued, despite promises to the I.O.C., to be materially rewarded for stellar performances. Cash payments were officially ended, but they went on clandestinely and the system of state support was never a secret.

This led to another brouhaha when Brundage visited the Soviet Union in 1954 (at their invitation but at his own expense) and published an account of this three weeks in the *Saturday Evening Post*. Traveling not only to the more accessible cities of Leningrad, Moscow, Kiev, and Odessa, which he had visited in 1912, but also to places like Tashkent, Samarkand, and Bukhara, he was immensely impressed by the strides made in the previous twenty years and by the huge scale of the Russian physical-education program, which was creating the "greatest mass army of athletes the world has ever known." As Moscow's annual sports parade, he saw 34,000 athletes perform. He was informed that Russia had 4,000,000 track-and-field specialists. "I saw volleyball courts even on hospital grounds." While he was bothered by the grimness and regimentation of the program, there was a spartan strain in his own character that responded sympathetically when a Russian athlete told him, "Sports without self-denial and self-conquest are merely amusement." In this context Brundage took up a theme which became an important one for him throughout the 1950s: in comparison with these toughened ascetics, Americans seemed a nation of spectators, "soft and flabby from too easy living, too much amusement, too many automobiles and television sets."[30]

Such remarks might have been interpreted as "un-American" in the heyday of McCarthyism, but other comments were even more controversial. Brundage related in the article that he had questioned his hosts Andrianov and Romanov about the system of "state amateurism." Specifically, he asked them about cash payments and about special camps for year-round training. Brundage's account of his conversation can be called, depending upon one's moral view, devious or subtle. "The charges were emphatically denied. . . . No special inducements or material rewards are given athletes in Russia, he [Romanov] told me." When Brundage pressed him and referred to the contrary testimony of exiles, Romanov answered, "These men are deserters, traitors."[31] Since few *Saturday Evening Post* readers were likely to distinguish between reporting and assenting, Romanov's denials, which Brundage did not challenge in his article, were taken as Brundage's, and the public response was explosive. Brundage was pilloried in the press as a naïvely imperceptive Communist dupe. When he criticized some of his critics, John T. McGovern, legal counsel to the U.S. Olympic Association, stepped in and chastized Brundage for his shoot-from-the-hip attacks on journalists who irritated him,[32] but Brundage reacted defensively, explaining that he had merely told the press "that *I was told* by the Russians that they knew the Olympic rules and followed them." Besides, journalists are a rather ignorant lot who often cannot understand English, French, or German. Defensiveness was then followed by ingenuousness: "I do not know what you mean when you say I have attacked the Press. This I have never done."[33] If he did not smile at this remark, he should have.

Since Brundage was no novice at making public statements or at writing articles for popular magazines, he must have known he would be misunderstood. In this case, he seems to have preferred the letter to the spirit. And this was, indeed, his solution to the entire knotty problem of "state amateurs." He knew perfectly well that the Communists had set up an entire system of state schools to cultivate an athlete elite and he knew that the athletes of the Warsaw Pact were seldom gainfully employed at vocations unrelated to their physical training, but he wanted the Olympic movement to be universal, to include everyone. When attacked as pro-Communist, he was always able to point to American or European infractions of the amateur rule, like the awarding of athletic scholarships to analphabetic bruisers. Thus, when the Swiss periodical *Sport* condemned him for his acceptance of the "state amateurs," he wrote to Otto Mayer, "There are probably abuses in the USSR, but there are also abuses in the USA and European countries."[34] From this state of affairs, one might reasonably have concluded that the amateur rule was an anachronism, that it was not amenable to enforcement, and that it ought to be abolished, but Brundage continued to hope that the Soviets might gradually move in the direction of true amateurism as he understood it—if only he could get them to listen, if only he had time to write the book on amateurism that was never written. The irony is that it was the Western nations which moved—towards the Communist model of state support.

It had been possible to integrate the Communists of the smaller Slavic nations into the Olympic movement because there was national and frequently personal continuity from prewar days and it was possible to bring the USSR into the movement by recognizing its newly formed national Olympic committee; but the Chinese situation was a novel one. There had been a Chinese Olympic Committee and Chinese athletes had participated in prewar games. There were also three Chinese members of the I.O.C. However, when Nationalist China collapsed in 1949, none of the three members followed Generalissimo Chiang Kai-shek in this flight to Taiwan. At the time of Brundage's election as I.O.C. president, C. T. Wang lived in Hong Kong (a British colony), H. H. Kung lived in New York, and Tung Shou-yi had chosen to stay in Peking. A similar division scattered the members of the national Olympic committee. Who should represent China in the I.O.C. and at the Olympic Games?

Edstrøm's position wavered. He thought in January of 1952 that *both* Olympic committees, the one on Taiwan and the one on the mainland, ought to be recognized.[35] In June he ruled that *neither* China had a right to participate at Helsinki.[36] Brundage agreed.[37] Then, on the occasion of the winter games in Oslo, an attaché of the embassy of the People's Republic of China spoke to Edstrøm and to Chancellor Mayer and requested recognition of the All-China Athletic Federation, which proposed to send a team to Helsinki.[38] Edstrøm told the attaché that recognition of the All-China Athletic Federation depended on that organization's accepting Olympic rules, especially those on amateurism and on the political independence of the national Olympic committee from its own government. When the attaché seemed unresponsive, Edstrøm struck the table with his cane and marched out of the room, leaving Mayer to explain the difference between sport and politics.[39]

The Chinese representative must have understood at least part of the explanation, for the various Chinese sports federations began to seek affiliation with the international federations, a necessary step. The Fédération Internationale de Football Association (F.I.F.A.) cabled its recognition on June 19, 1952, but the most important body, the I.A.A.F., did not accept the Chinese track-and-field federation until 1954, much too late for Helsinki.[40]

Failure to secure membership in the I.A.A.F. did not deter the Communists. (After all, the I.A.A.F. had let the Russians compete in the European championships prior to formal affiliation.) The question came to a head on the very eve of the 1952 Olympics in Helsinki. On July 17, two days before the contests began, the I.O.C. listened to the arguments of both Chinese claimants to the right to represent all of China. Taiwan's representative, Gunsun Ho, made his case enthusiastically but introduced political considerations that irritated the I.O.C. members. Shen Chi-pai, a diplomat from the People's Republic's embassy in Stockholm, was even more political and displeased the members even more. Edstrøm told him tartly that the committee made "all its decisions in complete independence" and that the Chinese Communists were in no position to impose conditions or to give advice or instruction to the committee."[41] At that there were loud cheers from the members.

But what was the I.O.C. to do? Of the 51 members present, 22 wanted to exclude both teams and 29 wanted to admit both to the Helsinki games. François Piétri of France moved that neither national Olympic committee be recognized but that both Chinas be allowed to compete in Helsinki, each in the sports for which its national federation had international recognition. This ingenious motion passed with 33 votes. The following day, Brundage spoke against recognizing either national Olympic committee and against the exception which authorized participation before recognition, but the I.O.C., "inspired by sentiments of sympathy toward the Chinese athletes already en route to Helsinki," refused to reconsider.[42]

It was all in vain. Forty-one athletes and officials from the People's Republic arrived on July 29th—ten days after the start of the games. They did not compete. Since the Nationalists decided to boycott the games because of the Communists' expected appearance no Chinese were able to participate.

The Chinese puzzle began to seem bizarre. Otto Mayer's *A Travers les anneaux olympiques* tells how Edström, at Helsinki, asked for I.O.C. member Tung Shou-yi, whose residence was given as Peking. He was still there. Said Edström, "His place is here. Have him come." He came, but he was accompanied by an interpreter from the Chinese embassy in Stockholm. Since he had formerly spoken excellent English, Edström rightly assumed that the "interpreter" was present in a political rather than a linguistic capacity. Once more, he banged the table with his cane, and he ordered the Chinese to leave. Mayer notes ironically that Tung Shou-yi had recovered his ability to speak English when he appeared at the I.O.C. meeting in Sofia in 1957.[43]

Prompted by the desire for universality, the I.O.C. returned to the problem and finally decided on May 14, 1954, at the 49th Session, in Athens, by a vote of 23–21, to recognize both committees, but not before a stormy scene during which Andrianov's praises of

Charles and Minnie Lloyd Brundage, 1884

Avery Brundage, aged five

The Young Graduate, ca. 1909

Pierre de Coubertin

Mon Repos: I.O.C. Headquarters in Lausanne from 1915 to 1968 (photo by the author)

In Uniform of the U.S. Olympic
Team of 1912

At the National All-Round
Championships, 1916

Gustavus Town Kirby

Greeting Lord David Burghley (later the Marquess of Exeter) before
the U.S.-British Empire Meet, Chicago, 1930

The Successful Businessman, ca. 1930

With Comte Henri de Baillet-Latour and Sigfrid Edstrøm, March 1, 1936

Carl Diem, ca. 1936

Founder of the Pan-American Games, 1940

Leaders of the American Olympic Association, Washington, 1950. Standing (left to right): John T. McGovern, Gustavus Town Kirby, J. Lyman Bingham. Seated (left to right): Asa S. Bushnell, Avery Brundage, Kenneth L. "Tug" Wilson, Owen V. Van Camp.

On the S.S. *Valais*, Ouchy-Lausanne to Montreaux, September 7, 1946. (Left to right): José Pontes (Portugal), Comte Melchior de Polignac (France), Avery Brundage, Sigfrid Edstrøm.

Elizabeth and Avery Brundage at Olympia, 1954

LaPiñeta, Santa Barbara, California

The LaSalle Hotel, Chicago

The President, 1952

The Executive Board, ca. 1960 (left to right): Armand Massard, Avery Brundage, the Marquess of Exeter, Karl Ritter von Halt

With Chancellor Otto Mayer, ca. 1956

The Art Collector, ca. 1968

Chateau de Vidy, Lausanne: I.O.C. Headquarters (photo by Doris Bargen)

With Willi Daume

The Executive Board, 1971–1972: (first row, left to right): Hermann van Karnebeek (Holland), Lord Killanin (Ireland), Avery Brundage, Comte Jean de Beaumont (France); (standing, left to right): Juan Antonio Samaranch (Spain). Konstantin Andrianov (U.S.S.R.), Sir Adetokunbo Ademola (Nigeria), Major Sylvio de Magalhaes Padilha (Brazil), Prince Takeda (Japan) (photo courtesy the International Olympic Committee)

With Monique Berlioux, Director of the I.O.C., Munich, 1972
(photo courtesy the International Olympic Committee)

The President and the Princess. Frankfurt, late 1973 or early 1974: (left to right): Richard Mandell, Liselott Diem, Hans-Joachim Körner, Princess Mariann von Reuss Brundage, Avery Brundage, Karin Diem (photo courtesy Liselott Diem)

sport in the People's Republic brought an angry retort from the Nationalist delegate, whom Andrianov then called "a political left-over."[44] In November, both Chinas were officially invited to the Melbourne games in 1956. The People's Republic accepted with alacrity on November 20, 1954, but their Nationalist rivals protested, rejected the invitation, and then changed their minds. Brundage's position was fundamentally the same as the one he had adopted toward the Soviet Union. He told Mayer that the "Communist Chinese have agreed to our rules and we will have to assume they are following them until we have evidence to the contrary."[45] The Communists, however, were no more satisfied with the I.O.C.'s "two Chinas" solution than the Nationalists were. Brundage explained and explained. "We do not recognize Chiang Kai-shek any more than we recognize Mao Tse-tung; we make no distinction between Communists and capitalists so long as they follow our regulations."[46] Mayer was correct when he summed up the situation four years after the recognition of both committees: "The quarrel of the 'two Chinas' has been, from 1954 on, the main burden of Olympism."[47]

Before the next great crisis in the Chinese story, there was a series of petty squabbles which frustrated and exasperated Brundage, who found the entire Chinese controversy a maddening distraction from the true purpose of the Olympic movement. At a meeting of the Executive Board with all the national Olympic committees and all the international federations, in Paris in 1955, Brundage discovered that someone had crossed out the words "Formosan China" from the attendance list that had been passed around. When he complained about the schoolboy trick, Jung Kao-tang of the Communists' national Olympic committee rose to proclaim that there was only one China, which represented the entire Chinese people: "Formosa" ought to be erased. And Formosa too. Brundage told him that his remarks were out of place.[48] Tung Shou-yi, looking forward to Melbourne in 1956, demanded on behalf of the People's Republic that the bandits from Taiwan be barred, a demand seconded by Jung Kao-tang of Pekings's Olympic committee.[49] The I.O.C. refused and the Communists boycotted the games. When the Chinese Nationalists arrived in Melbourne, the Communists' flag was mistakenly, or perhaps purposely, hoisted over their quarters. More protests followed.

Relations between the I.O.C. and the Peking government deteriorated. Brundage and Tung Shou-yi were soon mired in a prolonged exchange of insults, in a kind of epistolary shouting match. From Peking came complaints about the insinuations in the I.O.C. minutes to the effect that member Tung's remarks were political. From Chicago came the request that Mr. Tung desist from political remarks of the sort which he had made at Melbourne in 1956 and in Sofia in 1957. Mr. Tung retorted that Mr. Brundage had introduced politics into sports. Furthermore, "There is only one China in the world and that is the People's Republic of China." The riposte from Chicago went out on June 1, 1958, and the counterthrust from Peking was postmarked August 19:

I am most indignant at your letter dated June 1. Evading the questions I raised in my letter of April 23, you continued your mean practice of reversing right and wrong, wantonly slandered and threatened the Chinese Olympic Committee (All-China Athletic Federation) and myself, and shamelessly [sic] tried to justify your reactionary acts. This fully reveals that you are a faithful menial of the U.S. imperialists bent on serving their plot of creating "two Chinas."

A man like you, who are staining the Olympic spirit and violating the Olympic charter, has no qualifications whatsoever to be the IOC president . . . . I feel painful . . . that the IOC is today controlled by such an imperialist like you and consequently the Olympic spirit has been grossly trampled upon.

Tung ended the letter, and the entire correspondence, by resigning from the I.O.C.[50] Since the Communists had already, earlier that year, dropped out of F.I.F.A., one suspects that his final blast was not simply the personal response of an insulted gentleman. The suspicion is strengthened by the fact that the Communists simultaneously withdrew from the international federations for basketball, cycling, shooting, swimming, track and field, weight lifting, and wrestling.[51] They did not return to international sports, other than those of the "Third World," until the end of the "Great Cultural Revolution" of the 1960s and early 1970s. By that time, Brundage had retired as I.O.C. president.

The Chinese Communists were gone, but the Russians remained and they made an all-out effort to have the Chinese Nationalists expelled from the Olympics. Although their Chinese allies had announced their departure, the Russians nonetheless moved that their national Olympic committee be recognized as the sole legitimate representative of all Chinese athletes and that the Taiwanese committee lose its recognition (even for Taiwan). The issue was debated at the 55th Session, which began in Munich on May 23, 1959. Roby suggested that the Nationalists continue to be recognized as the group responsible for Taiwan and that they change their name from "Chinese National Olympic Committee" to something more appropriate. The debate was long and heated. Since the People's Republic had resigned from the international federations as well as from the I.O.C., there was no way for Andrianov and Romanov to win a majority for their motion. Still, the Nationalists were obviously not in charge of the mainland, where the vast majority of all Chinese lived. The majority finally voted a compromise:

The Chinese Olympic Committee having its seat in Taipeh (Taiwan) will be notified by the chancellor of the International Olympic Committee that it can no longer be recognized under this name because it does not administer sport in China. The name will be stricken from the official list. If the I.O.C. is presented with a request for recognition under another name, the I.O.C. will return to the question.[52]

Brundage explained to the press that there "was no *pressure* from anyone—the action was practically unanimous and it was a purely common sense discussion, not political in any sense of the word."[53]

The public response to this decision, especially but not only in the United States, was explosive. Newspapers reported that the Nationalists had been expelled from the Olympic movement, which was a not unreasonable interpretation of the words of the resolution, and Brundage suddenly found himself in the center of another political storm. The American press was now almost unanimous in its hostility to Brundage.

Because the press misinterpreted the substance of the decision, it was generally reported that the IOC had expelled Nationalist China . . . as a result of Communist pressure in order to make room for the readmission of the PRC. The outcry from the United States buried Brundage in vitriolic correspondence.[54]

Brundage brought much of the grief upon himself by his reference to the decision as "not political in any sense of the word" and as "practically unanimous." This latter claim was challenged by Roby at a press conference held immediately after his return to the United States. Estimating the number of members present at roughly fifty, Roby claimed that Brundage had counted aloud until he reached 28 and then announced that the decision was "practically unanimous." By Roby's calculation, 22 or 24 (both figures were published) opposed or abstained from the vote. The New York *World-Telegram and Sun* for June 10 headlined the controversy: "Olympic Vote Only 28–24, Against Nationalist China, Roby Refutes Brundage Account of Expulsion." Brundage was so furious that he continued to blame Roby for the next decade.[55] While still at the Dorchester Hotel in London; he began to scribble a circular letter dated June 23:

The I.O.C. refused to recognize that the Peking Chinese controlled sport in Taiwan and as a result they withdrew entirely from the Olympic Movement. It cannot very well recognize that the Committee with headquarters in Taipei controls sport in the mainland of China, which is not the fact.

Brundage went on to suggest that Roby resign from the I.O.C.: "If they are his views [those which Brundage cited from the *World-Telegram and Sun*], one cannot understand how he can wish to continue as a member of an organization whose members and whose actions command so little of his respect."[56] Brundage did more than suggest Roby's resignation. He attempted to force him out of the committee as Baillet-Latour had forced out Jahncke in 1936. As Roby bluntly commented, "He tried to bust me. . . . He tried to throw me out."[57] Brundage did not, however, press the issue. He had his hands full as telegrams and letters of protest came in upon him like an avalanche. Protests came from the Holy Rosary Rectory of Brooklyn and from the Yale Club of New York, from the First Evangelical United Brethren Church of Iola, Kansas, and from the United States Senate.[58] Daniel J. Ferris and Kellum Johnson transmitted an A.A.U. resolution to the I.O.C.: "That the action of the International Olympic Committee . . . be condemned, and . . . that the International Olympic Committee rescind immediately its unjustified action against Nationalist China."[59] The U.S.O.C. met and asked that the I.O.C. recognize the Nationalists "under their rightful name—the Republic of China Olympic Committee."[60] Senator Thomas Dodd of Connecticut subpoened Brundage to appear before the Judiciary Committee's Internal Security Subcommittee, apparently to learn whether or not the I.O.C. was a threat to the national security of the United States, but Senator Thomas Hennings of Missouri persuaded his colleague to drop the issue.[61] When the United Press International carried a dispatch to the effect that President Eisenhower condemned the I.O.C. for its political behavior, Brundage scribbled himself a note: "Everyone is Getting Into the Act."[62] It must have seemed that way. By August he wrote, "The country seems to have gone off on an emotional binge in unprecedented proportions."[63] He felt himself nearly alone, "confronting 175,000,000 misinformed people."[64]

By the time the newspapers had recovered from the binge, the Department of State had become aroused. The immediate cause for distress was a letter from Otto Mayer to the Italian Olympic Committee (March 21, 1960), on arrangements for the 1960 games. Mayer stated that the title of the Chinese Olympic Committee (on Taiwan) was "Olympic Committee of the Republic of China" (under which title the Nationalists had been readmitted), but the Chinese athletes were to march into Rome's Olympic stadium behind the placarded name "Taiwan." In the view of the Department of State, "The effort to force the athletes from the Republic of China to adopt the name 'Taiwan' in place of the name of their country . . . would . . . be offensive and unacceptable to the Chinese . . . and would be widely regarded as a politically discriminatory act designed in effect to exclude the free Chinese athletes from participation."[65] To this Brundage replied,

The International Olympic Committee does not deal with Governments and does not propose to become involved in political controversies. Its Executive Board has therefore recommended that its rules indicate more clearly that Olympic Committees represent the geographical areas in which they operate, about which there can be no dispute, and not Governments.[66]

Since the I.O.C. dealt only with geographical areas which had governments, it was not a very helpful distinction, but the diplomats in Washington had to be content with it. At approximately this time, Brundage showed his exasperation with the conflict in a handwritten note to himself:

AB
Clever fellow
Imperialist
Fascist
Capitalist
Nazi
& now Communist[67]

It is probably just as well that the Department of State had no inkling about Brundage's more private thoughts about the Chinese controversy. After nearly ten years of trying to settle, once and for all, the dust raised by political antagonisms, Brundage began to think the USSR was right: "There may be some merit to their position,"[68] i.e., let Peking represent China and forget about Taipei. Although the controversy was far from ended, Brundage had a respite until the mid-1960s (and it was his successor who had to deal with the Chinese problem that disrupted the 1976 Olympics in Montreal).

Brundage accepted the "two Chinas" policy, but he rejected a similar solution to the German problem. It was his attachment to German culture in general and to his German friends in particular which impelled him stubbornly to seek a single Germany in the world of sports when there were manifestly two Germanies in the domain of politics. This state of affairs was another result of the war, which ended with Nazi Germany divided and occupied by American, British, French, and Russian armies. The occupation zones of the three Western allies became the Federal Republic of Germany; that of the Russians became the German Democratic Republic. The Bonn government claimed jurisdiction for the whole of Germany and the I.O.C. was inclined to honor the claim.

The West Germans set up their national Olympic committee on September 24, 1949, one day after the establishment of the Federal Republic. The first president of the committee was Adolf Friedrich zu Mecklenburg, who was of course also an I.O.C. member, but he found the task too onorous and turned the office over to his colleague Karl Ritter von Halt on January 6, 1951. Another of Brundage's close friends, Carl Diem, became the committee's secretary.

Brundage was eager to have the Germans back in the Olympics and was shocked at the Copenhagen session in 1950 to find "so much bitterness and hatred" directed at Germany.[69] The resistance to the German I.O.C. members on the part of Holland's P. W. Scharroo and several other members has already been discussed. Some of it was allayed when Peco Bauwens, vice president of Bonn's new committee, read a statement, apparently drafted by Diem, in which he expressed sorrow for the atrocities committed under Nazi rule.[70] The Executive Board decided unanimously on August 29, 1950, to recommend speedy recognition of the West German commitee by the entire I.O.C.[71] The next opportunity was the I.O.C. session in Vienna in May of 1951.

On April 22, 1951, two weeks before the I.O.C. session, the East Germans founded *their* national Olympic committee and informed both the I.O.C. and the West German committee of their willingness to cooperate in the best interests of the Olympic movement.[72] Although their official sports journal, *Deutsches Sport-Echo*, had sneered at the 1948 Olympics as an example of "misleading cosmopolitanism," the East Germans had changed their minds (or had them changed by the new wind that blew from Moscow).[73] Willy-nilly, the I.O.C. found itself once again unable to avoid what it most disliked: political controversy. While the Federal Republic claimed to represent all Germans, even those living in what they referred to in those days as the "Soviet Occupied Zone," the German Democratic Republic maintained that it was a completely independent state with rights to diplomatic representation, United Nations membership, and, of course, its own Olympic team. The I.O.C. had three choices: it might agree with the Bonn government and thus follow the policy of the United States and other NATO nations; it might accept the East Germans as representatives of an independent state; it might act on the hint of willingness to cooperate and attempt to bring the two Germanies together as—for Olympic purposes—one nation. The I.O.C. chose the third option.

The Vienna session opened on May 7 and the I.O.C. recognized the national Olympic committee of the USSR without serious dissent. The next day, the German question was discussed for two and a half hours. Several influential members, including Exeter, Piétri, Seeldrayers, and Mezö, suggested recognition of *both* committees if they agreed to form a single German team and Brundage remarked that the formation of a united team would be "une nouvelle victoire pour le mouvement olympique." The I.O.C. determined to recognize West Germany's committee, which it did without dissent, and to invite representatives from both German committees to Lausanne later that month.[74] There, at I.O.C. headquarters in Chateau Mon Repos, they could explore the possibility of forming a single organization. Since the Federal Republic was larger, more advanced economically, and—at that time—more powerful in sports as well, it was the unspoken assumption of most I.O.C. members that the Federal Republic would be the dominant power in any combined team. The German Democratic Republic, on both ideological and practical grounds, was understandably reluctant to sacrifice its autonomy. The negotiations were prolonged and difficult.

The two sets of delegates met several times, and the road to a single team proved an extremely rocky one. When the first round of talks resulted in a stalemate, Brundage stepped in to facilitate the discussions. He met in Lausanne on May 22 with von Halt, Kurt Edel, and other members of the two rival committees. To West German Chancellor Konrad Adenauer, von Halt wrote that he had met privately with the entire Executive Board on the 21st and made sure of their support; Brundage was especially understanding.[75] Credit may be due to von Halt's stubbornness, to Brundage's persuasiveness, or perhaps to the effects of a Swiss ambiance; the East Germans agreed to be part of the team which Bonn planned to send to the 1952 games in Helsinki. The agreement was signed, but celebrations were premature. When the Communist delegation returned to the German Democratic Republic, it was berated for its weakness and the agreement was repudiated. Brundage was simultaneously outraged and relieved. He was able to feel, as with the People's Republic of China, that *he* had done his utmost to make the Olympic movement truly universal. If *they* persisted in petty, childish, and irresponsible behavior, it was not his fault.

The two committees resumed their negotiations in November, first in Kassel, then in Hamburg. And then came the fiasco of Copenhagen. Arrangements were made for the Executive Board to meet in the Danish capital with both delegations on February 8, 1952. Edstrøm was anxious to overcome the difficulties which had plagued the negotiations: "It is essential that East Germany participates in Helsinki."[76] Unfortunately, the emissaries from East Germany arrived late in Copenhagen and refused to walk the 300 meters that separated their hotel from the West Germans. Edstrøm, Brundage, Otto Mayer, and the Bonn delegation waited impatiently from 10:00 A.M. to 7:30 P.M., at which moment Edstrøm shouted "Finish!" He banged his cane on the table, and left. The East Germans later offered their official explanation: Kurt Edel and his associates had arrived in the Danish capital after a difficult plane ride and they were tired. The true explanation remains a mystery.[77] The German team which competed in Helsinki consisted entirely of athletes from the West.

With sponsorship from Andrianov, the East Germans renewed their quest for I.O.C. recognition at the 49th Session in Athens in 1954. Brundage noted at that time that the I.O.C. had endured torrents of abuse from the East German press, which had reviled the committee as a conspirational gang of imperialist thugs. Andrianov alleged that Edel wished to apologize for this journalistic mistreatment, but the Greek government had denied him a visa.

Von Halt complained that the Communists' committee was not fully independent of its own government, an odd objection from a man who had been a German member in the 1930s. The I.O.C. decided to postpone its decision for another year. The vote was 31–14.[78]

The Communists attained a part of their goal at the 50th Session in Paris in 1955. Edel, a former worker, had been replaced by Heinz Schöbel, a publisher and a man more conversant with the folkways of aristocrats and millionaires. The night before the session opened, Schöbel met with Brundage at the Hotel Carillon. Brundage asked bluntly, "Are you or are you not a political organization?" Schöbel gave a simple reply, "Nein." On June 17, the national Olympic committee of the German Democratic Republic was accorded provisional recognition by a vote of 27–7. They were told, however, that they must contest the 1956 games as part of a combined German team. In fact, the I.O.C. voted that "this recognition will lapse automatically" if an agreement on a combined team proved impossible.[79] Agreement was possible, largely due to the skillful efforts of Willi Daume of Bonn's committee (his reward was membership in the I.O.C.). The German team at Cortina d'Ampezzo was made up of 58 *Wintersportler* from the West and 18 from the East; at Melbourne, the numbers were 138 and 37.[80]

The agreements of 1956 held up—more or less—for the games of 1960, celebrated in Rome. There were, however, nasty quarrels about symbolism. Struggling to achieve diplomatic recognition on all fronts, the German Democratic Republic wanted to fly its own flag, which was anathema to the West Germans, who still maintained that they alone represented *all* Germans. Brundage suggested that both use the black-red-gold flag common to both but with the Olympic rings instead of the hammer and calipers which were emblazoned upon the center of the Communists' banner. The two sides agreed, the East quickly and the West reluctantly, only after Daume and von Halt were able to calm the enraged Adenauer.[81]

There was another matter which troubled Brundage. There were reports that athletes of the German Democratic Republic were rewarded with cash prizes. He wrote to Schöbel, "If the stories in the newspapers are true, of course all your athletes will be ineligible for Olympic . . . competition."[82] The reports were immediately denied; there was *no* professional sport of any kind in East Germany.[83] Subsequently, when defectors to the West offered sworn testimony to the effect that they had been paid while "amateur" athletes, Schöbel would respond that such charges were simply repetitions of lies and slanders that the German Democratic Republic had already refuted.[84]

Brundage's determination to overcome political obstacles can be gauged from an anecdote which he used on many occasions. As the combined German team marched into Rome's Stadio Olimpico, President Gronchi of Italy, standing beside Brundage during the opening ceremony, marveled that the I.O.C. had achieved the impossible; it had obtained—if but for a moment—the unification which had eluded the United Nations. Brundage beamed. Reunification had indeed proven impossible in politics, "But in sport, we do such things."[85] It was a moment he never forgot. It was for him the perfect symbol of the games as a social movement capable of bringing divided peoples together. He turned often to this theme in his speeches:

Another example of an important victory for sport over politics has been the united German team that has now appeared on four different occasions at the Olympic Games in 1956 and in 1960. . . . The spectacle of East and West German athletes in the same uniform marching behind the same leaders and the same flag is an inspiration under present political conditions and a great service to all the German people who wish for a united country.[86]

Then, on August 13, 1961, came *die Mauer*.

In a desperate attempt to halt the flow of mostly young and skilled workers and professionals that streamed from East to West, the German Democratic Republic literally walled itself off from the Federal Republic. Unready to act with military means and helpless to remove the Berlin wall diplomatically, Bonn's response was to impose economic and cultural sanctions. The national Olympic committee joined with the Deutscher Sport-Bund (German Sports Federation) in a boycott of inter-German athletic competition (August 16, 1961). Otto Mayer informed both sides, however, that the I.O.C. still insisted upon a combined team for the games to be celebrated in Tokyo in 1964.[87] A new series of meetings began, not to end until February 6, 1963, when Brundage brought both sides to a new agreement. (To carry out the agreement, fourteen meetings of the two national Olympic committees were required and ninety-six conversations among the national sports federations.[88])

The Olympic agreement was, however, undermined by the I.A.A.F., led since 1946 by Exeter, who was also vice president of the I.O.C. The track-and-field federation decided to recognize a fully independent East Germany in 1964 and allowed separate teams to compete in the European championships in 1966.[89] Andrianov asked the I.O.C. to follow suit, but the members dragged their feet.[90] At Madrid, on October 6, 1965, the I.O.C. gave up a little more ground—the German Democratic Republic was granted the right to enter a separate team at Mexico City in 1968, but both teams were to fly the flag with the Olympic rings and to share the choral theme from Beethoven's Ninth Symphony as their victory anthem.[91]

At Rome in the spring of 1966, indefatigable Andrianov achieved a goal he had labored toward since 1958, the election of Heinz Schöbel to the I.O.C. (to replace von Halt, who had died on August 5, 1964). Since Brundage had written a laudatory preface to Schöbel's book on the ancient Olympic Games, *Olympia und seine Spiele* (1966), and Schöbel was planning a lavishly illustrated and utterly uncritical biography called *The Four Dimensions of Avery Brundage* (1968), we can be certain that Brundage favored the affable publisher's election to membership. The Communists courted Brundage assiduously and he began to feel that the sports administrators of the Federal Republic were less cooperative than those of the German Democratic Republic.[92] When Albert Mayer opined that the former showed "bad will," Brundage agreed, "You are right about the situation in Germany."[93]

At the 67th Session in Mexico City in 1968, the I.O.C. finally voted 44–4 for full and complete and unqualified acceptance of the

German Democratic Republic, with its own team, its own flag, its own anthem. When in 1972 the East Germans marched into the Olympisches Stadion in Munich, they "achieved their ultimate objective";[94] they quite literally flaunted their flag before their hosts from the Federal Republic, who had publicly to acknowledge East German legitimacy as well as East German athletic prowess. For Brundage, however, it was a defeat, a reminder of the frailty of Olympic ideals and of their inability to dam the tides of *Realpolitik*.

Hours, days, months, years went by while the I.O.C. debated the Russian demand for a seat on the Executive Board, the Nationalist Chinese claim that Taipei's committee represented the mainland as well as Taiwan, the East German insistence upon full autonomy. None of these matters seemed of great importance to the man in the street, glancing as he does at the headlines of his newspaper before studying the sports pages to find out if the home team won. Brundage considered the Olympic movement as a secular religion distilling the ideals of fair play, good sportsmanship, and amateurism into an idealistic elixir, but the average American, Austrian, or Japanese was more interested in Wilma Rudolph winning the 100 meters in world-record time, in Tony Sailer sweeping downhill to three gold medals in skiing, or in Takashi Ono challenging Russia's Boris Schaklin for the gymnastics championship. All the rest was secondary.

For the man in the street, the integration of the Communists into the Olympic movement meant that the contests were athletically better because many of the greatest athletes were from Communist homelands and that the games were now more than ever "representative" sport in the sense that spectators now identified with this or that athlete or team on the basis of ideology as well as nationalism and racism. Emil Zatopek represented, willy-nilly, a way of life. That ideological and nationalistic identification often threatened to distort admiration for athletic achievement *per se* was, of course, a problem that bothered Brundage enormously, but one cannot miss the fact that the 1952 games in Helsinki had an excitement even greater than those of 1948 in London. A close contest between two Americans ought, theoretically, to be as attractive to spectators as one between an American and a Russian, but, practically, nationalism and ideology tend almost invariably to increase the emotional involvement—for better or for worse.

There were indications in 1952 that the Russians were not overwhelmed by the Olympic spirit. The Kremlin refused to allow the Olympic torch to be carried across the territory of the Soviet Union. The Russian athletes lived not in Helsinki's Olympic Village but in their own isolated quarters near the USSR's naval base at Porkkala. When Russian and American athletes embraced after their events, in mutual exhausted congratulations, there seemed always to be a Soviet official standing by to monitor the spontaneous admiration.

Despite the anxieties of officialdom, the athletes had a field day. Russian competition seemed to inspire the American track-and-field squad; the men won 14 gold medals, the Russians none. Perhaps everyone did better in the mood of intensified competition; in the 22 track-and-field events, 17 Olympic records were broken. Meanwhile, discus-thrower Nina Romaschkova and shot-putter Galina Zybina began a long tradition of Russian superiority in women's track and field. The Americans dominated the swimming, the Russians the gymnastics; the Americans did better at weight lifting, the Russians at wrestling. The most memorable performance of the games was that of Emil Zatopek of Czechoslovakia, who began with a victory in the 10,000-meter race. He lowered his own Olympic record from 1948 by 42 seconds. In the 5,000 meters he defeated the Algerian runner Alain Mimoun. (The same day Dana Zatopek set an Olympic record in the javelin and won a gold medal of her own.) Zatopek suddenly announced his intent to compete in the marathon as well. In that race, at about the 15-mile point, he is said to have remarked to the favored English runner James Peters, "Excuse me, I haven't run a Marathon before, but don't you think we ought to go a bit faster?"[95] Zatopek then accelerated and finished more than two minutes ahead of the runnerup.

It was probably inevitable that the newspapers concentrated on the "battle of the giants" and published daily statistics on the number of unofficial points harvested by the Russians and the Americans. Brundage deplored this, of course, just as he deplored the breakdown in sportsmanship in the soccer tournament when the Uruguayan team expressed its disappointment by assaulting the referee: "This is the most disgraceful thing that has ever happened at the Olympic Games."[96] Brundage wrote to Uruguay to demand that the offenders be punished for their "disgraceful" and "inexcusable" attack and he was assured that the players had been properly disciplined,[97] but there was no way for him to diminish the tendency to transform the games into a symbolic confrontation between "Communism and the Free World" or, as it was perceived from the other side of the fence, between "Capitalism and Socialism."

By no means were all of Brundage's Olympic problems political in origin. With each successive Olympiad, the games had grown larger and more complicated and more difficult to plan. The host city for a modern Olympic faces enormous logistical problems as well as a huge financial burden. Construction is always more complicated than expected, strikes delay progress, engineers discover flaws that need to be corrected, bureaucratic quibbles stall necessary decisions. At Rome in 1949, the games of the XVI Olympiad were awarded to Melbourne after a close contest with partisans of Buenos Aires. Brundage was happy about the prospects of an Olympic "debut" in the Far East, but Melbourne fell behind its construction schedule and began to hint at postponement. Brundage's characteristic response was to fly down to Australia in the spring of 1955 and let loose what he referred to as "a mild atomic explosion."[98] (Atomic tests were then common in the Pacific, but he may have picked up the image from a cartoon in the Adelaide *News* for April 12, 1955; the cartoon shows a mushroom-shaped cloud and a policeman shouting, "Quick! Shield those eyes—Mr. Brundage is in town making another statement on the Games!") He cajoled and berated the organizing committee and received promises of a speedup. Although he blithely assured the I.O.C. at its Paris session in 1955 that the "only regret expressed was that I had not come sooner,"[99] he had certainly stirred ire with his frank remarks about incompetence and he admitted to Otto Mayer that he had "never had such rude, uncouth and ill-mannered treatment in my life."[100]

Brundage had good reason to have been furious with the Australian organizers. On October 10, 1951, four years before his visit, the New York *Times* carried a Reuters dispatch proclaiming AUSTRALIAN OFFICIAL SEES OLYMPIC SHIFT POSSIBLE. Hugh R. Weir, an I.O.C. member since 1946, was quoted to the effect that Melbourne might not be able to carry out its commitments. Early in 1953 Brundage positively begged Weir for an honest answer to his questions:

I urge and beseech you, if there is the slightest doubt in your mind that the 1956 Games will be staged properly so that they will be a credit to Australia and to the Olympic Movement, to give them up now and let us select another venue before it is too late. Almost four years have been wasted and we cannot wait any longer.[101]

Weir telephoned Brundage and asked him to withhold judgment.[102] Brundage also kept after Australia's other I.O.C. member, Lewis Luxton (elected 1951). He sent Weir and Luxton a five-page letter of inquiry in March.[103] Brundage's temper rose several additional degrees when he discovered that it was impossible for Melbourne to arrange for the equestrian events that had been an important part of the Olympics since 1912 (and which were especially dear to many of the more aristocratic I.O.C. members). The problem was Australia's strict quarantine laws, which the government was unready to relax for the games. Brundage wrote to the head of the organizing committee, W. S. Kent Hughes, that the games had to be moved.[104] Weir was upset and pointed out that the I.O.C. certainly had the power to modify its own rules to allow the equestrian events to be contested elsewhere.[105] The I.O.C. was flexible on the matter and the Swedish Olympic Committee volunteered to carry out the events in Stockholm.

Although Brundage's visit probably stimulated the Australians to accelerate the pace of the construction, ill will lingered in the wake of the storm and Brundage had new occasions for indignation shortly before the games when Edgar S. Tanner, an Australian journalist, referred to him in the Sydney *Daily Express* as a "voluble old fusspot."[106] Chancellor Mayer rushed to defend President Brundage and Hugh Weir professed to be astonished at Mayer's intemperate language.[107] Brundage defended his defender and W. S. Kent Hughes entered the fray and remarked that Brundage's public assault on him at the time of Brundage's visit had caused the worst attacks, public and private, of his entire career.[108]

By this time the athletes and the officials were in Melbourne for what were, in November in the southern hemisphere, the summer games. The ruffled feathers were soon back in place and Brundage graciously thanked Hughes, Weir, and Luxton in his opening address to the I.O.C.'s 52nd Session: "It was a huge task to organize this vast and complicated enterprise and it required the concerted efforts of all for success." Brundage couldn't resist a last jab: "It is not to be denied that we were worried and had our doubts at times, until we discovered that Australians are different—that while they do insist on doing things their own peculiar way, when they say a thing will be done they mean it."

Brundage went on to speak of the Olympic truce:

. . . in the Golden Age there was an Olympic truce and all warfare stopped during the period of the Games, [but now] after two thousand years of civilization, we stop the Games and continue our wars. One of the objectives of the Games is to develop international goodwill. Alas, the Olympic Movement has no soldiers and no money. It, therefore, cannot stop warfare, but it can and does set a good example, and only when the politicians of the world adopt those principles of fair play and good sportsmanship which prevail on the fields of amateur sport will there no longer be necessity for wars.[109]

The remarks were topical and not merely the result of his interest in ancient history. The "Olympic peace" of November 1956 was violated not by one but by two wars.

After a lengthy controversy over Egypt's right to have seized the Suez Canal from its mostly British and French stockholders, Prime Ministers Anthony Eden of England and Guy Mollet of France conspired to arrange an Israeli attack upon Egypt (which, of course, had for eight years maintained that it was at war with Israel). The

Israelis struck on October 29. Within days, British and French forces parachuted in to "protect" the canal from the Israelis, and the entire Middle East seemed about to explode. The crisis was settled when the United States decided to join its principal adversary, the Soviet Union, to force its principal allies, Britain and France, to withdraw. The British, French, and Israeli governments gave in, with varying degrees of bitterness, but the effects of the war were felt in Melbourne when Egypt, Lebanon, and Iraq decided to boycott the games rather than compete against British, French, and Israeli athletes.

Two days before the Israeli attack, Prime Minister Imre Nagy of Hungary announced that his country wished to renounce its treaty of alliance with the Soviet Union and to hold free elections. Russian tanks rumbled into Budapest three days later. The non-Communist world watched nervously and ineffectually as the Hungarian people were slaughtered by their "ally." John Foster Dulles provided the Hungarians with unlimited amounts of verbal aid and thousands of refugees fled to Austria and from there to asylum in West Germany, France, England, and the United States.

Holland and Spain decided to boycott the Olympics in order to protest the Russian invasion. Switzerland's national Olympic committee asked that all belligerent nations be barred from the games and, when that request was turned down, voted to keep the Swiss team at home. When the Swiss I.O.C. member Albert Mayer persuaded the committee to change its decision, it was too late to arrange for transportation to Melbourne (at least this was the explanation Mayer offered to Brundage[110]).

Brundage's response was, once again, predictable:

Every civilized person recoils in horror at the savage slaughter in Hungary, but that is no reason for destroying the nucleus of international cooperation and goodwill we have in the Olympic Movement. The Olympic Games are contests between individuals and not between nations.

We hope that those who have withdrawn from the Melbourne Games will reconsider. In an imperfect world, if participation in sport is to be stopped every time the politicians violate the laws of humanity, there will never be any international contests. Is it not better to try to expand the sportsmanship of the athletic field into other areas?[111]

The I.O.C. voted unanimously to censure the national Olympic committees which boycotted the games: "The I.O.C., an organization concerned only with sports, expresses its sadness and regret at the abstentions, which it considers contrary to Olympic ideals."[112] There was some talk of punishment,—e.g., exclusion from the 1960 games,—but the proposals were quickly dropped. For his part, Holland's Scharroo took the view that the boycott was not "d'inspiration *politique*, mais seulement du *sentiment*,"[113] a distinction which must have made sense to him.

Ironically, the Hungarians *did* compete. It was not at all certain that Hungary would be represented. Part of the team was on a Russian ship bound for Melbourne; the rest was in Prague, waiting for air connections. Since the border between Czechoslovakia and Hungary was sealed, ruling out any return to Budapest, the officials and athletes decided to go on to Melbourne. Their travel was arranged by Otto Mayer, who persuaded Air France to provide the transportation.[114] When the athletes arrived in Melbourne, they were greeted by cheers from Hungarian exiles already in Australia.

Tensions were high as the games began, but there is a power in ritual and ceremony which exerts a force of its own. Gradually, most of the athletes were, most of the time, caught up in their competitions and able to forget wars and rumors of wars. While the Americans once again edged the Russians in weight lifting, the Japanese men and the Hungarian women gave the Russians a metaphorical run for their money in gymnastics. The most spectacular race was the 10,000 meters in which Russia's Vladimir Kuts defeated England's Gordon Pirie by confusing him with a series of slowdowns and speedups. Bobby Morrow of the United States earned more medals (100 meters, 200 meters, 400-meter relay), but Kuts became a legend on the basis of his Svengali-like tactics. Sprinting at 1500-meter pace, slowing, sprinting again, walking, waving Pirie ahead and then dashing past him, Kuts disoriented his rival and became the Soviet Union's first gold medalist in men's track and field.

Too psychologically distracted and distressed to concentrate upon sports, the Hungarian athletes did less well than in 1952. In water polo, however, they trounced the Russians by a score of 4–0 in a match definitely not characterized by Olympic goodwill. Shortly before the end of the contest, a Russian who had been pushed about by the Hungarians butted one of his tormenters in the eye. Blood streamed into the pool, tempers flared, and the Russians decided to leave the water and forfeit the match, which they could not have won in any event. For their part, 45 Hungarians elected to defect to the West.

That the Communist bloc lost another athlete, Czechoslovakia's Olga Fiktova, was due more to Venus than to Mars. She won a gold medal in the discus. Harold Connolly of the United States won one in the hammer throw. Each won the other's heart. Although the Czech team was closely watched by political agents, Olga managed to steal away several times and, by the time the games were over, the two were engaged. She returned to Prague, he followed, diplomatic problems were eventually overcome, and they were married on March 27, 1957, with Emil Zatopek as best man.[115] Venus also appeared in the guise of a CIA agent, at least in the version of Olympic history published by the Soviet journal *Literaturnaya Gazeta*, which alleged that American intelligence had used beautiful women to distract and befuddle Russian athletes.[116]

There was intentional as well as unintentional comedy. At a luncheon at the Menzies Hotel on November 26, Brundage explained to an amused audience that he preferred to speak in English because his German was dangerous: he had once referred to his friend Carl Diem as the rector of the "Hochschule für *Liebes*übungen" rather than "*Leibes*übungen" (i.e., erotic exercises rather than physical exercises)[117]. The good mood became general at the closing ceremony when the athletes spontaneously broke ranks, left their national teams, and mingled in *their* joyous celebration of the games they had experienced together, more or less peacefully, in a world that remained tragically bellicose. Even Brundage, stickler for the rules that he was, realized that the brotherhood and sisterhood demonstrated by the athletes was a moving embodiment of the Olympic spirit.

Even before the opening ceremony of the XVI Olympiad's

games, plans were well advanced for those of the XVII, a necessary consequence of the increased size and complexity of the games. In Paris, in 1955, the I.O.C. decided to have the 1960 summer games at Rome (by a vote of 35–24 over Lausanne) and the winter games at Squaw Valley, California (by a vote of 32–30 over Innsbruck).[118] It had been a disappointment to Coubertin that the Romans had been unable to carry through their commitment to host the games in 1908. Now, Brundage was elated that the modern Olympics were to be celebrated on an ancient site rich with classical associations. (That imagery drawn from the gladiatorial combats, far more popular among the ancient Romans than the Greek athletic festivals, was now available to critics of the games is something he simply had to accept.) Implicit in his later account of the games is the suggestion that the religion of Coubertin had come to Rome almost as a challenge to the religion of Pope John XXIII. Brundage wrote politely of John's hospitality (he entertained the I.O.C. and blessed the athletes), but Brundage also contrasted the games with the "medieval asceticism that considered all physical activity not only useless, but perhaps harmful to mental and spiritual development."[119] Citing the accomplishments of the games, Brundage concluded, once again, that Coubertin had been justified when he spoke of the Olympic movement as a "modern religion."[120]

The organizing committee commissioned Italy's most famous architect, Pier Luigi Nervi, to design a sports complex worthy of the occasion. The committee also made imaginative use of the old as well as the new: "Basketball, a modern game, was played in Nervi's modern Palazetto; wrestling, an ancient sport, was staged in the ancient Basilica of Maxentius."[121]

Preparations for the winter games at Squaw Valley went less smoothly. Shortly after Melbourne's delays sent Brundage into a rage and down to Australia, he was confronted by similar problems in what was more or less his backyard. In the summer of 1955 he expressed his fear that badly managed winter games might give the United States "a black eye."[122] Others who investigated the matter began to speak of the preparations as a pathetic mess of monumental proportions.[123] One of the difficulties seems to have been a conflict of interest that arose because the chairman of the organizing committee owned some of the land intended as a site for the games; another problem was that the predicted costs escalated in a now familiar pattern. Eventually, the chairman left the committee and the California legislature passed a series of bills in which the original commitment of $1,000,000 in state funds climbed gradually to the mountainous sum of $8,990,000.[124]

The embarrassment of the committee's repeated requests for more aid was ameliorated somewhat by the decision to omit the bobsled races and, thereby, to save the money necessary for bobsled facilities. The I.O.C. was ready to accept the organizing committee's request to drop the races because only two nations had indicated their desire to compete in this exotic event, but the bobsledders were given time to demonstrate that there was widespread support for their passion. A year later, however, the bobsled enthusiasts were able to report that a meager five nations wanted to compete; the I.O.C. voted 22–5 not to insist that Squaw Valley include the races.[125] This decision greatly upset the Comte R. de la Frégeolière of the Fédération Internationale de Bobsleigh et Tobogganing. He protested to the organizing committee and to the I.O.C., and Albert Mayer, who agreed with the Count, sent Brundage a letter full of accusations: He complained that Brundage had given up too easily on the bobsled question, that Brundage had never given Switzerland a fair chance to host the games, that Brundage had kept Swiss members from the Executive Board and from other important I.O.C. committees.[126] Mayer felt that Brundage helped his opponents more than his friends, a backhanded tribute to the American's attempts at fairness.

Even as Brundage worked to resolve the problems of Squaw Valley, he learned of a scandal that threatened to besmirch the reputation of the U.S.O.C. There was conclusive evidence that team members of the Los Angeles Water Polo Club had conspired among themselves to allow the Southern California Water Polo Club to win a ludicrously easy 15–2 victory and thus to qualify for the next stage of the elimination tournament which selected the American entry for Melbourne.[127] The Los Angeles players preferred to see another club from southern California advance rather than the rival team from San Francisco, which would have gone on if Los Angeles hadn't lost by such a lopsided score. Players who did not want to participate in a fixed contest testified that their coach had ordered them to play to lose. The U.S Olympic Water Polo Committee investigated and concluded that the game had indeed been fixed, but the investigators voted not to alter the results. Brundage felt that the decision was a coverup and that the case against the committee's decision was "a damning indictment of both the United States Olympic Committee and the Amateur Athletic Union."[128] Since one of the members of the investigating committee was Jay E. Mahoney, the son of Brundage's old antagonist Jeremiah T. Mahoney, the situation involved the clash of personalities as well as of principles. Young Mahoney, unconvinced by a stack of sworn testimony to the contrary, informed Brundage that there was no evidence of a fix. His father agreed and, moreover, threatened Brundage with a law suit if Brundage did not let sleeping dogs lie.[129] That seems to have been the end of the matter, except for Brundage's brooding sense that virtue was threatened on every side by vice, that cheaters were now coddled as they were not when *he* was president of the American Olympic Association.

Perhaps the 1960 games restored some of Brundage's faith. Both the winter and the summer games were celebrated without the political tensions that had marred the games of 1952 and 1956. There was no Korean War, no Suez War, no Hungarian Revolution to cloud the skies over Squaw Valley and Rome. The People's Republic of China had withdrawn to occupy itself with Mao's "Great Cultural Revolution" and the Russians were on their best behavior. In fact, the winter games were remarkable partly for their uneventfulness. The handsome Austrian skier Toni Sailer had dazzled the spectators at Cortina d'Ampezzo in 1956 with his victories in the downhill and slalom contests; at Squaw Valley, the Alpine medals went to three different men from three different countries while the Finns, Norwegians, and Swedes divided up the honors for men's cross-country and for ski-jumping. Hayes Jenkins and Carol Heiss, both Americans, were the best individual skaters while a Canadian couple won the pairs competition.

The summer games were the occasion of Brundage's proud boast that the I.O.C. had brought the two Germanies together. There were other signs of international amity, and Russian and American athletes seemed, almost as if by prepared script, to wish each other good luck before their contests and to rush tearfully into one another's arms after them. Among the unforgettable performers was Wilma Rudolph, whose acknowledged supremacy as a sprinter left great runners like England's Dorothy Hyman and Germany's Jutta Heine to race for the silver medals. Rudolph symbolized the arrival of the black female athlete as Jessie Owens had represented the importance of black male athletes a generation earlier; neither Rudolph nor Owens was the first black Olympian, but they, by their performances, by their personalities, perhaps even by their sheer physical beauty, became the symbols. Among the oarsmen, the *Weltwunder* was the German team, coached by the unorthodox Karl Adam. They won three gold medals and a silver one. While Italy's Francesco de Piccoli boxed his way to a gold medal in the heavyweight division, the best light-heavyweight fighter was a boy from Louisville, then named Cassius Clay, subsequently to be known as Muhammed Ali or simply as "The Greatest."

Inevitably, there were unhappy moments. The gymnastics and boxing matches were marred by what the spectators took to be biased judgments on the part of Russian judges. Curiously, at least one of the reporters, the novelist Rudolf Hagelstange, faulted Brundage for not stepping in to right the wrongs.[130]

From his perspective as apostle of amateurism, Brundage was able to take a somewhat vindictive pleasure in the defeat of the American athlete Ray Norton. A favorite in the 200-meter race, Norton lost to Italy's Livio Berruti and then added to his misery by a misstep in the finals of the 400-meter relay which caused the American team to be disqualified. In his private notes, Brundage wrote, "Failure of Norton at Rome, Divine retribution because he obviously had a contract with [the San Francisco] 49'ers, although he swore that he did not."[131] Once again, as in his undergraduate short story, thoughts of retribution. Brundage took pleasure of a less punitive sort when he was reelected president of the I.O.C. by acclamation.[132] If the world continued to misunderstand the amateur code, at least his colleagues appreciated him and his leadership.

In the aftermath of the Roman games, the I.O.C. decided to establish an International Olympic Academy, which Carl Diem and Jean Ketseas had advocated since 1947. The 43rd Session (1949) had accepted the idea in principle, the Deutsche Olympische Gesellschaft provided the financial support, and the Greek Olympic Committee took over the administration. The Academy opened on June 14, 1961. The president was Prince George of Hannover, until the Greek government decided that the I.O.A. had to be headed by a Greek citizen. The purpose of the Academy was purely educational. Distinguished scholars and experienced sports administrators expounded upon Olympic ideals and discussed Olympic problems.[133] It is curious that Brundage, while not opposing the institution, gave it relatively little attention.

CHAPTER X

NEW FORMS,
NEW LEADERS

From 1936, when Brundage was elected to the I.O.C. as a reward for his defense of the Berlin games against the threat of boycott, to 1972, when the end of his third term as president was marred by an act of terrorism, the members of the committee had maintained that the Olympic movement had to be protected from political interference (or, as they liked to say, *l'ingérence politique*). Many of the committee's most severe problems seemed to derive, either directly or indirectly, from the sphere of politics, which the members wanted devoutly to avoid. This was true not only in the I.O.C.'s relationship with the national Olympic committees but even within the committee itself. The most persistent pressure came from the Russians.

Even before their entry into the Olympic movement, the Russians had demanded a seat on the Executive Board. They had been rather indignantly refused, but they had every right, once admitted to the I.O.C., to repeat the request. In fact, they called for a complete reorganization of the entire I.O.C.

The Russians' view of I.O.C. membership was totally at variance with Coubertin's. His aristocratic conception was that the I.O.C., an organization free from all political ties, sent *its* delegates out to the various countries of the world to stimulate Olympic ideals and to encourage the formation of national Olympic committees. In no sense were the distinguished members of the I.O.C. to be considered representatives of governments or nations. Within the circle of like-minded aristocrats and wealthy patrons of sport, decisions were to be reached through a process of gentlemanly discussion, a process which presupposed a consensus on basic values. This consensus had been threatened by the rise of Fascism in the 1920s and 1930s, but the Nazi and Fascist members of the I.O.C. were either marginally active within the committee (like Italy's General Giorgio Vaccaro) or lukewarm in their commitment to official ideology (like Germany's Karl Ritter von Halt). The Russians were, ideologically, a different kettle of fish.

The Russian members, loyally supported by their colleagues from the other Communist nations, assumed political conflict between themselves and the members from the "capitalist" countries. They assumed differences in consciousness between those dedicated to the advancement of Communism and those entangled in the web of "bourgeois" ideology. They wished to articulate these differences and to institutionalize them within the bureaucratic structure of the I.O.C. Brundage's response to all of this was adamant opposition: "There must be no blocs and there must be no nationalism in the International Olympic Committee. . . . To allow countries to select their representatives on the Committee would be fatal. Political considerations would soon control and all the good work of the last sixty years would be destroyed."[1] Brundage advocated a small I.O.C. of no more than 80 members; he felt keenly that mail ballots and proxy votes disturbed the exchange of opinions necessary to discover consensus. Above all, "no blocs."

Andrianov's proposals all went in the opposite direction. In 1955, he asked that the Executive Board be increased to nine members, including a second vice president. There was no two-thirds majority for the first proposal, but the second passed. If Andrianov hoped to see a Communist elected, he was apparently ready to wait patiently; England's Exeter (then still Lord Burghley) was nominated and elected unanimously.[2] A year later, at the Melbourne session of the I.O.C., Bulgaria's Vladimir Stoytchev became the first Communist member to serve on the Executive Board.[3] Andrianov proposed major reorganization in 1959. He wanted an expanded I.O.C. made up of its present members (then 64 in number) plus representatives from *all* the national Olympic committees (then 115 in number) and from *all* the recognized international sports federations (which he wanted to raise from 25 to 35).[4] The effect of this plan would have been to triple the size of the I.O.C. and to increase drastically the influence of the Communist bloc and the "Third World." The plan was clearly analogous to Nikita Khrushchev's almost simultaneous proposal that the United Nations adopt a "troika" arrangement to allow executive power to be shared among Communist, non-Communist, and neutralist factions. The Munich session of 1959 referred the Russian plan to the Executive Board.[5] Once again, Brundage threw his weight against the attempt to institutionalize ideological difference and to adulterate the influence of the Europeans and Americans who had always controlled the I.O.C.[6]

Two years later, the plan was defeated by a vote of 35–7—i.e., the non-Communists versus the Communists.[7] In 1962, meeting in the politically favorable climate of Moscow, the Russians persuaded the others to agree in principle that the Executive Board should be broadly representative, at least in a geographical sense, but the majority then defeated the hosts' proposal to achieve this end by increasing the Executive Board to include the president, the two vice presidents, and eight members (the vote was a close 17–16).[8] The Russians failed at this time even in their campaign to have the presidents of the national Olympic committees and the international sports federations invited to I.O.C. sessions as nonvoting members.[9] There was, however, a sop; Andrianov was elevated to the Executive Board to replace Stoytchev. The Communists had clearly achieved de facto what the I.O.C. was reluctant to grant de jure.[10] Like the American political "ticket" that includes a mandatory rainbow of ethnic and religious and racial differences, the Executive Board was "balanced."

Three years later, Andrianov returned to the fray with a proposal for an Executive Board consisting of the president, three vice presidents, and nine members distributed among the five continents, each of which was to have two except for Oceania, which would have a single member.[11] (North and South America were to count as one continent.) By this time, Andrianov had persuaded Otto Mayer, who published his support in the *Bulletin du C.I.O.* for August 15, 1965. Andrianov's proposal was not acceptable in its entirety, but the I.O.C. did decide at its Rome session in 1966 to add the third vice president that Andrianov had called for.[12] Since France's Armand Massard was continuing in office as first vice president and the Marquess of Exeter had concluded his term as second vice president, there were two positions to fill—second vice president and third vice president. The positions went, respectively, to Andrianov and to General José de Clark Flores of Mexico, one of Brundage's confidants.[13].

By 1970, elections had become thoroughly politicized. Brundage's notes on those of the 69th Session at Amsterdam show that there were three ballots necessary to elect Comte Jean de Beaumont of France as second vice president and three more to choose Holland's Herman van Karnebeek as third vice president. (Ireland's Lord Killanin's term as first vice president had not expired.) To choose four members of the Executive Board required eleven ballots. The result was a nine-member Executive Board including representatives of every continent but Oceania.[14] Andrianov, the only member with a majority on the first ballot of the Executive Board voting, might well have concluded that he had won the battle even if there had never been a formal surrender.

Although Brundage had expressed strong opposition ("no blocs") to the organizational changes that accompanied the Russians' demand for greater power and influence within the I.O.C., his correspondence reveals no personal animosity against Andrianov or Romanov. It seems that Brundage recognized that the inclusion of previously excluded interest groups was a democratization as well as a politicization of the committee. Far different was his reaction to another challenge to European-American domination of the Olympic movement and to his personal authority as president.

When the Comite Olimpico Nazionale d'Italia (C.O.N.I.) led the way to the formation of an organization of all the national Olympic committees, Brundage reacted vehemently. When this organization evolved into the Permanent General Assembly of the National Olympic Committees (P.G.A.) and began to tussle with the I.O.C. for control of the Olympics, Brundage was furious. His anger was directed largely against his I.O.C. colleague Giulio Onesti, who was also the dynamic, imaginative, ambitious leader of the P.G.A.

As early as 1963, Onesti had urged the Executive Committee to arrange for regular annual meetings with the national Olympic committees.[15] Elected to the I.O.C. the following year, he arranged for C.O.N.I. to invite representatives of the national committees to meet among themselves just before the I.O.C. session in Tokyo in 1964.[16] In the past, the national committees had met frequently with the I.O.C. Executive Board, but the meetings had always been dominated by the latter and communication was not very satisfactory. As Douglas Roby recalled, "We'd have meetings with the national Olympic committees or the international federations and he'd say, 'We'll take it under advisement.' It was a brush-off. . . . He just wouldn't listen. . . . Let them talk, and then forget it."[17] The "he," of course, was Avery Brundage.

C.O.N.I.'s proposal was patently more than an attempt to clear blocked channels of communication. Onesti's statements of personal loyalty to the I.O.C. failed to allay Brundage's suspicions. Brundage warned the Italian from the start that "the formation of a permanent organization of NOC's is fraught with many dangers." Specifically, it institutionalized the one-country, one-vote rule which gave Dahomey, Mongolia, and Panama the same weight in Olympic affairs as Italy, the Soviet Union, and the United States.[18] This model of representation was familiar in the U.N. General Assembly, which Brundage considered an ineffective body, and in Andrianov's proposals for obligatory national Olympic committee representation in the I.O.C. Brundage invariably argued to the contrary that a nation's representation in the Olympic movement ought to be proportional to the stage of sports development, a position which ensured for the foreseeable future the continued dominance of Europe and the United States. In Onesti's suggestions,

Brundage saw the specter of domination by what is now loosely referred to as the "Third World."

Organization problems of a different sort beset Brundage in the months before the Tokyo session. His leadership was vigorous, which most of the members appreciated, but it verged frequently upon the dictatorial, which caused currents of resentment. Exeter, president of the I.A.A.F., was the logical person to challenge Brundage. The Englishman was eloquent, witty, vivacious, affable, gauntly handsome. He had the ease and confidence of an Olympic champion who was also an English lord. Unfortunately, his charm, his popularity among the members, and his undeniable eligibility as Brundage's successor tended to sour the relationship between the two men. Exeter must have seemed unfairly to have plucked without effort the fruits for which Brundage had labored. To one of the older members of the I.O.C., Brundage suddenly and unexpectedly admitted as much. Drawing the startled member aside, Brundage declared himself ready to step down as president—*if* Exeter were persuaded not to become a candidate. But Exeter *was* persuaded to stand, and the count in Tokyo was close. Brundage won and the *Bulletin* announced that his reelection had been unanimous.[19] Not satisfied with his victory, Brundage aspired to replace Exeter as president of the I.A.A.F., but he managed to restrain himself from an open challenge.[20] During the last years of Brundage's presidency, he and Exeter—once friends—"tended to avoid each other."[21]

Plans for an assembly of the national committees at Tokyo were premature and the foundation of a "Co-Ordinating and Study Committee" did not take place until the beginning of October 1965. Three days before the Executive Board's scheduled meeting with the national committees in Madrid, the representatives of 68 of the committees caucused in Rome as guests of C.O.N.I. The committee which they set up was headed by Onesti and included Weir (Australia), Andrianov, Jean-Claude Ganga (Congo), Tsuneyoshi Takeda (Japan), K. Sandy Duncan (Great Britain), Gabriel Gemayel (Lebanon), H. Corenthin (Mali), José de Clark Flores (Mex-

ico), R. W. Wilson (U.S.A.), and Jean Weymann (Switzerland).
The majority of the assembly resolved that the national committees
ought to receive 25 percent of whatever television revenue flowed
into I.O.C. coffers and that the question of amateurism should be
shifted from the I.O.C. to the international sports federations.

Onesti continued to assure Brundage that the Co-Ordinating and
Study Committee posed no threat to the I.O.C. He sent texts of
resolutions to Chicago and he was thanked by Brundage for his
"friendly personal references" and for the "sensitive phraseology"
of the initial report. Indeed, Brundage confided to the Italian that
he was "not very happy with our Madrid Session." The world
needed leadership. The implication was that the world needed people like the president of C.O.N.I.[22] The president of C.O.N.I.
wrote back that the new Olympic committees of Asia and Africa
were inexperienced and unhappy about their lack of representation
in the I.O.C. Onesti hoped not to alter the basic structure of the
organization but to integrate the newer units more closely within
the Olympic movement.[23] Brundage replied supportively.[24]

Meanwhile, Onesti involved himself—as a good-will emissary—
in a controversy within the Comité Olympique Français; he also
initiated a series of moves designed to bring the People's Republic
of China back into the Olympic family.[25] Once again, Rome kept
Chicago informed.[26] Forwarding Brundage a copy of an attack on
the I.O.C. president, Onesti commented that there were those who
thought of him as Brundage's deputy or ambassador.[27] Brundage's
tone remained cordial: "It is unfortunate that your trip to China
did not materialize."[28] Despite Onesti's assurances to the head of
the "All-China Sports Federation" in Peking that C.O.N.I. was in
full agreement vis-à-vis the "fugitives of Taiwan," the attempted
rapprochement failed.[29] Mao Tse-tung had led China into the
"Great Cultural Revolution" and there was little interest in athletic
encounters with Italy and other non-Asian nations.

While Onesti was involved in his overture to the East, plans
progressed for the second meeting of the Study and Co-Ordinating
Committee of the National Olympic Committees. When it did meet
in Rome, in 1966, the committee adopted a constitution incorpo-

rating most of the features which Andrianov had been advocating for the I.O.C.—a president, three vice presidents, an executive committee composed of these officers plus two representatives from each of the five continents.[30] A second general assembly was planned just before the I.O.C.'s Teheran session of April 1967.

By this time, there was unmistakable vehement opposition from Chicago.[31] There was also opposition from England's K. S. Duncan. Speaking for the British Olympic Association, he maintained there was no need for a new organization. This was a position taken also by José de Clark Flores, who tried to dissuade the Latin American delegates from attending the meeting, and by Denmark's Ivar Vind, who told Brundage in private that the Nordic committees were unanimously opposed to Onesti, whom he thought disloyal and motivated by personal ambitions.[32] When Onesti officially invited the representatives of the national committees to the assembly, he stressed that the planned meeting took place "with the agreement of the International Olympic Committee. . . . I should add that a preliminary visit to Teheran at the beginning of March will be made by Mr. Westerhoff, Secretary General of the I.O.C., who will be accompanied on such occasion by a collaborator of mine, Dr. Marcello Garroni."[33] Brundage wrote to the presidents of the national Olympic committees and denied Onesti's claim of I.O.C. sponsorship; he wrote also to Johann Westerhoff, the Dutch Secretary General of the I.O.C., and told him bluntly to disassociate himself from any collaboration with C.O.N.I.[34] A week later, Brundage sent out an official circular letter informing the national Olympic committees that the Executive Board had decided that no new organization was needed and repeating to them that the assembly of the national committees was not sponsored by the I.O.C.[35]

Onesti was annoyed but not deterred. Representatives of 64 national Olympic committees convened at Teheran on April 29 and voted to establish a permanent organization when they met in Mexico City in 1968. The effects of Brundage's opposition were visible in the changed proportion of Western to non-Western representatives. There had been 27 European delegates and 13 Americans at the Roman assembly; now there were 23 and 7. The number of African committees represented remained at 15 and the Asians increased from 12 to 18.[36] The shift in the organization's geographical center of gravity signaled that an ideological earthquake was not far off.

In Brundage's view, the official meeting of the Executive Board with the national Olympic committees, which took place on May 3,

was loaded with dynamite and there could have been a serious explosion. We were on the edge of a precipice and one slip . . . and we would have been over the edge. They were like a pack of hungry lions and only by talking louder and longer were they held at bay.[37]

The medley of images—dynamite, precipice, hungry lions—and the errors of syntax (who talked louder, we or they?) indicate that Brundage was thoroughly disconcerted. He suffered from his nightmare of an Olympic movement fallen into the hands of the smaller and more radical nations. The I.O.C. seemed about to go the way of the U.N. General Assembly. "Who got the applause? People we have never heard of. . . . representing new and very small countries: Ganga of the Congo with one-and-a-half million people and very little sport development."[38]

Brundage's Opening Address to the Teheran session was devoted almost exclusively to the national Olympic committees, which he praised for "the promulgation of Olympic principles and ideals, for the development of the Olympic Movement, and for the creation of the 'Olympic image' throughout the world."[39] (Since sociological research indicates that the national committees care rather little for these matters and much more for the sending of powerful Olympic teams to the games, Brundage was obviously hoping to flatter the delegates.) He praised individual Olympic committees, including those of Italy and the Congo, for their fine work. He offered reassurances:

Since the National Olympic Committees as agents of the International Olympic Committee are the organizations that control Olympic affairs in their respective countries, the International Olympic Committee is ever concerned with their well-being and is always eager to strengthen their powers and to help them with their work.[40]

At the session a subcommittee was formed under the chairmanship of Ivar Vind, whose mandate was to investigate the relations between the I.O.C. and the national committees. Although Onesti was named to this subcommittee, he was flanked and outvoted by Brundage supporters. He was also berated by them. Brundage's close friend Clark Flores told Onesti that there was not and had not been any tension between the I.O.C. and the national committees, and he attributed the present unrest to agitators, malcontents.[41]

Brundage's official address to the Session was sweetness and light. (It included lavish praise of the hosts—the Shah of Iran and his brother, who was —despite pieties about the autonomy of national committees—the head of the Iranian N.O.C. and also the I.O.C. member from Iran.) His less formal greetings to the members upon their arrival at the Royal Hilton Hotel contained ominous references to another unwelcome organization. As early as 1920, the international sports federations, led by the energetic and capable Henri Rousseau of the Fédération Internationale Amateur de Cyclisme, demanded greater influence in the direction of the Olympic movement. Now the representatives of the federations had decided to follow the example of the national Olympic committees and to meet among themselves as well as with the I.O.C. Executive Board. The General Assembly of the International Federations (G.A.I.F.) was founded barely a month before the Teheran session.[42] Led by Australia's Berge Phillips (representing the Fédération Internationale de Natation Amateur) and France's Roger Coulon (representing the Fédération Internationale de Lutte Amateur), this new organization had already, in Brundage's view, intruded into "matters which are not of their competence and only concern the I.O.C."[43] The Olympic movement was unmistakably in the midst of an organizational crisis. Perhaps Brundage found solace in the fact that the G.A.I.F. and the P.G.A. were often at odds not only with the I.O.C. but with each other.[44]

From Teheran the scene of the drama shifted to Grenoble, where the 1968 winter games were about to be celebrated. When the Executive Board met with the international federations immediately before the 66th Session, Phillips urged that the federations be given one-third of all television revenue and that an Olympic Congress be convened.[45] There had not been a congress since the one in Berlin in 1930, but Brundage's position was that such affairs are a waste of time and money. At the session itself, which began on February 1, Vind reported on behalf of his subcommittee on relations with the national Olympic committees that there was difficulty in communication but no necessity for a separate organization of national committees.[46] His point about communication was illustrated by Onesti, who delivered a major speech in which he gave a history of the P.G.A. and an ardent defense of his initiative. Proclaiming his loyalty to the I.O.C. and condemning the leaders of the international sports federations for *their* subversion of the I.O.C., Onesti resigned from the subcommittee on I.O.C.– N.O.C. relations.[47]

Preparations now went ahead for the Third General Assembly of the National Olympic Committees. Since Brundage's second term as president was due to expire in 1968, Onesti's supporters began to ponder an electoral coup. At a time when the Olympic movement was about to split apart on the issue of South Africa's right to participate, the I.O.C. was wracked with internal tensions.

Each side to the dispute over the role of the National Olympic committees gathered its forces. Drawing on the good will he had accumulated as a supporter of the Pan-American Games and of Latin American membership in the I.O.C., Brundage sent out a form letter in Spanish to the Hispanic committees; they were to announce to Onesti that they saw no need for a permanent organization of national committees. Brundage provided the language: "no requerimos de organismos internacionales paralelos o intermediarios ajenos al COI."[48] Almost every nation of the western hemisphere complied, some using Brundage's form, some composing their own letters. Brundage profited in another way from his Hispanic connections. In a ploy which reminds one more of backroom maneuvers at a political convention than of Olympic fair play, the president of the Mexican Organizing Committee for the 1968 games informed Onesti that there was no space available for a session of the general assembly of the national Olympic committees because the organization was not a part of the official program of events.[49] Brundage warned Onesti in person and by letter not to convene his organization in Mexico City, and Onesti let Brundage know about his sense of bitterness.[50] Brundage reiterated his stand: "No NOC in good standing had ever been refused I.O.C. support. All NOCs are and have been invited to submit their problems directly to the IOC at any time. . . . There is no reason whatsoever for any permanent association of NOCs."[51] When Andrianov cabled Brundage an appeal on Onesti's behalf, Brundage replied, "I have not interfered."[52] If Brundage thought of his actions as noninterference, one wonders what his notion of intervention was.

Andrianov was not the only person who felt that Brundage had been too inflexible and authoritarian in his response to the national Olympic committees. On September 7, Comte Jean de Beaumont, president of the Comité Olympique Français, chaired a meeting in Versailles with representatives of 22 European national committees. The Europeans agreed to participate in the work of the P.G.A. committees at Mexico City and to accept Onesti's invitation for a 1969 session in Dubrovnik, Yugoslavia.[53] The group also called for a new Olympic congress at some future date. Beaumont now emerged as a possible successor to Brundage. At a press conference, he remarked that Brundage looked upon the I.O.C. as if it were his child. (One of the younger members, Gunnar Ericsson of Sweden, remarked later that Brundage's attitude varied between that of a father and that of a god.[54]) Beaumont commented to the reporters that reelection of the eighty-one-year-old president would be "a challenge to common sense in the eyes of the world."[55] Stories about Beaumont's candidacy appeared in *Le Monde* and in *The Times* (London) and in other papers around the world.

There was no doubt that Beaumont was a forceful person and an attractive candidate for those who felt that Brundage had been president long enough. Brundage, who insulted Beaumont by calling him Onesti's "second lieutenant,"[56] failed to understand that Beaumont's harsh judgments were partly the result of frustration. The Frenchman considered himself a loyal follower not of Onesti but of Brundage, but he felt rebuffed, kept at a distance by the coldness that most members experienced whenever they attempted to express their more personal emotions to him.[57] Contrary to the usual stereotypes, it was the European aristocrats—Exeter and Beaumont—who were able to charm by gregarious informality. Brundage remained the loner. And it was apparently impossible for him to understand that his own personality was a factor within the committee. He saw only the alleged Machiavellianism of Onesti.

The atmosphere was one of intrigue, rumor, innuendo. There were newspaper stories about Onesti's candidacy for Brundage's office. Rome's *Il Messaggero* scoffed at the rumors in a way that made them seem plausible: "Onesti has not Brundage's money, nor his pride, nor the strain of continual travel. Onesti is interested neither in the burden of office nor is the I.O.C. destined to become a representative organization unless some changes are made."[58] Hearing the rumors, Brundage became even more hostile.[59]

Voices of dissatisfaction within the committee became stronger. Sir Reginald Alexander, one of the more directly outspoken members, approached Brundage and spoke candidly, "Avery, you're eighty; you're on the top. You've been at it now for sixty years and President for twenty years and when you're on the top, there's only one way to go, and that's down. Move now, and history will record you as one of the greatest." Brundage replied that many members had urged him to stay on for another term. "Avery, that's what they'd like you to hear. I'm telling you . . . what you don't like to hear."[60] Alexander and Roby were among those who asked Killanin to stand for the presidency. Indeed, Alexander sounded out the members and felt that there were at least thirty for the Irishman, but Killanin preferred to wait.[61] Brundage still had his devoted backers, especially among the Latin Americans and among some of the younger members like Csanadi of Hungary, whose warmth and generosity seemed to have encouraged Brundage to reveal his gentler features.[62]

At any rate, the "dump Brundage" campaign fizzled. On October 10, 1968, he was reelected by a wide margin and Killanin became vice president, defeating Beaumont by a vote of 29–27.[63] But the losers had won something too. Beaumont was made a member of the Executive Board and it was understood that Brundage would retire from office in 1972.

Brundage remained in office, but Onesti was now president of the Permanent General Assembly of the National Olympic Committees, which had been officially founded by a meeting of 78 committees on September 30 and October 1. The organization included not only Andrianov and Ganga, as leaders of the Communist and neutralist blocs, but also Duncan of Great Britain, Takeda of Japan, Weir of Australia, and even Douglas F. Roby.[64] The organization voted to meet again at Dubrovnik, immediately before the official I.O.C. session. It was obviously time for some sort of compromise if the conflicts among the I.O.C., the national Olympic committees, and the international sports federations were not to tear the Olympic fabric to shreds. The I.O.C.'s response was to set up five Joint Commissions with six I.O.C. and six N.O.C. members each. The fifth commission was devoted to relations among the three Olympic groups.[65]

As the date for the Dubrovnik session approached, however, tempers flared and confusion reigned. Onesti faulted Brundage for supposedly reneging on the agreement made at the Warsaw session to allow the national Olympic committees to meet among themselves.[66] While Monique Berlioux, the new French director of the I.O.C. headquarters in Lausanne, told Brundage, in regard to Onesti, "His meetings do not appear on *our* programme," Clark Flores was flabbergasted and shocked when the Yugoslav organizers of the session printed and distributed a program that had been created, allegedly, "in agreement with the International Olympic Committee and the Permanent General Assembly of the National Olympic Committees."[67] When Lord Killanin placed some of Onesti's spokesmen on the I.O.C. program, Clark Flores burst out, "These are not Lord Killanin's tactics, they are Mr. Onesti's."[68] By the time the session was underway, the five Nordic committees seemed to have reached a state of despair: "Where is our Headquarters? Is it in Mexico, Rom [*sic*], Chicago or Lausanne? Or is it in Paris? So many good plans and suggestions have been offered, everyone has done a good job, everyone has been carrying his colours, only—too many colours have been on parade."[69] President Gudmund Schack of the Danish Olympic Committee informed Edward Wieczorek, Secretary General of the P.G.A., that the Danes did not want to be a part of the new organization, but Wieczorek countered with the proposal that he and Onesti meet with the Danes in Copenhagen.[70]

The P.G.A. met on October 21–23 and busied itself with committee reports and suggestions for improved I.O.C.–N.O.C. relations. When Brundage addressed the national committees on the 25th, he asked for a return to high ideals:

Empires dissolve, governments disappear, kingdoms vanish, but the ancient Olympic Games lasted twelve centuries and they were not based on temporal power. And so will the modern Games survive if we stick together and adhere to the lofty ideals laid down by the Baron de Coubertin.[71]

Not even the magic name of the "renovateur" was able to exorcise the demons of conflict. Andrianov and others asked for official I.O.C. recognition of the P.G.A., but Brundage refused and repeated his argument that only the I.O.C. represented all 127 national Olympic committees.[72] At the closed meeting of the Executive Board, Beaumont too asked that the I.O.C. not fight the P.G.A., but Brundage was in no mood to make peace.[73]

Some of the most interesting insights into the controversy between the I.O.C. and the P.G.A. are to be found in a long letter addressed to Brundage by Khaw Kai-Bow, vice president of the Olympic Council of Malaysia. Referring to the P.G.A. meeting in Dubrovnik, Khaw Kai-Bow admitted that he had been disaffected from the I.O.C. He sent Brundage the thirteen-page speech which he had delivered at the P.G.A. meeting. He had condemned the I.O.C. because its leaders seemed inefficient, intolerant, arbitrary, and even "somewhat tyrannical and dictatorial." They had condescended to the national Olympic committees. There had been little dialogue. "Sending circulars is not enough." In Khaw Kai-Bow's vivid English, the leaders of the I.O.C. sat on pedestals like "tiny tin Gods—incommunicado to all and sundry." But the outsiders who felt themselves disregarded by the I.O.C. found the same haughty lack of regard within the P.G.A. Consequently, the Malaysians were "disillusioned, disappointed, dejected and deflated." Did Onesti and Beamont think them "ignorant and illiterate boys" to be carried away by emotional discourse? "By jove we are not." Nonetheless, he concluded his speech by affirming that Malaysia intended to remain within the P.G.A. to prevent it from becoming "a kingdom within a kingdom" or a "stepping stone to power and gain." In his letter, Khaw Kai-Bow noted that there had been a genuine I.O.C.–N.O.C. dialogue at Dubrovnik. If the I.O.C. would only meet annually with the national Olympic committees, the P.G.A. would die a natural death. The Malaysian also expressed his personal gratitude for the chance to have met Brundage privately in Dubrovnik.[74] Brundage, unfortunately, had become too emotionally involved to listen to the soft voices of compromise and reconciliation. He wrote back to Khaw Kai-Bow that there had been "a quite satisfactory dialogue between the NOCs and the IOC for some 50 years or more, until it was disrupted recently." All the trouble was due to dissident elements who sought their own advantage.[75] The atmosphere was so poisoned that, when Onesti visited Nairobi, Kenya, and was greeted as an important Olympic figure, which he was, Brundage fumed, "How much longer is the I.O.C. willing to tolerate such blatant disloyalty?"[76]

In 1971, at the Executive Board meetings in Luxembourg, Brundage "expressed his intention of recommending that any I.O.C. member associated with the P.G.A. should submit his resignation," but Andrianov, Killanin, and Takeda, who had all attended one or more P.G.A. meetings, protested.[77] Andrianov blamed the I.O.C. for the plain fact that many national committees felt a P.G.A. was necessary, a point which Killanin seconded.[78] Sir Ade Ademola of Nigeria was no backer of Onesti, but he commented that many African committees felt neglected by the I.O.C. and appreciated the attentions paid them by the P.G.A.[79] This same point had also been made by Sir Ade's countryman H. E. O. Adefope when the Executive Board met with the national Olympic committees two days earlier, and Adefope had made the additional important observation, "He underlined, however, that the N.O.C.'s had noticed that the I.O.C. was now giving active consideration to all their proposals and showed more concern."[80] This remark was followed by loud applause.

Despite the sound conciliatory advice of Olympic leaders like Andrianov, Beaumont, and Killanin, and from obscure but dedicated followers like Khaw Kai-Bow and H. E. O. Adefope, Brundage stayed on the warpath. To the three vice presidents of the I.O.C. he wrote, "The P.G.A. must be buried NOW and perhaps the three vice-presidents will have the courage to report that any I.O.C. member who [wishes] to participate in the P.G.A. activities must first resign from the I.O.C."[81] The following day, he told the vice presidents that Onesti had finally surrendered but that the Italian wanted to "bury" his organization in his own way.[82] Brundage certainly overstated Onesti's desire to capitulate. Killanin was probably close to the truth when he observed to Monique Berlioux that the I.O.C. really *had* granted the P.G.A. a kind of de facto recognition.[83] Of course, Brundage protested loudly that this was not the case:

This is certainly not true. Every time the organization has been mentioned in my presence, it has been stated that it is not recognized. If any communications are received from the PGA they will be returned and accepted only if they come from one or more NOC.[84]

Nonetheless, the P.G.A. lingered on as an important unofficial institution. Brundage won a less than total victory and Onesti suffered a far from complete defeat. The I.O.C. had become far more attentive to the national Olympic committees and to their interests, and that was what Onesti had called for in the first place.

Compared to the controversies over the structure and leadership of the Olympic movement, office quarrels are a very small part of the story, but they cannot be ignored entirely because they contributed to the level of irritation and often lay behind an otherwise inexplicable flash of temper. To an outsider it may have seemed that the Olympic headquarters in Lausanne was well organized and efficient, but Brundage remained dissatisfied through a whole series of changes until, near the end of his career as president, he found the person he wanted.

When he became president in 1952, Brundage found a helpful collaborator in Otto Mayer, a Lausanne businessman with a shop for jewelry and watches, who had been I.O.C. chancellor for six years. About Mayer's intelligence and dedication there was never any doubt, but Brundage began to feel that his aide was sometimes impetuous and indiscreet.[85] When Mayer reported, for instance, that Massard was unfairly annoyed with him for what Mayer thought were trivial disagreements, Brundage told him candidly that he was commendably eager to get things accomplished but sometimes too quick to act.[86] Mayer felt morally obliged during a trip to Italy to prevent a "revolution" by assuring the Italians that their favorite sports—soccer and cycling—would remain on the Olympic program for 1960.[87] Brundage was furious, partly because he disliked these highly commercialized sports and partly because he was jealous of his authority, and he warned Mayer about unauthorized or premature announcements.[88] Mayer's life was not easy. The I.O.C.'s headquarters from 1922 to 1968 was Chateau Mon Repos in downtown Lausanne. The chancellor and his secretarial help had to share the space with Coubertin's widow, who lived to be 101 years old and became very querulous.[89] Brundage was sympathetic and supportive, but he was also greatly relieved when Mayer was persuaded to resign in 1964.

His relief was tempered by anxiety because Brundage's weakness for attractive women had landed him, at precisely this time, in a minor imbroglio. He was on friendly terms with Myriam Meuwly, one of Mayer's staff at Mon Repos. Exeter told Brundage that the friendship with Meuwly was a regrettable disturbance.[90] There was gossip among the I.O.C. members to the effect that Brundage neglected official business during the 1963 session in Baden-Baden in order to spend time in Meuwly's company. Mayer referred to the members' comments and promised to do his best to pour oil on the troubled waters.[91]

Unfortunately, Mayer's brother Albert, I.O.C. member for Switzerland, seems to have felt that Meuwly was a factor in Otto's subsequent resignation.[92] The squabble was aired by Radio Lausanne and in the newspapers. The Chicago *Tribune* quoted Albert Mayer on the OLYMPICS SHAM and Brundage held Mayer responsible for the bad publicity in his hometown paper.[93] Mayer threatened to publicize the gossip that his brother had promised to scotch.[94] Albert Mayer's threats may have been prompted by Brundage's decision to fire Otto Mayer's *successor*, whom Albert Mayer had recommended.[95] The young man in question, Eric Jonas, had been given the title of I.O.C. Secretary, but he never won Brundage's confidence and he left with a sense of grievance and promptly sued his former employers.[96] The Lausanne headquarters began to look like a morass of gossip, innuendo, ill will, and recrimination.

Next came Johann Westerhoff, a 51-year-old Djakarta-born industrialist, who became I.O.C. secretary in May 1966. He seems to have had ideas about an administrative reorganization of the office, but Brundage thought him a lax worker who spent too little time on the job.[97] Brundage complained to Beaumont, who consulted with Clark Flores and reported back that Westerhoff had to go.[98] Vind thought that the president had been too openly hostile to the secretary, but the Executive Board concluded that it was best to end the relationship; Westerhoff was granted six months pay and was dismissed.[99]

At the same time, the Board hired Artur Takec as Technical Director and promoted Monique Berlioux to Director for Press and Public Relations. The latter soon revealed herself as the solution to the problems of the Lausanne office. When Vind worried about the administrative mess at the Chateau de Vidy (where the headquarters was moved in 1968), Brundage was able to assure him that the problems had finally been solved.[100] Of Berlioux's impact on the office, Meuwly commented, "While we had carried on in the modest Swiss way, she changed it all with her indomitable *esprit français*."[101] Originally hired by Westerhoff to work on the *Bulletin du C.I.O.*, she eventually earned the title of I.O.C. Director. She had been a champion swimmer and had also competed in track and field and a number of other sports. She had worked as a sports journalist in both print and electronic media, in both the private sector and for the French Secretariat d'État à la Jeunesse et aux Sports (under Maurice Herzog, later to become an I.O.C. member). She demonstrated administrative talent and got on well with Brundage.[102] Although she described her boss as a man who often acted with "despotic firmness," she also described occasions when she and Brundage joked and laughed together in a way that seemed almost conspiratorial to others. In such moods, "He's like a little boy."[103] Except for some minor friction between her and Takec, the Lausanne office seems to have caused Brundage little or no worry in the last three years of his presidency.[104]

CHAPTER XI

NEW GAMES AND OLD PROBLEMS

Organizational disputes about the composition of the International Olympic Committee or the relationship of the committee to the national Olympic committees and the international sports federations can be distinguished from disagreements over the sports which are to be organized and administered. Exactly what events should appear on the Olympic program? Coubertin's initial position had been that the I.O.C. should welcome *all* sports: "the Committee is not competent to judge that one sport is preferable to another. . . . The Committee's mission is to organize the Olympic Games, in which all sports are represented, and not to make choices among sports."[1] It was an overly generous position that the I.O.C. was forced to abandon as the games became more prestigious, as more athletes wished to compete, as more sports federations wanted their sports to be included in the program. Invidious distinctions were necessary.

The I.O.C.'s response to the problem of proliferation was to organize competitions only in those sports whose international federations were recognized as Olympic, but this simply shifted the moment of choice from one context to another. Hoping to encourage the spread of amateur sports, the committee recognized as "Olympic" more federations than it was prepared to see represented at any given Olympic celebration. The International Aeronautics

Federation, for instance, was recognized as "Olympic" in 1965, but airplanes have never flown in an Olympic race.[2] The committee distinguished between "obligatory" and "optional" sports; organizing committees were required to stage competitions in the first category and were allowed to in the second. It was a distinction that led to ill will and it was eventually dropped at the 53rd Session in 1957.[3]

As early as 1930, there was almost incessant knocking at the Olympic door. Representatives of the international federations for baseball, billiards, canoeing, lacrosse, pelota, and roller skating vainly sought admission to the festival of Olympic sports.[4] The demands for entry continued through Brundage's years on the committee. There was a major drive for recognition on the part of many sports enthusiasts immediately after World War II. At the first postwar session in Lausanne in 1946, the I.O.C. refused the requests made by the partisans of archery, baseball, gliding, team handball, polo, roller skating, table tennis, and volleyball.[5] Of these sports, volleyball was added to the program in 1964; team handball and archery arrived in 1972. Although roller skating probably never had a chance of adoption, a letter from Chancellor Mayer, who was also secretary of the roller skater's federation, seemed almost to sabotage the effort; he told Brundage that he personally didn't care a bit whether the group was admitted or not and he invited Brundage to ignore the letter of application![6] Volleyball's backers were more determined and less odd and contained among their number Massard of France and Stoytchev of Bulgaria, influential I.O.C. members who bombarded Brundage and others with appeals for their neglected sport.[7] After a lively debate at Melbourne in 1956, the volleyball players lost by a vote of 19–13, but Stoytchev kept the cause alive with a good-natured promise to stage a vigorous exhibition of the sport when the I.O.C. met in Sofia the following year.[8] The exhibition was convincing and volleyball became an Olympic sport.[9]

As a favor to the Japanese hosts, judo entered the Olympic program at the Tokyo games of 1964, but Brundage, despite his love of Japanese culture, regretted the addition because of his desire to reduce the size of the Olympic program.[10] In the 1960s, there seemed to be no end to the appeals for recognition. Badminton buffs and ballroom dancers, bowlers and flycasters, ski-bobbers, softball players, and sand-and-land yachtsmen were *some* of those who wanted their place in the Olympic sun. Brundage eventually lost patience with the requests, some of which he thought were absurd:

> Is ice dancing an athletic sport or not? The next thing we will have is an application to add synchronized swimming (which is a form of water vaudeville), fly casting for fishermen, billiards, bowling, sky diving, and baton twirling. Where does it stop?[11]

Brundage was not the only one who wanted to call a halt. In 1971, the I.O.C. firmly resolved to add no new sports to the program.[12] (The resolve was temporary; synchronized swimming will be a feature of the 1984 Olympics.)

Brundage's opposition to new sports was based partly on his sense that they somehow lacked legitimacy but more importantly on his conviction that the Olympics had become gargantuan affairs, too complex, too costly, too impersonal. Smaller cities were no longer able to bid for the games and, since Brundage was committed to the principle that the games should travel and that every part of the world should have a chance to celebrate an Olympiad and thus become converted by the Olympic spirit, the size of the games seemed a great evil. Speaking to the international federations and to the national Olympic committees, he emphasized the fact "that the Games are doomed and will certainly come to an end if the present overcrowded programme is not reduced."[13]

In the first year of his presidency, he began to campaign for reductions in the program and in the number of athletes and reserves allowed in those events which remained on the program.[14] He wanted those sports which were already a part of the Olympics to reduce the number of their contests. He thought, for instance, that there were too many weight divisions for boxers and wrestlers, too many races for swimmers.[15] He wanted to eliminate "artificial teams" like those in gymnastics, where athletes competed as individuals and simultaneously accumulated points for a team which might then be awarded an additional medal above and beyond the ones earned individually.[16]

Many I.O.C. members agreed that the games had become gargantuan. The committee decided in 1953 to exclude substitutes in individual events and in 1954 not to allow the officials accompanying a team to outnumber the athletes.[17] At the 53rd Session in Sofia in 1957 they resolved once again, by a vote of 22–9, that the program was too large and ought to be reduced.[18] The vote was like that of a legislature highmindedly determining that the budget *must* be cut. Somehow. Predictably, the campaign to implement the ringing resolution foundered on the rock of interest-group politics: "*Your* favorite sport has too many contests; *my* favorite sport has too few." Every international federation thought that *its* sport was underrepresented. The equestrians boldly decided to increase the number of contestants in the Grand Prix des Nations from 9 to 12 riders and the Executive Board tamely accepted the "fait accompli."[19] In 1965, Berge Phillips of the Fédération Internationale de Natation Amateur asked for 11 new swimming events because "the existing programme for the Olympic Games is entirely inadequate and does not represent the usual events which are held in the National Championships of all leading swimming nations in the world."[20] Of 14 international federations responding to an I.O.C. questionnaire, only the weightlifters thought there should be a general reduction in events.[21] Moving the other federations to such a conclusion was harder than hoisting the barbells. Thomas Keller, speaking as president of the General Assembly of the International Federations, maintained that the exclusion of softball, table tennis, and roller skating was unjustified, but Brundage answered that the international federations were "a little prejudiced" in this matter.[22] No doubt they were, but the prejudice was inerradicable and the secular-long-range tendency of the games was to grow, and grow, and grow. The last Olympics over which Brundage presided, those of Munich in 1972, were the largest of all, with the greatest number of events for the greatest number of athletes from the greatest number of countries.

Among the recurrent suggestions for reducing the program were three that would have produced large-scale results: eliminating women's sports, team sports, and winter sports. At various moments, Brundage listed all three suggestions as possibilities. He personally advocated the second and third options but *not*, as has been frequently charged, the first.

As women were admitted to more and more Olympic disciplines, there was an obvious tendency for the number of events and contestants to double. Because Brundage listed the exclusion of women as a logically possible means to reduce the program, he was often misunderstood.[23] He was said to have wanted to "kick the women out." Many sportswriters, like Arthur Daley of the New York *Times*, misread Brundage, praised what they took to be his anti-feminist views, and trotted out their own Victorian hobbyhorses:

There's just nothing feminine or enchanting about a girl with beads of perspiration on her alabaster brow, the results of grotesque contortions in events totally unsuited to female architecture. It's probably boorish to say it, but any self-respecting schoolboy can achieve superior performance to a woman champion.[24]

This had been the position, less boorishly expressed, of Pierre de Coubertin.

François Piétri, I.O.C. member from France, wrote that the exclusion of women was "la seule mesure réellement logique et efficace" if one wished to reduce the program.[25] Brundage did not agree. The truth is that he too cherished certain prejudices common to the Victorian era in which he had been born. He was, however, not among the conservatives on this issue. He was biased against females in some events, like shot putting, but his general inclination was to approve of women athletes. As we have seen, he firmly objected to Knute Rockne's sneers at women runners and he raved about the "lithe, supple, physically disciplined, strong, slender" women who participated in the London games of 1948.[26] Indeed, his objection to the shot putters was precisely that they did not conform to his image of *athletic* womankind. It is worth noting that it was at this time that the 61-year-old Brundage fell in love with 29-year-old Lilian Dresden, who might well have been described as "lithe, supple," etc. Arguing that one ought not underestimate "la force des femmes," Brundage was instrumental in the I.O.C.'s 1948 decision to allow mixed crews in yachting.[27] When Piétri argued in 1953 for the expulsion of female athletes, Brundage defended their right to remain.[28] While it may be an exaggeration to refer to his views as an "enigma,"[29] there were clearly moments of ambivalence. He found himself somewhere in the middle between those who affirmed total equality and those who wished to rid the games of "Amazons." While Piétri ridiculed women's sports as insignificant "contests which are of no interest to anybody," Andrianov and Exeter were among the influential members who thought that women's events should be increased.[30] Brundage was prepared, in 1957, to eliminate "events which are not truly feminine, like putting a shot, or those too strenuous for most of the opposite sex, such as distance runs."[31] His most negative remarks were probably those made to a group of women journalists in 1960. He referred to the "unfeminine" athletes of the Communist bloc as a special breed: "They carry bricks, labor in fields, clean the streets and do hard manual labor in their daily life. What do these Olympic lassies look like? Get a picture for yourself."[32] Nonetheless, he continued to feel that the modern Olympics would be incomplete without the female athletes. In his later years, he was puckishly apt to surprise the proponents of women's sports with signs of unexpected support. Despite the myriad demands on his time in Munich in 1972, he dropped in to visit a meeting of the Bundesausschuß für Frauensport (Federal Committee for Women's Sport) and stayed for an hour, to the astonishment of the members.[33]

Exeter, speaking for the I.A.A.F. but *not*, in this case, for Brundage, who referred back to the "disaster of 1928,[34] advocated restoration of the 800-meter race in 1960. The 400-meter race and the pentathlon were introduced in 1964, the 1500 meters and the 1600-meter relay at Brundage's last Olympics in 1972. The program for female swimmers was expanded in the 1960s. Perhaps the most significant sign of the gradual extinction of Piétri's attitudes was that men's and women's volleyball both entered the program in 1964, men's and women's archery returned in 1972. Inequalities still existed: women were still thought too frail for certain events, like races longer than 1500 meters; men were allowed 12 teams in their tournaments while women were allowed only 6 (unless the international federation decided in a burst of egalitarianism to hold both sexes to 9 teams).[35] The Executive Board was enlightened enough to spurn a proposed beauty pageant to elect a quadrennial "Miss Olympiad."[36] In his last opening address. Brundage indicated his pleasure that even Islamic women were at last free to participate in sports. He recalled the grace and strength of Enriqueta Basilio, the girl who carried the Olympic torch into the stadium in Mexico City in 1968, who "circled the track, climbed the 90 steps without slackening her pace and lighted the sacred Olympic flame."[37] No, he was not prepared to do without young women who were like the "Godesses of ancient Greece."[38]

Team sports were another matter. Coubertin had opposed them in 1921 and Edstrøm joined the opposition in 1924.[39] In the 1950s, Edstrøm and Brundage agreed that team sports were a special problem because many of them had professional as well as amateur manifestations. An Olympic medal in basketball, ice hockey, or soccer led all too frequently to a career in what Brundage usually referred to disdainfully as "the entertainment business."[40] That it was commercialism rather than simply the numbers of athletes involved that bothered him is clear. When naming sports to be eliminated, he also cited individual sports like boxing, cycling, and figure skating because they shared with basketball, ice hockey, and soccer the taint of professionalism.[41] There was, in his mind, still another argument against team sports. They had the capacity, far more than individual sports, to incite paroxysms of nationalism.[42] To reduce the program by eliminating commercialized team sports would therefore have been triply gratifying. With one mighty slash, one could sever the neck from which grew the hydra's heads of nationalism, professionalism, and excessive numbers.

Edstrøm and Brundage had important allies in Executive Board members Lord Porritt of New Zealand and Scharroo of Holland.[43] The latter "urged again and again the necessity of *eliminating all team sports*," but the majority remained committed to these sports for both good and bad reasons.[44] Some simply loved the sports; others pointed out that their popularity meant large ticket sales, a television audience, and huge revenues. The latter argument only exasperated Brundage because it seemed to prove the justice of his criticisms of commercialism, but he was helpless to impose his idealistic will upon the majority. It is probably just as well that he did not quite attain Edstrøm's age of 93; had he done so, he would have witnessed the chauvinistic frenzy that accompanied the 1980 victory of the U.S. hockey team and the post-Olympic stampede of the players to join the professionals of the National Hockey League.

In his crusade to do away with the winter games, Brundage was, once again, able to invoke the sacred name of Coubertin.[45] Edstrøm too had had doubts about the winter sports, which he expressed as early as 1937.[46] In the early years of his presidency, Brundage seemed resigned: "We should never have created the Winter Olympic Games, but how can we stop them now?"[47] The issue remained more or less dormant for a decade. Then, the inability or reluctance of the Fédération Internationale de Ski to withstand the onslaught of commercialism angered Brundage to the point where he resolutely set out to extirpate the evil.

Of the 1968 winter games, a writer in *Skiing* commented, "The Olympic idea died somewhere in Grenoble, France, because there are limits to what the human psyche can stand in the name of belief."[48] Citing this article as well as other evidence, Brundage fired off a circular letter complaining of violations of the rules requiring the games to be held in one place (they were scattered "over the entire district") and prohibiting commercial exploitation ("we had Olympic butter, Olympic sugar, Olympic petrol"). The F.I.S. was charged by Brundage with failure to fulfill its promise to remove advertisements from ski equipment.[49] (Although Brundage was on solid legal grounds in attempting to protect Olympic symbolism, he seems not to have had the law on his side in his quixotic attempts to remove or reduce in size internationally copyrighted trademarks.[50]) Two nations, charged Brundage in his circular, had won over half of all the gold medals ever awarded in the winter games, proof positive that winter sports were not really popular throughout the entire world. Figure skaters seemed to glide directly from the winter games into the commercial ice shows. Worst of all, numerous winter athletes boasted openly of their enormous subrosa incomes and, in effect, dared the I.O.C. to take punitive action against them.[51]

It was all too much. Brundage refused to attend the Alpine events at Grenoble. While scribbling furious notes to himself ("circus," "alpine extravaganza," "farce"), he issued press releases that were a declaration of war against the F.I.S.: "Alpine skiing does not belong in the Olympic Games! . . . Our regulations must be enforced and the program must be simplified."[52] When Brundage protested to Marceau Crespin that half the French skiers failed to live up to the amateur rule, Crespin answered, "You have been misinformed, Monsieur. No one on the French ski team lives up to your definition."[53] Irate, Brundage vowed a showdown at Sapporo in 1972. If the F.I.S. was unready to control its dishonest members, Brundage was ready to do "the dirty work."[54]

In his determination to force the F.I.S. to adhere to the amateur code and disqualify skiers who openly profited from their sport, he sent out a circular letter, dated January 18, 1971, which many members correctly interpreted as a mail ballot. Killanin, Beaumont, Raymond Gafner of Switzerland, van Karnebeek, Jan Staubo of Norway, and Tsuneyoshi Takeda of Japan all protested what they perceived as an act of lèse-majesté, and Brundage first promised that the results of the mail ballot would be sequestered and then maintained that the ballot was not a ballot but merely a questionnaire for advisory purposes.[55] Beaumont wrote frankly and bluntly and faulted Brundage for trying to disqualify skiers without properly discussing the matter with the Executive Board.[56] That Brundage might safely have trusted Beaumont to share his principles was proven by the latter's resignation as president of the French Olympic Committee, on December 8, 1971, when his hypocritical colleagues certified the eligibility of the French skiers.[57] Still, one can sympathize with Brundage's impatience. He had fought in the 1940s to prevent commercial interests from a takeover in ice hockey; he fought now to expose the commercialism of skiers. "By this time," he told van Karnebeek, "everyone knows both the French and Austrian ski teams are part of the . . . departments of tourism—and this is not sport. We are cognizant of enough violations to eliminate not only these teams—but, in fact, practically all prominent skiers from the Games."[58] This almost obsessive desire to take some kind of drastic action against the skiers led not to the disqualification of all the alleged professionals, which might have destroyed the entire winter games for 1972, but to the selection of Karl Schranz of Austria as scapegoat. Schranz certainly set himself up for the role. He communicated a brazen assurance that *he*, the greatest of skiers (which he was), was invulnerable (which he wasn't). Gafner, Staubo, and Marc Hodler all felt that Schranz deserved at least to be heard before he was thrown out of the games, but the desire to punish was too strong for procedural formality.[59] Although a cynic might have expected the Communists to rejoice at the prospect of getting rid of Schranz and clearing the slopes for the East Germans, Vladimir Stoytchev of Bulgaria and Vladimir Smirnov of the Soviet Union both argued that the evidence against Schranz was inconclusive. Ignoring such arguments and brushing aside the protests of Austria's national Olympic committee representative Rudolph Nemetschke, the I.O.C. expelled Schranz by a vote of 28–14.[60] The fury of outraged Austrian nationalism has already been described. Considering the intensity of the anger and the vileness of some of the retaliations, which included attacks upon the children of those who spoke up for him, Brundage must have realized how hopeless was his crusade to abolish the winter games.

CHAPTER XII

THE MIDDLE WESTERNER AND THE FAR EAST

At the I.O.C.'s Munich session in the spring of 1959, the majority favored Tokyo's bid to stage in 1964 the games that were once scheduled for 1940. With 34 votes, the Japanese easily defeated their American rivals, who had argued on behalf of Detroit (which received 10 votes).[1] It was a decision which eroded still further Brundage's domestic popularity. Critics, Douglas Roby among them, felt that his authority was certainly sufficient to have brought the games back to the United States if he had really wanted them for Detroit, but Brundage was no longer as concerned as he had been with his American reputation. His sphere of activity was international and his friends were more often European than American. And he had his own special reasons to be pleased with the selection of Tokyo.

He had been enthusiastic about the entry of the Japanese into the Olympic movement. It was an indication of the games' universality. He was genuinely pleased that the Japanese had swum to a series of upset victories in Los Angeles in 1932 and that Asian athletes, like marathon runner Kitei Son, had done remarkably well in Berlin in 1936. His was clearly the excitement of the missionary whose faith is justified by the conversion of the heathen. As the

Jesuits once brought Christianity to China and Japan, he wanted to bring the religion of Olympism.

Brundage's satisfaction with his colleagues' venue decision had other, more private sources as well. Although he was best known for his dedication to amateur sports, he was also recognized by connoisseurs as one of the world's foremost collectors of Asian art. If the number of magazine articles devoted to him is an accurate guide to interest, he may have been better known in the 1960s for his art collection than for his Olympic office. While *Sports Illustrated* mentioned him often and ran an occasional interview, journals like *Apollo* and *The Connoisseur* offered frequent accolades. There are those who maintain that he will be remembered not for his career in sports but for his jades and bronzes.[2] The dust jacket of Heinz Schoebel's biographical sketch, *The Four Dimensions of Avery Brundage* (1968), pictures him with a pair of carved dragons. In the background is a poster with a Doric column. The only hint of Olympic involvement is the symbolic set of interlocked Olympic rings which appears on the poster. Brundage liked the jacket because it suggested that his two passions were complementary. It was impossible to understand his commitment to Olympism without insight into his love of Asian art.

This love came upon him suddenly and quite unexpectedly. As a young traveler he had gone to European museums and bought black-and-white postcards of famous works of art. He had photographed Istanbul's Hagia Sophia and the Bargello in Florence. There is no indication that his pre-1936 response to art was more intense than the lukewarm one of most tourists. Then, while in Europe for the winter Olympics at Garmisch-Partenkirchen in 1936, he stopped in London and visited the exhibition of Chinese art sponsored by the Royal Academy at Burlington House. He later remembered that the visit had been in 1935, but the exhibition did not open until November of that year and there is no record of a visit to England in November or December. (The Brundages sailed on the *Bremen* on January 29.) Either before or after his visit to the exhibition, Brundage had a chance to share his enthusiastic reactions with Carl Diem, who was then at work on his *Asiatische Rei-*

terspiele (1941); Diem found the Burlington House show "over-whelming."[3]

The exhibition was unquestionably extraordinary. The Chinese government had sent 800 pieces from the imperial collection—jades, bronzes, scrolls, screens, vases, statues. To these treasures, not one of which had ever been shown in the West, the organizers in London added another 1200 items borrowed from almost every major European and American collection, public and private (the Boston Museum of Fine Arts and the Freer Gallery in Washington excepted).[4] The art magazines appearing in the winter of 1935–36 were full of astonished commentary as the experts attempted in a flood of superlatives to express their wonder at thirty-five centuries of Chinese art. Although Brundage had been a museum-goer and a "souvenir hunter," he was transformed into an art-lover.[5] He returned again and again to the exhibition. He wandered from bronze statues of the Chou dynasty to Sung scrolls like Hsia Kuei's famed "A Myriad Miles of the Yangtze." "We spent a week at the exhibition and I came away so enamored with Chinese art that I've been broke ever since."[6] This comment, written thirty-five years later, telescopes somewhat the sequence of events. At the time of his first visits he was not yet ready to embark on his avid, some might say fanatic, career as a collector, but he was certainly anxious to see more of Asian art and there was no better way to do that than to visit the Far East, which he and Elizabeth did in 1939.

The Brundages left from San Francisco on the *Tatuta Maru* and arrived in Yokohama on April 13. They left from Kobe on the *Suwa Maru* on April 27. Their two weeks in Japan were carefully planned by their hosts, who included Count Michimasa Soyeshima of the I.O.C. There were excursions to the elaborately polychromatic temples and shrines of Nikko in the wooded hills to the north of Tokyo (on the 16th and 17th). There was of course a visit to Kyoto, Japan's ancient capital and cultural center, from the 22nd to the 25th. The route to Kobe led through another ancient capital and treasure trove, Nara, and through Osaka ("the Japanese Chicago"). What Brundage made of Kyoto's Ryoanji temple and the unearthly stillness of its Zen Buddhist rock gardens or of the colossal Buddha in Nara's Todai-ji temple, we can only guess at. In his many speeches, he praised the Japanese for their peaceful religious life, without the "holy wars" that disgraced the West, for their love of nature, and for their "wholesome amateur outlook on life."[7] He seems, however, neither to have kept a diary nor to have written many letters to friends at home.

En route to Europe, the couple stopped in Shanghai and Hong Kong, but the war between Japan and China prevented them from seeing much more of Chinese civilization or its art. It was a disappointment that nagged at Brundage for the rest of his life. The Brundages left the boat at Saigon and motored westward through the Mekong Valley into Cambodia, where they were fortunate enough to visit Angkor Wat. From that mysterious complex of Khmer art and architecture they drove on to Bangkok and its exotic mix of Chinese and Indian artistic influence. From Penang, they boarded ship for Colombo, Aden, and Alexandria. From Egypt they flew to London and the 38th Session of the I.O.C., which took place on June 6 through 9 in their favorite hotel, the Dorchester. They were undoubtedly happy to relax into the familiar after their extensive venture into the strange.

By this time, Brundage had probably determined to become a serious collector of Asian art. It was a good time to buy. China was torn apart by a combination of civil and foreign war. Chiang Kai-shek's troops were fighting Mao Tse-tung's and both were fighting against the Japanese invaders. Chaotic conditions forced many wealthy Chinese to sell the *objets d'art* that they had collected in more peaceful times or that had been in their families for centuries. And Brundage bought. In fact, he was the ideal customer— a millionaire in love. His arrivals in London or Paris or (later) Tokyo or Taipei were occasions for art dealers to congregate, but they found him a canny customer despite his love affair with the Orient. He read more widely in the field of Asian art than he did elsewhere, pointing out to an interviewer that a "major library is an indispensable tool."[8] He admitted that collectors inevitably make mistakes. After all, "In this field, some of the fakes are [a] thousand years old,"[9] but he made relatively few blunders.

He acquired ceremonial bronzes, like a *ting* (food vessel) attributed to the reign of Ch'eng Wang (eleventh century B.C.), said to be "one of the best known square *Ting* in existence."[10] He specialized in such bronzes and in jades. His jade collection ranged from the Brancusi-like "Resting Bird" (neolithic period) to the intricately detailed narratives of the Ch'ing dynasty (1644–1912), in which, for instance, four separate groups of horsemen hunt deer and other prey through a forested mountain landscape.[11] The Asian Art Museum of San Francisco, to which Brundage left his collection in 1966 when the Art Institute of Chicago showed insufficient interest, has published an entire volume of over 400 plates simply on the Chinese, Korean, and Japanese sculptures, mostly Buddhas and Bodhisattvas.[12] His paintings were less impressive, but they included treasures as various as the stiffly symmetrical "Preaching Buddha and the Eight Great Bodhisattvas" (fourteenth-century Korea) and Tosa Mitsuoki's delicate courtiers, brightly colored little figures who seem almost lost in the sandy shore that contains them.[13] The painter he most admired was the Sung emperor Hsui-tung, but he was never able to acquire a work by him.[14] One of the most admired pieces in the collection, and one of Brundage's favorites, is a small rhinoceros-shaped bronze ceremonial wine vessel of the late Shang period (eleventh century B.C.). The work was excavated in 1843 in Shantung province, near the birthplace of Confucius, and was said to have been owned by the sage's descendents. Of the "fully zoomorphic" vessel, the curator of the Brundage Collection remarks, "We regard it as the mascot of our museum."[15].

This remark suggests the curator's own affection for the works of art he helped Brundage collect, but what was Brundage's attitude? Although there are collectors of art whose motives are materialistic, who buy in order to sell, who see their Rembrandts or their Warhols as investments or as a hedge against inflation, Brundage was not among them. He bought because he loved what he saw, or, on at least one occasion, because he wanted to restore a work of art to the land from which it had been stolen. (Bangkok's National Museum contains a finely carved temple lintel identified as a gift from Avery Brundage, who recognized it as a work smuggled out of Thailand.) When he sold, it was because he had changed his mind about the aesthetic value of the work and not because he saw the opportunity for capital gains. An anecdote told by Willi Daume suggests a psychological need for the kind of status wealthy businessmen attain by collecting art. Once, when Brundage was asked if he cared for Bach and Beethoven, Daume wisecracked, "No, he likes beer." Brundage was visibly hurt, "He didn't want to be taken as a Philistine."[16] Genuine as his love of art was, it served also as a means to overcome his origins. Queen Elizabeth II has her Vermeers, at Buckingham Palace; Avery Brundage had his jades and bronzes, at La Piñeta.

His advisor in these matters, once he had moved beyond the stage of impulsive purchase, was the French scholar René-Yvon Lefebvre d'Argencé, currently curator of the collection. Lefebvre d'Argencé had studied at the Sorbonne and at Cambridge and had directed museums in Saigon and Hanoi before taking over the famed Cernuschi Museum in Paris. When Brundage met him, he was teaching at the University of California in Berkeley. Once Brundage persuaded him to devote himself entirely to the Brundage collection, the two of them came to an agreement—each had the right to veto a purchase by the other. Brundage bought only what both of them desired.[17] Since no art collectors, not even millionaires, can ever be wealthy enough to acquire all the treasures they covet, Lefebvre d'Argencé was often at odds with Ruegsegger, who took charge of Brundage's financial affairs at approximately the same time that the Frenchman became Brundage's Berenson. Differences in temperament and personality undoubtedly contributed to the frictions between the two trusted advisors, who were not fond of each other.

The scholar's expertise was obviously superior to his employer's. That was, after all, the reason why he was employed. Brundage was in art as well as in sports an amateur in the etymological sense (which he was always ready to gloss) of someone who acted from love, but he was nonetheless—as dealers knew—well informed. Japanese friends marveled that he knew not only the chronology of European but also that of Chinese and Japanese art. Shown a Buddha of the Kamakura period, he was able immediately to comment upon the equivalent work done during the coeval Sung dynasty or in Medieval Europe.[18]

Brundage liked to say that his mission in Japan was to bring a love of sports to his art-collector friends and a love of art to his Olympic colleagues.[19] How far did he go with the possible equation of art and sports? To what degree did he see the visual arts as a complex which included both Chinese bronzes and the Olympic Games? Such questions raise problems over which philosophers have differed. Those, like Pierre Frayssinet, who have argued for the essential identity of sport and the fine arts, have not been able to overcome the objection that all true sports are contests but that the fine arts are not in and of themselves competitive (although they can be made into the occasion for contests).[20] It is, moreover, arguable that the fine arts are essentially expressive and require an audience while sports are intrinsically an activity sufficient in itself (which may, of course, like any activity, acquire spectators). If we reject the notion that sports are a category of art, we can nonetheless ask not about the sameness of the two phenomena but about their possible similarity. In other words, was Brundage attracted by something which he found in both sports and the visual arts or was he drawn rather to alternative and complementary modes of experience which have little in common? The answer seems to be that Brundage saw the two modes of experience as basically dissimilar but as alike in at least one aspect—both were alternatives to commercialism and materialism. Sports and the fine arts were both activities pursued for their own sakes, not for material gain. They were for the amateur. Speaking to the I.O.C.'s Tokyo session of 1958, he used a simple anecdote to assert a similarity in motivation:

The professional athlete must always win if he is to be successful and he must perform and win in the way that the public, who pays the bills, wants him to perform and win. He is a paid worker and not a free agent. It is the same with a commercial artist. To be successful he must make or paint things that can be sold. It is not his taste but the taste of the purchasers which governs.

No true artist or true amateur will submit to such dictation. An amateur-artist creates—he does not accept the standards of the mass—he refuses to follow the crowd. He is not primarily interested in dollars. . . .

Let us take as an example, *netsuke*, the small hand carved wood or ivory toggles used by all Japanese when they wore *kimono* a few generations ago, to suspend their tobacco pouches and *inro*. Originally these *netsuke* were carved with loving care for personal use. The carver conceived the design and built something of himself into the object. It may have taken him six months, but when he finished it was an original thing and bore the stamp of his own personality. He was an amateur carver. Later, after the demand for *netsuke* grew, there arose a class of professional carvers. These men were usually more accomplished and expert than the individuals referred to above; their work was perhaps more polished and displayed a superior technical skill. But it was ordinarily cold, stiff and without imagination. It was the labored effort of a craftsman and not the inspiration of an artist, a living thing. Missing was the element of his personality carved into them by the amateur carver which causes these *netsuke* to be esteemed so much higher by the collector, than the commercial product carved for money.[21]

The amateur, who acts for love rather than calculation, is the focus of Brundage's esteem. He never wrestled with the objection, easily raised, that great art has most often been produced by professionals, that is, by men and women like Shakespeare, Rembrandt, or Bach whose motives were material as well as spiritual and whose vocational pattern was clearly similar to that of a professional athlete. The closest that Brundage came to answering this objection that great artists have lived both for and from their art was to argue that amateurism is a thing of the spirit and that Rembrandt and Hsui-tung painted because they needed to create and to express and that pecuniary motives were secondary. This line of analysis led, however, to the embarrassing possibility that the professional athlete did the same, that he or she played as much from love of the game as from material motives. And Brundage did not even attempt to discuss the fact that professionalism is best defined not by whether or not one is paid but by whether or not the activity is one's vocation, the center of one's concern. Such a definition unquestionably includes Shakespeare, Rembrandt, and Bach among the professionals—along with most Olympic athletes. Brundage never thought the matter through. His projected book on amateurism was never written.

Can one reject Brundage's assertion that the artists and the Olympic athletes are both amateurs and still find similarities between art and sports? One can go beyond the discussion of the alleged motives and argue plausibly that Brundage was attracted to an aesthetic element in sports as well as to the shapes and colors and textures of the visual arts. There is an undeniable visual grace manifested in moments of athletic competition which is at least analogous to the form of a painting or a statue. There are physical actions in sports as well as in the dance which are felt to be faultless, perfect, the kinetic equivalents of the drawings of a bamboo grove that catch the ephemeral and the permanent in nature. There are also, in many sports, moments of stress, strain, and even agony, moments which distort the body and twist the athlete's face into grimace, but these moments too have their parallels in the visual arts, which capture the hideous as well as the conventionally lovely. If the delicate strength of the gymnast poised on the balance beam is an analogue to the momentary stasis caught in a brush stroke by Sesshu, then the tortured physiognomy of an Emil Zatopek finds its artistic parallel in the flayed portraits of Francis Bacon. Was Brundage's preference for Asian over European or American art motivated at least in part by the fact that Chinese and Japanese art was less prone to the depiction of horrors? Was this possibly reflected in Brundage's dislike of violent sports like football and ice hockey?

One can only speculate, but it is important to such speculation to note that Brundage was deeply involved in Asian philosophy and religion, which he more than once claimed to have begun to read as an undergraduate.[22] He called himself "a disciple of Lao Tzu" and, on sending a friend a copy of Witter Bynner's translation of the Chinese sage, he commented that he, Brundage, was "a fellow Taoist."[23] He followed the gift a few years later with a copy of Kakuzo Okakura's *The Book of Tea*, a work which embodies the Japanese approach to the tea ceremony as a formalized occasion for philosophic and aesthetic conversation.[24] On another occasion, jotting down notes to himself, he saw the irony of America's sending teachers to India, whose civilization was "thousands of years older than ours."[25] It seems clear that he was fascinated by a vision of the moral life which was worldly and humanistic without the crass materialism he loathed, that was, above all, aesthetic.

But how seriously can we take the alleged commitment to Taoism as a creed? There is certainly negative evidence for his attachment to Asian philosophy and religion in the sense that his adherence to Christianity was never more than superficial. His family was Episcopalian but he never joined and seldom attended a church.[26] Quite often, his references to Christianity are hostile. He noted that "all too often the Cross or the Crescent has been accompanied by the sword"[27] and he commented, in an official report, that ancient Greece, "not having had the benefits of 2,000 years of Christian civilization, always respected a sacred truce during the period of the Games and all warfare ceased."[28] Positive signs of a commitment to Taoism or to any other conventional religion are rare. In his notes to himself, he asks, "Are people born with a moral sense or not? If not, what are morals, such as the Ten Commandments?"[29] Such questions occur rarely and are never pursued.

If, however, we take Brundage at his word and assume that he believed in the philosophy of Lao Tzu, we are brought up short by the pervasive and fundamental quietism of *The Way of Life*, a quietism quite incompatible with Brundage's other faith, the unconventional religion of Olympism. The message of the poems is that the wise man accepts the world as it is and does not waste his substance in futile efforts to swim against the stream:

> Acceptance of quietism has been condemned as "fatalism."
> But fatalism is acceptance of destiny
> And to accept destiny is to face life with open eyes,
> Whereas not to accept destiny is to face death blindfolded.[30]

Another poem is more typical, working as it does through metaphor:

> How can a man's life keep its course
> If he will not let it flow?

Those who flow as life flows know
They need no other force:
They feel no wear, they feel no tear,
They need no mending, no repair.[31]

It is difficult to imagine a doctrine more opposed to the faith in-
capsulated in the bold motto "altius, citius, fortius" and embodied
in the I.O.C.'s restlessly active president, caught up in "slam bang
action twenty-four hours a day."[32] Perhaps it was the restless activity that sent him back to the quiet of Taoism and the silent
symbolism of carved jade. Perhaps we can conclude that Olympic
sports expressed the dynamic and modern elements of his personality while Taoism and Asian art expressed the contrasted values
of peace and quiet and "the majesty of nature and the minor role
played by man."[33] Except for their shared opposition to getting and
spending, the religions of Olympism and Taoism may have little
in common, but who among us is not drawn simultaneously toward
incompatible ideals? Had he been asked directly, Brundage might
have responded that Taoism and Olympism were the yin and yang
of his sensibility.

As the 1964 Olympics approached, Brundage must have felt as
if the two parts of his life were about to come together. Before the
twain met, disaster intervened. On September 22, 1964, a forest
fire broke out in the mountains east of Santa Barbara. Although it
seemed at first as if the winds might send the flames away from
La Piñeta, the weather shifted and the fire leapt over El Camino
Cielo and swept down upon Brundage's mansion. Ruegsegger and
the staff of the Montecito Country Club, which Brundage owned,
managed to save a few items, but the house and almost all of the
art treasures in it were destroyed. At 6:00 A.M. on the 23rd, Brundage surveyed the ruins. He had rushed back from San Francisco,
from where he was about to leave for Tokyo, but there was nothing
he could do. "The whole house was filled with irreplaceable treasures Mrs. Brundage and I collected from all over the world," he
told reporters. "There were dozens of pieces she particularly liked.
And there were ancient Greek and Japanese pottery, Etruscan
works, Japanese swords and Roman and Egyptian sculpture."[34] He

was, quite naturally, "sick at heart." Elizabeth was already in Tokyo, where Prince Takeda and other Japanese friends were careful to keep the news from her, hiding English-language newspapers before she saw them.[35] It was left to Brundage to break the news to his wife, which he did. (Returning from Japan, the Brundages decided not to rebuild La Piñeta. In its place, they purchased another mansion, this one at 415 Hot Springs Road in nearby Montecito. It remained their California home until Elizabeth's death at the age of 81, on July 1, 1971.[36])

Outwardly, Brundage remained calm and went about his Olympic duties, one of which was to welcome the athletes of the world at the opening ceremonies. He had spoken a few Italian sentences for the Roman games and was determined to follow his own precedent in Tokyo, but Japanese was a much greater challenge even in the *romanji* transliteration of the characters into the Western alphabet. He sought help from Sunichi Hirai, to whom he frequently turned while in Japan. An unusual problem was the need for a special honorific level of speech in the presence of the Emperor. Comically, Brundage begged Hirai not to consult with Prince Takeda: "He'll never be satisfied!"[37] If the Emperor was displeased, he kept his annoyance politely to himself.

The ceremony itself was marred somewhat by the behavior of the Iraqi team, which deviated from the prescribed order of march and refused to take its ordained place next to the Israeli team. Instead, the Iraqi athletes lined up side by side with the Iranians.[38] (For this blatantly political act, Brundage demanded an explanation and he was eventually mollified by a change in Iraq's Olympic Committee and by a promise that a "friendly relationship will be maintained with all N.O.C.s."[39])

It is unlikely that the Iraqi gesture was noticed by many. The track-and-field events were suitably thrilling. Peter Snell's double victory in the 800 and the 1500 meters was especially memorable. In the 800-meter final, the New Zealander had to drop back behind runners who had boxed him in before he was able to sprint to the outside and overtake his rivals George Kerr of Jamaica and Wilson Kiprigut of Kenya, both of whom had lowered Snell's Olympic record in the semifinals. Americans Robert Schul and William Mills unexpectedly won the 5,000 and 10,000 meters, races which Americans had never won before, and Ethiopia's Abebe Bikila triumphed for the second time in the marathon. The men of the Russian track-and-field team did rather poorly, winning only the hammer throw and the high jump, and the women did only somewhat better— Tamara Press won the shot put and the discus while her sister Irina won the pentathlon.

Collecting a chestful of medals, Donald Schollander was the star of men's swimming while Australia's Dawn Fraser continued to dominate the women's sprints. Among other American champions were a boxer named Joseph Frazier and a basketball player named William Bradley. Although Czechoslovakia's Vera Caslavska performed marvelously to win the combined gymnastics title as well as individual gold medals on the balance beam and the vaulting horse, she was destined to triumph even more dramatically four years later, in Mexico City, when history made a political allegory of her contest with her Russian rivals.

When it was all over, Brundage announced that Japan had been converted to Olympic principles. He was surely too optimistic, but 3.5 million Japanese had applied for the 60,000 opening-day tickets, and Brundage had some reason to think that the Asian nation was indeed unusually receptive to Olympic ideals.[40] Or perhaps it was simply his desire to think well of a people that had created the Zen Buddhist rock garden of Ryoanji temple.

CHAPTER XIII

OLYMPIC COMMERCE

When he heard names like "Rossignol" and "Adidas," Brundage frowned. The names had become, by the late 1960s, symbols of temptation. Manufacturers' colophons had become diabolical rivals to the Olympic rings. If skiers or runners took money to appear in advertisements or to display their skis or their shoes before the television cameras, they violated the amateur code and defiled the religion of Olympism. Brundage looked upon the fallen athletes as sinners or, when they openly defied him and boasted of their commercialism, as apostates. There were other aspects of commercialism too, and they too violated his principle that none should capitalize on the Olympic movement. One of these other aspects appears in Olympic minutes and committee reports under the rubric "emblems."

To the uninitiated historian who reads through the Olympic files, it will forever be a minor mystery that Brundage and his colleagues spent as much time as they did in the futile effort to prevent the commercial use of Olympic symbolism and even of the word "Olympic," which had been in the English language since 1610. For Brundage, the appropriation of the Olympic rings or the motto "altius, citius, fortius" for any purpose other than the Olympic movement was—in the strictest sense—blasphemy. His zeal in this matter was extraordinary if not wacky. When the Fannie May Candy Company of Chicago used the Olympic rings in a newspaper advertisement, he fired off a letter of protest.[1] When he discovered the Olympiad Skate Company of St. Paul, he dashed off another complaint.[2] He attempted to deprive Greece's Olympic Airlines of its name, but the Greek authorities retorted that their title to the symbolism was even more substantial than the I.O.C.'s.[3] His sense of betrayal was especially keen when he learned that Josef Neckermann, the German millionaire, had used his Olympic success as an equestrian to advertise his mail-order business: "Here is a clear capitalization of athletic fame that violates all of the Olympic ideals. It should be called to the attention of the German Olympic Committee, the International Equestrian Federation and our Eligibility Committee."[4] Brundage was reminded that Neckermann was very active in the Olympic movement and was at the time a candidate for I.O.C. membership.[5] It is likely that the contretemps over the commercial misuse of symbolism contributed to Neckermann's failure and to the election of Berthold Beitz of the Krupp concern. (Krupp has not yet advertised "Olympic steel.")

In his campaign to protect Olympic symbolism, Brundage did not rely simply on appeals and protests. As an Executive Committee member of the American Olympic Association he wrote to inquire if the motto and the Olympic rings were legally copyrighted.[6] They were not. As president of the association (renamed United States of America Sports Federation), he persuaded Representatives David I. Walsh of Massachusetts and James E. Van Zandt of Pennsylvania to introduce bills to prohibit the use of the word "Olympic" in any manner that was "likely to deceive the public."[7] Success came in 1950 when the United States Congress passed legislation guaranteeing the American representatives of the Olympic movement exclusive rights to its emblems. Neither for business nor for charity was anyone other than the U.S.A.S.F. allowed to use

an escutcheon having a blue chief and vertically extending alternate red and white bars on the base with five interlocked rings displayed on the chief, or any other sign or insignia made or colored in imitation thereof, or the words "Olympics," "Olympiad," or "Citius, Altius, Fortius" or any combination of these words.[8]

Brundage urged other national Olympic committees to follow the

American lead and he attempted to organize an international conference to that purpose.

Legislation is one thing; compliance with the law is another. John T. McGovern, attorney for the U.S.A.S.F., reported in 1951, a year after the American law had been passed, that there were 22,500 commercial enterprises in the United States which had a prior legal right to describe themselves as Olympic. The word, alas, was in the public domain. The U.S.A.S.F. was able to take action only against the infringements of the graphic design described in the law.[9]

This sober counsel came too late to keep Brundage from one of his most quixotic campaigns. The target was the Helms Bakery of Los Angeles, which used the Olympic rings in its advertising and proclaimed itself the Olympic bread.[10] Difficult as it is for an outsider to imagine, Brundage kept a folder of incriminating bread wrappers. He actually mailed out samples to prove his allegations.[11] One can look upon all of this as quirky if not demented behavior, but one must, once again, consider the religious context. It was as if a devout Christian had discovered a bakery advertising its products with pictures of Jesus using its whole wheat bread to perform the miracle of the loaves and fishes or enjoying its pumpernickel at the Last Supper. Whether Brundage's obsession seems admirable or ridiculous depends upon the beliefs of the observer. That he was not hopelessly Scrooge-like in his attitude toward Olympic symbolism can be seen in his generous response to the Kennedy family when the Joseph P. Kennedy Jr. Foundation staged its "Special Olympics" for handicapped children. Brundage arranged for the children to stay at the LaSalle Hotel and saw to it that Ruegsegger gave financial support through the Brundage Foundation.[12]

There was another aspect of Brundage's crusade against Olympic commerce. In addition to the problems caused by athletes who wished to capitalize upon their exploits and businessmen who seized upon Coubertin's symbolism to promote their products, there was a new phenomenon that became increasingly apparent in the 1960s. The I.O.C. itself began to sell the Olympic movement. When the Fédération Internationale de Ski decided to allow skiers to appear in advertisements if the F.I.S. or a national affiliate, not the athlete, was remunerated, Brundage protested vehemently, but as the Executive Board refused to back him he suffered what the press referred to as a "humiliating rebuff."[13] An I.O.C. which engaged in commerce was in a poor position to condemn international federations that engaged in commerce. National Olympic committees had for decades been involved in a small trade in Olympic pins and buttons and posters, items sold to raise money to send the American or the German or the Argentine team to the games. In the 1960s, new techniques created a new situation. The new medium—television—made it possible for hundreds of millions of people to watch the games more closely than thousands had in earlier days when the audience was limited to those who crowded into the Olympic stadia and halls. An audience of millions was one that neither advertisers nor bureaucrats were likely to ignore. The commercial networks of the United States and Japan and the state-owned agencies of Europe began to offer large sums for television rights. The I.O.C., which had been almost ludicrously indigent for half a century, was suddenly caught up in what can quite literally be termed an *embarras de richesse*.

It was truly a switch from rags to riches. Originally, the members of the I.O.C. paid their own expenses while Coubertin covered most of the costs of the Paris or (from 1915 on) the Lausanne office. "For the first 25 or 30 years of its existence," wrote Brundage, "the office of the I.O.C. was in the waist coat pocket of the Baron de Coubertin," and the committee was almost without financial resources.[14] Miscellaneous disbursements were covered by an annual assessment paid by the I.O.C. members; a sum was originally set at 25 Swiss francs and was gradually raised (but not regularly collected—dunning the remiss turned into a steady job). Brundage generously supported Olympism with his own money just as Coubertin had done, but the I.O.C. reached the middle 1950s with a financial basis little better than that provided by a bake sale. Exeter proposed to lay a small tax on tickets to athletic events; a surcharge of 5 percent would have been enough to rescue the I.O.C. from insolvency. He added that his plan might have had an additional benefit in that it would open up the I.O.C. to members who were not independently wealthy.[15]

Brundage's stand on the ticket tax was inconsistent. He had championed such a tax in the United States. When the A.A.U. turned down a proposed 5 percent Olympic tax on all tickets sold for A.A.U.-sanctioned events, Brundage objected to the organization's secretary, "As I recall it, the Executive Committee in San Francisco unanimously endorsed this proposal. Can you tell me why it was not accepted? I think it is most unfortunate that this proposal was not adopted."[16] Nonetheless, Brundage objected strongly to Exeter's suggested tax (3 percent to the international sports federations, 2 percent to the I.O.C.). Brundage actually maintained that the imposition of such a tax would mean the end of the I.O.C. "If we start taking part of the gate receipts . . . we are finished—the Olympic Games will never survive unless they remain amateur."[17] The Olympic movement is "an idealistic enterprise" which would be wrecked by schemes of taxation.[18] Exeter's responses—that the I.A.A.F. held no world track-and-field championships and badly needed the income from its share of the proposed tax, that the I.O.C. was not liable to tumble into the abyss because of a 5 percent tax—fell on deaf ears.[19] The contradictory responses to the A.A.U. tax which Brundage favored and the I.O.C. tax which he did not may have been motivated by his sense that the Olympic movement was especially sacrosanct even within the special world of amateur sports or by something as simple as growing hostility to Exeter. Since his feelings about his English rival were not allowed to endanger the Olympic movement, it is probable that the inconsistency was the result of Olympic piety. Brundage did not want the I.O.C. to enter into the world of commerce in any way, shape, or form. His conversion to the religion of Coubertin had come about when he perceived the realm of Olympism as a shining place apart from the sordid domain of commerce. To have the I.O.C. reap the benefits of any sort of taxation was to breach the dike that separated the Olympic vale from the flood waters of materialism. When the I.O.C. debated Exeter's scheme, Brundage persuaded the majority to table the motion.[20]

Brundage was ready to accept the dismal consequences of such high-mindedness. Gafner recalls a moment, during a meeting at Dubrovnik, when the president announced that the I.O.C. was bankrupt, "and he was rather pleased."[21]

Given this obsessive desire to defend the purity of the Olympic Games from the stain of commercialism, Brundage was not entranced by the sugarplum dream of television revenue. At first, he did not imagine that there really was much of a prospect for such revenue: "It isn't going to be easy to get money for the television rights to the Olympic Games," he predicted in 1957.[22] Did he unconsciously hope that the games were not vendable? If he did, his hopes were quickly disappointed. Doubts about commercial possibilities were dispelled in 1960 when the Comite Olimpico Nazionale d'Italia (C.O.N.I.), which was itself well funded by a national lottery, offered the I.O.C. 5 percent of the expected million dollars in television money from the sale of rights to the 1960 games. The I.O.C.'s first reaction was to defer a decision on whether or not to accept C.O.N.I.'s offer.[23] The Executive Board decided a few months later to take the money, but Brundage's fear was that the Olympic coffers were about to become a Pandora's box, and he was right.[24] One historian has observed, "As the Games were big business, a business-like attitude began to pervade this sport organization's approach to the Games and the Olympic movement."[25]

The year 1960 was, in the words of the director of "émissions sportives" for French television, "the year of the Olympic Games and the triumph of sports television."[26] The pictures from Rome proved that the games were marvelously telegenic. NBC was encouraged, in 1961, to offer the Japanese organizers $660,000 for the American rights to the 1964 games. Technological progress accelerated and satellite transmission of televised images enormously increased the potential audience for live coverage. From Olympiad to Olympiad, the income from the sale of rights skyrocketed from millions to tens of millions and eventually to hundreds of millions of dollars. By 1966, there were already debates about the division of the pie for 1972. The Executive Board decided to divide the first million dollars (from the summer games) into three equal parts, with the thirds going to the international federations, the national committees, and the I.O.C. For the second million, the organizing committee was to receive one third of the total and the others were to divide the rest. For the third million, the organizing committee was to receive two thirds of the total, etc.[27] A similar plan was adopted for the income from the winter games. As the complaints from the interest groups became a clamor of dissatisfaction, Brundage was able to say that he had told them so: "The minute we handle money, even if we only distribute it, there will be trouble, as we have already discovered."[28] Nostalgic for the more idealistic days when the members reached into their own pockets to defray Olympic expenses, Brundage was worried that television money might "lead to a disaster for the Olympic movement as it had already proved to be a disaster for amateur sports in the United States where, as Brundage noted to Ivar Vind, rights to televise college football sold for tens of millions of dollars."[29] By the time he repeated this gloomy thought to Albert Mayer, the I.O.C. was already involved in bargaining with the Permanent General Assembly of the National Olympic Committees (the P.G.A.) and the General Assembly of the International Federations (G.A.I.F.). They had *their* ideas on how the money should be divided. It was an additional worry to Brundage that the I.O.C. had begun, by 1969, to live beyond its income in anticipation of future revenues.[30] The Olympic movement had mortgaged itself to the television networks. Distressed and disillusioned, Brundage watched as the I.O.C. adopted first the financial procedures and then the fiscal attitudes of a modern corporation.

As the "profit and loss mentality"[31] emerged, monetary considerations began to distort the Olympic movement in unexpected ways. As early as 1965, Exeter pointed out to Brundage that the games were more likely to attract large sums if they were held in the United States.[32] Were the decisions to hold the games in Montreal, Moscow, and Los Angeles influenced by calculations of profit and loss? It is impossible to say.

Infractions of the amateur rule were certainly not new, but the new electronic technology transformed the scale of the problem in the 1960s. Athletes had for decades been tempted to accept small sums of money for advertisements painted or sewn on their equipment or clothing, but the opportunity to reach a global television audience made advertisers frantic. Athletes were corrupted, rules and regulations were mocked, money flowed, hypocrisy flourished. When Jean-Claude Killy skied to victory at Grenoble in 1968, he was forbidden to flash his trademarked skis before the TV cameras. No matter. One of his associates rushed up to hug him. The associate wore gloves which were visible to the viewers around the world, and the gloves bore the trademark of the ski manufacturer. That the manufacturer was French can be credited to Crespin of the French Olympic Committee, who is said by one authority to have paid 300,000 francs to free Killy from a 5,000-franc contract with an Italian company.[33] The hug which greeted victorious Killy was a long one, even by Gallic standards, and the TV audience had ample time to realize which make of ski they should buy if they too dreamed of Olympic gold (and television hugs). Observing this "sordid little stunt," one of Brundage's critics wrote, "I sympathized with him and for the first time in my life I felt intense admiration for him."[34] After the Grenoble games, wrote Brundage, "many of the Alpine skiers had the impudence to brag about how they broke the Olympic rules."[35] It was a classic case of insult and injury.

It was not just that the Olympics had become commercialized. It was also that nationalism interacted with commerce in ways that seemed to seduce the I.O.C. into a dance of death. From London in 1948 to Munich in 1972, the cost of the games spiraled upward. Charles de Gaulle had felt that the French athletes at the 1964 games had done little to enhance, "la gloire française" and the general wanted a better showing in 1968. Brundage noted that the French invested $240 million in the winter games at Grenoble, "and when you consider that this was for ten days of amateur sport, it seems to be somewhat out of proportion. With that kind of money involved there is bound to be commercialization of one kind or another."[36] The summer games of 1976 are alleged to have cost almost ten times as much. One must be cautious, however, about accepting such allegations at face value. Since few economists have studied the Olympics to distinguish carefully between sums spent for necessary urban developments which remain tangible assets (like a subway system) and money expended solely for the games (like the salaries of the multilingual guides), one must discount some of the more sensational claims of fiscal catastrophe. Reports that the 1976 games cost $2 billion make good headlines but contain little precise information about real costs. Still, urban and national pride are at stake and each city seems determined to outdo its predecessor. Each organizing committee seems intoxicated by dreams of grandeur. And there is only one apparently inexhaustible source of money to defray the routinely underestimated costs—television. The networks pay and the athletes perform. Who calls the tune?

Although Brundage seems never to have commented on the problem either in writing or in talks with his colleagues, the coverage of the Olympics by commercial television means that the tens of millions of dollars paid by the networks will be matched and exceeded by the tens of millions paid by the advertisers which means, inexorably, that the most marvelous athletic achievements will be followed, preceded, and interrupted by the admen, at least in the United States and other countries which rely mainly on commercial rather than state-owned television. Olga Korbut competed against Karin Janz and Ludmilla Tourescheva in the gymnastic contests of 1972, and the three of them, and all the other athletes at Munich, had to share their triumphs with the advertisers who destroyed the drama in order to hawk their wares. Had advertisers halted the competitions in order to display their goods and tout their services on the 400-meter track, Brundage and the whole I.O.C. would have been enraged, but the American television viewer experiences such interruptions routinely—and no one, save for a handful of intellectuals, seems to mind. A marathon or a soccer match broken up by cigarette ads strikes almost no one as absurd. In comparison to this travesty, the commercialism of the Helms bakery's Olympic bread seems trivial. By 1972, Olympism was not dead, but it had come increasingly to resemble what Brundage had for fifty years inveighed against, a branch of the entertainment industry. That the 1980 Olympics were less commercialized than those of 1972 and 1976 was due not to the revival of idealism but to political interference and Communist ideology. It is indeed difficult not to wax ironic.

CHAPTER XIV

DEALING WITH
THE THIRD WORLD

When Coubertin designed the Olympic rings symbolizing the interconnectedness of the five continents and when Diem created the Olympic bell summoning the youth of the world, they expressed universalistic aspirations. When Edstrøm and Brundage decided to welcome the athletes of the Communist bloc into the Olympic community, they too acted ecumenically. To Brundage, perhaps even more than to Edstrøm, the Third World was an opportunity and a challenge to the Olympic movement. The underdeveloped world was also, although Brundage did not initially realize it, a grave threat and a source of vexation. The new nations of Africa and Asia were eager to participate in the games, but they were also determined that other nations, which they branded as racist or zionist, be cast out of the Olympic family. There was no way for the I.O.C. to escape new political entanglements.

As one dimension of its program for amateur sports, the I.O.C. offered its patronage for regional games to be conducted on Olympic principles. It offered encouragement and technical assistance and, in the 1960s, financial support as well. These regional games were thought to be valuable as a kind of mini-Olympics at which nations unlikely to see their flags hoisted in the victory ceremonies of the regular games might nonetheless enjoy their triumphs, gain experience, and imbibe the lessons of fair play and good sportsmanship. Cities like Bangkok and Beirut, which acted as hosts for regional games, acquired organizational knowhow that might enable them to stage the real thing one day. In theory, regional games were an integral part of the Olympic movement; in practice, they often engendered destabilizing political conflict.

Until after Brundage's retirement, there were relatively few problems connected with the Pan-American Games. Anti-Americanism, expressed in jeering, hooting crowds and in biased judging, became a serious concern only in the 1970s. The Mediterranean Games, however, were a forecast of what was to come. When Mohammed Taher Pacha of Egypt initially proposed "les Jeux Mediterranées" in 1948, he assured his I.O.C. colleagues that "every country bordering on the Mediterranean would be included in the games."[1] By the time that plans were set to hold the first of the series in Alexandria in October of 1951, there was a new nation on the shores of the Mediterranean—Israel. The Israelis had formed a national Olympic committee and had requested recognition by the I.O.C. the previous year, but the Copenhagen Session which accepted the Federal Republic of Germany rejected the State of Israel. (The irony of this did not escape the American Jewish Labor Council, the New York *Daily Worker*, and a number of private citizens who probably hurt their own cause when they denounced Brundage's friends Diem and von Halt as former Nazis.[2])

By the time the second festival was being planned, Israel's Olympic Committee had won official recognition. In simple geographical terms, all the region should have been invited to the games, but the existence of the State of Israel was an abomination in Arab eyes. The Palestinian sense of displacement and dispossession had further poisoned Arab–Israeli relations. The Spanish hosts of the second games invited the Israelis to Barcelona, then withdrew the invitation under Arab pressure.[3] The Spanish pretext was the equivalent of the infamous "grandfather clause" of Reconstruction days: since Israel had not been at the first games, it had no right to be at the second. The Israeli Olympic Committee protested to Brundage, citing the I.O.C.'s own rules and regulations for its patronage of regional games.[4]

Otto Mayer supported the Israelis, but when they took their grievance to the I.O.C. Executive Board, Brundage was unready to act upon the principle of universalism: "We can not become involved in a matter of this kind. Those who organize Regional Games are quite within their rights to include or exclude any country."[5] He then advised the Executive Board that the "I.O.C. should not become involved in the administration of events other than the Olympic Games."[6] Encouraged perhaps by Exeter's agreement with him on this point, Brundage demonstrated his least attractive side and speculated sarcastically that Israel might also claim the right to participate in the British Empire Games because Lord David Balfour had once promised them a Palestinian homeland.[7] A few months later, however, Brundage changed his mind on the rights and wrongs of the situation. He now took the line that the exclusion of Israel was politically motivated, which it certainly was, and counter to the conditions of I.O.C. patronage. "As a matter of principle," he wrote, "we had to oppose them in 1936 and we may have to support them in 1955."[8] (It was unfortunately typical of him to have lumped American Jews and Israelis into a single "them.") Despite I.O.C. support, the second games were celebrated without Israeli participation.

By the time the third festival was in preparation, Brundage had switched back to his original laissez-faire attitude. How could anyone expect Lebanon to invite the Israelis to Beirut "when there is practically a state of war between the latter country and all its neighbors?"[9] Since Brundage had argued the opposite view vis-à-vis Chinese participation in the 1940 Olympics and Russian participation in the 1956 Olympics, it is difficult not to suspect him of at least vestiges of anti-Semitic prejudice. His exasperated comments parallel those of segregationists in the United States, "I cannot understand why anyone wants to go where he is not wanted."[10] Others did understand. The I.A.A.F., led by Exeter, decided not to sanction track-and-field events for the Mediterranean Games unless Israeli athletes were invited to Beirut.[11] Brundage was not happy with the edict: "you will remember that we looked the other way when you did not want to invite the Germans to the 1948

Games in London."[12] Gabriel Gemayel of Lebanon made exactly the same point in a letter of protest to the I.A.A.F.[13] Nonetheless, Gemayel compromised under pressure from the federation and agreed that the Mediterranean Games would not include track-and-field events—but there were simultaneous "Jeux Libanais" which consisted of precisely these events, and (to the surprise of no student of legal subterfuge) Israel was not invited to them.[14] It is unlikely that anyone in the stands realized that the 400-meter race was not officially a part of the Mediterranean Games. Brundage offered his sympathy to Gemayel because of the I.A.A.F.'s "unwarranted restrictions" and accepted a personal invitation to attend the Beirut Games.[15]

By late 1962, Brundage had rejoined Exeter in the opinion that regional games under Olympic patronage must include *all* the nations of the region.[16] Perhaps he was as tired as Exeter of ethnic, racial, and religious hatreds. When an Asian official complained that the word "marathon" was an unwelcome reminder of a military defeat inflicted upon his ancestors in 490 B.C., Exeter wondered ironically to Brundage how a team of French athletes might feel upon arrival at London's Waterloo Station.[17] The immediate context of Brundage's revived support for Israel was Libya's desire to participate in the Mediterranean Games. Since Libya had not participated in 1951, it was technically liable to exclusion on the same grounds as Israel. Brundage was consistent enough to acknowledge that the two nations were both barred by the "founders only" rule, but the Italian organizers of the games, held in Naples, were reluctant to anger the Arab nations and Israel was not invited to the IV Mediterranean Games.[18]

Finally, on February 7, 1963, the Executive Board announced that free access to participation was an absolute precondition of I.O.C. patronage for all regional games.[19] At the next meeting of the Executive Board, Gemayel explained that Israel had not been invited because its national Olympic committee had not applied for admission two years in advance. Brundage answered that regional games had achieved their purposes and ought to be replaced by world championships.[20] No patronage was extended to the V Mediterranean Games held at Tunis in 1967, to which Israel was not invited.[21]

Why did the I.O.C. decide, after more than a decade of controversy, to act upon its ideals? One reason was undoubtedly that the breach in the wall of principle was followed by other breaches that threatened to bring the entire Olympic ramparts tumbling down. If the walls *had* come down, the Joshua for this particular Jericho would have been President Sukarno of Indonesia, who had vigorously sounded the trumpet of his defiance. Only minutes before Brundage reported to the international federations that the Executive Board had become adamant about free access to regional games, he announced that the Board had suspended the Indonesian Olympic Committee because of "the deplorable incidents which took place in Djakarta on the occasion of the celebrations of the IVth Asiatic Games."[22] The incidents were the result of the national committee's refusal to protest its government's denial of visas for Israeli and Nationalist Chinese athletes. Brundage exhibited none of the hesitation which had characterized his stand on the Mediterranean Games. He denounced the exclusion of Israel and Taiwan as "scandalous."[23] When the Indonesian committee explained to Chancellor Mayer that the committee had sent out invitations but that the Indonesian government had confiscated the letters, Brundage remained strict: "It may be, and probably is true, that the Government was at fault, but how can we induce Governments to change if we do not take action and invoke penalties when violations occur [?]"[24] When the Executive Board met later that year with representatives of the national Olympic committees, the suspension of Indonesia was hotly debated. Brundage's opponents, citing the frequent refusal of visas to East Germans, were indignant. In the words of a recent historian, "A double standard was apparent in the IOC suspension. It suspended Indonesia for virtually the same crime committed by France and the United States."[25] Asian delegates protesting the suspension were supported by Roman Kiselev of the Soviet Union, who expressed his astonishment that the Executive Board had committed an act of political interference.[26] Iraq quit the Olympic movement in protest and the entire Arab bloc considered a boycott of the 1964 games,[27] but the I.O.C. retained the full support of its Indian member, G. D. Sondhi. Before the games, he had persuaded the Executive Board of the Asian Games Federation, in an all-night emergency session, to adhere to Olympic rules. The games were to have been renamed "The Jakarta Games." On August 28, four days after the games began, the Asian Games Federation had met and overruled its own Executive Board. Sondhi became persona non grata in the eyes of the Indonesian government. Sukarno's Minister of Trade announced economic reprisals against India and the Ministry of Foreign Affairs may have been the instigator of the mob which gathered on September 3, attacked the Indian Embassy, and invaded the Hotel Indonesia, from which Sondhi managed to flee in the nick of time. He reached the airport and flew to Singapore. The disappointed Indonesians had had to content themselves with execrations of the Indian athletes still in Djakarta.[28]

Stung by the political rebuke from Lausanne, Sukarno announced Indonesia's withdrawal from the Olympic movement. With moral and financial support from the People's Republic of China, Sukarno now began grandly to plan what he called the "Games of the New Emerging Forces" (G.A.N.E.F.O.).[29] These games were to be based "on the spirit of the 1955 Bandung Conference," i.e., on the solidarity of the Third World against its imperialist oppressors. As if to rub salt in the I.O.C.'s wounds, Sukarno now proclaimed that sports and politics are inseparable: "Let us declare frankly that sport has something to do with politics. And Indonesia now proposes to mix sport with politics."[30] Sports were to become an instrument of emancipation from imperialist fetters, including the chains fastened upon the Third World by the I.O.C.

Sukarno had unmistakably thrown down the gauntlet and G. D. Sondhi, for one, was eager to accept the challenge. He noted that governments often allege "Reasons of State, *at a very late hour*, to forbid the entry of a team or teams. In such a case very firm action is essential. The Games or Championship must be *forthwith cancelled* . . . . Desperate situations call for desperate remedies."[31] Sondhi scorned the I.A.A.F. compromise which allowed participation if the games were given another name. Discrimination was discrimination no matter what the games were called. The I.A.A.F., the Fédération Internationale de Natation Amateur, and the Fédération Internationale Haltérophile ("International Weightlifting Federation") all decided to refuse their sanction of the G.A.N.E.F.O. A. D. Touny of Egypt, an I.O.C. member and also vice president of G.A.N.E.F.O., protested the I.A.A.F. action and defended Sukarno so energetically that Otto Mayer referred to him as a spy.[32] Brundage wrote to Touny to condemn "public statements of defiance" and transgressions of common courtesy. He specifically praised G. D. Sondhi.[33]

Eventually, 48 nations sent teams to the first G.A.N.E.F.O. (68 had been invited). The Soviet Union prudently sent second-string athletes to prevent the disqualification of its stars by the international federations. The games were celebrated November 10–22, 1963, complete with G.A.N.E.F.O. torch, flag, hymn, and doves of peace. They were successful enough for a permanent organization to set itself up in Djakarta with the Indonesian minister of sports as president of its executive board. Although the I.O.C.'s Executive Board lifted its ban on Indonesia in 1964 in return for a promise to respect Olympic rules, Touny was given two years to decide whether he wished to continue as G.A.N.E.F.O.'s vice president or remain an I.O.C. member.[34] Before Touny made up his mind, Indonesia underwent an abortive coup d'état by its Communist Party, a repressive counterrevolution, and a change of government. Sukarno was gone and plans for G.A.N.E.F.O. II foundered when Cairo, the prospective host, backed out because of "the financial strain"; the games "sank into quiet oblivion."[35]

There was, however, an aftermath to the G.A.N.E.F.O. episode. A number of individual athletes were suspended when they defied the ban laid down by the I.A.A.F., the F.I.N.A., and the F.I.H. Some of these athletes were then selected to take part in the 1964 Olympics in Tokyo. The I.O.C. turned them away and Brundage had to deal with the irate head of the North Korean team, six of whose athletes were among the suspended. The Koreans threatened to withdraw their entire team if the suspended six were not allowed to compete. Brundage cautioned them, "You are complaining because we keep six people out of the Games and you are keeping 174 out. Who is right?"[36] The Koreans thought that they were right, and they withdrew from competition. When representatives of the Olympic committees of Egypt, Morocco, and the Soviet Union expressed their sympathy for the North Koreans, Sondhi remarked that he "sympathized with the suspended athletes but . . . no one seemed to sympathize with the two whole countries which were prevented [from participating] in the Asian Games." Sondhi's remarks were more just and humane than the propagandistic vituperation of the I.O.C. for its "pro-U.S. stranglehold on world sport."[37] The V and VI Asian Games were celebrated in 1966 and 1970 without serious political flareups. By the time that politics returned to plague the VII games in 1974, Brundage's problems had become Killanin's.

Of all the family of man, the last major group to be integrated into the Olympic movement were the black peoples of Africa. Ali Mohammed Hassanein of Egypt was the first African to compete when he entered the sabre and foil competitions in 1912. His countrymen Ibrahim Mustafa and Said Nasser won gold medals in 1928 in Greco-Roman wrestling and in weight lifting. That same year, A. B. El Quafi won the marathon as a member of the French team. The first black African to win a gold medal was Abebe Bikila of Ethiopia, who won the marathon in 1960 and 1964.

I.O.C. member Angelo Bolanchi hoped to arrange for the first African Games at Alexandria in 1927, but there was a series of delays and regional festivals were not inaugurated until after World War II. The first important African games were the Jeux de l'Amitié, which were sponsored by the French in conjunction with their former colonies. The first celebration of these games was at Tananarive, Madagascar (1960), the second at Abidjan on the Côte d'Ivoire (1961). At the third Jeux de l'Amitié, held at Dakar in Senegal (1963), Brundage and Beaumont attended and thus showed support for the games (whose official poster showed a white hand passing a baton to a black one). Brundage's commitment to the inclusion of Africa within the Olympic movement impressed the brilliant young Senegalese jurist, Kéba Mbaya; when he met Brundage for the second time, at Munich in 1972, he was astonished by Brundage's recollection of the details of their first encounter. Brundage himself was impressed by Senegal's president, Léopold Senghor, a francophone poet who read Pindar in Greek and had visited Olympia.[38] A few months after the Jeux de l'Amitié, Brundage nominated Nigeria's Sir Adetokunbo Ademola to become the first black African member of the I.O.C.[39]

When thirty nations competed two years later at the Jeux Africains at Brazzaville, Congo, leaders of the Olympic movement came to offer their moral support. Brundage was there with Exeter, Onesti, and the presidents of eight international sports federations. Brundage was unimpressed by Reginald Honey's complaint that South Africa, Rhodesia, Angola, and Mozambique were excluded from the African games; he told the South African I.O.C. member that his country had violated the rules and that the other three were not independent states.[40] More important to Brundage was the fact that teams from Congo-Brazzaville and Congo-Leopoldville both competed despite the "strained relations" between the two countries.[41] The apostle of amateurism was also pleased that the hosts had cancelled a lucrative contract "in order to keep the stadium free from advertising."[42] On his way to the 5th Session of the International Olympic Academy in Olympia, Brundage stopped to confer with President Jomo Kenyatta of Kenya and to inspect the athletic facilities of Uganda and Ethiopia. He was unquestionably eager to bring black Africa into the "Olympic family."

That the first African games went well was due in large part to Jean-Claude Ganga of the Congo (Brazzaville), a man who soon came to play an important role in Olympic history. Ganga greatly appreciated Brundage's support in 1965, but the two men were destined to clash. When representatives of 32 African nations founded the Supreme Council for Sport in Africa (at Mamako,

Mali, in December, 1966), Ganga became secretary general of the new organization. The Supreme Council issued a fairly pugnacious statement of purpose:

It is the firm decision of the Supreme Council to use every means to obtain the expulsion of the South African sports organizations from the Olympic Movement and from International Federations should South Africa fail to comply fully with the IOC rules.

Finally, the Supreme Council invites all its members to subject their decision to participate in the 1968 Olympic Games to the reservation that no racialist team from South Africa takes part. . . .[43]

Brundage and Exeter, fearing that the African nations might desert the Olympic movement en bloc and go over to Sukarno's G.A.N.E.F.O., had reluctantly acquiesced in the exclusion of South Africa and Rhodesia from the African Games, but they were not yet ready to recommend the final expulsion of either country from the international sports community.[44]

South Africa's sports were undeniably segregated under the racist doctrine of apartheid. Whites enjoyed excellent facilities, high levels of participation, and considerable international success dating back to Reginald Walker's win in the 100 meters at London in 1908. Blacks, on the other hand, were badly disadvantaged. Those with leisure enough to play and money enough to acquire equipment, like cricket star Basil D'Oliveira and golfer Papwa Sewgolum, were denied the opportunity to test their skills against their athletic peers within South Africa or in international competition. The ban on interracial matches was strictly applied to visiting foreigners too; New Zealand's rugby teams were invited to South Africa with the proviso that they leave behind their Maori players (a stipulation which caused great controversy in New Zealand).

Although patent violation of the Olympic rules was obvious, apartheid had never been a serious issue within the I.O.C. The first significant protests came from the blacks of South Africa. Under the leadership of Dennis Brutus, a distinguished poet of mixed ancestry, blacks and a few sympathetic whites organized the South African Non-Racial Olympic Committee (S.A.N.R.O.C.) to challenge the mandate of the South African National Olympic

Committee (S.A.N.O.C.). Immediately upon its formation in 1962, the new organization petitioned the I.O.C. for recognition on the irrefutable ground that the official committee practiced discrimination forbidden by Olympic rules. The petition was no surprise to Brundage. Early in 1958, Olaf Ditlev-Simonsen had informed Brundage that Norway's Olympic committee was prepared to exclude South Africa from the games and Brundage replied sympathetically, "Sooner or later the subject will be on our agenda, and there can be only one answer, unless changes are made."[45] In 1959 he said to Otto Mayer, "This . . . is another situation that we cannot evade much longer."[46] Only three weeks after this candid remark, I.O.C. member Romanov of the Soviet Union raised the issue at an Executive Board meeting.[47] The person to whom the hard questions were addressed was Reginald Honey, who maintained that S.A.N.O.C. was on excellent terms with colored sports organizations and treated colored athletes as equals. When J. Ferreira Santos of Brazil objected that his country's soccer team had been barred from South Africa because of its black players, Honey replied that there had really been no problem as far as S.A.N.O.C. and the South African Football Association were concerned—the trip was cancelled by Brazil.[48] No one seems to have probed into the reasons for the cancellation, which was quite plainly the result of South Africa's apartheid policies.[49]

No action was taken against S.A.N.O.C., which assured the I.O.C. that "no South African of Olympic calibre will be barred from the South African Olympic team by reason of race, religion [or] political affiliations."[50] Celebrations were, however, premature. The following month S.A.N.O.C. received a severe jolt when the Fédération International de Football Association voted 52–10 to suspend the Football Association of South Africa within one year if racial discrimination did not end. The Football Association ignored the threat and was suspended in 1961. Any thoughts about government flexibility were proven naïve on March 29, 1962, when Minister of the Interior Jan de Klerk announced that South Africa intended to continue its ban on mixed sport within its borders and to send separate white and black teams to international meets.[51]

By this time, Brundage had become impatient. He told the Executive Board that Honey had not made good on his promises and that no progress had been made.[52] At the 59th Session, which took place in Moscow in June of 1962, the I.O.C. voted to suspend S.A.N.O.C. "if the policy of racial discrimination practiced by their government . . . does not change before our Session in Nairobi takes place in October 1963. . . ."[53] It is to Brundage's credit that pressure on S.A.N.O.C. came *before* the formation of the South African Non-Racial Olympic Committee. In fact, in a letter which indicated worry about Israel's and Taiwan's exclusion from the IV Asian Games, Brundage commented approvingly on the plan to challenge apartheid from within:

I note the formation of a new colored sport association in Port Elizabeth, South Africa which intends to apply for IOC recognition. You might write the South African Olympic Committee and ask it for [its] views on this subject. It will give them something to think about.[54]

The Nairobi session of October 1963 turned out to be the Baden-Baden session instead when the Kenyan government, despite the efforts of I.O.C. member Reginald Alexander, denied visas for Honey and other South African officials.[55] In Baden-Baden, the representatives of S.A.N.O.C. made their case: they maintained that the apartheid was an internal matter and none of the I.O.C.'s business, that qualified nonwhites were able to participate in the Olympics but that the trials had to take place outside of South Africa, and that opposition to South African policy came not from athletes but from political agitators. Dennis Brutus was not able to present S.A.N.R.O.C.'s rebuttal because he had been shot by the South African police (but not fatally). After the South African delegation left the room, the I.O.C. voted by a margin of 30–20, with 3 abstentions, to suspend them if there was no change in official policy by December 31, 1963:

The South African National Olympic Committee must pledge itself to declare categorically that it recognizes and submits to the spirit of the Olympic Charter and in particular to Rules No. 1 and No. 24. It must also receive from its Government between now and December 31st 1963 a modification of its policy of discrimination in sports matters and in competitions in its country.[56]

The deadline was not met and the I.O.C. had to decide at its Innsbruck session whether or not to make good on its threats. Frank Braun of S.A.N.O.C. appeared before the Executive Board on January 26 and argued that his government had "categorically refused to see the point of view of the I.O.C."[57] Andrianov, Exeter, Massard, and Vind all indicated their view that S.A.N.O.C. had not fulfilled its obligations. The Board recommended suspension and the I.O.C. voted it:

It was pointed out to the representatives of the South African National Olympic Committee by a number of speakers at the International Olympic Committee Meeting at Baden-Baden that to fulfill this obligation it was essential that it should collectively, clearly and publicly disassociate itself from the policy of non-competition in sport and non-integration in the administration of sport in South Africa between whites and non-whites, and would continue to urge this point of view.

The International Olympic Committee considers that the South African National Olympic Committee has not carried out this obligation adequately.

Under these circumstances, the resolution passed at Baden-Baden still stands and the invitation to the South African team to compete in Tokyo is withdrawn.[58]

The I.O.C. invited the South Africans to apply for reinstatement as soon as they were in compliance with the resolution. Hugh Weir of Australia confided to Brundage that there really *had* to be some way to keep South Africa in the games for 1964 and Brundage agreed with him, but it was already too late.[59]

The question of South African participation in 1968 now occupied the I.O.C. Braun appeared before it in Rome in 1966 and promised a nonracial team picked by a nonracial committee, but the I.O.C. decided to postpone its decision on S.A.N.O.C. until there was an investigation. Once again, progress was impeded by ill will and petty delay. Braun and other S.A.N.O.C. officials were apparently convinced that time was on their side.[60] The Johannesburg *Star* quoted defiant speeches by Braun, who praised the International Rugby Federation because it, unlike the I.O.C., did not "pander to Afro-Asians."[61] S.A.N.O.C. failed to supply the prospective investigators—Killanin, van Karnebeek, and Ademola—with the preliminary information they had requested; they were forced to postpone their visit. Before the commission had a chance to leave for South Africa, Braun appeared once more before the Executive Board, at the Teheran Session in 1967, to appeal for readmission to the games. Jean-Claude Ganga argued with Brundage and begged him not to turn his back on the Africans whom he had encouraged at Dakar and Brazzaville. Before the Executive Board, Ganga was caustic: "We do not wish that the Blacks of Africa appear like costumed apes presented at a fair and then, when the fair is over, sent back to their cages."[62] Braun was now conciliatory. He promised that there would be a single team for South Africa, that whites and nonwhites would travel together, wear the same uniform, and compete under the same flag. He added that they could compete against each other "at the Olympic Games and other international meetings." He thought that these concessions indicated "tremendous strides to meet the requirements of the IOC," and they were indeed unprecedented on the part of the Afrikaaner-dominated regime.[63] Had the concessions come earlier, they might have forestalled the investigation and achieved their goal, but the best that Braun was able to obtain was another postponement of the I.O.C.'s decision on 1968 participation.

While commission prepared for its delayed investigation, a group of Afro-American athletes and civil-rights activists joined together under the leadership of Harry Edwards—a University of California sports sociologist—in order to bring pressure on the U.S. Olympic Committee to take a stand against South African participation. It was a preview of the boycott movement that had begun to take form.[64]

Killanin, Ademola, and Alexander (who replaced van Karnebeek) met in Nairobi on September 9, 1967, and went to Johannesburg, where they were met by Honey and Braun. They spent ten days in South Africa and met all the major parties in the controversy over apartheid sport, including Prime Minister B. J. Vorster, R. W. J. Opperman of S.A.N.O.C., and Wilfred Brutus of the anti-apartheid forces (his brother Dennis had fled the country). After leaving South Africa, they spent three days discussing their findings in Nairobi, then met again in Lausanne on the 24th, where they interviewed Dennis Brutus. The commission prepared a 114-page report which described the investigation and concluded that S.A.N.O.C. had attempted, with some success, to change the government's policy:

The overwhelming evidence from sports administrators and competitors of all communities in Olympic sports inside South Africa is that the Teheran proposals of S.A.N.O.C. are an acceptable basis for a multiracial team to the Mexico Olympic Games.[65]

The report was issued on January 30, 1968, shortly before the Grenoble session. Braun appeared before the session and once again pledged a multiracial team selected on merit. Behind the scenes, Jean-Claude Ganga tussled again with Brundage, who confronted the secretary general of the Conseil Supérieur du Sport Africain with the testimony of Reginald Alexander and Sir Ade Ademola. The secretary general told Brundage that *he*, not they, was in touch with the realities of African sport. Brundage stuck to his guns, and the I.O.C. now decided to reinstate the South Africans. It passed a motion by Weir to the effect that S.A.N.O.C. had made it possible for a multiracial team to be selected on merit and that this team should be allowed to compete in Mexico City. The I.O.C. also resolved to reconsider the question before the end of 1970.[66] In his press conference at Grenoble on February 16, Brundage accentuated the positive: "it was only the power of the Olympic movement that could have secured this change, and this is the first time . . . that anything has been accomplished, for the non-whites in South Africa."[67] On the 25th, he sent out a press release noting that it was not South Africa that had been invited to Mexico City but "a multiracial team of individuals selected by a multiracial committee."[68] Dennis Brutus, the most articulate and perhaps the most stubborn opponent of apartheid sport, went privately to Brundage's hotel room in a vain attempt to persuade him to change his mind. Brundage was adamant; Brutus was equally adamant: "South Africa will not be at Mexico City."[69]

Brundage soon had reason to think that Brutus was the better prophet. The 32 nations of the Organization of African Unity called for a boycott of the 1968 Olympics. Initially, Brundage pretended indifference and announced, "The Games will go on. There is no doubt they'll proceed and will be a tremendous success."[70] Onesti called for a special I.O.C. session, but Brundage was opposed to the idea and informed I.O.C. Secretary Westerhoff, "We have not accepted South Africa—we have merely invited a multi-racial team."[71] Words for the wind to bear away. The boycott movement snowballed as the Caribbean nations, the Islamic world, and the Communist bloc, led by the USSR, all threatened to stay away if the South Africans came.[72] The New York *Times* appraised the situation shrewdly:

The Russian dilemma involves more than just a decision that may kill the Games. It bears directly on their rivalry with the Chinese for the loyalty of the left in the underdeveloped world. If Moscow turns its back on Africa now, in the face of the South African challenge, it would be a major victory for Peking, which does not even participate in the Games.[73]

Although Brundage still resisted the call to convene an I.O.C. emergency session, he decided to fly down to South Africa. His official pretext was his desire to visit a game park: "In view of the climate existing in some parts of the civilized world, I thought it might be refreshing to spend a few days with the animals in their natural habitat."[74] He conferred with Braun and allegedly promised to resign rather than see injustice done. Gaston Meyer, editor of the influential French sports journal *L'Equipe*, reported that Brundage's mission had failed, that he had to go empty-handed to the Executive Board meeting in Lausanne, that he had now lost his chance for reelection as I.O.C. president.[75]

The Executive Board met in Lausanne on April 20th. Its task was threefold. The Board had to

[P]reserve the honour and integrity of the I.O.C. and avoid a breach within the amateur sports world. . . . Save the Mexican Games. . . . Not yield to any threats of boycotts or to any political pressure.[76]

Within the meeting, Brundage argued that S.A.N.O.C. had done all that was humanly possible and that discrimination per se—outside the realm of sport—was no reason to expel a nation from the

Olympic movement. After all, the United States, the Soviet Union, India, the Arab world can all be accused of discrimination. Whatever the Executive Board thought of this argument, which was of course precisely the same one that Brundage used when the boycotters threatened in the 1936 Olympics, they were fully aware that South Africa's presence might indeed wreck the games. Sir Reginald Alexander of Kenya, whose candor and openness on the question of race had often made him unpopular with whites in South Africa, now urged Brundage to persevere against those who demanded more than simply compliance with Olympic rules. "Once, for any reason, you allow a technique of boycott, for *any* reason, you're on the slippery slide."[77] But Brundage had become resigned, for better or worse, to what he, very much under the influence of his Mexican friend Clark Flores, felt was now the inevitable: "we have to face the facts of life—political powers have more to say than we do."[78] Arguing that Clark Flores "wants a decision, not a session," he urged the Executive Board to act on its own authority, but Andrianov, despite his long opposition to South African participation, insisted that only the whole I.O.C. had the power to undo what the whole I.O.C. had done.[79] The Board decided to poll the I.O.C. members and to recommend to them withdrawal of the invitation:

In view of all the information on the international climate received by the Executive Board at this meeting, it is unanimously of the opinion that it would be most unwise for a South African team to participate in the Games of the XIX Olympiad.[80]

The Chicago *Tribune* portrayed Brundage as a shaken man who came before the press with tears in his eyes:

The Olympic games have lost their purpose and Mr. Brundage his valiant fight. His voice shaking, he confessed his disappointment, recalling his long dedication to fair play in sport, regardless of politics. As he talked, those who voted him down toasted each other with whisky and gin and tonic in the living room of the chateau where the vote was taken.[81]

To an interviewer for British television, Brundage remarked, "We seem to live in an age when violence and turbulence are the order of the day."[82] On the 28th, reporters were called to the I.O.C. headquarters at the Chateau de Vidy. A saddened I.O.C. president told them that not all members had replied but that the majority was already apparent. It was against South African participation. "It is a sad commentary on the state of the world today."[83] When the last ballots came in, the final tally was 47–16, with 8 abstentions. South Africa's support had come mainly from the American members, Garland and Roby, from the Australians, from Germany, and from Scandinavia.[84] Brundage later sought to minimize the defeat: "The proposal in the cablegram, which neither yielded Olympic principles in the face of the boycott threat nor criticized anyone, was adopted by the members of the IOC . . . The Games of the XIX Olympiad were saved without sacrifice of Olympic principles."[85] Perhaps claiming victory made defeat easier to accept.

There were further blows to come before the Olympic torch arrived in Mexico City. On May 29, the United Nations Security Council condemned the white-dominated government of Rhodesia, which had unilaterally declared its independence from Great Britain, and asked that Rhodesian passports not be honored. Mexico's foreign minister instructed Pedro Ramirez Vazquez, head of the organizing committee, of the government's intention to bar visitors presenting Rhodesian passports.[86] Ramirez Vazquez and Clark Flores telephoned Brundage, who felt that the government's move was "a flagrant violation of international law."[87] It was obviously impossible for the Rhodesians to participate and there was "not much that we can do, except to deliver a strong protest to the United Nations."[88] Brundage tried to persuade the organizing committee at least to send the entry forms and identity cards to Rhodesia, but communications between Mexico City and Salisbury mysteriously broke down and letters and cables either went astray or arrived too late to do any good. What made this particular defeat especially hard to bear was that sports facilities in Rhodesia were *not* segregated. The team which had been selected for the 1968 games included 14 whites and 2 blacks. Brundage's protests were in vain. "His voice," wrote the president of the Rhodesian Olympic Committee, "cries in a wilderness of spite."[89]

The wilderness grew wilder and more spiteful. In August, the Soviet Union and the German Democratic Republic invaded Czechoslovakia to smash the possibility of "socialism with a human face." It was 1956 all over again and Brundage responded just as he had in 1956, when Russian tanks destroyed the dream of humane socialism in Hungary:

The world, alas, is full of injustice, aggression, violence and warfare, against which all civilized persons rebel, but this is no reason to destroy the nucleus of international cooperation and good will we have in the Olympic Movement. . . .

If participation in sport is to be stopped every time the politicians violate the laws of humanity, there will never be any international contests. Is it not better to maintain and support the Olympic Games, one of the most priceless and powerful instruments of our present civilization and try to expand the fair play and sportsmanship of the athletic field into other areas?[90]

There was some disagreement on this even within the I.O.C. Jan Staubo cabled Brundage that the Norwegian Olympic Committee wanted the I.O.C. to see that the invitations sent to the Soviet Union and the German Democratic Republic were withdrawn.[91] The games ought to be celebrated, but the aggressors should not be among the celebrants. Brundage answered that "there is no provision in Olympic rules to permit such an action."[92] Since the invitation issued to South Africa *had* been withdrawn, there certainly *was* a precedent, but Brundage simply did not want to exclude nations whose human-rights violations were not specifically infractions of the Olympic rules. Eventually, it was necessary to modify arrangements in the Olympic Village so that the Russians and East Germans ate in one room and the Czechs in another. When the competition for women's gymnastics was held, it happened that five of the top six contestants were Russians or East Germans and the sixth, Vera Caslavska, was from Czechoslovakia. Inevitably, Caslavska—who won—was transformed into a political symbol as well as a metaphor for the possibilities of human movement.

Still another blow came only days before the games were to begin. On September 25, the Chicago newspapers headlined the

news: "MEXICO CITY FIGHT KILLS 15" and "15 DIE IN MEXICO CITY STU-
DENT-ARMY CLASH."[93] A week later, there were new headlines:
"FIRE ON MEXICO RIOTERS!" and "HUGE NEW BATTLE ROCKS MEXICO
CITY."[94] Brundage, who had arrived in Mexico City on September
29, met with Ramirez Vazquez of the organizing committee and
issued reassurances:

> The Games of the 19th Olympiad, a friendly gathering of the youth
> of the world in amicable competition, will proceed as scheduled. . . .
> We have conferred with the Mexican authorities and we have been
> assured that nothing will interfere with the peaceful entrance of the Olym-
> pic flame into the stadium . . . nor with the competitions which follow.[95]

The Chicago *Daily News* entitled its story "Avery rides to rescue."[96]

Three days later, Brundage strode into Mexico City's Palace of
Fine Arts and opened the 67th Session of the I.O.C. He repeated
the familar convictions of his press statements. When the I.O.C.
was not actually in session, he busied himself with interviews, re-
ceptions, and visits to museums. He was especially delighted by
the emphasis on Indian art and music, proof to him that the Third
World was increasingly integrated into the Olympic movement.
On October 11, the torch arrived and on the 12th—Columbus
Day—the games were opened. Competition began the next day,
and even as the New York *Times* proclaimed "Brundage's triumph,"
there were signs of new trouble.

Although the ostracism of South Africa and Rhodesia had de-
fused some of the smoldering rage felt by black Americans, 1968
was a year of frustration. The "Tet Offensive" of the Viet Cong
and North Vietnamese demonstrated that the cause of the government in Saigon was hopeless, despite the presence of half a million
American soldiers. The political pressures which forced Lyndon
Johnson to drop out of the presidential race in the midst of the
primaries were stymied by the assassination of Robert Kennedy.
Students at Columbia and other universities exploded in rage
against the war, against racism, against unresponsive academic bu-
reaucracies. The murder of Martin Luther King Jr. touched off
another series of violent and nonviolent demonstrations. The tu-
mults of Paris and Mexico City seemed linked to those of New
York and Los Angeles in a vast earthquake of protest.

The Olympic boycott, which Harry Edwards led and Jesse Owens opposed, fizzled because most of the athletes, black and white, were reluctant to sacrifice years of preparation in what they felt was a misdirected gesture aimed at an institution which was, at best, peripherally responsible for the world's ills. Nonetheless, many of the black athletes arrived in Mexico in an angry mood. Before the games, spokesmen of the National Conference on Black Power accused Brundage of racism and demanded his resignation as I.O.C. president. In Mexico City, black athletes blocked white runners from the tartan track and prevented them from training. Tommy Smith told reporters on the 15th: "I don't want Brundage presenting me any medals."[97] Then, on the 16th, Smith and John Carlos mounted the victory podium to receive (from I.A.A.F. president Exeter) their medals for first and third in the 200 meters. As the "Star-Spangled Banner" was played, Smith and Carlos turned their eyes down and raised their black-gloved fists. The photograph of this black-power demonstration became one of the most famous in Olympic history. The U.S. Olympic Committee, then headed by Roby, responded with relative moderation; it strongly reprimanded the two athletes. The I.O.C. then brought pressure to bear and the U.S.O.C. announced on the 18th that Smith and Carlos had been suspended from the team and expelled from the Olympic Village. The same day, Lee Evans set a world record over 400 meters and mounted the podium with Larry James and Ron Freeman. The three black athletes wore black berets which they doffed during the anthem. They stood at attention until the music ended, then waved their berets and walked away. The U.S.O.C. did not react. Bob Beamon, whose leap of 8.9 meters was probably the most spectacular athletic feat of the games, ignored the protests. George Foreman, upon winning the heavyweight title in boxing, pranced about the ring waving a small American flag. He and other black boxers ostentatiously invited Brundage to their victory celebration.

Brundage had absolutely no sympathy for the black-power protests. His comment: "Warped mentalities and cracked personalities seem to be everywhere and impossible to eliminate."[98] Was he a racist, as Harry Edwards and many others charged? In that he stood for the egalitarian principles implicit in the nature of modern sports and explicit in the Olympic rules, he was not. In a thousand speeches he repeated his conviction that sports are a realm in which racial discrimination has no place. Early in his career, he had opposed racial segregation in American sports. When the Southern Association of the A.A.U. condemned Nazi racism, he commented that "the Southerners who won't register a negro do not realize how ridiculous they have made themselves."[99] He was enthusiastic about Jesse Owens and other American blacks whose achievements became a large part of Olympic history. He encouraged African sports and welcomed African participation in the games. He condemned South Africa's apartheid policies—in sports. It was precisely this distinction which made him unpopular with activists who refused to separate sports and politics into two hermetically sealed compartments. If the sports administrators of Birmingham and Johannesburg opened tracks, fields, pools, and arenas to black and white alike, Brundage was satisfied. If black athletes were not legally barred from competition, he did not inquire into the social factors that determined their dominance in sports like boxing and their absence in fencing or tennis. He was, moreover, not especially sensitive to discrimination outside of sports. In reply to a correspondent who had sent him a virulently racist letter, he sent a criticism of *Brown versus Board of Education*, the U.S. Supreme Court decision which struck down segregation in American schools.[100] He seems not to have asked himself about the injustice done to a black athlete who competed on the field as a member of a racially integrated team and was then turned away from the hotel where his teammates sat down to their victory banquet.

Given his commitment to the preservation of sports as a sacred realm apart, unsullied by commerce or politics, he was utterly unsympathetic to the argument that sports are an *implicit* affirmation of the political and economic status quo, and he was bristlingly hostile to the attempt on the part of black activists to use their athletic fame as a weapon against injustice in other domains. The threat of an Olympic boycott because of racism in American business struck him as crass ingratitude. To use the Olympic ceremony as a protest against discrimination when Olympism itself was a symbol of equality seemed completely irrational. The bowed heads and raised fists simply *had* to have been the result of "warped mentalities." They represented a form of heresy that Brundage, not unlike the early Fathers of the Church, wanted to banish even from the pages of history. The official report of the U.S.O.C., lavishly illustrated, omits the Smith-Carlos photograph. Brundage protested stridently to Ramirez Vazquez about the appearance of Smith and Carlos in the official Olympic film sponsored by the organizing committee: "The nasty demonstration against the United States flag by negroes . . . had nothing to do with sport, it was a shameful abuse of hospitality and it has no more place in the record of the games than the gunfire" at the riots just before the games. "Should the Mexican flag and Mexican athletes have been involved, I am sure, it would not be featured."[101] To Beaumont and Exeter he suggested that Olympic rules be changed to empower the I.O.C. to veto the film: "The immediate reason for this is the fact that the Mexicans included the demonstration by Negro athletes in the film despite our disapproval. There is also always the possibility of political propaganda and we should see the film before it is released to the public."[102] Brundage was clearly unable in this instance to apply the aesthetic criteria that he relied upon in his eloquent defense of Leni Riefenstahl's film of the 1936 games. The Nazi salute and the swastika were part of the *Gesamtkunstwerk* of the Olympic ceremony, but the black-power salute and the black berets were somehow "political."

There were signs now that Brundage had begun to lose support even within the I.O.C. He had won reelection with much less difficulty than one might have inferred from newspaper accounts of the opposition to him, but his last four years in office were not happy ones. There was a time when Vind had encouraged him to be more forceful in his leadership,[103] but the members now began to murmur that he had become too authoritarian in his behavior. Arthur Porritt of New Zealand, who thought Brundage did more good for amateur sports than anybody else in the entire century, also commented that Brundage's "rule of the I.O.C. was that of

The Dictator . . . and it went on too long by probably 8 years—
certainly 4. As he got older, his judgment became more fallible.
He developed quite untypical foibles and petty jealousies."[104] Roby
commented later, "Personally, I think Avery should have gotten
out years ago. He has stayed too long."[105]

Unfortunately, the political crises became graver as Brundage's
leadership became less effective. The dream of Olympic universalism became a nightmare in which Brundage was haunted by
ghosts shrieking "South Africa! Rhodesia!" Brundage tried vainly
to silence the voices calling for the permanent expulsion of these
two members. The first I.O.C. session after Mexico City was in
Warsaw in June of 1969. Even before the members assembled,
Brundage predicted South Africa's expulsion, which prompted Reginald Honey into expostulation:

It is not the President's duty to prophesy the outcome of a meeting before
it is held. . . . For the President of the IOC to make such a prediction
. . . is not only a disgrace, but typical of the IOC's misconception of
power. South Africa has never broken an IOC rule. There is no possible
reason why we should be expelled, except for political reasons. . . . The
IOC is a farce today, as they do whatever they want and break their own
rules every day.[106]

The I.O.C. decided in Warsaw to postpone its decision until the
Amsterdam session of May 1970. Between the two sessions, there
was a meeting in Dubrovnik of the Executive Board with representatives of the national Olympic committees and another sign of
the white Africans' deteriorating position. At this meeting, Y. Tas-
sema of Ethiopia moved that the delegates from Rhodesia and South
Africa be expelled from the room. Brundage argued that this was
contrary to Olympic rules because only the full I.O.C. had the
power to expel. The black Africans demanded a vote and the majority was against the physical presence of the Rhodesians and
South Africans who were then allowed to remain on the condition
that they refrain from participation in matters not directly concerned with their status.[107]

A year later, the I.O.C. met in Amsterdam and the knotty matter
of South Africa was once again on the agenda. In his opening ad-

dress, Brundage praised Olympism as "a golden philosophy" that incorporated the highest ideals of East and West. He asked, almost wistfully, for an end to the political dissension that had tormented the I.O.C.: "Perhaps in the charming Dutch countryside, inspired by the gorgeous polychromy of the beautiful blossoms of the tulip festival, we can find the correct solution to our thorny problems."[108] The prospects for a peaceful solution disappeared when Brundage's flowery rhetoric was followed by an inflammatory speech given by S.A.N.O.C.'s Frank Braun, who attacked Brundage personally and dissipated his own support. By a vote of 35–28, with 3 abstentions, recognition was withdrawn from the South African National Olympic Committee.[109]

Brundage had mixed emotions. While he had fought long and hard for years to keep the South Africans within the Olympic movement, he had to admit that the blacks had made a better presentation and that the delegation from Johannesburg "certainly dug their own grave."[110] He had mixed emotions about another matter as well—the choice of his successor. Although Lord Killanin had for years been an important Olympic figure, Brundage's attitude was contemptuous. In his eyes, Killanin was an intellectual lightweight, a former journalist and filmmaker without the depth of character necessary for the office held by Coubertin, Baillet-Latour, Edström, and Brundage. To Daume, Brundage remarked scornfully, "We need a leader, and Michael isn't a leader."[111] Whether *anyone* was enough of a leader in Brundage's eyes is questionable. His attitude resembled that of Charles de Gaulle in regard to Georges Pompidou, whom "Charles le Grand" considered the least unworthy to succeed him. "What he would most have liked," commented Daume, "was to have been reelected once more."[112] Brundage's successor was, in Monique Berlioux's words, "Irish, Catholic, liberal, jovial,"[113] terms which suggest a character diametrically opposed to Brundage's. Killanin himself remarked, "One thing I can tell you. . . . I am not Avery Brundage."[114] Perhaps that was exactly what the members wished. Feeling that twenty years of Brundage were enough,[115] they turned not to the charismatic Comte de Beaumont but to the "jovial" Killanin, who was elected president on August 4, 1972. Brundage's own ballot was blank. His coldness toward Killanin in the weeks that followed had unfortunate consequences.

Having settled the South African question at Amsterdam, the I.O.C. hoped to find the solution to the Rhodesian problem as well. There was no evidence that Rhodesia had failed to comply with Olympic rules. A special I.A.A.F. investigation of 1971 found that there were no separate clubs for whites, no special facilities, and no separate championships.[116] Nonetheless, in order "to mollify any extremists, the I.O.C. decided to have the Rhodesian athletes participate as British subjects."[117] The athletes and officials were to travel with British passports, which the U.N. Security Council considered the only valid ones for Rhodesians, and were to march behind the same flag that had waved in Tokyo in 1964—a blue banner with the union jack in one corner. The sports officials of the African Olympic committees were satisfied with this arrangement, but their political counterparts were interested neither in Rhodesia's compliance with Olympic rules nor in the niceties of passports and flags. For the Organization of African Unity and the Supreme Council for Sports in Africa, the issue was the government of Ian Smith, which had declared its independence of Great Britain in order to preserve white domination.

As always, there were public stands. Dennis Brutus, who had led the fight for the expulsion of South Africa from the Olympics, spoke out against Rhodesia. He also went to the LaSalle Hotel and called on Brundage privately and was told that Brundage was ready to change his mind *if* the African national Olympic committees reversed *their* decision. Brutus informed the Organization for African Unity of his talk with Brundage, and the O.A.U. sent two officials to Munich, where the national Olympic committees were assembling just before the 1972 games.[118] Meanwhile, Lance Cross, member from New Zealand since 1969, sought Brundage out to counsel him not to meet with the Supreme Council unless he arranged to hear the Rhodesians as well. Brundage, however, remained confident that he was in control of the situation—as he had been confident before the South African debacle of 1968.[119]

When the Rhodesian team arrived in Munich with Olympic identity cards rather than the agreed-upon British passports, the black Africans had the technicality with which to scuttle them:

The United Nations Security Council sanctions committee told West Germany the presence of Rhodesians might violate the 1968 resolution and asked it to inform the I.O.C. that the resolution applied to individuals and private organizations as well as to governments. The West German government, concerned that the issue might damage its relations with black Africa, pressured the I.O.C. to reverse its decision.[120]

The British embassy in Bonn confirmed that the Rhodesians were bona fide British subjects, but Andrianov pointed out, when the I.O.C. convened to face the newest crisis, that the Rhodesians had Olympic identity cards rather than British passports and that the cards had been altered en route to Munich; the words "British Subject" had been added in a spurious attempt to deny political reality. Brigadier H. E. O. Adefope of Nigeria agreed that only passports could prove nationality and Brundage protested vainly that the I.O.C. had fought for twenty-five years to win acceptance of the identity cards that Andrianov and Adefope now found unacceptable. When Daume reported that twenty-one African committees were threatening a boycott, Weir and Cross spoke up for the Rhodesians and urged that the I.O.C. not be degraded to "a political whipping boy." In an emotional appeal, Brundage referred to his sixty years of involvement in the Olympic movement and asked that the movement not be allowed to disintegrate before his eyes. When the bitter debate was terminated by the secret ballot, Brundage had lost, 36–31 with 3 abstentions. Barely in control of himself, Brundage told his colleagues that "it was obviously time . . . to leave the presidency."[121] The threat of a boycott was "naked political blackmail," he asserted, "a savage attack on basic principles."[122] To Prime Minister Smith he confessed, "For the first time in twenty years, the Committee failed to follow my recommendation. . . . This action was denounced unanimously by the whole world of sport. . . . The general public has announced emphatically that it will not tolerate interference in amateur sport and the Olympic Games."[123] That Brundage no longer commanded a majority of the I.O.C. was true; that the "whole world of sport" (minus the majority of the I.O.C.) was on his side was questionable. He was a deeply wounded man.

Munich, long one of his favorite cities, was to have been the balm. The choice of the Bavarian capital was meant to be symbolic as well as practical. Brundage's election to the committee had taken place on German soil after he had fought strenuously to defend Germany's right to host the 1936 games despite Hitler's rise to power. Now, a new Germany, reborn from the ashes of the old, wanted to demonstrate to the world that there was indeed democracy where dictators once had ruled. The *heitere Spiele* (cheerful games) were to erase memories of the Nazi misuse of sports. The emphasis was to be where Coubertin had meant it to be.

The summer games opened in a joyous mood. Bavarian bands went umpah-pah and yodelers yodeled and the boys and girls danced their way through the impressively modern Olympic stadium. Daume and his fellow organizers were able to take satisfaction in their display of efficiency without inflexibility or impersonality. As the swimming events were contested, Mark Spitz began, almost systematically, to set world records and to reap gold medals. By the time he churned his way to a seventh medal in the 400-meter medley relay, the television cameras had made his face familiar to hundreds of millions of viewers. In track and field, the U.S.A. and the USSR continued their twenty-year-old rivalry, with the Russian men winning the 100 meters, 200 meters, high jump, triple jump, and decathlon while the Americans won the 400 meters, the 800 meters, the 110-meter hurdles, the 400-meter relay, the long jump, and—unexpectedly—the marathon. It was, not for the first or last time, the Russian women who made the difference as they carried off the prizes in the first Olympic 1500-meter race ever, in the discus, and in the shot put. Since this was the debut of the German Democratic Republic competing in its own uniforms with its own flag and anthem, the games also became a symbolic battle for the claim to represent the "real" Germany. The track-and-field contests were close enough to spare the hosts from humiliation on their own grounds. The Communists won the pole vault and the

20-kilometer walk, the women's 100 meters, 200 meters, 400 meters, 100-meter hurdles, 1600-meter relay, and javelin, but Bonn's representatives won the men's javelin and 50-kilometer walk, the women's 800 meters, 400-meter relay, long jump, and the high jump. (Sixteen-year-old Ulrike Mayfahrt was so surprised at her own victory in the high jump that her bewildered smile became one of the most famous pictures from Munich.)

While the journalists emphasized the "pixie" charm of tiny gymnast Olga Korbut, thus corroborating the suspicion that female athletes were still prized as something other than athletes, her muscular teammate Ludmilla Tourescheva regally carried off the gold in the women's combined gymnastics contest. While they flew around the uneven bars as if they were weightless, their countryman Vasseli Alexeev grunted, groaned, and hoisted a total of 640 kilos in his discipline's three lifts. There were bad moments, of course, like those that followed the realization that the Americans Eddie Hart and James Robinson had been given the incorrect time for their race, which they missed, but the games seemed likely to become the most marvelous Olympic celebration of all if they had not become—suddenly, shockingly—the most tragic.

In the predawn hours of September 5, a small group of Palestinian terrorists approached the fence ringing the Olympic Village, clambered over it, and made their way to 31 Connollystraße, a street named for a man and a woman whose union symbolized sport's ability to bring people together.[124] The Palestinians knocked on the door and pushed their way into the apartment. "Black September" had begun. While the terrorists rounded up their Israeli hostages, Gad Tsobari escaped and alerted the police. At a little after 5:00 A.M., the Palestinians announced their demands: freedom for 234 prisoners in Israel and for the German terrorists Andreas Baader and Ulrike Meinhof. At 9:00 A.M., they threw Moshe Weinberg's mutilated body into the street.

Brundage was wakened before 6:00 A.M. and rushed to the Olympic Village, where the police authorized I.O.C. member Touny to offer the terrorists ransom money and a safe conduct out of Germany. The best the Egyptian was able to obtain was a postponement of the ultimatum to noon and then, when his appeals were seconded by those of the director of the Arab League, to 1:00 P.M. While Touny negotiated with the Palestinians, Brundage and Daume conferred with Foreign Minister Hans-Dietrich Genscher, Bavaria's Minister of the Interior Bruno Merk, and other German officials. Although the press began almost immediately to refer to the *Krisenstab*, there was no officially constituted "crisis-staff." There was rather a constant, uninterrupted discussion in which Brundage played a modest role. Pointing out that he, a Chicagoan, knew something about criminality, he suggested knocking the terrorists out with a quick-acting gas known to the Chicago police, but a telephone call to Chicago proved that the police had no such gas.[125] The momentous decisions were made not by Brundage but by the German officials. They decided how to respond to the Palestinian demands. They set the terms of the negotiations with the terrorists and arranged for the move to Fürstenfeldbruck airfield at 10:00 P.M. They planned and carried out the mismanaged attack forty minutes later. When the shooting stopped, three of the captors and all of the captives were dead.

It was the I.O.C.'s task to decide another matter. Should the games be broken off? To continue despite the atrocity seemed heartless, callous; to abort the celebration was to fulfill the aspirations of the terrorists. Initially, there was indecision and confusion. In Munich and in Kiel, where Killanin and several others had gone for the yacht races, the members conferred with each other. Many felt that the Executive Board should be called into session, but Brundage resisted the notion of an emergency meeting, and for this he was sharply and justly criticized by Beaumont ("To Brundage, he is the I.O.C.—no one else, just him!"[126]). After consulting with Brundage, Daume announced at 3:51 P.M. the cancellation of the remainder of that afternoon's events. He also announced a memorial service for 10:00 A.M. the next day. Brundage told Killanin by telephone that there was no need for the Executive Board to meet, but those in Kiel flew back to Munich in a plane put at their disposal by Berthold Beitz, Germany's new I.O.C. member. When Killanin arrived, he was "furious."[127] The Executive Board, which consisted of Killanin, Beaumont, Andrianov, van Karnebeek, Ademola, Padilha, Takeda, and Juan Antonio Samaranch of Spain, met at 7:00 P.M. Brundage's colleagues were critical of his involvement in the negotiations with the terrorists; their view was that the matter should have been left entirely to the German government and to the organizing committee. But the Executive Board was unanimous in its endorsement of the memorial services announced by Brundage and Daume. The entire I.O.C. was then called together, a little after 10:00 P.M., at the Hotel Zu den Vier Jahreszeiten in Maximilienstraße. Many of the members were annoyed at Brundage and it was a "knock-down-drag-out session."[128]

Killanin told the committee that he had been in Kiel with Takeda and van Karnebeek and that they had been called back to Munich and that Brundage had attempted to countermand the instructions. He also condemned Brundage's involvement in the *Krisenstab*, arguing that "this was a matter of internal security for the German Government and the Organizing Committee." Whatever their feelings about the quarrel between their president and his successor, the members were practically unanimous in their support of the Executive Board: the games should not be broken off, there should be a memorial service. Suddenly, at midnight, Daume, relying on news reports, announced the complete success of the rescue attempt: "Wir haben gewonnen!" (We've won!). In false euphoria, the meeting broke up at 12:15 A.M.[129]

By the time the memorial service was held, the entire world knew that the rescue mission had failed and that all the hostages were dead. As Brundage rose to speak, all the world's flags hung at half-mast—except those of the Arab nations, which insisted that their banners be hoisted in the usual manner.[130] Brundage had stood proudly four years earlier in Mexico City when Beethoven's ninth symphony was used as the victory anthem of the combined German team. Now the stadium was filled with the tragic strains of the second movement of Beethoven's "Eroica." On such occasions, tears must be accompanied by words. Standing before the mourning thousands in the stadium and before countless millions of television viewers, Brundage uttered the credo of his life:

Every civilized person recoils in horror at the barbarous criminal intrusion of terrorists into peaceful Olympic precincts. We mourn our Israeli friends[,] victims of this brutal assault. The Olympic flag and the flags of all the world fly at half mast. Sadly, in this imperfect world, the greater and the more important the Olympic Games become, the more they are open to commercial, political and now criminal pressure. The Games of the XX Olympiad have been subject to 2 savage attacks. We lost the Rhodesian battle against naked political blackmail. We have only the strength of a great ideal. I am sure that the public will agree that we cannot allow a handful of terrorists to destroy this nucleus of international co-operation and good will we have in the Olympic Movement. The Games must go on and we must continue our efforts to keep them clean, pure and honest and try to extend the sportsmanship of the athletic field into other areas.

We declare today a day of mourning and will continue all the events one day later than originally scheduled.[131]

It was the most public of many moments in which Brundage had shown the world glimpses of his innermost self, the tactless self ("We lost the Rhodesian battle") as well as the idealistic self ("The Games must go on"). Liselott Diem, who had known Brundage for decades, thought this was "the greatest moment of his life."[132] His colleagues on the I.O.C., even those who had had doubts about his suitability for continued leadership, were all but unanimous in their sense that Brundage, with his sixty years of involvement in the Olympic movement, was the right person, perhaps the only person, to have spoken their nearly unanimous convictions. He spoke with authority and with "a strength that was his own." It was their decision he communicated, but he gave that decision what Gafner aptly called "brightness."[133]

Brundage's brief words were "a testament,"[134] the revelation of character in the intensity of commitment. For him, there really was no other possibility. He had been involved in the Olympic movement for sixty years as athlete, administrator, spokesman, leader, trustee. The games were for him the religion of Coubertin and the vision of a better world. Sports were not only an alternative to the sordid routines of business and politics but an elixir to transform the grubby into the grand. The games represented for him the fact that a self-made millionaire from the United States had been chosen to carry on the idealistic crusade begun by a French baron. The games represented for him the fact that a fatherless boy from Chicago was able to win the western decathlon championship and sail to Stockholm to compete with other young men symbolizing the bewildering diversity of mankind and the marvelous, momentary, exemplary unity of sports. To have stopped the games would have been to have lost the dream.

A GERMAN PRINCESS

The Israeli officials in Munich, including national Olympic committee president J. Lindbar, endorsed the decision to continue the games[1] and there was applause from the mourners in the stadium when Brundage finished his brief memorial remarks, but there were many critics who thought the games should have been halted. Among the most influential of them was the sportswriter Red Smith, who published an angry column in the New York *Times*:

This time surely, some thought, they would cover the sandbox and put the blocks aside. But, no. "The Games must go on," said Avery Brundage, high priest of the playground, and 80,000 listeners burst into applause. The occasion was yesterday's memorial service for eleven menbers of Israel's Olympic delegation murdered by Palestinian terrorists. It was more like a pep rally.[2]

Perhaps a man who thought of the Olympic Games as a sandbox in a playground was not the best judge in this case, but one of the historians of the games has called the speech "puzzling ramblings," neither dignified nor rational.[3] At any rate, the games went on and Brundage presided at the closing ceremony, where German efficiency broke down once again, this time comically: "Auf Wiedersehen, Avery Brandage" read the scoreboard lights. The athletes paraded, mixed and mingled, and expressed their joy and sadness. Thoughts turned to Montreal in 1976, where Lord Killanin would welcome the youth of the world and where the Canadians would do their best to protect the world's youth from terror. Had Brundage known that the Montreal games were to be jeopardized by Ottawa's denial of visas to athletes from Taiwan and by another African boycott, this one triggered off by the I.O.C.'s refusal to expel New Zealand for playing rugby against South Africa, had Brundage known that the President of the United States was to order a meekly compliant U.S. Olympic Committee to boycott the 1980 Olympics because of the USSR's invasion of Afghanistan, he might well have shown more sympathy than he did for Killanin, beset as Killanin was by the same problems that tormented him.

Brundage's years of retirement were not quiet ones. Although he was now free of the burdens of official responsibility, it was impossible for him not to remain emotionally involved in the Olympics. I.O.C. Director Monique Berlioux reported that he haunted the Chateau de Vidy and waited, pathetically, for Killanin to turn to him for help:

> The Olympic movement had been his life. . . . He kept on turning up at his IOC office in Lausanne, answering calls, reading correspondence. He simply could not believe it was finished. It was a bit embarrassing for Lord Killanin.
>
> He would call me from Geneva and ask me to keep him company. I would just wander through the streets with him, aimlessly, for hours on end. He would not speak much. He was totally lost. He was desperately lonely.[4]

Frederick Ruegsegger has described a somewhat different Brundage, more like an abdicated Japanese emperor, tranquil in chosen retirement.[5]

If Berlioux was closer to the truth, there were other than Olympic reasons contributing to the restlessness. Following his wife's death in 1971, Brundage had not remarried. There seems to have been no desire on his part to legitimize his relationship with Lilian Dresden, whom he no longer saw. What affairs he conducted were more or less discreet, more or less private. For years he had felt more at home in Europe than in America. He was especially fond of Germany. In jest, he once remarked to Willi Daume that his ambition was to marry a German princess.[6]

Perhaps it was more than a jest. Princess Mariann Charlotte Katharina Stefanie von Reuss was the daughter of Heinrich XXXVII of Reuss, a tiny (15 square kilometers) principality in the Thüringer Wald, between Weimar and Dresden, in what is now the German Democratic Republic. By a truly extraordinary coincidence, she was born in Berlin on July 29, 1936—the day before the I.O.C., meeting in Berlin for the Olympic Games, elected Avery Brundage as a member. At sixteen she had come to the United States as an exchange student, after which she had a commercial rather than an academic education. Before the 1972 Olympics, she worked as an interpreter for the organizing committee. In her work, she occasionally encountered Brundage, whom she said she had first met in 1955 when she was a girl of nineteen.[7] She was not a conventional film-star beauty, but her blond hair and blue eyes fulfilled the Germanic stereotype. She was tall, athletic, vivacious, charming. In February of 1973, she and Brundage danced together at Munich's fashionable Ball des Sports. The boulevard press reported her denials of an engagement to be married: "I don't know who started this wicked rumor. Why I can't let myself be seen in Munich now. I'll have to leave town."[8] Leave she did, for Chicago, where Brundage suddenly announced their engagement on June 11. (She claimed it was a surprise.) Queried about the difference in their ages, Brundage told the reporters—with more humor than tact—that the two were closer than it seemed: "she is very mature for her age. People say I am young for my age. I think instead of it being 85–37, it is more like 55–46."[9]

They were married on June 20 in a civil ceremony in Garmisch-Partenkirchen, site of the 1936 winter Olympics and thus another place of Proustian memory for him. They were remarried in a religious ceremony in the Erlöserkirche in the nearby town of Grainau on July 28:

Brundage had asked Ruegsegger to be his best man, but Ruegsegger had replied archly, "I will do no such thing," and refused even to attend. Indeed, when Brundage first told him of the engagement, Ruegsegger had said, "Mr. Brundage, I have one message for you: there is no fool like an old fool." Therefore, Daume did the honors.[10]

After the second ceremony, the guests were invited to the reception at the town's *Kursaal*. He wore a tuxedo, she a rose-colored Bavarian dirndl, with a silver neckband. The guests feasted on king crab from Alaska, Scottish salmon, smoked ham from Holstein, and other suitably international delicacies. At midnight, the bride turned thirty-seven. The honeymoon was spent in Sweden, visiting Bo Ekelund, and on the ship *Hanseatic*, cruising up to Norway's North Cape.[11] Brundage bought a house in Santa Barbara at 767 Pichacho Lane and another in Garmisch at Dreitorspitzstraße 43, where the couple lived when not traveling.[12] The Bavarian house was a short walk from the site of the 1936 games.

Some of Brundage's friends were delighted with the marriage. Liselott Diem had not seen Brundage often after the death of her husband in 1962, but she had known the Chicagoan for nearly forty years. She was struck by his new wife's devotion, by her constant concern for his comfort.[13] Other friends were surprised that Brundage, presumably under Mariann's influence, suddenly abandoned the sombre black suits and white shirts that had been a kind of trademark for decades. As Ruegsegger's refusal to act as best man suggests, some were hostile to the young wife. They hinted that the bride and her mother, who lived with the couple, were a pair of fortune-hunters interested not in Avery's welfare but in his wealth. At a trial held in conjunction with quite another matter, Ruegsegger testified that the couple spent nearly $2 million in a period of roughly eighteen months. "I informed him in March [1975] that he was bankrupt or near bankrupt."[14] (It should be noted that the two houses Brundage purchased cost over $500,000 and that large sums spent for jewelry should probably be considered as investments rather than simply as expenses.) Mariann's frank comment on the marriage was that they sometimes fought "until the feathers flew—but not for long."[15] It is impossible for an outsider to judge without the kind of evidence (letters, diaries) which seems not to exist. Fortunately, it is not necessary to judge because the marriage took place after Brundage's retirement from Olympia.

Although marriage to a German princess was the fulfillment of an ambition, another ambition remained unrealized. Brundage had always wanted to visit China, whose art he had loved and collected for forty years. Tsuneyoshi Takeda attempted to arrange a visit for him when Chinese envoys came to Tokyo in the days of "Ping Pong Diplomacy"[16] and Daume also raised the question when China opened up ties with the Federal Republic of Germany.[17] The visit never materialized, and it was probably no treat for Brundage to receive a cheery card from Peking—from his quondam gadfly Giulio Onesti.[18] The consolation was a final three-week trip to Japan with Mariann, her mother, and the faithful Ruegsegger, now resigned if not reconciled to the boss's marriage.[19] This trip was the occasion of Brundage's pilgrimage to the Ise Shrine, Japan's most sacred place, where only the imperial family is allowed to worship. Brundage too bowed his head in prayer, and his hosts marveled, "It was as if he had become a Japanese!"[20] It was a splendid visit and one of the last happy times of Brundage's life.

His eyesight had been poor since childhood. In his later years, he suffered from acute glaucoma which was especially hard to treat because of his reluctance to take time out from his crammed schedule.[21] Now, in January of 1974, he underwent a badly needed operation for glaucoma and cataracts. Arrangements were initially made by Juan Antonio Samaranch, the younger I.O.C. member from Spain, a man whom Brundage liked and trusted. Samaranch had come to Brundage's attention during the 1965 Session in Madrid while still a member of the Spanish Olympic Committee. In 1966 he was nominated by Brundage for I.O.C. membership. Two years later, Brundage made him Chief of Protocol (Samaranch was by profession a diplomat). In 1970 he was elected to the Executive Board (and in 1980 he followed Killanin as seventh president of the I.O.C.). Samaranch chose Dr. Joaquin Barraquer for the delicate operation and was astonished, just before Brundage was due to enter the hospital in Barcelona, to receive a telex cancelling the arrangements.[22]

Brundage had decided to undergo surgery at an *Augenklinik* in the Arabella-Haus, a luxurious hotel-and-apartment complex in Munich. The operation took place on January 13, 1974.[23] After forty-six days in the clinic, during which time Mariann and her mother lived in a room next to his, Brundage was visited by Rueg-

segger, whom he asked to take him back to Chicago.[24] Brundage
left for Chicago without his wife, but he called for her soon after
his arrival and asked her to join him.[25]

According to Mariann Brundage, her husband's operation was a
success—his color vision returned and he was able to read without
glasses.[26] Ruegsegger, on the contrary, asserted that the operation
had actually hurt Brundage's vision.[27] Brundage himself wrote to
Samaranch that he was unable to see well, but he did not go into
details.[28]

Brundage recovered sufficiently for his last trip to the Far East,
but he was no longer robust, which is scarcely surprising for a man
of eighty-seven. In April of 1975 he entered the hospital at Garmisch, complaining of the flu and a severe cough. He seemed to
improve. Talking with his friend Walther Tröger, who had been
Mariann's boss during the preparations for the 1972 games, Brundage commented, "I'm glad that I feel better. Now I want to get
out of the clinic. I look forward to some peaceful years with my
family."[29] Then, at 9:40 P.M. on May 8, his heart failed. Mariann
was at the deathbed.[30]

What we make of the last three years is less important than how
we interpret the sixty years of Olympic involvement. At Munich
in 1972, Brundage entered the realm of mythic history. Speaking
to his fellow mourners, appealing one last time for a world of fair
play and good sportsmanship where race and religion are as irrelevant as political commitment and economic condition, for a world
beyond the power even of hooded terrorists, he spoke his mind and
heart. Whether we think of him as idealistically inspired or as quix-
otically unrealistic, he was one with his vision. Thanks largely to
him, for better or for worse, the games have gone on.

MEMBERS OF THE INTERNATIONAL OLYMPIC COMMITTEE—1894–1972

NAME	COUNTRY	DATES			
		Member	President	Vice President	Executive Board
Baron Pierre de Coubertin	France	1894–1925	1896–1925		
Ernest Callot	France	1894–1913			
Dimetrius Bikelas	Greece	1894–1897	1894–1896		
Alexander Butowsky	Russia	1894–1900			
Viktor Balck	Sweden	1894–1921			
William M. Sloane	U.S.A.	1894–1925			
Jiri Guth-Jarkovsky	Bohemia	1894–1943			1921–1923
Ferenc Kemeny	Hungary	1894–1907			
Arthur Oliver Villiers Russell, Lord Ampthill	U.K.	1894–1898			
Charles Herbert	U.K.	1894–1906			
José Benjamin Zubiaur	Argentina	1894–1907			
Leonard A. Cuff	New Zealand	1894–1905			
Comte Lucchesi Palli	Italy	1894–1895			
Comte Maxime de Bousies	Belgium	1894–1901			
Riccardo Carafa, Duke d'Andria	Italy	1894–1898			

My information is taken mainly from *Le Comité International Olympique* (Lausanne, 1981), pp. 146–147, and Karl Adolf Scherer, *Der Männerorden* (Frankfurt, 1974), pp. 228–238.

NAME	COUNTRY	DATES			
		Member	President	Vice President	Executive Board
Willibald Gebhardt	Germany	1895–1909			
R. S. de Courcy Laffan	U.K.	1897–1927			
Count Alexandre Mercati	Greece	1897–1925			
Count Brunetta d'Usseaux	Italy	1897–1919			
Baron F. W. de Tuyll de Serooskerken	Holland	1898–1924			
Graf de Talleyrand Périgord	Germany	1899–1903			
Colonel N. V. S. Holbeck	Denmark	1899–1906			
Prince Georges Bibesco	Romania	1899–1901			
Baron Godefroy de Blonay	Switz.	1899–1937		1921–1937	1921–1937
Theodore Stanton	U.S.A.	1900–1904			
Caspar Whitney	U.S.A.	1900–1905			
H. Hébrard de Villeneuve	France	1900–1911			
Prince Serge Beliosselsky de Beliozersk	Russia	1900–1908			
Count de Ribeaupierre	Russia	1900–1910			
Count Clarence de Rosen	Sweden	1900–1948			
Prince Edouard de Salm-Horstmar	Germany	1901–1905			
Commandant Reyntiens	Belgium	1901–1903			
Sir Howard Vincent	U.K.	1901–1907			
Miguel de Beistegui	Mexico	1901–1931			
Gonzalo de Figueroa y Torres, Conde de Mejorada del Campo	Spain	1902–1921			
Graf Caesar von Wartensleben	Germany	1903–1913			
Comte Henri de Baillet-Latour	Belgium	1903–1942	1925–1942		1921–1926
James Hyde	U.S.A.	1903–1908			
Carlos F. de Candamo	Peru	1903–1922			
Comte Albert Bertier de Sauvigny	France	1904–1920			
Graf von der Asseburg	Germany	1905–1909			
R. Coombes	Australia	1905–1932			
Prince Alexandre de Salms Braunfels	Austria	1905–1909			
Heinrik Angell	Norway	1905–1907			
E. N. Tzokow	Bulgaria	1906–1912			
Captain Torben Grut	Denmark	1906–1912			
Lord Desborough of Taplow	U.K.	1906–1909			
Duc de Lancastre	Portugal	1906–1912			
Manuel Quintana	Argentina	1907–1910			
Count Geza Andrassy	Hungary	1907–1938			

NAME	COUNTRY	DATES			
		Member	*President*	*Vice President*	*Executive Board*
Thomas Heftye	Norway	1907–1908			
Allison Armour	U.S.A.	1908–1919			
Baron R. Willebrand	Finland	1908–1920			
Prince Scipion Borghese	Italy	1908–1909			
Comte Albert Gautier Vignal	Monaco	1908–1940			
Johan T. Sverre	Norway	1908–1927			
Georges A. Plagino	Romania	1908–1949			
Prince Simon Trobetzkoi	Russia	1908–1910			
Selim Sirry Bey	Turkey	1908–1930			
Baron de Wenningen	Germany	1909–1914			
Sir Theodore Cook	U.K.	1909–1915			
Jules de Muzza	Hungary	1909–1946			
Attilio Brunialti	Italy	1909–1913			
Jigoro Kano	Japan	1909–1938			
Graf A. F. Sierstorpft	Germany	1910–1919			
Angelo C. Bolanaki	Greece	1910–1963			
Maurice Pescatore	Luxemburg	1910–1929			
Prince Leon Ouroussoff	Russia	1910–1933			
Prince Othon de Windischgraetz	Austria	1911–1919			
Sir John Hanbury Williams	Canada	1911–1921			
Evert Jansen Wendell	U.S.A.	1911–1921			
Abel Ballif	France	1911–1913			
Graf Rudolf de Colloredo Mansfeld	Austria	1912–1919			
O. N. Garcia	Chile	1912–1919			
Comte de Penha Garcia	Portugal	1912–1940			
S. W. Djoukitch	Serbia	1912–1949			
Graf Hermann von Arnim-Muskau	Germany	1913–1919			
Raoul de Rio Branco	Brazil	1913–1938			
Dimitrius Stancioff	Bulgaria	1913–1929			
Sydney Farrar	South Africa	1913–1919			
Colonel Fritz Hansen	Denmark	1913–1922			
Albert Glandaz	France	1913–1944			
Duke Algernon of Somerset	U.K.	1913–1920			
Carlo Montu	Italy	1913–1939			
Georges Duperron	Russia	1913–1915			
Marquis Melchior de Polignac	France	1914–1950			1921–1950
P. J. de Matheu	Central America	1918–1941			
Baron de Laveleye	Belgium	1919–1939			

NAME	COUNTRY	Member	President	Vice President	Executive Board
Carlos Silva Vidosola	Chile	1920–1922			
Dorn y de Alsua	Ecuador	1920–1929			
Bartow Weeks	U.S.A.	1920–1921			
Ernst Krogius	Finland	1920–1948			
Comte Justinien de Clary	France	1920–1933			
R. J. Kentish	U.K.	1920–1933			1926–1931
Sir Dorabji J. Tata	India	1920–1930			
Marquessa Guglielmi	Italy	1920–1930			
Arthur Marryatt	New Zealand	1920–1925			
Henry Nourse	South Africa	1920–1943			
Franjo Bucar	Yugoslavia	1920–1947			
J. Sigfrid Edstrøm	Sweden	1920–1952	1942–1952	1937–1942	1921–1952
J. G. Merrick	Canada	1921–1946			
Horacio Echevarrieta	Spain	1921–1923			
Nizam Eddin Khoi	Iran	1921–1923			
F. Ghigliani	Uruguay	1921–1937			
T. de Alvear	Argentina	1922–1932			
C. T. Wang	China	1922–1957			
Ivar Nyholm	Denmark	1922–1931			
Santiago Guell, Baron de Guell	Spain	1922–1954			
William May Garland	U.S.A.	1922–1948			
Charles H. Sherrill	U.S.A.	1922–1936			1926–1931
Gerald, The Earl Cadogan	U.K.	1922–1929			
J. J. Keane	Ireland	1922–1951			
Prince Casimir Lubomirski	Poland	1922–1930			
Ricardo C. Aldao	Argentina	1923–1949			
Arnaldo Guinle	Brazil	1923–1961			
Ferreira Santos	Brazil	1923–1962			1960–1962
J. Marte Gormaz	Chile	1923–1928			
Porfirio Franca	Cuba	1923–1938			
Marquis de Guadelupe	Mexico	1923–1924			
Alfredo Benavides	Peru	1923–1957			
Theodor Lewald	Germany	1924–1938			1927–1937
Oskar Ruperti	Germany	1924–1929			
James Taylor	Australia	1924–1944			
Martin Haudek	Austria	1924–1928			
Jacobo Stuart FitzJames, Duque de Alba	Spain	1924–1927			
P. W. Scharroo	Holland	1924–1957			1946–1953
S. Kishi	Japan	1924–1933			
Jorge Gomez de Parada	Mexico	1924–1927			
Prince Samad Khan	Iran	1924–1927			
David Kinley	U.S.A.	1925–1927			
Baron A. Schimmelpennick von der Oye	Holland	1925–1943			

NAME	COUNTRY	Member	President	Vice President	Executive Board
Count Alberto Bonacossa	Italy	1925–1953			1935–1952
J. P. Firth	New Zealand	1925–1927			
Herzog A. F. zu Mecklenburg-Schwerin	Germany	1926–1956			
Georges Averoff	Greece	1926–1930			
J. Dikmanis	Latvia	1926–1947			
Manuel Falco, Marques de Pons	Spain	1927–1930			
Ernest Lee Jahncke	U.S.A.	1927–1936			
Lord George Rochdale	U.K.	1927–1933			
M. Saenz	Mexico	1927–1932			
Sir Thomas Fearnley	Norway	1927–1950			
Theodor Schmidt	Austria	1928–1939			
Sir George McLaren Brown	Canada	1928–1940			
F. Akel	Estonia	1928–1932			
Lord Bernard Freyberg	New Zealand	1928–1930			
Ignace Matuszewski	Poland	1928–1939			
Karl Ritter von Halt	Germany	1929–1964			1957–1963
Stephan G. Tchaprachikov	Bulgaria	1929–1944			
Don Alfredo Ewing	Chile	1929–1933			
Lord Clarence Aberdare	U.K.	1929–1957			1931–1951
M. Politis	Greece	1930–1933			
Augusto Turati	Italy	1930–1931			
Kremalettin Sami Pacha	Turkey	1930–1933			
Fernando Suarez de Tangil, Conde de Vallellano	Spain	1931–1952			
C. J. Wray	New Zealand	1931–1934			
General Rouppert	Poland	1931–1946			
Horacio Bustos Moron Jr.	Argentina	1932–1952			
Prince Axel of Denmark	Denmark	1932–1958			1952–1956
G. D. Sondhi	India	1932–1966			1961–1965
Count Paolo Thaon di Revel	Italy	1932–1964			1954–1960
Sir Harold Luxton	Australia	1933–1951			
David Burghley, the Marquess of Exeter	U.K.	1933–1982		1954–1966	1951–1970
Sir Noel Curtis Bennett	U.K.	1933–1950			
Jotaro Sugimoura	Japan	1933–1936			
Rechid Saffet Atabinen	Turkey	1933–1952			
François Piétri	France	1934–1966			
Lord Arthur Porritt	New Zealand	1934–1967			1956–1961
Mohammed Taher Pacha	Egypt	1934–1968			1952–1964
Count Michimasa Soyeshima	Japan	1934–1948			

NAME	COUNTRY	Member	President	Vice President	Executive Board
Segura Marte R. Gomez	Mexico	1934–1973			
AVERY BRUNDAGE	U.S.A.	1936–1972	1952–1972	1946–1952	1937–1952
Prince Franz Josef	Lichtenstein	1936–1980			
Joakim Puhk	Estonia	1936–1942			
Prince Iesato Tokugawa	Japan	1936–1939			
Jorge B. Vargas	Philippines	1936–1980			
Frederic-René Coudert	U.S.A.	1937–1948			
Henri Guisan	Switzerland	1937–1939			
Joaquin Serratosa Cibils	Uruguay	1937–1958			
Walther von Reichenau	Germany	1938–1942			
Miguel A. Moenck	Cuba	1938–1969			1953–1957
Antonio Prado Jr.	Brazil	1938–1955			
Johan Wilhelm Rangell	Finland	1938–1967			
Baron de Trannoy	Belgium	1939–1957			
H. H. Kung	China	1939–1955			
Giorgio Vaccaro	Italy	1939–1949			
M. Nagai	Japan	1939–1950			
Sh. Takaishi	Japan	1939–1967			
A. V. Lindbergh	South Africa	1939–1939			
Nicolas de Horthy Jr.	Hungary	1939–1948			
Hugh Richard Weir	Australia	1946–1975			
R. W. Seeldrayers	Belgium	1946–1955			
Jean-Claude Patterson	Canada	1946–1954			
Joseph Gruss	Czechoslovakia	1946–1965			
Armand Massard	France	1946–1970		1952–1968	1950–1968
C. F. Pahud de Mortanges	Holland	1946–1964			
Benedikt J. Waage	Iceland	1946–1966			
Le grand duc Jean de Luxembourg	Luxemburg	1946–			
Jose Pontes	Portugal	1946–1956			
J. Dowsett	South Africa	1946–1951			
Reginald Honey	South Africa	1946–1982			
Albert Mayer	Switzerland	1946–1969			
Jean Ketseas	Greece	1946–1965			
Manfred M. Ritter von Markhof	Austria	1947–1969			
Sidney Dawes	Canada	1947–1967			
Shou-Yi-tung	China	1947–1958			
Raja Bhalindra Singh	India	1947–			
Bo Ekelund	Sweden	1948–1965			1958–1962
Georges Loth	Poland	1948–1961			
Stanko Bloudek	Yugoslavia	1948–1959			
Ferenc Mezö	Hungary	1948–1961			
Enrique O. Barbosa Baeza	Chile	1948–1952			
John Jewett Garland	U.S.A.	1948–1969			
Erik von Frenckell	Finland	1948–1976			

NAME	COUNTRY	Member	President	Vice President	Executive Board
Miguel Ydigoras Fuentes	Guatamala	1948–1952			
Olaf Christian Ditlev-Simonsen, Jr.	Norway	1948–1967			
Prince Rainier III	Monaco	1949–1950			
Ahmed E. H. Jaffer	Pakistan	1949–1956			
Ryotaro Azuma	Japan	1950–1969			1960–1964
James Brooks B. Parker	U.S.A.	1950–1951			
Prince Pierre de Monaco	Monaco	1950–1964			
Ian, Lord Luke of Pavenham	U.K.	1951–			
Comte Jean de Beaumont	France	1951–		1970–	1968–
Giorgio de Stefani	Italy	1951–			1964–1968
Konstantin Andrianov	U.S.S.R.	1951–		1966–1970	1962–
Lewis Luxton	Australia	1951–1974			
Vladimir Stoytchev	Bulgaria	1952–			1956–1961
Michael Morris, Lord Killanin	Ireland	1952–1980	1972–1980	1968–1972	1967–1980
Gabriel Gemayel	Lebanon	1952–			1964–1969
José de J. Clark Flores	Mexico	1952–1971		1966–1970	1963–1971
Alexsei Romanov	U.S.S.R.	1952–1971			
Enrique Alberdi	Argentina	1952–1959			
Julio Gerlein Comelin	Columbia	1952–			
Pedro Ibarra Mac-Mahon, Baron de Guell	Spain	1952–			
Douglas F. Roby	U.S.A.	1952–			
Augustin Sosa	Panama	1952–1967			
Gustaf Dyrssen	Sweden	1952–1970			
Julio Bustamante	Venezuela	1952–1968			
Alejandro Rivera Bascur	Chile	1955–			
Suat Erler	Turkey	1955–			
Ki Poong Lee	Korea	1955–1960			
Prince Gholam Reza Pahlavi	Iran	1955–1980			
Alexandru Siperco	Romania	1955–			
Willi Daume	Germany	1956–		1972–	1972–
Saul Christovao Ferreira Pires	Portugal	1957–1962			
Prince Albert de Liege	Belgium	1958–1964			
Eduardo Dibos	Peru	1958–			
Syed Wajid Ali	Pakistan	1959–			1966–1970
Ivar Emil Vind	Denmark	1959–1977			1963–1967
Reginald Stanley Alexander	Kenya	1960–			
Boris Bakrac	Yugoslavia	1960–			
Mario L. Negri	Argentina	1960–1977			

NAME	COUNTRY	Member	President	Vice President	Executive Board
Ahmed Eldemerdash Touny	Egypt	1960–			
Wlodimierz Reczek	Poland	1961–			
Mohammed Benjelloun	Morocco	1961–			
Sir Adetokunbo Ademola	Nigeria	1963–			1969–1973
Raul Pereira de Castro	Portugal	1963–			
João Havelange	Brazil	1963–			
Marc Hodler	Switzerland	1963–			
Alfredo Inciarte	Uruguay	1963–1975			
King Constantine of Greece	Greece	1963–1974			
Arpad Csanadi	Bulgaria	1964–			
Prince Aexandre de Mérode	Belgium	1964–			
Sylvio de Magalhães Padiha	Brazil	1964–			1970–
Giulio Onesti	Italy	1964–			
Herman A. van Karnebeek	Holland	1964–1977		1970–1976	1968–1977
Sang Beck Lee	Korea	1964–1966			
Amadou Barry	Senegal	1965–1969			
Gunnar Ericsson	Sweden	1965–			
Frantisek Kroutil	Czechoslovakia	1965–			
Pyrros Lappas	Greece	1965–1980			
Mohamed Mzali	Tunisia	1965–			
Georg von Opel	Germany	1966–1971			
Juan Antonio Samaranch	Spain	1966–	1980–		1970–
Heinz Schöbel	Germany	1966–1980			
Jan Staubo	Norway	1966–			
Prince Georg von Hannover	*	1966–1971			
Key Young Chang	Korea	1967–1977			
Paavo Honkajuuri	Finland	1967–			
Prince Tsuneyoshi Takeda	Japan	1967–			1970–
James Worrall	Canada	1967–			
Agustin Carlos Arroyo Yerovi	Ecuador	1968–			
Jose Beracasa	Venezuela	1968–			
Abdel Mohamed Halim	Sudan	1968–			
Sultan Hamengku Buwono IX	Indonesia	1968–1976			
René Rakotobe	Madagascar	1968–1971			
C. Lance S. Cross	New Zealand	1969–			

* Prince Georg represented the International Olympic Academy (Olympia, Greece).

NAME	COUNTRY	DATES			
		Member	President	Vice President	Executive Board
Raymond Gafner	Switzerland	1969–			
Louis Guirandou-N'Diaye	Ivory Coast	1969–			
Masaji Kiyokawa	Japan	1969–			
Virgilio de Leon	Panama	1969–			
Rudolf Nemetschke	Austria	1969–1976			
Maurice Herzog	France	1970–			
Henry Hsu	Taiwan	1970–			
Sven Thofelt	Sweden	1970–1976			
Prabhas Charusathiara	Thailand	1971–1974			
Ydnekatchew Tessema	Ethiopia	1971–			
Berthold Beitz	Germany	1972–			
Pedro Ramirez Vazquez	Mexico	1972–			

SESSIONS OF THE INTERNATIONAL OLYMPIC COMMITTEE—1894–1972

SESSION	PLACE	DATES
1	Paris	June 23, 1894[a]
2	Athens	April 4, 6–7, 9, 14, 1896
3	LeHavre	July 23–August 1, 1897
4	Paris	May 21–24, 1901
5	Paris	May 23, 1903
6	London	June 20–21, 1904
7	Brussels	June 9–14, 1905
8	Athens	1906[b]
9	The Hague	May 1907[b]
	London	1908[e]
10	Berlin	July 13–16, 1909
11	Luxemburg	June 11–13, 1910
12	Budapest	May 23–28, 1911
13	Basel	March 27–28, 1912

[a] Date Pierre de Coubertin was empowered to select a committee.
[b] Exact dates unknown.
[c] The meetings of the 23rd took place in Olympia.
[d] The meetings actually took place on shipboard on the Nile.
[e] Discovering that the sessions had for decades been incorrectly numbered because of the failure to count one in London in 1908, the I.O.C. apparently decided, rather than to renumber all the sessions, to skip a number.

SESSION	PLACE	DATES
14	Stockholm	July 4–5, 12, 18, 23, 1912
15	Lausanne	May 6–7, 1913
16	Paris	1914[b]
17	Lausanne	1919[b]
18	Antwerp	August 18–30, 1920
19	Lausanne	June 3–6, 1921
20	Paris	June 7–10, 1922
21	Rome	May 7–12, 1923
22	Paris	June 25–July 12, 1924
23	Prague	May 26–28, 1925
24	Lisbon	May 2–7, 1926
25	Monaco	April 22–27, 1927
26	Amsterdam	July 25–27—August 3, 1928
27	Lausanne	April 8–11, 1929
28	Berlin	May 22–24, 1930
29	Barcelona	April 26–27, 1931
30	Los Angeles	July 28–29, 1932
31	Vienna	June 7–9, 1933
32	Athens	May 15, 17–19, 23[c]
33	Oslo	February 25–28—March 1, 1935
34	Garmisch-Partenkirchen	February 11, 1936
35	Berlin	July 29–31—August 15, 1936
36	Warsaw	June 7–11, 1937
37	Cairo	March 13–18, 1938[d]
38	London	June 6–9, 1939
39	Lausanne	September 3–6, 1946
40	Stockholm	June 19–21, 1947
41	St. Moritz	January 29–31—February 4–8, 1948
42	London	July 27–29—August 13, 1948
43	Rome	April 24–29, 1949
44	Copenhagen	May 15–17, 1950
45	Vienna	May 7–9, 1951
46	Oslo	February 12–13, 25, 1952
47	Helsinki	July 16–18, 27, 1952
48	Mexico City	April 17–18, 20, 1953
49	Athens	May 11–14, 1954
50	Paris	June 13–18, 1955
51	Cortina d'Ampezzo	January 23–24, 1956
52	Melbourne	November 19–21—December 4, 1956
53	Sofia	September 23–28, 1957
54	Tokyo	May 14–16, 1958
55	Munich	May 25–28, 1959

SESSION	PLACE	DATES
56	San Francisco	February 15–16, 1960
57	Rome	August 22–23, 1960
58	Athens	June 19–21, 1961
59	Moscow	June 5–8, 1962
60	Baden-Baden	October 10–14, 1963
61	Innsbruck	January 26–28, 1964
62	Tokyo	October 7–8, 1964
63	Madrid	October 7–9, 1965
64	Rome	April 25–28, 1966
65	Teheran	May 6–8, 1967
66	Grenoble	February 1–5, 1968
67	Mexico City	October 7–11, 1968
68	Warsaw	June 7–10, 1969
69	Amsterdam	May 12–16, 1970
71[e]	Luxemburg	September 15–17, 1971
72	Sapporo	January 31–February 1, 1972
73	Munich	August 21–24, September 5, 1972

NOTES

The following abbreviations are used in the notes:

A.B.C.   The Avery Brundage Collection, Urbana, Illinois
C.D.I.   The Carl-Diem-Institut, Cologne
I.A.A.F.   Archives of the International Amateur Athletic Federation, London
I.O.C.   Archives of the International Olympic Committee, Lausanne

The I.O.C.'s official magazine changed its name several times; I have referred to it as the *Bulletin du C.I.O.* or, after September 1967, as the *Newsletter*. Since the issues were usually quite short, I have often omitted page references when citing.

PREFACE

1. *The Speeches of Avery Brundage* (Lausanne: Comité International Olympique, 1968), p. 80. For earlier references to the "virile, dynamic" religion and/or philosophy of sports, see "For Honor of Country and Glory of Sport," *Olympic News* (August 1934), p. 11; "Baron Pierre de Coubertin," manuscript speech dated August 5, 1964 (A.B.C., Box 244).

I EARLY YEARS OF A SELF-MADE MAN

1. Brundage to Murray Hulbert, October 29, 1946 (A.B.C., Box 26).
2. Robert Shaplen, "Profiles: Amateur," *New Yorker* (July 23, 1960) 35:50.
3. *Ski Survey* (September 1972), p. 22.
4. Brundage to Otto Mayer, October 27, 1953, quoted in "The President of the I.O.C. and the Press," *Bulletin du C.I.O.* (December 15, 1953), no. 43, p. 16.
5. Information in this and the next four paragraphs is drawn largely from Hans Klein, ed., *Avery Brundage: Die Herausforderung* (Munich; Pro Sport, 1972), pp. 25–51; Richard Lee Gibson, "Avery Brundage: Professional Amateur" (Ph.D., Kent State University, 1976), pp. 13–14; Interview with Frederick Ruegsegger, Chicago, July 21, 1979; Brundage to Mrs. Murrell R. Wheeler, May 8, 1968 (A.B.C., Box 41); Obituary clipping on Chester L. Brundage (A.B.C., Scrapbook 12 C).
6. Information on Edward J. Brundage is drawn from *Notable Men of Chicago* (Chicago; Daily Journal, 1910), p. 31; Edward Fitzsimmons Dunne, *Illinois: The Heart of a Nation*, 5 vols. (Chicago: Lewis Publishing Co., 1933), 4:45; Alex Gottfried, *Boss Cermak of Chicago* (Seattle: University of Washington Press, 1962), pp. 363–64: Photograph album 104 (A.B.C.).

7. Interview with Monique Berlioux, Baden-Baden, October 3, 1981.

8. Brundage to Hans Lagerloef, November 7, 1951 (A.B.C., Box 31).

9. "A Sound Mind in a Sound Body," *American Boy* (May 1919), pp. 9–10.

10. *Ibid.*

11. Quoted in Gibson, "Avery Brundage," p. 15.

12. Brundage's high-school and college transcripts are in the University of Illinois Alumni Office; his senior project is referred to in the *Daily Illini*, June 2, 1909.

13. *Handbook of the International Amateur Athletic Federation 1932–1934*, p. 51 (I.A.A.F.); *Minutes of the 14th Congress of the International Amateur Athletic Federation*, February 28–March 1, 1938, p. 34 (I.A.A.F.); Brundage to Bo Ekelund, March 29, 1937 (I.A.A.F.).

14. "Is There Something Wrong with Current Engineering Education?" *The Technograph* (1907–1908), 22(22):151.

15. Brundage to Amund M. Korsmo, March 1, 1969 (A.B.C., Box 31).

16. *Ibid.*

17. *The Illini*, March 20, 21, April 23, 1907; *The Scribbler* (January 1909) 2(1); *The 1910 Illio*, p. 258.

18. Amund M. Korsmo to Brundage, February 21, 1969 (A.B.C., Box 31).

19. *Daily Illini*, October 28, 29, November 11, 25, 1905; February 22, October 7, 21, November 4, 1906; February 3, 17, March 2, April 28, June 5, November 5, 10, 11, 26, December 15, 1907; January 5, 11, March 31, May 5, 15, 16, 23, September 26, October 11, 29, November 4, 20, 1908; February 11, May 9, 16, 22, June 6, 1909.

20. The *Daily Illini*, May 9, 1909.

21. *The 1910 Illio*, pp. 163–64.

22. *Ibid*. The *Daily Illini* for June 6, 1909, lists Brundage 1st with a throw of 127', but the *Illio* refers to him as 2nd with 127' 1¼" (p. 200).

23. The *Daily Illini*, January 8, 1908.

24. "The Retribution," *The Scribbler* (April 1909), 2(4):124–28.

25. Klein, *Avery Brundage*, pp. 31–32; "Application for Examination for Commission in Ordnance Officers' Reserve Corps," December 28, 1917 (A.B.C., Box 334).

26. *Ibid.*; Carl W. Condit, *Chicago: 1910–1929: Building, Planning, and Urban Technology* (Chicago: University of Chicago Press, 1973).

27. "The Olympic Story," Chapter I, p. 17 (A.B.C., Boxes 330–31).

28. Steven A. Riess, *Touching Base* (Westport: Greenwood Press, Connecticut, 1980), pp. 55–56.

29. "The Olympic Story," Chapter I, p. 17 (A.B.C., Boxes 330–331).

30. Quoted in Robert Creamer, "The Embattled World of Avery Brundage," *Sports Illustrated* (January 30, 1956), 4:57.

31. *Chicago Tribune Magazine*, November 19, 1972.

32. "Address at Hotel Sherman, Chicago, September 16, 1929" (A.B.C., Box 247).

33. Newspaper clippings (A.B.C., Scrapbook 18). Brundage ran 100 yards in 11 seconds and a mile in 5:56. He performed the 800-yard walk in 4:02, high jumped 5'3¾", long jumped 19'7", shot putted 36'1½" and threw the hammer 112'9" and the 56-pound weight 22'1¼".

34. "The Olympic Story," Chapter I, pp. 1–2 (A.B.C., Boxes 330–331).

II COUBERTIN AND THE OLYMPIC IDEAL

1. See Joachim K. Ruehl, *Die Olympischen Spiele Robert Dovers* (Heidelberg: Winter Verlag, 1975).

2. My chief sources for this chapter are Pierre de Coubertin, *Une Campagne de Vingt-et-Un Ans* (Paris: Libraire de l'éducation physique, 1909); Coubertin, *Mémoires olympiques* (Lausanne: Bureau international de pédagogie sportive, 1931); Marie-Thérèse Eyquem, *Pierre de Coubertin: L'Épopée olympique* (Paris: Calmann-Lévy, 1966); John A. Lucas, "Baron Pierre de Coubertin and the Modern Olympic Movement" (Ph.D., Pennsylvania State University, 1963); Yves-Pierre Boulongne, *La Vie et l'oeuvre pédagogique de Pierre de Coubertin* (Ottawa: Le Méac, 1975); S. P. Lambros and N. G. Polites, eds., *The Olympic Games* (Leipzig: C. Beck, 1896–1897); Richard D. Mandell, *The First Modern Olympics* (Berkeley: University of California Press, 1976); Karl Adolf Scherer, *Der Männerorden: Die Geschichte des Internationalen Olympischen Komitees* (Frankfurt: Limpert, 1974); Bill Henry, *An Approved History of the Olympic Games* (New York: Putnam's, 1948); Ferenc Mezö, *Les Jeux Olympiques modernes* (Budapest: Pannonia, 1956); Otto Mayer, *À Travers les anneaux olympiques* (Geneva: Cailler, 1966).

3. Coubertin distinguished between his personal loyalty to France and his official position of neutrality as president of the I.O.C.

4. Mayer, *À Travers*, p. 17.

5. Norbert Müller, *Von Paris Bis Baden-Baden: Die Olympischen Kongresse 1894–1981* (Niedernhausen: Schors-Veriag, 1981), pp. 25–26. Other sources, which Müller discusses (pp. 25n-26n), give other numbers for the delegations.

6. Eyquem, *Pierre de Coubertin*, p. 133.

7. *Ibid.*, p. 136; Coubertin, *Une Campagne*, p. 96; Coubertin, *Mémoires olympiques*, p. 18.

8. *Ibid.*, pp. 22–23.

9. *Bikelas* is also transliterated as *Vikelas*.

10. Mandell, *The First Modern Olympics*, p. 116.

11. *Ibid.*, p. 110.

12. John T. MacAloon, *This Great Symbol* (Chicago: University of Chicago Press, 1981), p. 198.

13. Quoted in Henry, *An Approved History*, p. 45.

14. Thomas Curtis, "The Glory That Was Greece," *The Sportsman* (July 1932), 12(1):22. It should be noted that this was written 36 years after the event.

15. Eugen Weber, "Pierre de Coubertin and the Introduction of Organized Sport in France," *Journal of Contemporary History* (1970), 5(2):24.

16. Eyquem, *Pierre de Coubertin*, p. 159.

17. Quoted in Dick Schaap, *An Illustrated History of the Olympics*, 3rd ed. (New York: Knopf, 1975), p. 67.

18. *Une Campagne*, p. 161; Henry, *An Approved History*, p. 78.

19. *Mémoires olympiques*, p. 65; Mayer, *À Travers*, p. 51.

20. Henry, *An Approved History*, p. 98.

21. See George R. Matthews, "The Controversial Olympic Games of 1908 as Viewed by the *New York Times* and the *Times* of London," *Journal of Sport History* (Summer 1980), 7(2):40–53.

22. James Coote and John Goodbody, *The Olympics 1972* (London: Robert Dale, 1972), p. 38.

23. Mayer, *À Travers*, p. 71.

III STOCKHOLM AND AFTER

1. The *Daily Illini*, May 29, 1908; October 1, 1908.

2. Richard Lee Gibson, "Avery Brundage," (Ph.D., Kent State University, 1976), pp. 25–27.

3. "The Olympic Story," Chapter I, p. 1 (A.B.C., Boxes 330–331).

4. A.B.C., Scrapbook 18, Box 311.

5. Gibson, "Avery Brundage," p. 28.

6. James E. Sullivan, *The Olympic Games Stockholm 1912* (New York: American Sports Publishing Co., 1912), p. 41.

7. "The Olympic Story," Chapter I, p. 4 (A.B.C., boxes 330–331).

8. *Ibid.*

9. *Ibid.*, p. 5; Brundage to Robert Wheeler, September 13, 1967 (A.B.C., Box 41).

10. *Ibid.*

11. "The Olympic Story," Chapter I, p. 7 (A.B.C., Boxes 330–331).

12. Sullivan, *The Olympic Games*, pp. 9, 11.

13. From a speech delivered during the 44th Session of the I.O.C., Copenhagen, May 1950 (A.B.C., Box 245).

14. "The Olympic Story," Chapter I, p. 14 (A.B.C., Boxes 330–331).

15. "Amateur Sport," a speech given on numerous occasions in 1930 (A.B.C., Box 247).

16. "The Olympic Story," Chapter I, p. 12 (A.B.C., Boxes 330–331).

17. *Minutes of a Special Congress of the International Amateur Athletic Federation June 9, 1947*, p. 3 (I.A.A.F.).

18. On Thorpe and the fact that Warner paid $9,233 to his 1907–1908 football team, see Reet A. and Maxwell L. Howell, "The Myth of 'Pop Warner': Carlisle Revisited," *Quest Monograph* (Summer 1978), 30:19–27.

19. Jack McCallum, "The Regilding of a Legend," *Sports Illustrated* (October 25, 1982), 57:49; Mark Kram, "Thorpe and the man who shadowed him," Washington *Times*, October 28, 1982.

20. "The Olympic Story," Chapter I, pp. 6, 18–19 (A.B.C., Boxes 330–331).

21. The passport application, dated July 16, 1912, is in Scrapbook 2 (A.B.C.). The programs for the Finnish and the Russian track meets are in Scrapbook 18 (A.B.C.). In the program, Anderson's initials are given as "A.R."

22. On Taipaly, see Sidney Mautner to Brundage, March 24, 1947 (A.B.C., Box 27).

23. On Pihkala, see Brundage to Erkki Lahdepera, June 17, 1949 (A.B.C., Box 34).

24. "Remarks Made at Dinner in Honor of Sheldon Clark, December 10, 1941" (A.B.C., Box 244).

25. "Opening Address to the 59th Session of the I.O.C., Moscow, June 5, 1962," *Speeches of Avery Brundage* (Lausanne: Comité International Olympique, 1968), p. 59.

26. Brundage to Suat Erler, August 29, 1970 (A.B.C., Box 54).

27. "Travel to 1932" (A.B.C., Box 243).

28. A printed version of the chronology appears in Hans Klein, ed., *Avery Brundage: Die Herausforderung* (Munich: Pro Sport, 1972), pp. 52–55. The photographs taken by Brundage are in Scrapbook 18.

29. January 14, 1926.

30. Seattle *Post-Intelligencer*, October 8, 1916.

31. September 20, 1914.

32. "The Olympic Story," Chapter I, p. 4 (A.B.C., Boxes 330–331).

33. September 17, 1916.

34. Gibson, "Avery Brundage," pp. 31–32.

35. "A Sound Mind in a Sound Body," p. 9.

36. November 25, 1933.

37. "Notes on Athletic Policy—C.A.A.," dated February 25, 1931 (A.B.C., Box 244); Chicago *Tribune*, April 17, 1931.

38. Arnold Flath, "A History of the Relations between the National Collegiate Athletic

Association and the Amateur Athletic Union of the United States" (Ph.D., University of Michigan, 1963), p. 32; see also Robert Korsgaard, "A History of the Amateur Athletic Union of the United States" (Ph.D., Teacher's College-Columbia University, 1952) and Paul Stagg, "The Development of the National Collegiate Athletic Association . . ." (Ph.D., New York University, 1947).

39. Flath, "A History," p. 52.
40. A. C. Gilbert to Gustavus T. Kirby, December 22, 1937 (A.B.C., Box 26).
41. Flath, "A History," p. 120.
42. New York *Times*, May 4, 1923.
43. Quoted in Flath, "A History," p. 160.
44. Undated notes (A.B.C., Box 245).
45. "Address, September 16, 1929" (A.B.C., Box 247).
46. Kirby to Brundage, December 17, 1929 (A.B.C., Box 28).
47. Brundage to Lee Combs, July 25, 1970 (A.B.C., Box 39).
48. Flath, "A History," pp. 173, 176.
49. "Address, December 31, 1930" (A.B.C., Box 247).
50. *Annual Report*, p. 12 (A.B.C., Box 247).
51. Quoted in Flath, "A History," p. 180.

IV MONEY AND LOVE

1. Homer Hoyt, *One Hundred Years of Land Values in Chicago* (Chicago: University of Chicago Press, 1933), p. 237.
2. Carl W. Condit, *Chicago, 1910–1929* (Chicago: University of Chicago Press, 1973), p. 165.
3. From a brochure, *Avery Brundage Company* (A.B.C., Box 242).
4. Hans Klein, ed., *Avery Brundage: Die Herausforderung* (Munich: Pro Sport, 1972), p. 32.
5. *Ibid*.
6. Obituary notice (A.B.C., Scrapbook 12 C).
7. "The Olympic Story," Chapter VI, p. 3 (A.B.C., Boxes 330–331).
8. W. A. Starrett to Brundage, August 21, 1918; Brundage to Starrett, September 3, 1918 (A.B.C., Box 334).
9. A.B.C., Box 334.
10. "Olympic Story," Chapter VI, p. 3 (A.B.C., Boxes 330–331).
11. Certificate dated October 21, 1920 (A.B.C., Scrapbook 3).
12. *Hill's Reports*, undated copy (A.B.C., Box 334).
13. "Applies Athletics to Business," *Cherry Circle* (September 1926), p. 20.
14. Frederick J. Ruegsegger, Interviewed by Richard L. Gibson, Chicago, August 9, 1975, quoted by Richard Lee Gibson, "Avery Brundage: Professional Amateur" (Ph.D., Kent State University, 1976), p. 47.
15. A.B.C., Box 334.
16. *Avery Brundage Company*, pp. 7, 9, 23, 29.
17. Shaplen, "Profiles: Amateur," p. 52.
18. "Olympic Story," Chapter VII, p. 7 (A.B.C., Boxes 330–331).
19. Gibson, "Avery Brundage," p. 49.
20. Al Chase, "Corporation Leases Hotel LaSalle for Eleven Years," Chicago *Tribune*, December 24, 1939; Brundage to Joseph E. Raycroft, February 9, 1940 (A.B.C., Box 34).
21. Brundage to Daniel J. Ferris, July 1, 1946 (A.B.C., Box 24).

22. Gibson, "Avery Brundage," p. 50; Tonapha (Nevada) *Times-Bonanza*, February 20, 1953.

23. Chicago *Sun-Times*, April 25, 1961.

24. Interview, Chicago, July 21, 1979.

25. Obituary notice (A.B.C., Scrapbook 12 C): Gibson, "Avery Brundage," p. 40; Last Will & Testament, November 7, 1974.

26. Santa Barbara *News-Press*, January 23, 1949; January 3, 1950; September 27, 1956; June 8, 1958.

27. Undated notes (A.B.C., Box 245).

28. A.B.C., Box 243.

29. Undated notes (A.B.C., Box 245).

30. Gibson, "Avery Brundage," p. 36; Klein, *Avery Brundage*, pp. 42–43; Santa Barbara *News-Press*, July 1, 1972.

31. "Brundage Calls on Boreas," *The Homecomer* (July 1927), 4(1):1.

32. "The Alaskan Hunting Trip," *The Cherry Circle* (November 1927), 44:9–12, 42–43.

33. Brundage to Ferris, May 5, 1938 (A.B.C., Box 23).

34. Raycroft to Brundage, February 8, 1938 (A.B.C., Box 34).

35. Karl Gustav Wahamaki, Petition for Naturalization No. 123594, April 24, 1956, U.S. Department of Justice—Immigration and Naturalization Service. Her name appears here as "Lillian," with a double "l."

36. A. R. Catton, Judge of the Superior Court, Decree of Annulment, Superior Court of the State of California in and for the County of San Mateo, September 16, 1952.

37. Certificates of Live Birth, Nos. 51–180456 and 52–178394, Office of the State Registrar of Vital Statistics.

38. Acknowledgement of Paternity, June 20, 1952, San Mateo County, California.

39. Trust Agreement, Bank of America National Trust and Savings Association, March 30, 1955.

40. Agreement of Settlement and Release, signed by Avery Gregory Dresden (May 5, 1980), Gary Toro Dresden (May 14, 1980), Ralph E. Davis (May 1, 1980), Frederick J. Ruegsegger (May 1, 1980).

41. William Oscar Johnson, "Avery Brundage: The Man Behind the Mask," *Sports Illustrated* (August 4, 1980), 53(6):52.

42. Interview with Willi Daume, Cologne, August 25, 1980.

43. Johnson, "Avery Brundage," pp. 49–52, 55–58, 60, 63.

44. Interviews with Sir Reginald Alexander and Douglas Roby, Baden-Baden, September 29, 1981, September 30, 1981.

V   THE OLYMPIC MOVEMENT FROM ANTWERP TO LOS ANGELES

1. Mayer, *À Travers les anneaux olympiques* (Geneva: Cailler, 1966), pp. 84–85.

2. David Benjamin Kanin, "The Role of Sport in International Relations" (Ph.D., Fletcher School of Law and Diplomacy, Tufts University, 1976), pp. 53–54.

3. Mayer, *À Travers*, p. 89.

4. Donald E. Fouss, "An Analysis of the Incidents in the Olympic Games from 1924 to 1948 . . ." (Ph.D., Teacher's College, Columbia University, 1951), pp. 54–56.

5. New York *Times*, July 1, July 22, 1924.

6. See Norbert Müller, *Von Paris bis Baden-Baden: Die Olympischen Kongresse, 1896–1981* (Niederhausen: Schors-Verlag, 1981), pp. 95–109.

7. Mayer, *À Travers*, p. 111.

8. *Ibid.*, p. 115.

9. On the workers' sports movement, see Robert F. Wheeler, "Organized Sport and Organized Labour: The Workers' Sport Movement," *Journal of Contemporary History* (1978), 13:191–210; David A. Steinberg, "The Workers' Sport Internationals 1920–1928," *Journal of Contemporary History* (1978), 13:233–251; Jürgen Fischer, "Die Olympiade der Sozialistischen Arbeitersport-Internationale in Frankfurt 1925," *Die Zukunft der Olympischen Spiele*, ed. Hans-Jürgen Schulke (Cologne: Pahl-Rugenstein, 1976), pp. 96–126.

10. On formal similarities between the two movements, see Henning Eichberg et al., *Massenspiele* (Stuttgart: Friedrich Frommann, 1977), esp. pp. 19–180.

11. Although there is no adequate history of women's sports, see Auguste Hoffmann, *Frau und Leibesübungen im Wandel der Zeit* (Schorndorf: Karl Hofmann, 1965); Ellen W. Gerber, "Chronicle of Participation," in Gerber, Jan Felshin, Pearl Berlin, and Waneen Wyrick, *The American Woman in Sport* (Reading, Massachusetts: Addison-Wesley, 1974), pp. 3–176.

12. Quoted by Edmund Neuendorff, *Geschichte der Neueren Deutschen Leibesübungen*, 4 vols. (Dresden: Limpert, 1930), 3:538.

13. Mary Hanson Leigh, "The Evolution of Women's Participation in the Summer Olympic Games, 1900–1948" (Ph.D., Ohio State University, 1974), p. 55.

14. Mayer, *À Travers*, p. 109.

15. On Milliat and the F.S.F.I., see Mary H. Leigh and Thérèse M. Bonin, "The Pioneering Role of Madame Alice Milliat and the FSFI in Establishing International [Track] and Field Competition for Women," *Journal of Sport History* (Spring, 1977), 4(1):72–83.

16. Edstrøm to Brundage, January 3, 1935 (A.B.C., Box 42).

17. Leigh, "The Evolution of Women's Participation," pp. 173–78.

18. "Minutes of the Session of the I.O.C. at Lisbon," *Bulletin du C.I.O.* (July 1926), 1(3):14.

19. "The Olympic Story," Chapter VI, p. 6 (A.B.C., Boxes 330–331).

20. *Session de 1923: Rome* (A.B.C., Box 90); on Garland's role in the 1932 Olympics, see Steven A. Riess, "Power without Authority: Los Angeles' Elites and the Construction of the Coliseum," *Journal of Sport History* (Spring 1981), 8(1):50–65.

21. "The Olympic Story," Chapter VII, p. 2 (A.B.C., Boxes 330–331).

22. *Ibid.*, p. 3.

23. *Ibid.*

24. Procès-Verbale, Commission exécutive, July 23–25, 1929 (A.B.C., Box 90).

25. Kirby to Howard S. Braucher, June 9, 1930 (A.B.C., Box 75).

26. *Ibid.*

27. Rockne, "Campus Comment," *Chicago Herald-American*, July 17, 1930.

28. Brundage to Rockne, July 17, 1930 (A.B.C., Box 8).

29. Program, Staatsoper, May 25, 1930 (A.B.C., Box 75).

30. *Handbook of the International Amateur Athletic Federation 1929–1931*, pp. 43–44 (I.A.A.F.).

31. *Ibid.* p. 49; see also Leigh, "The Evolution of Women's Participation," pp. 185–186.

32. *Minutes of the Olympic Congress of Berlin 1930: May 25–30, 1930* (Lausanne, 1930), p. 25.

33. Edstrøm to Milliat, October 12, 1936, quoted in Leigh, "The Evolution of Women's Participation," pp. 203–204.

34. *Handbook of the International Amateur Athletic Federation 1932–1934*, pp. 40–41 (I.A.A.F.).

35. Edstrøm to Brundage, April 9, 1934 (A.B.C., Box 42).

36. Dick Schaap, *An Illustrated History of the Olympics*, 3rd ed. (N.Y.: Knopf, 1976), p. 204.

VI   "THE NAZI OLYMPICS"

1. Otto Mayer, À Travers les anneaux olympiques (Geneva: Cailler, 1966), p. 131.
2. On the Deutsche Turnerschaft's hostility to modern sports, see Hajo Bernett, ed., Der Sport im Kreuzfeuer der Kritik (Schorndorf: Karl Hofmann, 1982), pp. 15–42.
3. Bruno Malitz, quoted in Bernett, Der Sport im Kreuzfeuer, p. 219.
4. Arnd Krüger, Die Olympischen Spiele 1936 und die Weltmeinung (Berlin: Bartels & Wernitz, 1972), p. 36, quoting Otto Dietrich.
5. On Lewald and his relationship with the Nazis, see Arnd Krüger, Theodor Lewald (Berlin: Bartels & Wernitz, 1975).
6. For Diem the best source is his posthumous autobiography, Ein Leben für den Sport (Ratingen: A. Henn, 1976); his apologia for his role during the Hitlerzeit appeared, edited by L. Pfeiffer, as Der Deutsche Sport in der Zeit des Nationalsozialismus (Cologne: Carl-Diem-Institut, 1980).
7. Diem, "Amerikareise 1929," pp. 64–69 (C.D.I.); Diem, Sport in Amerika (Berlin: Weidmannsche Buchhandlung, 1930), pp. 192–193.
8. Diem, Ein Leben, p. 127.
9. Lewald to Brundage, April 29, 1933 (A.B.C., Box 33).
10. Krüger, Die Olympischen Spiele 1936, pp. 12, 63.
11. Ibid., p. 49.
12. "International Olympic Committee," Bulletin du C.I.O. (September 1933), 8(24):9.
13. Sherrill to Frederick W. Rubien, June 11, 1933 (A.B.C., Box 35).
14. Deutsch to Brundage, October 8, 1933; New York Times, October 9, 1933 (A.B.C., Box 153).
15. A.B.C., Box 28.
16. Kirby to A. C. Gilbert, December 14, 1933 (A.B.C., Box 26).
17. A.B.C., Box 28.
18. Kirby to Brundage, November 2, 1933 (A.B.C., Box 29).
19. Henri de Baillet-Latour to Brundage, December 1, 1933, transmitting an English translation of an order dated November 21, 1933 (A.B.C., Box 42). On the Reichssportführer, see Dieter Steinhöfer, Hans von Tschammer und Osten (Berlin: Bartels & Wernitz, 1973).
20. Brundage to Baillet-Latour, December 28, 1933 (A.B.C., Box 42).
21. "International Olympic Committee," Bulletin du C.I.O. (October 1934), 9(26):8.
22. Ibid.
23. See Hans Joachim Teichler, "Coubertin und das Dritte Reich," Sportwissenschaft (1982), 12(1):25n.
24. Brundage to Diem, July 13, 1934 (A.B.C., Box 22).
25. Brundage to William May Garland, October 5, 1934 (A.B.C., Box 56).
26. "Reise nach Schweden 1934", p. 51 (C.D.I.).
27. Ibid., p. 52.
28. Avery and Elizabeth Brundage to Jean Harper, September 9, 1934 (A.B.C., Box 240).
29. Edström to Brundage, December 4, 1933 (A.B.C., Box 42).
30. Brundage to Karl Ritter von Halt, October 22, 1934 (A.B.C., Box 57).
31. New York Post, September 26, 1934.
32. See Friedrich Bohlen, Die XI Olympischen Spiele Berlin 1936 (Cologne: Pahl-Rugenstein, 1979), p. 52.
33. Frederick W. Rubien to Diem, October 8, 1934 (A.B.C., Box 35). Rubien was secretary of the A.O.C.
34. New York Times, September 27, 1934.
35. Brundage to Kirby, March 3, 1934 (A.B.C., Box 28).

36. Teichler, "Coubertin und das Dritte Reich," pp. 23–24.

37. Brundage to Elias Brailas, January 14, 1936 (A.B.C., Box 153).

38. Brundage to B. Halbach, March 17, 1936 (A.B.C., Box 153).

39. September 24, 1935 (A.B.C., Box 42).

40. Quoted in Hajo Bernett, *Guido von Mengden* (Berlin: Bartels & Wernitz, 1976), p. 47.

41. Moshe Gottlieb, "The American Controversy over the Olympic Games," *American Jewish Historical Quarterly* (March 1972), 61:181–213.

42. For the opposite view of the matter, see Arnd Krüger, "'Fair Play for American Athletes': A Study in Anti-Semitism," *Canadian Journal of the History of Sport and Physical Education* (May 1978), 9(1):48.

43. Kirby to Brundage, May 27, 1936 (A.B.C., Box 29).

44. October 26, 1935 (A.B.C., Box 243).

45. New York *American*, October 9, 1935.

46. October 28, 1935 (A.B.C., Box 56).

47. December 7, 1935 (C.D.I.).

48. "Opening Address to the 55th Session of the I.O.C., Munich, May 23, 1959," *Speeches of Avery Brundage* (Lausanne: Comité International Olympique, 1969), p. 41.

49. Lee Ballinger, *In Your Face: Sports for Love and Money* (Chicago: Vanguard, 1981), p. 32.

50. New York *Times*, November 27, 1935.

51. Baillet-Latour to Brundage, October 10, 1935, and December 10, 1935 (A.B.C., Box 42); Baillet-Latour to Jahncke, December 13, 1935 (A.B.C., Box 42). Brundage told Baillet-Latour that the reply to Jahncke was "straight from the shoulder" (January 6, 1936; A.B.C., Box 42).

52. Kirby to Brundage, March 17, 1936 (A.B.C., Box 29).

53. See Judith Holmes, *Olympiad 1936* (New York: Ballantine Books, 1971), pp. 44–49.

54. Ferris to Brundage, June 5, 1936 (A.B.C., Box 23).

55. On the "Olimpiada," see David A. Steinberg, "Workers' Sport and United Front, 1934–1936," *Arena Review* (February 1980), 4(1):1–6; Bruce Kidd, "The Popular Front and the 1936 Olympics," *Canadian Journal of the History of Sport and Physical Education* (May 1980), 11(1):1–18.

56. "Statements by May Lou Petty and Ada Taylor Sackett" (A.B.C., Box 235).

57. See Chicago *Sunday Times*, July 26, 1936; Chicago *Daily News*, July 25, 1936; Chicago *American*, July 25, 1936; Chicago *Tribune*, July 28, 1936 (A.B.C., Box 235, contains these and other articles).

58. For a retrospective view, see Paula Welch, "Where Are They Now?" *The Olympian* (November 1980), 7(5):15.

59. Krüger, *Die Olympischen Spiele 1936*, pp. 154–55.

60. November 3, 1933 (A.B.C., Box 42).

61. André Poplimont, "Berlin 1936," *Bulletin du C.I.O.* (October 15, 1956), no. 56, pp. 46–47.

62. *Bulletin du C.I.O.* (August 15, 1955), no. 51, pp. 34–35.

63. *Bulletin du C.I.O.* (January 15, 1953), no. 37, pp. 14.

64. "The Olympic Story," Chapter VIII, p. 18 (A.B.C., Boxes 330–331).

65. "Report of the President," *Games of the XIth Olympiad* (New York; U.S. Olympic Association, 1937), p. 27.

66. Jean M. Leiper, "The International Olympic Committee . . ." (Ph.D., University of Alberta, 1976), pp. 59–60.

67. See William E. Dodd Jr., and Martha Dodd, eds., *Ambassador Dodd's Diary, 1933–*

1938 (New York: Harcourt, Brace, 1941), pp. 339–344; Brundage to Heinz Schöbel, January 7, 1963 (A.B.C., Box 62).

68. Mayer, *À Travers*, p. 142.

69. "Olympic Games," *Spectator* (August 7, 1936), 157(5641):230.

70. Hans-Joachim Teichler, "Berlin 1936—Ein Sieg der NS-Propaganda?" *Stadion* (1976), 2(2):285.

71. *Die Olympischen Spiele 1936*, 2 vols. (Altona-Bahrenfeld: Reemtsma, 1936), 2:17, 23, 26–27, 46–47.

72. *Ibid.*, pp. 22–23.

73. *"Revue de Deux Mondes*, 8th Series (August 15, 1938), 46:935.

74. Hajo Bernett, *Untersuchungen zur Zeitgeschichte des Sports* (Schorndorf: Karl Hofmann, 1973), pp.

75. Richard Mandell, *The Nazi Olympics* (New York, 1971), p. 165; see also William Oscar Johnson, *All That Glitters Is Not Gold* (New York: Putnam's 1972), pp. 177–184.

76. Quoted by Teichler, "Coubertin und das Dritte Reich," pp. 35–36.

77. "Procès-Verbale de la 35ième Session du Comité International Olympique," Berlin, July 30–31 and August 15, 1936, p. 2 (I.O.C.).

VII   PRESERVING THE IDEAL, 1936–1948

1. Edstrøm to Brundage, July 8, 1943 (A.B.C., Box 42).

2. Garland to Brundage, February 24, 1937 (A.B.C., Box 56).

3. June 26, 1936 (A.B.C., Box 29).

4. Gilbert to Kirby, December 22, 1937 (A.B.C., Box 26).

5. Kirby to Brundage, October 26, 1936 (A.B.C., Box 29).

6. October 31, 1936 (A.B.C., Box 29).

7. Kirby to Brundage, February 3, 1937; Garland to Brundage, November 2, 1936 (A.B.C., Boxes 29, 56).

8. New York *Times*, December 7, 1936.

9. Brundage to Edstrøm, February 15, 1937 (A.B.C., Box 42).

10. Brundage to Garland, July 17, 1937; Brundage to Kirby, December 13, 1937 (A.B.C., Boxes 56, 29).

11. A.B.C., Box 42.

12. Brundage, "Brief Summary of Proceedings" (A.B.C., Box 75).

13. Edstrøm to Brundage, January 1, 27, 1938 (A.B.C., Box 42).

14. Brundage's undated notes, 1938 (A.B.C., Box 244).

15. Brundage to Bonacossa, April 25, 1938 (A.B.C., Box 51).

16. Gilbert to Brundage, February 7, 1938; Brundage to Gilbert, February 10, 1938 (A.B.C., Box 26).

17. Hajo Bernett, "Das Scheitern der Olympischen Spiele von 1940," *Stadion* (1980), 6:260.

18. *Ibid.*, p. 254.

19. June 6, 1938 (A.B.C., Box 29).

20. Chicago *Journal*, June 9, 1938.

21. A.B.C., Box 156.

22. Otto Mayer, *À Travers les anneaux olympiques* (Geneva: Cailler, 1966), p. 167.

23. Bernett, "Das Scheitern," p. 271.

24. Brundage to Baillet-Latour, April 23, 1940 (A.B.C., Box 42).

25. September 12, 1939 (A.B.C., Box 30).

26. Brundage to Boyd Comstock, October 10, 1939 (A.B.C., Box 22).

27. March 27, 1940 (A.B.C., Box 42).

28. Brundage to Kirby, December 2, 1939 (A.B.C., Box 30).

29. Bernett, "Das Scheitern," pp. 277–78.

30. J. Lyman Bingham to Curtis Ray Emery, April 5, 1963, quoted in Emery, "The History of the Pan-American Games" (Ed.D., Louisiana State University, 1964), p. 8.

31. Brundage to Emery, March 28, 1964, quoted in Emery, "The History," pp. 12–13.

32. *Ibid.*

33. "Pan-American Message," *Amateur Athlete* (January 1942), p. 4. The address was broadcast on December 3, 1941.

34. Hull to Brundage, October 2, 1939 (A.B.C., Box 26).

35. Bushnell to Brundage, February 24, 1942; Brundage to Bushnell, February 28, 1942 (A.B.C., Box 19).

36. April 20, 1942 (A.B.C., Box 21).

37. March 10, 1942 (A.B.C., Box 38).

38. March 13, 1942 (A.B.C., Box 38).

39. Brundage to Philip Badger, April 18, 1942 (A.B.C., Box 332).

40. Chicago *Times*, October 5, 1936.

41. February 13, 1939 (A.B.C., Box 56).

42. Simms to Brundage, November 15, 1938; Brundage to Simms, November 26, 1938 (A.B.C., Box 38).

43. Brundage to Werner Klingeberg, May 16, 1938 (A.B.C., Box 31).

44. Kirby to Brundage, November 10, 1938 (A.B.C., Box 29).

45. Brundage to Garland, December 8, 1938 (A.B.C., Box 56).

46. Garland to Brundage, December 17, 1938 (A.B.C., Box 56).

47. "Procès-Verbale," June 9, 1939 (A.B.C., Box 75).

48. A.B.C., Box 152.

49. Undated memorandum (A.B.C., Box 243).

50. Rosen to Brundage, May 23, 1947 (A.B.C., Box 62).

51. Varney, "The Red Road to War," *The American Mercury* (May 1937), 41(161):8.

52. *Ibid.*, p. 10.

53. *Ibid.*, p. 14.

54. *Ibid.*, p. 17.

55. May 12, 1937 (A.B.C., Box 41).

56. Brundage to Paul Palmer, July 19, 1937 (A.B.C., Box 41).

57. Brundage to Varney, September 8, 1937 (A.B.C., Box 41).

58. Brundage to Garland, September 12, 1939 (A.B.C., Box 56).

59. "Remarks of Avery Brundage," Soldiers Field, August 4, 1940 (A.B.C., Box 325).

60. Undated notes (A.B.C., Box 246).

61. June 17, 1940 (A.B.C., Box 56).

62. Brundage to George Horace Lorimer, November 5, 1935 (A.B.C., Box 31).

63. "Why I'll Vote for Willkie," Chicago *Herald-American*, September 10, 1940.

64. Outline for a talk at the LaSalle Hotel, December 12, 1942 (A.B.C., Box 248).

65. Brundage to Boyd Comstock, December 22, 1944 (A.B.C., Box 22).

66. Klein, Avery Brundage, p. 41; Chicago *Tribune*, February 18, 22, 1944.

67. See *American Digest* (March 1952), 14(1):1; *American Commentator*, (September 25, 1952), 5(14):3.

68. Memoranda (A.B.C., Box 245).

69. John T. Flynn, "America's Unknown War," *Clover Business Letter*, August 1951.

70. *Ibid.*

71. "What I Saw During Three Weeks Behind the Iron Curtain" (A.B.C., Box 245).

72. Hans Joachin Teichler, "Coubertin und das Dritte Reich," *Sportwissenschaft* (1982), 12(1):50–51.

73. Greta von Halt to Brundage, September 1, 1946; Brundage to Greta von Halt, February 8, 1950 (A.B.C., Box 57).

74. Liselott Diem to Brundage, February 17, 1947 (A.B.C., Box 22).

75. Interview with Liselott Diem, Cologne, December 7, 1981.

76. December 29, 1944 (A.B.C., Box 70).

77. "Address to the Annual A.A.U. Convention," December 1945 (A.B.C., Box 248).

78. Aberdare to Brundage, October 28, 1944 (A.B.C., Box 50).

79. Brundage to Garland, October 9, 1945 (A.B.C., Box 56).

80. September 17, 25, 1945 (A.B.C., Box 54).

81. Brundage to Nadia Lekarska, March 20, 1964 (A.B.C., Box 31).

82. Henry L. Seldis, "Avery Brundage: Olympian Patron of Art," *Los Angeles Times West Magazine*, September 11, 1966.

83. Greta von Halt to Brundage, September 1, 1946 (A.B.C., Box 57).

84. October 14, 1950 (A.B.C., Box 57).

85. Scharroo to Edstrøm, July 2, 1950; Albert Mayer to Brundage, February 24, March 7, 1951; Brundage to Mayer, April 9, 1951 (A.B.C., Boxes 62, 60).

86. Scharroo to Edstrøm, July 2, 1950 (A.B.C., Box 62).

87. Edstrøm to Executive Board, January 28, February 13, 1947 (A.B.C., Box 42).

88. Scharroo to Edstrøm, July 2, 1950 (A.B.C., Box 62).

89. Edstrøm to Brundage, April 24, 1947 (A.B.C., Box 42).

90. Burghley (Exeter) to Brundage, February 26, 1946 (A.B.C., Box 54).

91. Edstrøm to Scharroo, June 13, 1950 (A.B.C., Box 43).

92. "Procès-Verbale," May 8, 1951 (A.B.C., Box 76).

93. *Bulletin du C.I.O.*, Nr. 11 (September 15, 1948).

94. "Procès-Verbale," May 17, 1950 (A.B.C., Box 76).

95. "Procès-Verbale de la Session de Copenhagen," May 15–17, 1950.

96. Brundage to William J. Bingham, October 15, 1947 (A.B.C., Box 19).

97. Brundage to R. N. LeCron, June 24, 1946 (A.B.C., Box 236).

98. André Poplimont to Daniel J. Ferris, March 3, 1947 (A.B.C., Box 236).

99. Brundage to Otto Mayer, July 15, 1947 (A.B.C., Box 46).

100. November 10, 1947 (A.B.C., Box 236).

101. Edstrøm to Brundage, December 17, 1947 (A.B.C., Box 42).

102. Brundage to Edstrøm, December 27, 1947 (A.B.C., Box 42).

103. December 1, 1947 (A.B.C., Box 236).

104. Brundage to U.S.O.C., December 30, 1947 (A.B.C., Box 236).

105. A.B.C., Box 236. The carbon copy in the collection, dated March 1, 1948, is marked "to be revised," but it shows Brundage's views better than do later, more tactful comments.

106. Mayer, *À Travers*, p. 183.

107. September 27, 1949 (A.B.C., Box 24).

108. Undated report of the chairman (A.B.C., Box 24). Ferris sent it to Brundage on September 26, 1952.

109. "The Olympic Story," Chapter X, p. 10 (A.B.C., Boxes 330–331).

110. Kirby, "Report of the Chef de Mission," *U.S.O.C. Report* (New York: U.S. Olympic Association, 1949), pp. 241–48.

111. Carl Diem to Liselott Diem, August 1, 1948, "Londoner Briefe" (C.D.I.).

VIII   PRESIDENT AND APOSTLE OF AMATEURISM

1. Comité International Olympique, *Le Comité International Olympique* (Lausanne, 1981), p. 62; Edstrøm to Brundage, August 29, 1929 (A.B.C., Box 42).

2. April 3, 1934 (A.B.C., Box 42).

3. Circular Letter, December 29, 1944 (A.B.C., Box 70).

4. See the minutes of the 15th through 18th congresses of the I.A.A.F., 1946–1952 (I.A.A.F.).

5. "Extrait du Procès-Verbale de la Session du Comité International Olympique," *Bulletin du C.I.O.* (October 1946), No. 1, pp. 14–24.

6. November 2, 1945 (A.B.C., Box 42).

7. Interview with Douglas Roby, Baden-Baden, September 30, 1981.

8. May 28, 1949 (A.B.C., Box 56).

9. Interview with Douglas Roby, Baden-Baden, September 30, 1981.

10. Interview with Lord Porritt, Baden-Baden, September 29, 1981.

11. Interview with Alexandru Siperco, Baden-Baden, October 2, 1981.

12. Interview with Herman van Karnebeek, The Hague, June 10, 1982.

13. Interview with Giorgio de Stefani, Baden-Baden, September 27, 1981; de Stefani to Brundage, December 19, 1957 (A.B.C., Box 63).

14. Interview with Herman van Karnebeek, The Hague, June 10, 1982.

15. September 7, 1951 (A.B.C., Box 56).

16. December 6, 1951 (A.B.C., Box 56).

17. March 8, 1952 (A.B.C., Box 60).

18. "Extrait du Procès-Verbale," May 15–17, 1950, *Bulletin du C.I.O.*, (June-August 1950) nos. 21–22.

19. June 1, 1952 (A.B.C., Box 62).

20. "The Olympic Story," Chapter VI, p. 10 (Boxes 330–331).

21. John Jewett Garland to Brundage, October 6, 1952 (A.B.C., Box 56).

22. *Ibid.*

23. Brundage's notes (A.B.C., Box 76).

24. John Jewett Garland to Brundage, October 6, 1952 (A.B.C., Box 56).

25. Brundage's notes (A.B.C., Box 76).

26. Otto Mayer, *À Travers les anneaux olympiques* (Geneva: Cailler, 1966), p. 210.

27. Quoted from Brundage's address to the 1929 annual convention of the A.A.U. (A.B.C., Box 8); see also speeches given in 1940, 1941, 1948, and 1956 (A.B.C., boxes 247–249, 311).

28. "Opening Address to the 58th Session of the I.O.C., Athens, June 16, 1961," *Speeches of Avery Brundage* (Lausanne: Comité International Olympique, 1969), pp. 61–62.

29. "Opening Address to the 62nd Session of the I.O.C., Tokyo, October 6, 1964," *Speeches of Avery Brundage*, p. 80.

30. "Lofty Spirit of Ancients Imbues Olympics," *Think*, September 1936, p. 18 (A.B.C., Box 243).

31. Circular Letter, "On the Olympic Games and Payment for Broken Time," April 12, 1954 (A.B.C., Box 70).

32. Address to the 1929 annual convention of the A.A.U. (A.B.C., Box 8).

33. "The Olympic Story," Chapter II, pp. 4–6 (A.B.C., Boxes 330–331).

34. *Ibid.*, p. 11.

35. "Opening Address to the 55th Session of the I.O.C., Munich, May 23, 1959," *Speeches of Avery Brundage*, p. 45.

36. "The Social Significance of Amateur Sport" (1940) (A.B.C., Box 247); see also "Olympic Spirit" (1956) (A.B.C., Box 249).

37. See both of the above and also "Amateur Sport and the Olympic Games" (1948) (A.B.C., Box 247).

38. Burghley (Exeter) to Brundage, May 8, August 7, 1971 (A.B.C., Box 55).

39. Brundage to Burghley (Exeter), May 19, August 13, 1971 (A.B.C., Box 55).

40. Howard J. Savage, *Games and Sports in British Schools and Universities* (New York: Carnegie Foundation, 1927), p. 186; on the entire question of amateurism, see Eugene A. Glader, *Amateurism and Athletics* (West Point, New York: Leisure Press, 1978), which discusses the development of the rules in a historical perspective.

41. See *France-Soir*, September 29, 1956; Otto Mayer to Brundage, September 20, October 26, 1956 (A.B.C., Box 47); "Minutes of the Executive Board Meeting," Lausanne, October 3–4, 1956 (A.B.C., Box 78).

42. Brundage to Donald F. Hull, October 8, 1963; Hull to Brundage, October 10, 1963 (A.B.C., Box 1).

43. Richard Espy, *The Politics of the Olympic Games* (Berkeley: University of California Press, 1979), p. 138.

44. *Sport Belgique*, March 15, 1972 (A.B.C., Box 117).

45. E.g., *Wiener Kurier*, February 15, 1972.

46. Brundage to Arthur Takec, July 12, 1972 (A.B.C., Box 45).

47. Turkish Olympic Committee to Johann Westerhoff, October 10, 1967; Suat Erler to Westerhoff, October 31, November 1, 1967 (A.B.C., Boxes 45, 54).

48. Brundage to Armand Massard, February 7, 1959 (A.B.C., Box 60).

49. "Extract of the Minutes," *Bulletin du C.I.O.* (June 15, 1953) nos. 39–40.

50. Albert Mayer to Otto Mayer, August 31, 1954 (A.B.C., Box 47).

51. "Minutes of the 50th Session of the I.O.C.," Paris, June 13–18, 1955 (A.B.C., Box 77).

52. "Opening Address to the 56th Session of the I.O.C., San Francisco, February 13, 1960," *Speeches of Avery Brundage*, p. 48.

53. Deutscher Sportbund, ed., *Willi Daume: Deutscher Sport, 1952–1972* (Munich: Pro Sport, 1973), p. 188.

54. "Extracts of the Minutes of the 47th Session—Helsinki 1952," *Bulletin du C.I.O.* (September 15, 1952), nos. 34–35, p. 29.

55. "Extracts of the Minutes of the Meeting of the Executive Committee of the I.O.C. with the Delegates of the International Federations," *Bulletin du C.I.O.* (September 15, 1952), nos. 34–35, pp. 32–34; see also the I.O.C. minutes referred to in the previous note.

56. Brundage to Dan Roruzescu and N. Floresco, January 27, 1954 (A.B.C., Box 116).

57. "Minutes of the 53rd Session in Sofia of the International Olympic Committee," *Bulletin du C.I.O.* (February 15, 1958), no. 61, pp. 71–78.

58. "The Olympic Games and the Question of Broken Time," *Amateur Athlete*, May 1947, no pagination.

59. Circular Letter, August 30, 1957 (A.B.C., Box 70).

60. Circular Letter, November 6, 1970 (A.B.C., Box 71).

61. Transcript of a B.B.C. broadcast, July 4, 1967, *Transatlantic Forum*, no date (A.B.C., Box 249).

62. Brundage to Daniel J. Ferris, January 13, 1967 (A.B.C., Box 24).

63. Albert Drix, "The Problems of Altitude and Doping in Mexico," *Bulletin du C.I.O.* (February 15, 1967), no. 97, pp. 43–46.

64. For an instance of concern, see his Circular Letter, September 14, 1968 (A.B.C., Box 71).

65. New York *Herald Tribune*, March 6, 1956; May 16, 1956; "Names, Places and Pay-Offs—Santee Blows the Whistle," *Life*, November 19, 1956.

66. Brundage to Murray Hulbert, April 26, 1932 (A.B.C., Box 27). It is still widely assumed that Brundage wanted severe punishment; see Hans Gebhardt, *Die 80 Tage des Gunder Hägg* (Munich: Bertelsmann, 1976), p. 82.

67. On Adhemar Ferreira da Silva, see E. J. H. Holt to Brundage, November 10, 1952

(A.B.C., Box 26); Brundage, Circular Letter, *Bulletin du C.I.O.* (November 15, 1952), no. 36. On the Argentine players, see Brundage to Confederación Argentina de Deportes— Comite Olimpico Argentino, June 19, 1952 (A.B.C., Box 116). On Barbara Ann Scott, see Brundage to Edstrøm, April 12, 1947 (A.B.C., Box 42); also folders in Box 37.

68. Interview with Arpad Csanadi, Baden-Baden, October 2, 1981.

69. Brundage to Daniel J. Ferris, May 1, 1952 (A.B.C., Box 24).

70. Dorothy Hyman, *Sprint to Fame* (London, 1964), ch. 14; Brundage to Asa S. Bushnell, July 16, 1953 (A.B.C., Box 21).

71. Gudmund Schack to Brundage, November 13, 1971 (A.B.C., Box 125).

72. "Minutes of the Executive Board Meetings," Munich, September 9, 1971/Luxembourg, September 12–17, 1971" (A.B.C., Box 95); Philip to Burghley (Exeter), November 2, 1971 (A.B.C., Box 55).

73. Brundage, Circular Letter, November 7, 1970 (A.B.C., Box 71); see also Brundage to Marc Hodler, January 31, 1969 (A.B.C., Box 86); Arthur Takec to Austrian Olympic Committee, December 16, 1971 (A.B.C., Box 116).

74. Brundage to Bingham, July 16, 1963; Bingham to Brundage, December 18, 1963 (A.B.C., Box 20).

75. Christopher Brasher, *Mexico 1968* (London: St. Paul, 1968), pp. 25–26.

76. Brundage to Roby, December 7, 1967; Roby to Brundage, December 11, 1967 (A.B.C., Box 62).

77. Brundage to Board of Governors, A. A. U., January 25, 1932 (A.B.C., Box 1).

78. Brundage to Baillet-Latour, September 2, 1938 (A.B.C., Box 42).

79. Brundage to Robert P. Booth, November 23, 1946 (A.B.C., Box 19).

80. Brundage to Edstrøm, May 7, 1946 (A.B.C., Box 42); see also André Poplimont to Brundage, July 4, 1958, and Brundage to Poplimont, July 12, 1958 (A.B.C., Box 34).

81. Brundage to Roland Palmedo, April 24, 1951, September 11, 1959; January 15, 1960 (A.B.C., Box 32).

82. Brundage to André Poplimont, May 5, 1953 (A.B.C., Box 118).

83. "The Fumbled Ball," *Phi Delta Kappan* (March 1952), 33(7): 351; see also "College Football: An International Scandal," *Amateur Athlete* (February 1962), 33(2):6–7, 36–37.

84. "Eligibility Rules of the International Olympic Committee," *Bulletin du C.I.O.* (November 15, 1962), no. 80, p. 45.

85. "Opening Address to the 60th Session of the I.O.C., Baden-Baden, October 16, 1963," *Speeches of Avery Brundage*, p. 69.

86. Brundage to Stephen M. Archer, Secretary, A.A.U., March 20, 1964 (A.B.C., Box 1).

87. James Counsilman to R. M. Ritter, May 21, 1964 (A.B.C., Box 34).

88. See Joe Marshall, "Little Sister Wins a Race of Her Own," *Sports Illustrated* (December 8, 1980), 53:57–76, 79.

89. *Bulletin du C.I.O.* (September-December 1927), 2(8–9).

90. *Minutes of the Olympic Congress of Berlin 1930* (Lausanne, 1930), p. 53; Brundage, "Payment for Broken Time: A History," Circular Letter, November 28, 1961 (A.B.C., Box 70).

91. "Report of the Special Commission," 35th Session of the I.O.C., Cairo, 1938 (A.B.C., Box 75).

92. "The Olympic Games and the Question of Broken Time," *Amateur Athlete* (May 1947), 18(5):4–5, 16.

93. Brundage to Daniel J. Ferris, October 25, 1950 (A.B.C., Box 24).

94. "On the Olympic Games and Payment for Broken Time," Circular Letter, April 12, 1954 (A.B.C., Box 70).

95. "Idées revolutionnaires," *Bulletin du C.I.O.* (July 15, 1956), no. 55, 20–23.

96. Brundage to Armand Massard, June 30, 1964 (A.B.C., Box 60).

97. Brundage to Daniel J. Ferris, January 6, 1972 (A.B.C., Box 4).

98. April 12, 1954 (A.B.C., Box 70); see also notes for speeches (Boxes 245–246).

99. Brundage to Ivar Vind, January 22, 1962 (A.B.C., Box 64).

100. "Eligibility Rules of the International Olympic Committee," *Bulletin du C.I.O.* (November 15, 1962), no. 80, p. 45.

101. Brundage to A.A.U., September 27, 1962 (A.B.C., Box 1).

102. "Minutes of the Meeting of the Executive Board, March 22–23, 1969," Annex IV, "Amateurism and Eligibility," p. 7 (A.B.C., Box 94).

103. The article appeared in the issue for December 29, 1958; see also René Bondoux to Brundage, December 12, 1959; P. Morel to Brundage, May 24, 1960 (A.B.C., Box 334). Sending the centime to Brundage, Morel commented on behalf of the Comité Olympique Français that the sum "consacre l'hommage rendu au Président BRUNDAGE par la Justice française!"

104. "Självporträttet 67: Avery Brundage," *Vecko-Journalen*, February 23, 1972 (A.B.C., Box 250).

105. Hans Klein, ed., *Avery Brundage: Die Herausforderung* (Munich: Pro Sport, 1972), p. 26.

IX   THE OLYMPIC GAMES AND THE COLD WAR

1. Edstrøm to Brundage, December 7, 1945 (B.B.C., Box 42).

2. *Session de Rome* (Lausanne, 1923), p. 28.

3. Carolyn Marvin, "Avery Brundage and American Participation in the 1936 Olympic Games," *Journal of American Studies* (April 1982), 16(1):105.

4. March 27, 1944 (A.B.C., Box 50).

5. March 17, 1944 (A.B.C., Box 36).

6. September 12, 1944 (A.B.C., Box 42).

7. Brundage to L. di Benedetto, August 31, 1943 (A.B.C., Box 23).

8. Rudolf E. Cahn, "Establishment of National Council of Sports," report dated April 23, 1941 (A.B.C., Box 118).

9. See, for example, Brundage to Brazil's Conferacio Brasileira de Desportos, March 31, 1944 (A.B.C., Box 118).

10. "Procès-Verbale," April 21, 1949 (A.B.C., Box 76).

11. Edstrøm to Brundage, December 7, 1945 (A.B.C., Box 42).

12. April 7, 1950 (A.B.C., Box 31).

13. Edstrøm to Brundage, November 25, 1946 (A.B.C., Box 42).

14. "The Olympic Story," Chapter X, p. 1 (A.B.C., Boxes 330–331).

15. "Procès-Verbale," September 2, 1946 (A.B.C., Box 75).

16. Circular Letter, September 20, 1946 (A.B.C., Box 75).

17. "The Olympic Story," Chapter X, p. 3 (A.B.C., Boxes 330–331).

18. Edstrøm to Brundage, December 4, 1946 (A.B.C., Box 42).

19. Brundage to Edstrøm, March 4, 1947 (A.B.C., Box 42).

20. Burghley (Exeter) to Edstrøm, July 31, 1947 (A.B.C., Box 54).

21. Brundage to R. M. Ritter, July 15, 1947 (A.B.C., Box 34).

22. Edstrøm to Brundage, December 4, 1946 (A.B.C., Box 42).

23. Brundage to Brutus Hamilton, March 3, 1949 (A.B.C., Box 26).

24. Brundage to Arnold Lunn, June 21, 1951 (A.B.C., Box 31).

25. "Procès-Verbale," May 7, 1951 (A.B.C., Box 76).

26. Interview with Douglas Roby, Baden-Baden, September 30, 1981.

27. Interview with Lord Porritt, Baden-Baden, September 29, 1981.

28. "Minutes of the Executive Board," Athens, June 18, 1961 (A.B.C., Box 92).

29. Ferris to Brundage, December 14, 1962 (A.B.C., Box 24).

30. Brundage, "I Must Admit—Russian Athletes Are Great!" *Saturday Evening Post*, April 30, 1955, pp. 28, 111, 114.

31. *Ibid.*, p. 29.

32. McGovern to Brundage, July 18, 1955, (A.B.C., Box 32).

33. Brundage to McGovern, August 3, 1955 (A.B.C., Box 32).

34. March 10, 1954 (A.B.C., Box 46).

35. Edstrøm to Brundage, January 17, 1952 (A.B.C., Box 43).

36. Edstrøm to Executive Board, June 10, 1952 (A.B.C., Box 43).

37. Brundage to Edstrøm, June 16, 1952 (A.B.C., Box 43).

38. Otto Mayer, *À Travers les anneaux olympiques* (Geneva: Cailler, 1966), p. 208.

39. *Ibid.*

40. On F.I.F.A., see Brian B. Pendleton, "'The Mantis and the Chariot': A Case Study: F.I.F.A. and the Football Association of the Peoples' Republic of China," *Arena Review* (October 1979), 3(4):15–26; on the I.A.A.F., see Daniel J. Ferris to Brundage, September 21, 1954 (A.B.C., Box 24).

41. "Minutes of the 47th Session of the I.O.C.," Helsinki (A.B.C., Box 90).

42. Mayer, *À Travers*, p. 211.

43. *Ibid.*, pp. 211–212.

44. New York *Times*, May 11, 1954.

45. January 3, 1955 (A.B.C., Box 47).

46. Brundage to Vladimir Stoytchev, December 4, 1958 (A.B.C., Box 63).

47. Circular Letter, September 5, 1958 (A.B.C., Box 70).

48. "Minutes," June 11, 1955 (A.B.C., Box 77).

49. Mayer, *À Travers*, p. 266; Mayer to Brundage, October 22, 1956. (A.B.C., Box 47).

50. Brundage to Tung, January 8, 1958; Tung to Brundage, April 23, 1958; Brundage to Tung, June 1, 1958 (A.B.C., Box 64); Tung to Brundage, August 19, 1958, see also Geoffrey Miller, *Behind the Olympic Rings* (Lynn, Mass.: H. O. Zimman, 1979), p. 162.

51. Pendleton, "'Mantis and Chariot,'" p. 17; Jonathan Kolatch, *Sport, Politics and Ideology in China* (Middle Village, New York: Jonathan David, 1972), pp. 184–185.

52. Mayer, *À Travers*, p. 297.

53. Press Release, June 3, 1959; "About the Chinese Problem (Taiwan)," *Bulletin du C.I.O.* (August 15, 1959), no. 67, p. 63.

54. Richard Espy, *Politics of the Olympic Games* (Berkeley: University of California Press, 1979), p. 64.

55. Brundage to Roby, January 5, 1968; Roby to Brundage, January 9, 1968 (A.B.C., Box 62); Interview with Douglas Roby, Baden-Baden, September 30, 1981.

56. Circular Letter, June 23, 1959 (A.B.C., Box 70).

57. Interview, Baden-Baden, September 30, 1981.

58. See A.B.C., Box 121.

59. June 23, 1959 (A.B.C., Box 313; Scrapbook 38).

60. Kenneth L. Wilson and Asa S. Bushnell to Brundage, July 31, 1959 (A.B.C., Box 313; Scrapbook 38).

61. Santa Barbara *News-Press*, July 26, 1959.

62. A.B.C., Box 313; Scrapbook 38.

63. Brundage to Grenville Clark, August 1, 1959 (A.B.C., Box 313; Scrapbook 38).

64. Brundage to Roland Palmedo, September 11, 1959 (A.B.C., Box 32).

65. Raymond A. Hare to Brundage, June 8, 1960 (A.B.C., Box 333).

66. Brundage to Hare, June 27, 1960 (A.B.C., Box 333).
67. A.B.C., Box 120.
68. Brundage to Mayer, April 24, 1960 (A.B.C., Box 48).
69. Brundage to Edstrøm, July 3, 1950 (A.B.C., Box 43).
70. Ulrich Pabst, *Sport--Medium der Politik?* (Berlin: Bartels & Wernitz, 1980), p. 179.
71. "Procès-Verbale," August 29, 1950 (A.B.C., Box 76).
72. Peter Kühnst, *Der Miß brauchte Sport* (Cologne: Verlag Sport und Wissenschaft, 1982), pp. 79–80; Pabst, *Sport*, p. 180–181.
73. Cited by Kühnst, *Der Miß brauchte Sport*, p. 179.
74. "Procès-Verbale," May 8, 1951 (A.B.C., Box 76).
75. Von Halt to Adenauer, May 25, 1951, quoted by Pabst, *Sport*, p. 185.
76. Edstrøm to Executive Board, January 22, 1952 (A.B.C., Box 43).
77. Pabst, *Politik*, p. 188.
78. "Minutes of the 49th Session of the International Olympic Committee, Athens, May 11–15, 1954" (I.O.C.).
79. "Minutes of the 50th Session of the International Olympic Committee, Paris, June 13–18, 1955" (I.O.C.).; Pabst, *Politik*, pp. 175–191.
80. G. A. Carr, "The Involvement of Politics in the Sporting Relations of East and West Germany, 1945–1972," *Journal of Sport History* (Spring 1980), 8(1):45.
81. Karl Adolf Scherer, *75 Olympische Jahre* (Munich: Pro Sport, 1972), p. 119; Pabst, *Politik*, p. 252–256.
82. December 7, 1959 (A.B.C., Box 62).
83. December 29, 1959 (A.B.C., Box 62).
84. Brundage to Schöbel, January 26, 1963; January 13, 1964; Schöbel to Brundage, January 24, 1964 (A.B.C., Box 64).
85. "The Olympic Movement," speech given September 17, 1968 (A.B.C., Box 249).
86. "Opening Address to the 60th Session of the International Olympic Committee, Baden-Baden, October 16, 1963," *Speeches of Avery Brundage*, p. 67.
87. Scherer, *75 Olympische Jahre*, p. 120.
88. *Ibid.*, p. 122.
89. *Ibid.*, p. 124.
90. "Minutes of the 62nd Session," October 7–8, 1964, Tokyo, *Bulletin du C.I.O.* (February 15, 1965), no. 89.
91. "Minutes of the 63rd Meeting of the I.O.C.," Madrid, October 7–9, 1965, *Bulletin du C.I.O.* (November 15, 1965), no. 92.
92. See Gunter Holzweißig, *Diplomatie im Trainingsanzug* (Munich: Oldenbourg, 1981), p. 40.
93. Albert Mayer to Brundage, March 6, 1967; Brundage to Mayer, March 20, 1967 (A.B.C., Box 60).
94. Carr, "The Involvement," p. 50.
95. Dick Schaap, *An Illustrated History of the Olympics* 3rd ed. (N.Y.: Knopf, 1975), p. 249.
96. Brundage to Otto Mayer, September 10, 1952 (A.B.C., Box 46).
97. Brundage to Joaquin Serratosa Cibils, October 21, 1952; Serratosa Cibils to Brundage, December 19, 1952 (A.B.C., Box 63).
98. Brundage to Ralph C. Craig, May 26, 1955 (A.B.C., Box 22).
99. "Minutes of the 50th Session of the International Olympic Committee, June 13–18, 1955," p. 21 (I.O.C.).
100. Brundage to Otto Mayer, August 3, 1956 (A.B.C., Box 47).
101. Brundage to Weir, January 17, 1953 (A.B.C., Box 164).

102. Weir to Brundage, January 19, 1953 (A.B.C., Box 164).
103. March 18, 1953 (A.B.C., Box 164).
104. November 3, 1953 (A.B.C., Box 164).
105. Weir to Brundage, November 24, 1953 (A.B.C., Box 164).
106. July 18, 1956.
107. Weir to Brundage, August 2, 1956 (A.B.C., Box 164).
108. Brundage to Lewis Luxton, August 7, 1956; Hughes to Brundage, August 31, 1956 (A.B.C., Box 164).
109. "Opening Address to the 52nd Session of the International Olympic Committee, Melbourne, November 19, 1956," *Speeches of Avery Brundage*, pp. 25–26.
110. Albert Mayer to Brundage, November 19, 1956 (A.B.C., Box 60).
111. Press Release, November 9, 1956 (A.B.C., Box 249).
112. Otto Mayer to National Olympic Committees, January 4, 1957 (A.B.C., Box 47).
113. Scharroo to Brundage, April 27, 1957 (A.B.C., Box 62).
114. Otto Mayer to Kent Hughes, November 18, 1956 (A.B.C., Box 164).
115. Olga Connolly, *The Rings of Destiny* (New York: David McKay, 1968).
116. New York *Times*, April 3, 1957.
117. Carl Diem, "Briefe aus Melbourne 1956", p. 23 (C.D.I.).
118. "Minutes of the 50th Session of the I.O.C.," Paris, June 15, 1955 (A.B.C., Box 77).
119. "The Olympic Story," Chapter XII, p. 13 (A.B.C., Boxes 330–331).
120. *Ibid.*, p. 15.
121. Schaap, *Illustrated History*, p. 287.
122. Brundage to Kenneth Wilson, August 20, 1955 (A.B.C., Box 165).
123. Cortlandt T. Hill to Brundage, October 19, 1955; Albert E. Sigal to Brundage, November 23, 1955 (A.B.C., Box 165).
124. "Summary of Facts Concerning Awarding and Financing of VIII Olympic Winter Games" (A.B.C., Box 165).
125. "Minutes of the 53rd Session in Sofia of the International Olympic Committee," September 23–28, 1957, *Bulletin du C.I.O.* (February 15, 1958), no. 61; "The Tokyo Session," May 14–16, 1958, *Bulletin du C.I.O.* (August 15, 1958), no. 63.
126. Frégéolière to Alan E. Bartholemy, October 12, 1957, *Bulletin du C.I.O.* (February 15, 1958) no. 61; Albert Mayer to Brundage, July 28, 1958 (A.B.C., Box 60).
127. The account of the water-polo controversy is taken from folders in the A.B.C., Box 239.
128. Brundage to Kenneth Wilson et al., April 21, 1958 (A.B.C., Box 239).
129. May 8, 1958 (A.B.C., Box 239).
130. Rudolf Hagelstange, *Römisches Olympia* (Munich: Piper, 1961), pp. 150, 190–199.
131. Notes (A.B.C., Box 246).
132. "Extracts of the Minutes of the 56th Session of the International Olympic Committee," August 22–23, 1960, *Bulletin du C.I.O.* (November 15, 1960), no. 72.
133. "The I.O.A.," *Newsletter* (June 1968), no. 9, 209–217.

X NEW FORMS, NEW LEADERS

1. Circular Letter, January 30, 1954 (A.B.C., Box 70).
2. "Extracts from the Minutes of the 50th Session of the International Olympic Committee," Paris, June 13–18, 1955, *Bulletin du C.I.O.* (November 15, 1955), no. 52.
3. "Extract of the Minutes of the 52nd Session of the International Olympic Committee in Melbourne," November 19–21, December 4, 1956, *Bulletin du C.I.O.* (May 15, 1957), no. 58.

4. "Plan for Reorganizing the International Olympic Committee . . . ," *Bulletin du C.I.O.* (August 15, 1959), no. 67, pp. 86–87.

5. "Minutes of the 55th Session," May 28, 1959 (A.B.C., Box 91).

6. Circular Letter, March 1960 (A.B.C., Box 70).

7. "Minutes of the 58th Session of the International Olympic Committee," Athens, June 19–21, 1961, *Bulletin du C.I.O.* (August 15, 1961), no. 75.

8. "Extracts of the Minutes of the 59th Session," June 5–8, 1962 *Bulletin du C.I.O.* (November 15, 1962), no. 80.

9. *Ibid.*

10. *Ibid.*

11. Proposal dated March 1, 1966 (A.B.C., Box 74).

12. "Minutes: 64th Session of the International Olympic Committee," April 25–28, 1966 (A.B.C., Box 93).

13. *Ibid.*

14. Brundage's notes, May 14, 1970 (A.B.C., Box 88).

15. "Minutes," October 15, 1963 (A.B.C., Box 92).

16. C.O.N.I. to National Olympic Committees, October 3, 1964 (A.B.C., Box 61).

17. Interview with Douglas Roby, Baden-Baden, September 30, 1981.

18. Onesti to Brundage, March 20, 1965; Brundage to Onesti, September 14, 1965 (A.B.C., Box 61).

19. "Minutes of the 62nd Session," *Bulletin du C.I.O.* (February 15, 1965), no. 89.

20. Interview with Willi Daume, Cologne, December 16, 1981.

21. *Ibid.*; Lord Killanin, *My Olympic Years* (London: Secker & Warburg, 1983), p. 62.

22. Onesti to Brundage, October 2, 1965; Brundage to Onesti, January 5, 1966 (A.B.C., Box 61).

23. January 7, 1966 (A.B.C., Box 80).

24. January 26, 1966 (A.B.C., Box 80).

25. Onesti to Ma Yueh-han, June 6, 1966 (A.B.C., Box 82).

26. March 17, 1966 (A.B.C., Box 61).

27. August 27, 1966 (A.B.C., Box 61).

28. September 22, 1966 (A.B.C., Box 61).

29. Onesti to Ma Yueh-han, June 6, 1966 (A.B.C., Box 82).

30. "Study and Co-Ordinating Committee of N.O.C.'s" (A.B.C., Box 81).

31. Brundage to Johann Westerhoff, July 7, 1966 (A.B.C., Box 45).

32. Duncan to Onesti, March 10, 1966; Clark Flores, "Minutes: 66th Session of the International Olympic Committee," February 2–5, 1968; Vind to Brundage, January 14, 1967 (A.B.C., Boxes 82, 93, 64).

33. Onesti to Presidents of National Olympic Committees, February 21, 1967 (A.B.C., Box 61).

34. Brundage to National Olympic Committees, March 23, 1967; Brundage to Westerhoff, March 23, 1967 (A.B.C., Box 61).

35. March 29, 1967 (A.B.C., Box 71).

36. "Minutes: 66th Session of the International Olympic Committee," February 2–5, 1968 (A.B.C., Box 93).

37. "Report to the Session in Teheran on the Meeting with the NOCs Delegates the Day Before" (A.B.C., Box 93).

38. *Ibid.*

39. "Opening Speech to the 65th Session of the International Olympic Committee, Teheran, May 3, 1967," *Speeches of Avery Brundage* (Lausanne: Comité International Olympique, 1969), p. 93.

40. *Ibid.*, p. 98.

41. Clark Flores, José Beracase, and Agustín C. Arroyo to Onesti, December 9, 1967 (A.B.C., Box 52).

42. Phillips and Coulon to Brundage, April 26, 1967 (A.B.C., Box 86).

43. "Minutes: 65th Session of the International Olympic Committee," May 6–9, 1967 (A.B.C., Box 93).

44. See Roger Coulon to Onesti, December 10, 1969 (A.B.C., Box 90).

45. "Minutes of the IOC Executive Board Meeting with the International Sports Federations," January 27–28, 1968 (A.B.C., Box 93).

46. Minutes: 66th Session of the International Olympic Committee," February 1–5, 1968 (A.B.C., Box 93).

47. *Ibid.*

48. Copies are in A.B.C., Box 93.

49. José Saenz to Onesti, August 29, 1968 (A.B.C., Box 52).

50. Brundage to Onesti, August 19, 1968; Onesti to Brundage, August 30, 1968 (A.B.C., Box 93).

51. Brundage to Onesti, September 11, 1968 (A.B.C., Box 93).

52. Andrianov to Brundage, September 19, 1968; Brundage to Andrianov, September 20, 1968 (A.B.C., Box 93).

53. "Resume of the Report of European National Olympic Committees Meeting in Versailles" (A.B.C., Box 93).

54. Interview with Gunnar Ericsson, Baden-Baden, September 28, 1981.

55. *Times* (London), May 3, 1968; *Le Monde*, May 3, 1968.

56. Brundage to Burghley (Exeter), May 23, 1968 (A.B.C., Box 55).

57. Interview with Jean de Beaumont, Baden-Baden, October 2, 1981.

58. November 14, 1968.

59. Interview with Giorgio de Stefani, Baden-Baden, September 27, 1981.

60. Interview with Sir Reginald Alexander, Baden-Baden, September 29, 1981; Alexander to author, October 8, 1982.

61. *Ibid.* Interview with Douglas Roby, Baden-Baden, September 30, 1981.

62. Interview with Arpad Csanadi, Baden-Baden, October 2, 1981.

63. "Extracts from the Minutes of the 67th Session, October 7–11, 1968," *Newsletter* (December 1968), no. 15.

64. "Assemblée Générale des Comités Nationaux Olympiques: Documents" (A.B.C., Box 87).

65. "Minutes of the 67th Session of the International Olympic Committee," October 7–11, 1968 (A.B.C., Box 93).

66. Onesti to Brundage, September 2, 1969 (A.B.C., Box 87).

67. Berlioux to Brundage, September 24, 1969 (A.B.C., Box 87); Clark Flores to Brundage, September 19, 1969 (A.B.C., Box 87); Brochure, Yugoslav organizing committee (A.B.C., Box 87).

68. Clark Flores to Brundage, September 28, 1969 (A.B.C. Box 52).

69. Gudmund Shack to Brundage, October 9, 1969 (A.B.C., Box 87).

70. Gudmund Shack to Brundage, July 28, October 9, 1969; Edward Wieczorek to Shack, November 25, 1969 (A.B.C., Box 87).

71. "Minutes of the Meeting between the Executive Board of the IOC and the Representatives of the National Olympic Committees," October 25–26, 1969 (A.B.C., Box 87).

72. *Ibid.*

73. "Minutes of the Meeting of the Executive Board," October 23–27, 1969 (A.B.C., Box 94).

74. Khaw Kai-Bow to Brundage, April 2, 1970 (A.B.C., Box 73).

75. April 25, 1970 (A.B.C., Box 73).

76. Brundage to Alexander, January 14, 1970 (A.B.C., Box 50).

77. "Minutes of the Executive Board Meetings," September 13, 1971 (A.B.C., Box 95).

78. *Ibid.*

79. *Ibid.*

80. "Minutes of the Meeting between the Executive Board of the IOC and the Representatives of the National Olympic Committees," September 11, 1971 (A.B.C., Box 89).

81. October 8, 1971 (A.B.C., Box 58).

82. October 9, 1971 (A.B.C., Box 58).

83. August 16, 1971 (A.B.C., Box 59).

84. Brundage to Killanin, August 17, 1971 (A.B.C., Box 59).

85. Memoranda (A.B.C., Boxes 49, 245).

86. Mayer to Brundage, November 4, 1954; Brundage to Otto Mayer, November 19, 1954 (A.B.C., Box 46).

87. Otto Mayer to Brundage, March 19, 1957 (A.B.C., Box 48).

88. April 1, 1957 (A.B.C., Box 48).

89. Otto Mayer to Brundage and Edstrøm, October 15, 1953 (A.B.C., Box 46).

90. February 19, 1964 (A.B.C., Box 55).

91. February 20, 1964 (A.B.C., Box 44).

92. Marc Hodler to Brundage, July 1, 1965 (A.B.C., Box 44).

93. *Tribune*, February 15, 1964; Circular Letter, March 3, 1964 (A.B.C., Box 49).

94. Albert Mayer to Brundage, June 10, 1965 (A.B.C., Box 44).

95. Marc Hodler to Brundage, July 1, 1965 (A.B.C., Box 44).

96. Brundage to Albert Mayer, March 11, 1965 (A.B.C., Box 60); see also the folder "The Affair Jonas" (A.B.C., Box 44); "Minutes of the 62nd Session," October 7–8, 1964, *Bulletin du C.I.O.* (February 15, 1965), no. 89; "Minutes of the 63rd Meeting of the I.O.C.," October 7–9, 1965, *Bulletin du C.I.O.* (November 15, 1965), no. 92.

97. Brundage to Beaumont, December 31, 1968 (A.B.C., Box 51).

98. Brundage to Beaumont, November 29, 1968; Beaumont to Brundage, December 18, 1968 (A.B.C., Box 51).

99. Vind to Beaumont, August 7, 1968; "Minutes of the Meeting of the Executive Board," March 22–23, 1969 (A.B.C., Box 94).

100. Vind to Brundage, March 3, May 15, 1969; Brundage to Vind, May 21, 1969 (A.B.C., Box 64).

101. Quoted by Anita Verschoth, "Carrying the Torch," *Sports Illustrated* (April 13, 1981), 54(16):70.

102. Hans Klein, ed. *Avery Brundage: Die Herausforderung* (Munich: Pro Sport, 1972), p. 47.

103. Berlioux, "The History of the I.O.C.," *The Olympic Games*, ed. Lord Killanin and John Rodda (New York, 1976), p. 17; Interview with Monique Berlioux (by Richard L. Gibson), Chicago, August 9, 1974, quoted in Gibson, "Avery Brundage: Professional Amateur" (Ph.D., Kent State University, 1976), p. 36.

104. Killanin to Brundage, January 26, 1970 (A.B.C., Box 59).

XI NEW GAMES AND OLD PROBLEMS

1. Otto Mayer, *À Travers les anneaux olympiques* (Geneva: Cailler, 1966), p. 44.

2. "Minutes of the 63rd Meeting of I.O.C.," October 7–9, 1965; *Bulletin du C.I.O.* (November 15, 1965), no. 92.

3. "53rd Session, Sofia, September 23–28, 1957" (A.B.C., Box 78).

4. *Bulletin du C.I.O.* (July 1930), 5(16):19.

5. "Extrait du Procès-Verbale de la Session du Comité International Olympique," *Bulletin du C.I.O.* (October 1946), no. 1.

6. June 20, 1953 (A.B.C., Box 46).

7. Massard to Brundage, September 14, 1955; Stoytchev to Brundage, February 2, 1957 (A.B.C., Boxes 60, 63).

8. "52nd Session: Melbourne," November 21, 1956 (A.B.C., Box 78).

9. "Minutes of the 53rd Session in Sofia of the International Olympic Committee," September 23–28, 1957, *Bulletin du C.I.O.* (February 15, 1958), no. 61.

10. Brundage to Otto Mayer, February 4, 1961 (A.B.C., Box 48).

11. Brundage to Otto Mayer, May 16, 1962 (A.B.C., Box 48).

12. "Minutes of the 71st Session of the International Olympic Committee," September 15–17, 1971 (A.B.C., Box 95).

13. "Minutes," June 7, 1957 (A.B.C., Box 78).

14. "Extract of the 48th Session," April 17–18, 20, 1953, *Bulletin du C.I.O.* (June 15, 1953), nos. 39–40; "Extract of the Conference of the Executive Board and the National Olympic Committees," May 10–11, 1954, *Bulletin du C.I.O.* (June 15, 1954), no. 46.

15. "Minutes of the 53rd Session in Sofia . . . . ," September 23–28, 1957, *Bulletin du C.I.O.* (February 15, 1958), no. 61.

16. "The Tokyo Session," May 14–16, 1958, *Bulletin du C.I.O.* (August 15, 1958), no. 63.

17. "Extract of the 48th Session," *Bulletin du C.I.O.* (June 15, 1953), nos. 39–40; "Extract of the 49th Session," *Bulletin du C.I.O.* (June 15, 1954), no. 46.

18. "53rd Session, Sofia," June 23–28, 1957 (A.B.C., Box 91).

19. "Procès-Verbale," February 12, 1960 (A.B.C., Box 79).

20. Quoted in L. Zanchi, Circular Letter, September 10, 1965 (A.B.C., Box 70).

21. "Minutes," Executive Board, Lausanne March 13–14, 1971 (A.B.C., Box 95).

22. "Minutes of the Meeting of the IOC Executive Board with . . . the International Federations," May 29, 1972 (A.B.C., Box 95); see also Uriel Simri, *Women at the Olympic Games* (Netanya: Wingate Institute, 1979), p. 38.

23. Brundage, "Should We Prune the Games?" *World Sports* (January 1953), 19(1):5.

24. Daley, "More Deadly Than the Male," New York *Times*, February 8, 1953.

25. "Message du Baron Pierre de Coubertin à tous les athlètes et participants aux Jeux Olympiques," Amsterdam, 1928, *L'Idee olympique*, ed. Liselott Diem and O. Andersen (Cologne: Carl-Diem-Institut, 1966), p. 104; Piétri to Brundage, March 3, 1953 (A.B.C., Box 71).

26. "The Olympic Story," Chapter X, p. 10 (A.B.C., Boxes 330–331).

27. "Extraits du Procès-Verbale," July 26–27, 1948, *Bulletin du C.I.O.* (September 15, 1948), no. 11.

28. "Extract of the Minutes," April 15–16, 1953, *Bulletin du C.I.O.*, (June 15, 19 3), nos. 39–40.

29. Mary H. Leigh, "The Enigma of Avery Brundage and Women Athletes," *Arena Review* (May 1980), 4(2):11–21.

30. Piétri, "Women's Sports in the Olympic Games," *Bulletin du C.I.O.* (May 15, 1957), no. 58; "50th Session, Paris," June 13–18, 1955 (A.B.C., Box 77); Burghley (Exeter) to Brundage, October 22, 1954 (A.B.C., Box 54).

31. Circular Letter, August 30, 1957 (A.B.C., Box 70).

32. San Francisco *Examiner*, May 11, 1960.

33. Interview with Ilse-Marie Sabath, Münster, December 17, 1981.

34. San Francisco *Examiner*, May 9, 1960.

35. "Minutes of the Meetings between the Executive Board . . . and the National Olympic Committees," September 12–17, 1971 (A.B.C., Box 95).

36. *Ibid.*

37. "Speech at 73rd Session, Munich, 1972" (A.B.C., Box 247).

38. "The Olympic Story," Chapter X, p. 10 (A.B.C., Boxes 330–331).

39. "Session de 1924: Paris" (A.B.C., Box 90); Edstrøm to Brundage, July 15, 1957 (A.B.C., Box 43).

40. Brundage to Edstrøm, March 20, 1952; Edstrøm to Brundage, March 26, 1952 (A.B.C., Box 43).

41. Brundage to Otto Mayer, March 30, 1961 (A.B.C., Box 48).

42. Brundage to Georg von Opel, August 25, 1970 (A.B.C., Box 71).

43. Porritt to Brundage, September 10, 1965; Scharroo to Brundage, January 15, 1956 (A.B.C., Box 62).

44. *Ibid.*

45. Mayer *À Travers*, p. 87.

46. "International Olympic Meeting of 1937, Warsaw," June 7–11, 1937, *Bulletin du C.I.O.* (July 1937), 12(35).

47. Brundage to Edstrøm, May 16, 1957 (A.B.C., Box 43).

48. John Henry Auran, "The Sour Olympics," *Skiing*, October 1968, p. 67.

49. Circular Letter, April 26, 1969 (A.B.C., Box 71).

50. Luc Silance, "L'Organization de spectacles sportifs et l'athlète," *Le Spectacle Sportif* (Paris: Presses universitaires de Paris, 1981), pp. 152–158.

51. Circular Letter, April 26, 1969 (A.B.C., Box 71).

52. Notes (A.B.C., Box 95); "The Olympic Games in Danger," Press Release, May 10, 1970 (A.B.C., Box 247).

53. Quoted in "Olympics," *Time*, March 15, 1968.

54. Brundage to Daniel J. Ferris, March 15, 1972 (A.B.C., Box 4).

55. Killanin to Brundage, January 27, 1971; van Karnebeek to Brundage, January 27, 1971; Beaumont to Brundage, January 28, 1971; Gafner to Brundage, January 27, 1971; Takeda to Brundage, February 12, 1971; Staubo to Brundage, February 4, 1971; Brundage to Killanin, Beaumont, and van Karnebeek, January 28, 1971 (A.B.C., Boxes 55, 59, 63).

56. Beaumont to Brundage, February 2, 1971 (A.B.C., Box 51).

57. "Minutes, Executive Board, Tokyo and Sapporo, January 28–29, February 1, 1972," Annex 3 (A.B.C., Box 95).

58. December 20, 1971 (A.B.C., Box 51).

59. Interview with Raymond Gafner, Baden-Baden, September 25, 1981; "Minutes of the 72nd Session of the I.O.C., Sapporo, January 31 and February 1, 1972" (I.O.C.).

60. *Ibid.*

XII   THE MIDDLE WESTERNER AND THE FAR EAST

1. "55th Session of the International Olympic Committee," May 25–28, 1959, *Bulletin du C.I.O.* (August 15, 1959), no. 67.

2. Interview with René-Yvon Lefebvre d'Argencé, San Francisco, January 7, 1980.

3. Diem, *Asiatische Reiterspiele* (Berlin: Deutscher Archiv-Verlag, 1941), p. 132.

4. *A Commemorative Catalogue of the International Exposition of Chinese Art* (London, 1936).

5. Interview with Avery Brundage, *Newsweek*, June 20, 1966.

6. "The Olympic Story," Chapter VIII, p. 13 (A.B.C., Boxes 330–331).

7. "The Position of Japanese Culture in the World" (A.B.C., Box 244).

8. Quoted by Henry J. Seldis, "Avery Brundage: Olympian Patron of Art," *Los Angeles Times West Magazine*, September 11, 1966.

9. *Ibid.*

10. René-Yvon Lefebvre d'Argencé, *Bronze Vessels of Ancient China in the Avery Brundage Collection* (San Francisco: Asian Art Museum, 1977), p. 76; illustration, p. 77.

11. See d'Argencé, *Chinese Jades in the Avery Brundage Collection* (San Francisco: Asian Art Museum, 1977), pp. 16–17, 144–45.

12. See d'Argencé and Diane Turner, *Chinese, Korean, and Japanese Sculpture in the Avery Brundage Collection* (San Francisco: Asian Art Museum, 1974).

13. See d'Argencé, *Rarities of the Asian Art Museum of San Francisco* (San Francisco: Asian Art Museum, 1978), pp. 15, 18–19.

14. See the interview with Avery Brundage published in *Vecko-Journalen* (Stockholm), February 23, 1972 (A.B.C., Box 250).

15. Illustrated in Heinz Schöbel, *The Four Dimensions of Avery Brundage* (Leipzig: Edition Leipzig, 1968), plate 70; *Rarities*, p. 2; d'Argencé, *Bronzes*, p. 43. Comment is from d'Argencé, p. 42. See also Hans Klein, ed., *Avery Brundage: Die Herausforderung* (Munich: Pro Sport, 1972), p. 48.

16. Interview with Willi Daume, Cologne, December 16, 1981.

17. Interview with René-Yvon Lefebvre d'Argencé, San Francisco, January 7, 1980.

18. Interview with Sunichi Hirai and Tsuneyoshi Takeda, Tokyo, June 30, 1980.

19. *Ibid.*

20. See Pierre Frayssinet, *Le Sport parmi les beaux-arts* (Paris: Arts et Voyages, 1968); Allen Guttmann, *From Ritual to Record: The Nature of Modern Sport* (New York: Columbia University Press, 1978), pp. 1–14.

21. "Opening Address to the 54th Session of the International Olympic Committee, Tokyo, May 14, 1958," *Speeches of Avery Brundage* (Lausanne: Comité International Olympique, 1969), p. 38.

22. See Seldis, "Avery Brundage."

23. Brundage to Rufus Trimble, November 6, 1947 (A.B.C., Box 40); Brundage to J. W. Rangell, February 23, 1956 (A.B.C., Box 62).

24. Brundage to Rangell, January 28, 1959 (A.B.C., Box 62); another copy went to Mrs. Alexander Cushing, May 4, 1960 (A.B.C., Box 165).

25. Notes (A.B.C., Box 246).

26. Klein, *Avery Brundage*, p. 49.

27. "The Olympic Story," Introduction, p. 1 (A.B.C., Boxes 330–331).

28. U.S.O.C., *Report, 1948* (New York: U.S. Olympic Association, 1949), p. 22.

29. Notes (A.B.C., Box 245).

30. Lao Tzu, *The Way of Life*, translated by Witter Bynner (New York: John Day, 1944), p. 34.

31. *Ibid.*, p. 33.

32. Brundage to Joseph E. Raycroft, May 13, 1940 (A.B.C., Box 34).

33. Brundage to Ralph C. Craig, March 23, 1962 (A.B.C., Box 22).

34. Richard E. Praul, "Brundage Sees Treasures Burn," Los Angeles *Times*, September 25, 1964.

35. Interview with Sunichi Hirai and Tsuneyoshi Takeda, Tokyo, June 30, 1980.

36. Santa Barbara *News-Press*, July 2, 1971; December 14, 1971.

37. Interview with Sunichi Hirai and Tsuneyoshi Takeda, Tokyo, June 30, 1980.

38. "Minutes of the Executive Board Meeting," April 11, 1965 (A.B.C., Box 92).

39. "Minutes," Executive Board, Paris, July 9, 1965 (I.O.C.).

40. "The Olympic Story," Chapter XIII, p. 4 (A.B.C., Boxes 330–331).

XIII   OLYMPIC COMMERCE

1. Brundage to James F. Simms, January 17, 1941 (A.B.C., Box 38).
2. Brundage to Olympiad Skate Co., March 16, 1950 (A.B.C., Box 238).
3. Brundage to Jean Ketseas, December 1, 1958 (A.B.C., Box 48).
4. Brundage to Artur Takec, March 29, 1972 (A.B.C., Box 45).
5. Takec to Brundage, April 14, 1972 (A.B.C., Box 45).
6. Brundage to Frederick W. Rubien, August 5, 1931 (A.B.C., Box 35).
7. Brundage and Frederick W. Rubien to U.S.A.S.F., June 3, 1941 (A.B.C., Box 38).
8. Brundage, Circular Letter, January 17, 1962 (A.B.C., Box 70).
9. McGovern to Brundage, February 19, 23, 1951 (A.B.C., Box 238).
10. Brundage to McGovern, March 2, April 5, June 6, 1949 (A.B.C., Box 32).
11. Brundage to McGovern, February 20, 1951 (A.B.C., Box 31).
12. Brundage to Eunice Shriver, March 18, 1968 (A.B.C., Box 28).
13. Chicago *Sun-Times*, June 10, 1969; Brundage to Marc Hodler, January 31, 1969 (A.B.C., Box 87).
14. Brundage to Johann Westerhoff, September 6, 1966 (A.B.C., Box 45).
15. Burghley (Exeter) to Brundage, January 31, 1957 (A.B.C., Box 55).
16. Brundage to Daniel J. Ferris, December 12, 1951 (A.B.C., Box 24).
17. Brundage, Circular Letter, August 22, 1957 (A.B.C., Box 70); Brundage to Edstrøm, April 21, 1958 (A.B.C., Box 43).
18. Brundage, Circular Letter, May 14, 1959 (A.B.C., Box 70).
19. Burghley (Exeter) to Brundage, August 30, 1957 (A.B.C., Box 70).
20. "55th Session . . . ," May 25–28, 1959, *Bulletin du C.I.O.* (August 15, 1959), no. 67.
21. Interview with Raymond Gafner, Baden-Baden, September 25, 1981.
22. Brundage to Otto Mayer, March 2, 1957 (A.B.C., Box 47).
23. "Extract of Minutes of 56th Session in San Francisco," February 15–16, 1960, *Bulletin du C.I.O.* (May 15, 1960), no. 70.
24. "Minutes of the Meeting of the Executive Board," August 19, 1960 (A.B.C., Box 91).
25. Richard Espy, *Politics of the Olympic Games* (Berkeley: University of California Press, 1979), p. 73.
26. Raymond Marcillac and Christian Quidet, *Sport et télévision* (Paris: Albin Michel, 1963), p. 155.
27. "Minutes of the 64th Session . . . ," April 25–28, 1966, *Bulletin du C.I.O.* (August 15, 1966), no. 95.
28. Brundage, Circular Letter, April 17, 1967 (A.B.C., Box 71).
29. Brundage to Albert Mayer, May 19, 1969 (A.B.C., Box 60).
30. "Minutes of the Executive Board Meetings," June 6, 1969 (A.B.C., Box 94).
31. Espy, *Politics of the Olympic Games*, p. 118.
32. Burghley (Exeter) to Brundage, June 10, 1965 (A.B.C., Box 55).
33. Pierre Georges, *Champions à vendre* (Paris: Calmann-Lévy, 1974), pp. 87–88.
34. Christopher Brasher, *Mexico: 1968* (London: Stanley Paul, 1968), pp. 17–18.
35. Brundage, Circular Letter, April 26, 1969 (A.B.C., Box 71).
36. *Ibid.*

XIV   DEALING WITH THE THIRD WORLD

1. "Extrait du Procès-Verbale . . . ," January 29–31, February 4–8, 1948, *Bulletin du C.I.O.* (March 15, 1948), no. 9.
2. See A.B.C., Box 154.
3. Nahum Heth and A. Sarig to Brundage, January 23, 1955 (A.B.C., Box 134).

4. *Ibid.*

5. Otto Mayer to Brundage, October 30, 1954; Brundage to Mayer, December 20, 1954 (A.B.C., Box 46).

6. February 16, 1955 (A.B.C., Box 134).

7. Brundage to Burghley (Exeter), September 24, 1955 (A.B.C., Box 54); Burghley (Exeter) to Brundage, March 23, 1955 (A.B.C., Box 54).

8. Brundage to Otto Mayer, May 30, 1955 (A.B.C., Box 47).

9. Brundage to Otto Mayer, November 29, 1958 (A.B.C., Box 48).

10. Brundage to Otto Mayer, January 30, 1959 (A.B.C., Box 48).

11. Burghley (Exeter) to Brundage, September 1, 1958 (A.B.C., Box 54).

12. Brundage to Burghley (Exeter), November 8, 1958 (A.B.C., Box 54).

13. Gemayel to D.T.P. Pain, December 20, 1958 (A.B.C., Box 56).

14. Burghley (Exeter) to Brundage, April 8, 1959 (Gemayel to Brundage, April 17, 1959 (A.B.C., Box 54, 56).

15. Brundage to Gemayel, March 6, September 5, 1959 (A.B.C., Box 56).

16. Brundage to Burghley (Exeter), November 27, 1962 (A.B.C., Box 54).

17. Burghley (Exeter) to Brundage, February 3, 1961 (A.B.C., Box 54).

18. Brundage to Otto Mayer, November 26, 1962 (A.B.C., Box 49).

19. "Minutes of the Conference of the Executive Board . . . with the International Federations," *Bulletin du C.I.O.* (May 15, 1963), no. 82.

20. "Minutes of the Meeting of the Executive Board," June 6, 1963, *Bulletin du C.I.O.* (August 15, 1963), no. 83.

21. "Extracts of the Minutes of the 65th Session . . . ," May 6–8, 1967, *Bulletin du C.I.O.* (August 15, 1967), nos. 98–99.

22. "Minutes," February 8, 1963, *Bulletin du C.I.O.* (May 15, 1963), no. 82.

23. Brundage to Otto Mayer, October 3, 1962 (A.B.C., Box 49).

24. Brundage to Otto Mayer, December 7, 1962 (A.B.C., Box 49).

25. Richard Espy, *The Politics of the Olympic Games* (Berkeley: University of California Press, 1979), p. 80.

26. "Minutes," October 15, 1963 (A.B.C., Box 92).

27. *Gazette de Lausanne*, May 13, 1964.

28. See Willard A. Hanna, "The Politics of Sport," *Southeast Asia Series*, (1962), 10(19):197–207.

29. See Swampo Sie, "Sports and Politics: The Case of the Asian Games and the G.A.N.E.F.O.," *Sport and International Relations*, ed. Benjamin Lowe, David B. Kanin, Andrew Strenk (Champaign, Illinois: Stipes, 1978), 279–96.

30. Quoted in Jonathan Kolatch, *Sport, Politics and Ideology in China* (Middle Village, N.Y.: Jonathan David, 1972), p. 191; see also Ewa T. Pauker, *GANEFO I* (Santa Monica, California: Rand, n.d.), p. 7.

31. Circular Letter, January 15, 1963 (A.B.C., Box 70).

32. Touny to Burghley (Exeter), September 10, 1963; Mayer's note on a Blind Copy to Brundage of Otto Mayer to Touny, December 13, 1963 (A.B.C., Boxes 54, 64).

33. Brundage to Touny, May 25, 1963 (A.B.C., Box 64).

34. "Minutes of the 61st Session," January 26–28, 1964, *Bulletin du C.I.O.* (May 15, 1964), no. 86; "Minutes," June 26–27, 1964 (A.B.C., Box 80).

35. David B. Kanin, *A Political History of the Olympic Games* (Boulder, Colorado: West-View, 1981), p. 87; Sie, "Sports and Politics," p. 294.

36. Brundage, "Address to America-Japan Society and American Chamber of Commerce in Japan," October 9, 1964 (A.B.C., Box 246).

37. "Meeting of the Executive Board . . . with the Delegates of the National Olympic

Committees," October 3, 1964, *Bulletin du C.I.O.* (February 15, 1965), no. 89; Phillip Shinnick, "Latest Politics on the Admission of the People's Republic of China to the 1980 Moscow Olympics," *Arena Review* (October 1979) 3(4):50.

38. Interview with Kéba Mbaya, Baden-Baden, September 27, 1981.

39. Interview with Adetokunbo Ademola, Baden-Baden, September 29, 1981. Details for this and the following paragraph are also taken from Achot Melik-Chakhnazarov, *Le Sport en afrique* (Paris: Présence africaine, 1970); Desire Malet, "Les Jeux Africains," *Sport de France* (Paris: Service de Presse, 1971), pp. 503–7; Ramadhan Ali, *Africa at the Olympics* (London: Africa Books, 1976); Brundage to Otto Mayer, May 13, 1963 (A.B.C., 49).

40. "Minutes of the 63rd Meeting . . . ," *Bulletin du C.I.O.* (November 15, 1965), no. 92.

41. "Opening Address to the 63rd Session of the International Olympic Committee, Madrid, October 6, 1965," *Speeches of Avery Brundage* (Lausanne: Comité International Olympique, 1969), pp. 85, 84.

42. *Ibid.*, p. 84.

43. Quoted in Richard Edward Lapchick, *The Politics of Race and International Sport: The Case of South Africa* (Westport, Connecticut: Greenwood, 1975), p. 80.

44. Brundage to Burghley (Exeter), November 28, 1964; Burghley (Exeter) to Brundage, December 7, 1964; Burghley (Exeter) to Jean-Claude Ganga, January 5, 1964; Burghley (Exeter) to Brundage, February 12, 1965 (A.B.C., Box 54).

45. Ditlev-Simonsen to Brundage, March 5, 1958; Brundage to Ditlev-Simsonsen, April 8, 1958 (A.B.C., Box 64).

46. April 30, 1959 (A.B.C., Box 48).

47. "Minutes," May 19, 1959 (A.B.C., Box 78).

48. "Minutes: 55th Session," May 27, 1959 (A.B.C., Box 91).

49. See Lapchick, *Politics of Race*, p. 30.

50. Circular Letter, July 5, 1960 (A.B.C., Box 70).

51. Lapchick, *Politics of Race*, p. 45.

52. "Procès-Verbale," March 2–3, 1962 (A.B.C., Box 92).

53. "Extracts of the Minutes 59th Session," June 5–8, 1962, *Bulletin du C.I.O.* (November 15, 1962), no. 80.

54. Brundage to Otto Mayer, August 14, 1962 (A.B.C., Box 49).

55. Reginald Alexander to Brundage, July 8, 26, 31, 1963 (A.B.C., Box 50).

56. "Minutes of the 60th Session," October 14–20, 1963, *Bulletin du C.I.O.* (February 15, 1964), no. 85.

57. "Minutes," January 25–26, 1965 (A.B.C., Box 80).

58. "Minutes of the 61st Session," January 26–28, 1964, *Bulletin du C.I.O.* (May 15, 1964), no. 85.

59. Weir to Brundage, February 28, 1964; Brundage to Weir, March 17, 1964 (A.B.C., Box 64).

60. Ira Emery to Brundage, February 15, March 8, 1966 (A.B.C., Box 82); "Minutes of the 64th Session . . . ," April 25–28, 1965, *Bulletin du C.I.O.* (August 15, 1966), no. 95.

61. March 24, 1966.

62. Jean-Claude Ganga, *Combats pour un sport africain* (Paris: L'Harmattan, 1979), pp. 198–99.

63. "Minutes: 65th Session . . . ," Annex VI: Statement from the South African Olympic Games Association Delegation" (A.B.C., Box 93).

64. Lapchick, *Politics of Race*, p. 96.

65. *Report of the I.O.C. Commission on South Africa* (Lausanne, 1968), p. 14.

66. "Statement Presented by the South African Delegation to the I.O.C. Meeting on 3rd February 1968"; "Minutes: 66th Session . . . ," February 1–5, 1968, Annex VI (A.B.C. Box 93).

67. "Press Conference Given by Mr. Avery Brundage . . . ," *Newsletter* (February 1968), no. 5.

68. "About the South African Team," *Newsletter* 5 (February 1968), no. 5.

69. Interview with Dennis Brutus, Amherst, Massachusetts, February 16, 1981.

70. New York *Herald-Tribune*, February 27, 1968.

71. February 29, 1968 (A.B.C., Box 45).

72. Lapchick, *Politics of Race*, pp. 115–17.

73. February 6, 1968.

74. Port Elizabeth *Eastern Province Herald*, April 16, 1968, quoted by Lapchick, *Politics of Race*, p. 118.

75. "Les Ressous de Quinze Heures de Marchandage," *L'Equipe*, April 23, 1968.

76. "Mexico Without the South Africans," *Newsletter* (May 1968), no. 8.

77. Interview with Sir Reginald Alexander, Baden-Baden, September 29, 1981.

78. "Notes on the Executive Board Meeting," April 21, 1968 (A.B.C., Box 93).

79. *Ibid.*

80. Cable, April 22, 1968 (A.B.C., Box 179).

81. April 23, 1968.

82. "An Interview with President Brundage," *Newsletter* (May 1968), no. 8.

83. "Mexico Without the South Africans," *Newsletter* (May 1968), no. 8.

84. Brundage's notes (A.B.C., Box 179).

85. "The Olympic Story," Chapter XV, p. 21 (A.B.C., Boxes 330–331).

86. Antonio Carillo Flores to Pedro Ramirez Vazquez, June 6, 1968 (A.B.C., Box 179).

87. Brundage to Prince George of Hannover, June 15, 1968 (A.B.C., Box 179).

88. Brundage to Westerhoff, June 10, 1968 (A.B.C., Box 179).

89. Douglas Downing, quoted by John Cheffers, *A Wilderness of Spite* (New York: Vantage Press, 1972), p. 15.

90. Press Release, August 23, 1968 (A.B.C., Box 176).

91. September 29, 1968 (A.B.C., Box 176).

92. December 17, 1968 (A.B.C., Box 176).

93. Chicago *Tribune*, September 25, 1968; Chicago *Sun-Times*, September 25, 1968.

94. Chicago *Tribune*, October 3, 1968; Chicago *Sun-Times*, October 3, 1968.

95. Chicago *Daily News*, October 4, 1968.

96. *Ibid.*

97. New York *Times*, October 16, 1968.

98. "The Olympic Story," Chapter XV, p. 23 (A.B.C., Boxes 330–331).

99. Brundage to Patrick J. Walsh, October 5, 1935 (A.B.C., Box 10).

100. Brundage to Donald Day, May 18, 1957 (A.B.C., Box 22).

101. August 19, 1969 (A.B.C., Box 178).

102. March 10, 1970 (A.B.C., Box 51).

103. Vind to Brundage, November 27, 1965 (A.B.C., Box 64).

104. Lord Porritt to author, December 23, 1979.

105. William O. Johnson, *All That Glitters Is Not Gold* (N.Y.: Putnam's; 1972), p. 100; see also interviews with Giorgio de Stefani and Raymond Gafner, Baden-Baden, September 27 and 28, 1981.

106. Durban *Sunday Times*, June 1, 1969, quoted by Lapchick, *Politics of Race*, p. 143.

107. "Minutes . . . ," October 25, 1969 (A.B.C., Box 87).

108. "Speech, May 12, 1970" (A.B.C., Box 88).

109. On the vote, see Monique Berlioux, Circular Letter, June 10, 1970 (A.B.C., Box 71).

110. Brundage to Burghley (Exeter), May 28, 1970 (A.B.C., Box 55).

111. Interview with Willi Daume, Cologne, December 16, 1981.

112. *Ibid.* Lord Killanin, *My Olympic Years* (London: Secker & Warburg, 1983), p. 60.
113. Berlioux, "History of the I.O.C.," p. 22.
114. Geoffrey Miller, *Behind the Olympic Rings* (Lynn, Massachusetts: H. O. Zimman, 1979), p. 21.
115. Interview with Monique Berlioux, Baden-Baden, October 3, 1981.
116. Burghley (Exeter) to Brundage, September 3, 1971 (A.B.C., Box 88).
117. Espy, *Politics of the Olympic Games*, p. 129.
118. Interview with Dennis Brutus, Amherst, Massachusetts, February 16, 1981.
119. Interview with Lance Cross, Baden-Baden, October 3, 1981.
120. Espy, *Politics of the Olympic Games*, p. 130.
121. "Minutes of the 73rd Session of the International Olympic Committee, Munich, August 21–24, September 5, 1972" (I.O.C.).
122. Brundage to Pamela Richwine, March 19, 1973; Brundage to Hugh Weir, October 11, 1972 (A.B.C., Boxes 34, 64).
123. Brundage to Ian Smith, October 30, 1972 (A.B.C., Box 184).
124. Many details of this and the next three paragraphs are taken from Serge Groussard's *The Blood of Israel*, Translated Harold J. Salmeson (New York: William Morrow, 1975).
125. Interview with Willi Daume, Cologne, December 16, 1981.
126. Groussard, *Blood of Israel*, p. 161; Killanin, *My Olympic Years*, p. 92.
127. Interviews with Monique Berlioux and Douglas Roby, Baden-Baden, October 3 and September 30, 1981.
128. Interview with Douglas Roby, Baden-Baden, September 30, 1981.
129. "Extraordinary Meeting of the 73rd Session of the International Olympic Committee, September 5, 1972" (I.O.C.); interview with Monique Berlioux, October 3, 1981.
130. Groussard, *Blood of Israel*, p. 288.
131. "Address, September 6, 1972" (A.B.C., Box 249).
132. Interview with Liselott Diem, Cologne, December 7, 1981.
133. Interview with Raymond Gafner Baden-Baden, September 25, 1981.
134. Interview with Walther Tröger, Frankfurt, January 19, 1982.

EPILOGUE: A GERMAN PRINCESS

1. Interview with Walther Tröger, Frankfurt, January 19, 1981.
2. September 8, 1972.
3. John Apostle Lucas, *The Modern Olympic Games* (New York: A. C. Barnes, 1980), pp. 170, 210.
4. Quoted in William O. Johnson, "Avery Brundage: The Man behind the Mask," *Sports Illustrated* (August 4, 1980), 53(6):58.
5. Frederick J. Ruegsegger to author, September 12, 1980.
6. Interview with Willi Daume, Cologne, August 25, 1980.
7. Many details are taken from Johnson, "Avery Brundage."
8. *Die Abendzeitung*, April 2, 1973.
9. New York *Times*, June 12, 1973.
10. Johnson, "Avery Brundage," p. 60.
11. Ekelund to author, December 10, 1979; *Bild*, July 30, 1973.
12. Santa Barbara *News-Press*, October 29, 1974; *Bild*, January 23, 1976.
13. Interview with Liselott Diem, Cologne, August 13, 1980.
14. Ruegsegger's testimony, August 16, 1979, in the case of *Mariann Brundage v. Donald R. Pate* (wrongly given in some transcripts as "Page"), Superior Court of the State of California for the County of Santa Barbara, Department No. 6, Hon. Patrick McMahon, Judge-Pro Tempore, No. 116891; pp. 49, 51.

15. *Bild*, July 13, 1974.
16. Interview with Tsuneyoshi Takeda, Tokyo, June 30, 1980.
17. Interview with Willi Daume, Cologne, December 16, 1981.
18. Onesti to Brundage, July 24, 1972 (A.B.C., Box 120).
19. Ruegsegger's testimony, August 16, 1979, *Brundage v. Pate*, p. 19.
20. Interview with Tsuneyoshi Takeda, Tokyo, June 30, 1980.
21. Interview with Dr. Kenneth L. Roper, Chicago, June 28, 1979.
22. Interview with Juan Antonio Samaranch, Baden-Baden, October 3, 1981.
23. Mariann Brundage's testimony, August 15, 1979, *Brundage v. Pate*, p. 140.
24. Mariann Brundage's testimony, August 16, 1979, *Brundage v. Pate*, pp. 209–215.
25. *Ibid..*, p. 219.
26. Testimony, August 20, 1979, *Brundage v. Pate*, p. 397.
27. Testimony, August 18, 1979, *Brundage v. Pate*, p. 73.
28. June 15, 1974 (A.B.C., Box 62).
29. Interview with Walther Tröger, Frankfurt, January 19, 1982.
30. *Bild*, May 10, 1975.

Index